Völkerrecht und Außenpolitik

Herausgegeben von
Prof. Dr. Oliver Dörr
Prof. Dr. Jörn Axel Kämmerer
Prof. Dr. Markus Krajewski

Band 97

Sabrina Klein

Out means Out?

Brexit as a Case of Treaty Succession

Nomos

The research for this book was funded by the Deutsche Forschungsgemeinschaft (DFG, German Research Foundation) - DFG-Graduiertenkolleg „Dynamische Integrationsordnung. Europa und sein Recht zwischen Harmonisierung und Pluralisierung (DynamInt)" (397044234).

The publication of this book was supported by the Deutsch-Britische Juristenvereinigung e.V., the Konrad-Redeker-Stiftung and the Open Access Publication Fund of Humboldt-Universität zu Berlin.

The Deutsche Nationalbibliothek lists this publication in the Deutsche Nationalbibliografie; detailed bibliographic data are available on the Internet at http://dnb.d-nb.de

a.t.: Berlin, Humboldt-Universität zu Berlin, Juristische Fakultät, Diss., 2023
Original title: Out means Out? The Effect of Brexit on the International Agreements of the EU and its Member States

1st Edition 2025

© Sabrina Klein

Published by
Nomos Verlagsgesellschaft mbH & Co. KG
Waldseestraße 3–5 | 76530 Baden-Baden
www.nomos.de

Production of the printed version:
Nomos Verlagsgesellschaft mbH & Co. KG
Waldseestraße 3–5 | 76530 Baden-Baden

ISBN 978-3-7560-1602-0 (Print)
ISBN 978-3-7489-4521-5 (ePDF)
DOI https://doi.org/10.5771/9783748945215

Onlineversion
Nomos eLibrary

This work is licensed under a Creative Commons Attribution 4.0 International License.
https://creativecommons.org/licenses/by/4.0/deed.de

Für Friedrich, Eva und Ute

Vorwort

Die Idee zu dieser Arbeit entstand während meiner Tätigkeit im Referat für Völkervertragsrecht des Auswärtigen Amts. Dort kam ich nicht nur zum ersten Mal mit den völkerrechtlichen Fragen des Brexit in Berührung. Ich durfte auch mit großartigen Kolleginnen und Kollegen und begeisterten Völkerrechtlern zusammenarbeiten. Ihnen allen und insbesondere meinen damaligen Referatsleitern Jens Lorentz und Dr. Reinhard Haßenpflug möchte ich für den fachlichen Austausch danken, der die Grundlage für diese Arbeit gelegt hat.

Verwirklichen konnte ich meine Idee zu dieser Arbeit dank der hervorragenden Forschungs- und Promotionsbedingungen des DFG-Graduiertenkollegs *DynamInt* an der Humboldt-Universität zu Berlin. Diesem habe ich nicht nur tolle Kolleginnen und Kollegen zu verdanken, die aus der Promotion eine Gemeinschaftserfahrung gemacht haben. Dank *DynamInt* konnte ich auch Forschungsaufenthalte am *Amsterdam Center for International Law* und am *King's College London* verbringen, die nach der Covid-Zeit nicht nur fachlich eine große Bereicherung waren. Für die freundliche Aufnahme dort möchte ich mich insbesondere bei Prof. Catherine Brölmann und Prof. Holger Hestermeyer herzlich bedanken.

Zudem möchte ich mich bei denjenigen bedanken, die die Veröffentlichung meiner Arbeit möglich gemacht haben: Bei den Mitarbeitern von Nomos für ihre Geduld bei all meinen Anliegen, der Deutsch-Britischen Juristenvereinigung e.V. und der Konrad-Redeker-Stiftung für ihre großzügigen Druckkostenzuschüsse sowie dem Team des Open-Access-Publikationsfond der Humboldt-Universität zu Berlin, dank dem meine Forschung frei zugänglich ist.

Mein besonderer Dank gilt meinen beiden Betreuern: Prof. Georg Nolte, an dessen Lehrstuhl meine Begeisterung für das Völkerrecht entstanden ist und der mich zum Schreiben dieser Arbeit ermutigt hat, und Prof. Matthias Ruffert, der mit *DynamInt* ein besonderes Promotionsumfeld geschaffen hat und mir während meiner Zeit dort jederzeit mit Rat und Tat zur Seite stand.

Darüber hinaus möchte ich mich von ganzem Herzen bei meiner Familie und meinen Freunden bedanken. Meinen Eltern danke ich für den Ansporn, das Projekt Promotion zu wagen, für die Unterstützung während

Vorwort

der gesamten Zeit und für das gemeinsame Feiern des Abschlusses. Meiner Schwester danke ich für ihre Anrufe, Besuche und die notwendige Ablenkung. Kerstin Schuster hat mich durch meine gesamte Zeit an der Humboldt-Universität begleitet – ohne ihre Herzlichkeit wäre weder meine Zeit am Lehrstuhl von Prof. Georg Nolte noch bei *DynamInt* die Gleiche gewesen. Prof. Lena Riemer hat mich für immer mit dem Jessup-Fieber infiziert. Sie war während meiner Promotionszeit nicht nur mein großes Vorbild, sondern auch die beste Mittagessensbegleiterin, die ich mir hätte wünschen können.

Schließlich gilt mein größter Dank Roland Klein, der mir immer zur Seite steht. Ich könnte nicht stolzer sein, am Ende unserer Promotionszeit nicht nur einen Namen, sondern auch die Aufnahme in diese Reihe mit ihm zu teilen.

Berlin 2024   *Sabrina Klein*

Content Overview

Table of Contents	13
List of Abbreviations	19
Introduction	23
§ 1 Setting the Scene: Brexit and EU Treaty Practice	27
I. Background: The EU as a Global Actor	27
II. Brexit Practice: Out Means (Almost Always) Out	37
III. The Research Question: What's International Law Got to Do with It?	53
Part I: Brexit and the Law of Treaties	**61**
§ 2 EU Withdrawal: Exiting an International Organisation	67
I. (Un)Identified Legal Object? The EU as an International Organisation	68
II. Art. 50 TEU: A Regular Withdrawal Clause	74
III. Brexit as Treaty Withdrawal	80
§ 3 Automatic Treaty Termination: A Legal Consequence of EU Withdrawal?	83
I. Lex generalis: Legal Consequences of Exiting an International Organisation	84
II. Lex specialis: Arrangements between Member States	88
III. EU Withdrawal: Applying the Treaty Law Template	93
IV. Brexit and its (Limited) Automatic Consequences	105

Content Overview

§ 4   EU Withdrawal: Grounds for Treaty Termination?   107

    I. Termination by Design: EU Membership as a Resolutory Condition?   109

    II. Termination by Invocation: EU Withdrawal as a Fundamental Change of Circumstances   136

    III. Brexit and its (Practical) Effects   156

Concluding Remarks: Brexit and Treaty Law – Match or Misfit?   159

Part II: Brexit and the Law of Succession   163

§ 5   EU Withdrawal and Succession: The Case for an Analogy   165

    I. The Law of Succession: An Alternative Framework?   165

    II. Methodical Excursus: Analogical Reasoning in International Law   187

    III. EU Withdrawal and Separation: Treating Like Cases Alike   191

    IV. Applying Art. 34 VCSSRT to the Case of Brexit   204

§ 6   EU Withdrawal and Succession: Justifying the Analogy   207

    I. Methodical Excursus: Valid Analogical Reasoning and International Law   208

    II. On Dissimilarities: The Irrelevance of the EU's Lack of Statehood   212

    III. On Similarities: The Relevance of the Concept of Treaty Stability   248

    IV. Countervailing Considerations: The Principle of Consent   263

    V. Brexit Practice: Between Treaty Stability and Consent?   269

§ 7   Brexit and Recent Practice. Brexit as Recent Practice?   271

    I. Post-1978 Practice: Putting Art. 34 VCSSRT to the Test   274

    II. Brexit and Succession Practice: Applying a New Template   292

    III. Brexit and the Law of Succession: Match or Misfit?   303

Concluding Remarks: Towards a Law of EU Succession   309

Summary and Outlook   319

References   331
    Literature   331
    Cases   345
    International Agreements and Legislation   347
    Documents and Miscellaneous Sources   351

Table of Contents

List of Abbreviations — 19

Introduction — 23

§ 1 Setting the Scene: Brexit and EU Treaty Practice — 27
    I. Background: The EU as a Global Actor — 27
        A. EU Treaty Practice: A Formal Categorisation — 29
        B. The Global Scale of EU Treaty Practice — 32
    II. Brexit Practice: Out Means (Almost Always) Out — 37
        A. The UK Position: From Continuity to 'Global Britain' — 38
        B. The EU Position: Of Guidelines and Directives — 40
        C. The UK-EU Withdrawal Agreement: Transitioning International Agreements — 43
        D. Rolling Over: The UK's (Re)Conclusion of International Agreements — 48
    III. The Research Question: What's International Law Got to Do with It? — 53

Part I: Brexit and the Law of Treaties — 61

§ 2 EU Withdrawal: Exiting an International Organisation — 67
    I. (Un)Identified Legal Object? The EU as an International Organisation — 68
    II. Art. 50 TEU: A Regular Withdrawal Clause — 74
        A. The International Law Template and Art. 50 TEU — 75
        B. Unionalisation of the Withdrawal Procedure? — 78
    III. Brexit as Treaty Withdrawal — 80

Table of Contents

§ 3 Automatic Treaty Termination: A Legal Consequence of EU Withdrawal? ... 83

    I. Lex generalis: Legal Consequences of Exiting an International Organisation ... 84

    II. Lex specialis: Arrangements between Member States ... 88
        A. The Practice: Conventions Concluded between Member States ... 88
        B. The Limits: Agreements Concluded with Non-Member States ... 91

    III. EU Withdrawal: Applying the Treaty Law Template ... 93
        A. Art. 50 TEU: *Lex specialis* Arrangements for International Agreements? ... 94
        B. *Inter se* Agreements: The UK-EU Withdrawal Agreement as *lex specialis*? ... 96
        C. The EU's External International Agreements ... 98
            1. The EU's International Agreements and Art. 216(2) TFEU ... 99
            2. *Lex mixity*? The Status of EU Member States in Mixed Agreements ... 100

    IV. Brexit and its (Limited) Automatic Consequences ... 105

§ 4 EU Withdrawal: Grounds for Treaty Termination? ... 107

    I. Termination by Design: EU Membership as a Resolutory Condition? ... 109
        A. Explicit Termination and Withdrawal Clause ... 110
            1. The EU's *inter se* Agreements ... 112
            2. The EU's Mixed Agreements ... 114
        B. Implicit Termination Clauses ... 118
            1. Definition of Parties: EU Member State Status in International Agreements ... 119
            2. Territorial Scope of Application ... 124
            3. Frustration of the Object and Purpose ... 125
            4. Legal Consequences of Changes to An International Agreement ... 131

Table of Contents

II. Termination by Invocation: EU Withdrawal as a Fundamental Change of Circumstances	136
A. Automatic Termination: The Inappropriateness of Art. 62 VCLT	137
B. Invoking Art. 62 VCLT: Terminating International Agreements Post-Withdrawal	140
1. Possible Obstacles in the Case of EU Withdrawal	140
a. The Applicability of Art. 62 VCLT	141
b. The Consequences of Invoking Art. 62 VCLT	144
c. *Lex mixity* again? Art. 62 VCLT and Bilateral Mixed Agreements	148
2. The Substantive Conditions of Art. 62 VCLT: EU Withdrawal as a Fundamental Change of Circumstances?	152
III. Brexit and its (Practical) Effects	156
Concluding Remarks: Brexit and Treaty Law – Match or Misfit?	159
Part II: Brexit and the Law of Succession	**163**
§ 5 EU Withdrawal and Succession: The Case for an Analogy	165
I. The Law of Succession: An Alternative Framework?	165
A. Brexit as Separation?	167
B. The EU, its Member States and Statehood	170
C. Exiting the European Union: A Legal Lacuna	177
1. Beyond the VCSSRT: A Broader Customary Law of Succession?	178
2. *Lex EU*: A Specific Customary Law of EU Succession?	180
3. Filling a Legal Lacuna: Recourse to Legal Reasoning	185
II. Methodical Excursus: Analogical Reasoning in International Law	187
III. EU Withdrawal and Separation: Treating Like Cases Alike	191
A. The Source: Unions of States	192
B. The Target: The European Union	198

Table of Contents

C. The Inferred Characteristic: Continuity of International Agreements	201
IV. Applying Art. 34 VCSSRT to the Case of Brexit	204
§ 6 EU Withdrawal and Succession: Justifying the Analogy	207
I. Methodical Excursus: Valid Analogical Reasoning and International Law	208
II. On Dissimilarities: The Irrelevance of the EU's Lack of Statehood	212
A. Changing Sovereignty? Brexit and the Definition of Succession	212
1. The Irrelevance of Sovereignty to a Succession of States	213
2. The Relevance of Competence and Responsibility to Succession	217
3. Replacing in Relevant Aspects	220
B. Locating Sovereignty: Unions of States and the EU	225
1. The Relevance of Unions of States to Art. 34 VCSSRT	226
2. The Irrelevance of Statehood to Unions of States	230
a. Classical Dichotomy versus Federal Middle Ground	231
b. A Reasonable Systematisation of Practice?	236
C. Due to Sovereignty? Differences in the Practice of Unions of States and the EU	240
1. The (Ir)Relevance of the EU's Accession Practice to Codification	241
2. The Practice of the EU and Unions of States: Relevantly Similar	243
III. On Similarities: The Relevance of the Concept of Treaty Stability	248
A. The Relevance of the Law of Treaties to the Law on Succession	249
B. The Relevance of Treaty Stability to the Drafting of Art. 34 VCSSRT	252
C. The Relevance of Treaty Stability in the Case of EU Withdrawal	260

Table of Contents

  IV. Countervailing Considerations: The Principle of Consent 263
   A. The Irrelevance of the Principle of Consent in Drafting Art. 34 VCSSRT 263
   B. The Relevance of the Identity of the Treaty Partner in Bilateral Agreements 266
  V. Brexit Practice: Between Treaty Stability and Consent? 269

§ 7 Brexit and Recent Practice. Brexit as Recent Practice? 271
  I. Post-1978 Practice: Putting Art. 34 VCSSRT to the Test 274
   A. The Practice: Considering Instances of Separation 275
   B. The Evaluation: Considering the Reception of the Practice 282
    1. Distinguishing between Separations and Dissolutions 283
    2. Distinguishing between Bilateral and Multilateral Agreements 285
    3. Devolution Agreements, Unilateral Declarations and Good Faith Negotiations 288
  II. Brexit and Succession Practice: Applying a New Template 292
   A. Procedural Similarities? From Unilateral Declarations to Rollovers 292
   B. Brexit and International Agreements: Between Continuity and a Clean Slate? 298
  III. Brexit and the Law of Succession: Match or Misfit? 303

Concluding Remarks: Towards a Law of EU Succession 309

Summary and Outlook 319

References 331
 Literature 331
 Cases 345
 International Agreements and Legislation 347
 Documents and Miscellaneous Sources 351

List of Abbreviations

AA	Association Agreement
AG	Advocate General
CETA	Comprehensive Economic and Trade Agreement
CoE	Council of Europe
DARIO	Draft Articles on the Responsibility of International Organizations
DoC	Declaration of Competences
ECHR	European Convention on Human Rights
ECJ	European Court of Justice
ECSC	European Coal and Steel Community
EDF	European Development Fund
EDF Agreement	Internal Agreement between the Representatives of the Governments of the Member States of the European Union, meeting within the Council, on the Financing of European Union Aid
EEC Treaty	Treaty Establishing the European Economic Community
EPA	Economic Partnership Agreement
ES Convention	Convention Defining the Statute of the European Schools
EU	European Union
EUI	European University Institute
EUI Convention	Convention Setting up a European University Institute
EU-UK TCA	Trade and Cooperation Agreement between the European Union and the European Atomic Energy Community, of the one part, and the United Kingdom of Great Britain and Northern Ireland, of the other part

List of Abbreviations

FTA	Free Trade Agreement
GPA	Agreement on Government Procurement
ICJ	International Court of Justice
ILC	International Law Commission
ILO	International Labour Organization
ILO Constitution	Constitution of the International Labour Organization
OEEC	Organisation for European Economic Cooperation
PCA	Partnership and Cooperation Agreement
PCIJ	Permanent Court of International Justice
REIO	Regional Economic Integration Organisation
RIO	Regional Integration Organisation
SFRY	Socialist Federal Republic of Yugoslavia
SR	Special Rapporteur
TA	Trade Agreement
TEU	Treaty on European Union
TFEU	Treaty on the Functioning of the European Union
UAR	United Arab Republic
UK	United Kingdom of Great Britain and Northern Ireland
UK-EU WA	Agreement on the Withdrawal of the United Kingdom of Great Britain and Northern Ireland from the European Union and the European Atomic Energy Community
UNCLOS	United Nations Convention on the Law of the Sea
UNCSSRT	United Nations Conference on the Succession of States in Respect of Treaties
UNFCCC	United Nations Framework Convention on Climate Change
USA	United States of America
USSR	Union of Soviet Socialist Republics
VCLT	Vienna Convention on the Law of Treaties

List of Abbreviations

VCLT-IO	Vienna Convention on the Law of Treaties between States and International Organizations or between International Organizations
VCSSRT	Vienna Convention on Succession of States in Respect of Treaties
WTO	World Trade Organization
WTO	Agreement Agreement Establishing the World Trade Organization

Introduction

On June 23, 2016, a referendum was held in the United Kingdom (UK) on whether or not the UK should remain in the European Union (EU[1]). A narrow majority of 51.9 per cent voted to leave the EU, setting in motion a process known as Brexit.[2] Following domestic discussions on the path to pursue to become a non-Member State,[3] then British Prime Minister Theresa May submitted the official notification of withdrawal under Art. 50 *Treaty on European Union*[4] (TEU) to Brussels on March 29, 2017.[5] Pursuant to Art. 50(3) TEU, the notification kicked off a two-year phase of withdrawal negotiations, which, however, ended on March 29, 2019, without the UK having left. With the British parliament having rejected the draft of a UK-EU withdrawal agreement, the UK had requested – and been granted – an extension of the negotiation period under Art. 50(3) TEU.[6]

---

1 Throughout this study, the term 'EU' is used to refer to the current European Union but also its predecessors. In some instances, for example in case of quotations or where it is relevant for the historical background, reference is made to the exact name of a predecessor organisation of the current EU.
2 For the results of the referendum in detail, see UK Electoral Commission, 'Results and Turnout at the EU Referendum' (08.02.2023) <https://www.electoralcommission.org.uk/who-we-are-and-what-we-do/elections-and-referendums/past-elections-and-referendums/eu-referendum/results-and-turnout-eu-referendum>.
3 For an initial UK government report on the process of withdrawal, see UK Government, 'The Process for Withdrawing from the European Union' (February 2016) Cm 9216. The domestic process was delayed, *inter alia*, by court proceedings. In UK Supreme Court *R (on the Application of Miller and Another) v Secretary of State for Exiting the European Union* [2017] UKSC 5, for example, the Court held that the UK government required an Act of Parliament before officially notifying the EU of its withdrawal pursuant to Art. 50 TEU.
4 Consolidated Version of the Treaty on European Union (26 October 2012) OJ C326/13 [TEU].
5 UK Government, 'Prime Minister's Letter to Donald Tusk Triggering Article 50' (29.03.2017) <https://www.gov.uk/government/publications/prime-ministers-letter-to-donald-tusk-triggering-article-50>.
6 For a full timeline of the Brexit negotiations, including links to the relevant documents, see European Council, 'Timeline – The EU-UK Withdrawal Agreement' <https://www.consilium.europa.eu/en/policies/eu-relations-with-the-united-kingdom/the-eu-uk-withdrawal-agreement/timeline-eu-uk-withdrawal-agreement/>.

Introduction

Following changes of government in the UK and further intense negotiations, both necessitating additional deadline extensions, the *Agreement on the Withdrawal of the United Kingdom of Great Britain and Northern Ireland from the European Union and the European Atomic Energy Community*[7] (UK-EU WA) was finally signed on January 24, 2020. Following the agreement's subsequent ratification by the EU and the UK, the UK ceased to be a Member State of the EU on January 31, 2020. Its final 'goodbye', however, would not take place until the end of that year. During this agreed-upon transition period, the UK continued to be treated like an EU Member State, albeit without enjoying full Member State status, until December 31, 2020.[8] Thus, the foremost goal of the transition period – to gain time for the negotiations on future relations – was only just achieved with the signing of the *Trade and Cooperation Agreement between the European Union and the European Atomic Energy Community, of the one part, and the United Kingdom of Great Britain and Northern Ireland, of the other part*[9] (EU-UK TCA) on December 30, 2020, and its provisional application on January 1, 2021. Following completion of the EU and the UK's internal procedure, the EU-UK TCA entered into force on May 1, 2021.

Regardless of the exact shape and depth of their future relationship, the UK's exit from the EU resulted in a profound process of disintegration between the UK, on the one hand, and the EU and its Member States, on the other. The relationship between the UK and many continental European states, 27 at the time of its exit, had for nearly 5 decades rested on common participation in a 'new legal order'[10], the level of integration of which – regardless of how its nature is perceived[11] – is unprecedented and unique. In the future, however, this relationship will again rest solely upon

---

7 Agreement on the Withdrawal of the United Kingdom of Great Britain and Northern Ireland from the European Union and the European Atomic Energy Community (12 November 2019) OJ C384 I/1 [UK-EU WA].
8 Cp Art. 126 UK-EU WA.
9 Trade and Cooperation Agreement between the European Union and the European Atomic Energy Community, of the one part, and the United Kingdom of Great Britain and Northern Ireland, of the other part (30 April 2021) OJ L149/10 [EU-UK TCA].
10 A notion repeatedly employed by the European Court of Justice (ECJ), see rather recently in ECJ, Opinion 2/13 *Accession to the ECHR* [2014] ECLI:EU:C:2014:2454, [157].
11 On the nature of the EU and its legal order, see below Part I § 2 section I.

and be shaped by 'ordinary'[12] international law and agreements. Brexit, however, not only means a return to international law in the relations between the UK, EU, and EU Member States, it is also necessary to turn one's gaze to international law to fully grasp the withdrawal's consequences. Brexit was not only an 'earthquake' in EU–UK relations, the 'rubble [of which] will take years to clear'[13] – its seismic waves also reverberated beyond these entities and into the international legal order, shaking a main pillar of the EU and UK international relations: international agreements.

According to Art. 216 *Treaty on the Functioning of the European Union*[14] (TFEU), the EU 'may conclude [...] agreement[s] with one or more third countries or international organisations' (paragraph 1), which are 'binding upon the institutions of the Union and on its Member States' (paragraph 2). As simple as this provision may sound at first, the network of international agreements that has evolved over the years is widespread and complex. The EU maintains international agreements with most states in the world and many international organisations, with its Member States participating in some of these agreements as contracting parties alongside the EU. Moreover, internally – among Member States – international agreements serve as an additional layer of cooperation, often in the interest of deeper integration. What *all* these agreements have in common, however, is that the UK once participated in them – either by way of Art. 216(2) TFEU or itself as a treaty party. What *most* of these agreements have in common is, moreover, that the UK did so *because* it was an EU Member State. Since March 29, 2017, the question has therefore also arisen as to what effect withdrawal from the EU has on this network of international agreements. Can a former EU Member State continue to participate in international agreements of the EU? Can it remain a party to international agreements it concluded in the context of its EU membership?

As with many issues in the context of EU withdrawal, the question of the effect of a Member State leaving the EU on international agreements was asked for the first time in the wake of Brexit. But while the UK's

---

12 In ECJ, *ECHR Accession* (n 10) [157], the ECJ had separated the EU Treaties from other international agreements, stating that 'the founding treaties of the EU, unlike *ordinary international treaties*, established a new legal order' (emphasis added).
13 R Behr, 'Brexit earthquake has happened, and the rubble will take years to clear' (*The Guardian,* 24.06.2016) <https://www.theguardian.com/politics/2016/jun/24/brexit-earthquake-has-happened-the-rubble-will-take-years-to-clear>.
14 Consolidated Version of the Treaty on the Functioning of the European Union (26 October 2012) OJ C326/47 [TFEU].

Introduction

exit provided the opportunity, the question has so far still been only insufficiently answered. The reason is two-fold: firstly, most scholarly contributions aiming to provide answers were written following the UK's referendum but before Brexit took place, and therefore many of them could not consider the actual practice. In hindsight, the actual practice of Brexit contradicts many of the answers given in these earlier contributions. Secondly, most of these works also took only one particular perspective on the EU and withdrawal therefrom as a starting point for their analysis: namely that the EU is an international organisation the consequences of withdrawal from which must be considered in light of international institutional and treaty law. However, against the backdrop of Brexit practice, this approach has proven to be inadequate. The possibility of applying alternative legal frameworks to the situation of a state leaving the EU, on the other hand, is vastly underexplored.

The aim of this study is, therefore, not simply to show the deficiencies of earlier scholarship, but, following a deconstruction of previous arguments, it offers an alternative approach. Given the nature of the relationship between the EU and its Member States and the corresponding nature of the international agreements they conclude, this study argues that the framework of the law of state succession is better suited to address the challenges of such a disintegration for international agreements. While a direct application of the rules on *state* succession fails due to the EU's lack of statehood, this study makes the first attempt to comprehensively investigate the possibility of an analogical application. Based on a comparison between the EU and so-called 'unions of states', applying the framework of state succession by analogy is justifiable and the results of such an application arguably correspond better with the actual practice witnessed in the case of Brexit.

The argument is divided into three. The first chapter sets the scene: following a brief overview of the EU and its Member States' treaty practice in general, it looks at their specific practice in the context of Brexit and demonstrates the divergence between this practice and previous scholarship on the issue (§ 1). The following chapters form two parts. *Part I* engages with the traditional international institutional and treaty law approach to EU withdrawal and international agreements (§§ 2–4). *Part II* introduces and argues in favour of the alternative path of taking recourse to the framework of state succession (§§ 5–7). The study closes with a summary and outlook.

§ 1 Setting the Scene: Brexit and EU Treaty Practice

The UK's exit from the EU raised a plethora of (legal) questions. Some of these questions were of a fundamental nature: how could the EU and the UK square their ideas of future cooperation with the British–Irish border? Others were of a very practical character: what technological solutions could facilitate border controls? Many of them were politically charged and almost all of them – at least indirectly and in the long term – concerned the lives of British and EU citizens. Amidst the heated debates on citizens' rights, financial settlements, the future role of the European Court of Justice (ECJ), and the British-Irish border – of what relevance is the question of the effect of Brexit on international agreements?

To best understand the relevance of the topic covered in this study, it is first necessary to understand what is at stake. Over recent decades, the EU has become a global actor. This is not least thanks to its ever-growing network of international agreements in which its Member States – by way of EU or international law – participate (I.). With respect to many of these agreements, the EU and the UK took a sweeping approach expressed in their withdrawal agreement as well as in post-Brexit UK treaty practice (II.). This approach, however, raises serious questions under international law which have yet to be answered by the EU or UK and which have not been adequately addressed in the literature (III.).

I. Background: The EU as a Global Actor

The EU is increasingly depicted as a global actor. It is a characterisation that the EU ascribes to itself,[1] but also one that gradually found its way into the political and legal discourse about the Union.[2] An essential feature of this depiction and understanding is the EU's practice of concluding inter-

---

1 See only the EU's strategic communication on its international role, EU External Action Service, 'The EU as a Global Actor' (13.03.2022) <https://www.eeas.europa.eu/eeas/eu-global-actor_en>.
2 Recent publications include SB Gareis, G Hauser and F Kernic, *The European Union – A Global Actor?* (Verlag Barbara Budrich 2012); S Lütz and others (eds), *The European Union As a Global Actor: Trade, Finance and Climate Policy* (Springer 2021) and E

national agreements. The legal background and pre-condition for this is its treaty-making capacity. Art. 47 TEU establishes the EU's legal personality, while Art. 216 TFEU specifies the scope of its competences. According to Art. 216(1) TFEU, the EU has both explicit external competences, those provided for in the EU Treaties or secondary legislation, and implicit ones.[3] Moreover, its competences are always related to those of its Member States.[4] The question is thus not only whether the EU has the competence to conclude an international agreement, but also whether (simultaneous) action by Member States is precluded or still admissible.

In theory, this division of competences between the EU and its Member States should be an internal matter, irrelevant to their treaty partners.[5] In practice, however, it manifests itself in a variety of treaty constellations, some of which are unique to the EU's treaty practice. Moreover, the EU's specificities are not only regularly catered to in treaty practice: the EU's very own categorisation of international agreements – EU-only, mixed, *inter se* – has also diffused into international law-speak, underlining in a formal manner the weight of the EU as a global (treaty) actor. First and foremost, however, the said characterisation originates from the EU's practice of concluding international agreements with a wide variety of actors and on a broad range of topics. As put by Fahey and Mancini, '[f]rom tax

---

Fahey and I Mancini (eds), *Understanding the EU as a Good Global Actor: Ambitions, Values and Metrics* (Edward Elgar Publishing 2022).

3 Art. 216(1) TFEU: 'The Union may conclude an agreement with one or more third countries or international organisations where the Treaties so provide or where the conclusion of an agreement is necessary in order to achieve, within the framework of the Union's policies, one of the objectives referred to in the Treaties, or is provided for in a legally binding Union act or is likely to affect common rules or alter their scope.'

4 HG Schermers and N Blokker, International Institutional Law: Unity within Diversity (5th edn, Martinus Nijhoff Publishers 2011) para 1752.

5 In general, an international agreement between states – such as the EU Treaties – cannot and shall not impose any rights or obligations on non-treaty parties. On the principle of *res inter alios acta*, see further below Part I § 3 section II.B. In the context of the EU's division of competences, also Art. 46(2) of the Vienna Convention on the Law of Treaties between States and International Organizations or between International Organizations (adopted and opened for signature 21 March 1986) UN Doc A/CONF.129/15 [VCLT-IO] is often cited whereby '[a]n international organization may not invoke the fact that its consent to be bound by a treaty has been expressed in violation of the rules of the organization regarding competence to conclude treaties as invalidating its consent unless that violation was manifest and concerned a rule of fundamental importance.' For a good example, see E Steinberger, 'The WTO Treaty as a Mixed Agreement: Problems with the EC's and the EC Member States' Membership of the WTO' (2006) 17(4) *European Journal of International Law* 837, 844–848.

I. Background: The EU as a Global Actor

evasion to spam to gender to climate change to fisheries to passenger name records, nothing is beyond being included in trade agreements by the EU anymore.'[6]

Before considering the practice with regard to international agreements in the context of Brexit, it is necessary to understand these manifestations of the EU's role as a global treaty actor. It is necessary to know the EU's specific categorisation of international agreements (A.), because the EU and the UK have treated them differently in their Brexit practice. Moreover, it is necessary to understand the extent of the EU's treaty practice, both in terms of the quantity and quality of the international agreements concerned (B.), in order to understand the momentousness of the EU's and UK's Brexit approach for international (treaty) relations.

A. EU Treaty Practice: A Formal Categorisation

There are a number of ways to categorise international agreements in international law. These range from the laterality of the agreement (bi-, tri-, pluri- or multilateral), to its geographical scope (regional or universal), to its subject matter (particular or general), and to the quality of its obligations (contractual or law-making).[7] The EU categorises international agreements with the labels EU-only, mixed or *inter se*, the difference between these categorisations lying in the constellation of treaty parties on the EU side.

'EU-only' refers to international agreements which the EU concludes with one or more non-EU states or an international organisation. Although the Member States are involved in the internal EU conclusion procedure via the Council,[8] they do not act as (additional) contracting parties *vis-à-vis* non-EU state(s). Their obligation to implement these agreements, thus, does not stem from international law, but follows from Art. 216(2) TFEU, binding the Member States to international agreements concluded by the Union.[9]

---

6 E Fahey and I Mancini, 'Introduction: Understanding the EU as a Good Global Actor: Whose Metrics?' in E Fahey and I Mancini (eds) (n 2) 3.
7 K Schmalenbach, 'Article 2' in O Dörr and K Schmalenbach (eds), *Vienna Convention on the Law of Treaties: A Commentary* (2nd edn, Springer 2018) para 8.
8 Cp Art. 218 TFEU.
9 Art. 216(2) TFEU: 'Agreements concluded by the Union are binding upon the institutions of the Union and on its Member States.'

International agreements where the Member States *do* act as contracting parties together with the EU are referred to as mixed agreements.[10] Here, the EU and its Member States conclude the agreement with one or more non-EU treaty partners, thus all are bound under international law. Within the category of mixed agreements, it is common to differentiate between *bilateral* mixed agreements and *multilateral* mixed agreements. In the international law sense of the terms,[11] both of these subcategories are, of course, multilateral agreements, counting several treaty parties – the EU, its Member States, and at least one non-EU treaty party. By referring to some of these agreements as *bilateral* mixed agreements, however, the EU alludes to their structure: these agreements create reciprocal rights and obligations between the EU and its Member States, on the one hand, and one or more non-EU states, on the other hand.[12] In contrast, in *multilateral* mixed agreements, the EU and its Member States do not form such a 'single contracting party'[13] and, in general[14], all treaty obligations are owed *vis-à-vis* all other contracting parties.

While EU-only and mixed agreements are directed outward, meaning that there is always at least one non-EU treaty party, *inter se* agreements are an instrument of intra-union cooperation.[15] As phrased by Heesen, '[i]n this sense, the agreements, regardless of their legal nature under international law, are part of the law of the European association between the Union and

---

10 For three seminal contributions to the many questions surrounding these agreements, see the edited volumes D O'Keeffe and HG Schermers (eds), *Mixed Agreements* (Kluwer 1983); C Hillion and P Koutrakos (eds), *Mixed Agreements Revisited: The EU and its Member States in the World* (Hart Publishing 2010); N Levrat and others (eds), *The EU and its Member States' Joint Participation in International Agreements* (Hart Publishing 2021).
11 To illustrate the difference between agreements with two parties and those structured in a bilateral manner, McNair preferred the terms 'bipartite' and 'multipartite' instead of 'bilateral' and 'multilateral', when referring to the laterality (AD McNair, *The Law of Treaties* (Clarendon Press 1961) 29).
12 See further on this below at Part I § 4 section I.B.1 and section II.B.1.c.
13 ECJ, Case C-53/96 *Hermès International v FHT Marketing Choice BV* [1998] EU:C:1998:292, [14].
14 In some instances, the EU and its Member States seek to exclude the application of multilateral mixed agreements among themselves. A commonly used instrument for this is the so-called disconnection clause. See in detail, J Odermatt, *International Law and the European Union* (Cambridge University Press 2021) 82–87.
15 For an extensive study of the *inter se* agreements, see J Heesen, *Interne Abkommen: Völkerrechtliche Verträge zwischen den Mitgliedstaaten der Europäischen Union* (Springer 2015).

the Member States. They form its horizontal dimension.'[16] Within the *inter se* agreements, a distinction can be made between agreements solely among Member States and agreements between Member States and the EU.

The choice of treaty constellation depends essentially on the division of competences within the Union.[17] According to Art. 216(1) TFEU, the EU may conclude international agreements only in cases in which it has the external competence to do so. The EU may thus become a party to an agreement (alongside the Member States) only where the content of the agreement also touches upon its competences; it may become the sole party to the agreement (without the Member States) where this applies to the entire content of the agreement. Said another way – where the EU does not possess the necessary competences for all subject matters of the agreement, the Member States must become parties alongside it.[18]

Considering these different categorisations, it becomes clear that they convey information only about internal EU matters – that is whether the subject matter of the agreement falls within the competence of the EU or (also) that of its Member States. For international law, however, these categories are *prima facie* irrelevant.[19] Nonetheless, the categorisation of

---

16 Ibid 187 ('In diesem Sinne sind die Abkommen, ungeachtet ihrer völkerrechtlichen Rechtsnatur, Bestandteil des Rechts des europäischen Verbundes aus Union und Mitgliedstaaten. Sie bilden seine horizontale Dimension.' Translated by the author).
17 A vast amount of literature covers the issue of the EU's external competences. See for an instructive recent contribution, M Cremona, 'External Relations of the European Union: The Constitutional Framework for International Action' in P Craig and G de Búrca (eds), *The Evolution of EU Law* (3rd edn, Oxford University Press 2021). The development of the EU's external competences in the jurisprudence of the ECJ can be retraced in a number of contributions in G Butler and RA Wessel (eds), *EU External Relations Law: The Cases in Context* (Hart Publishing 2022).
18 There are two exceptions to this rule where the Member States co-conclude international agreements without any legal necessity. The first exception is the so-called 'facultative mixed agreement'. Here, the EU possesses the competence to conclude the agreement, but the scope of its *exclusive* competences does not cover the whole agreement. Opting for a mixed agreement is thus a political choice; the EU could have also concluded an EU-only agreement, exercising its shared competences. The second exception is the so-called 'false mixed agreement'. Here, co-conclusion is legally speaking the wrong procedure; the agreement falls completely within the EU's exclusive competence. On these two categories, see J Heliskoski and G Kübek, 'A Typology of EU Mixed Agreements Revisited' in N Levrat and others (eds) (n 10) 31–34 On false mixity, see also HG Schermers, 'A Typology of Mixed Agreements' in D O'Keeffe and HG Schermers (eds) (n 10) 27–28.
19 But see the discussion on the division of international responsibility in case of mixed agreements, eg in MD Evans and P Koutrakos (eds), *The International Responsibility*

international agreements as EU-only or mixed has been adopted by many treaty partners[20] and is meanwhile quite naturally used in international legal scholarship.[21] One could consider the adoption of these categories as harmless, seeing that 'the undertaking to classify treaties is [in any case] primarily of academic interest'. However, toying with existing categories such as 'bilateral' or 'multilateral' not only leads to confusion if not legal uncertainty[22] – the consequences of such classification can also be witnessed in the context of Brexit, where different legal outcomes were attached to the different categories of agreements.[23]

B. The Global Scale of EU Treaty Practice

The EU has concluded international agreements since the year of its nascency. Only 7 months after the entry into force of the *Treaty of Rome*[24] on January 1, 1958, the EU signed the *Agreement on Relations between the International Labour Organization and the European Economic Community*[25]. Since then, not only the number of international agreements has exponentially increased, also the subject areas covered by these agreements have significantly grown. Both aspects are essential to understanding not only the relevance of these agreements for the EU, but also the significance of the question what happens with them post-Brexit.

At the time of Brexit, the EU's treaty database counted a total of 1262 international agreements.[26] These agreements encompassed 266 mixed

---

     of the European Union: European and International Perspectives (Hart Publishing 2013).

20 This is not, however, without criticism on especially the concept of mixed agreements. See eg P Olson, 'Mixity from the Outside: The Perspective of a Treaty Partner' in C Hillion and P Koutrakos (eds) (n 10).

21 See eg the two standard works on international organisation that both include a section on mixed agreements, J Klabbers, *An Introduction to International Institutional Law* (2nd edn, Cambridge University Press 2009) 263–266; HG Schermers and N Blokker (n 4) paras 1756–1762.

22 See eg below Part I § 4 section II.B.1.c.

23 See below § 1 section II.

24 Treaty Establishing the European Economic Community (adopted on 25 March 1957, entered into force 1 January 1958) 294 UNT 3 [TEEC].

25 Agreement on Relations between the International Labour Organization and the European Economic Community (27 April 1959) OJ 27/521 [ILO-EEC Agreement].

26 The EU's External Action Service used to provide a treaty database on its official website (https://www.eeas.europa.eu/_en). This database was recently removed. The

agreements, of which 158 can be categorised as bilateral mixed and 108 as multilateral mixed agreements. The vast majority of international agreements – 873 – were EU-only agreements.[27] In addition, the database listed 26 agreements which cannot definitely be placed in one of the aforementioned categories. These are international agreements which, for example, the EU and only some EU Member States have concluded, because the subject matter does not pertain to all Member States.[28] The geographical scope of these 1262 international agreements is close to global. Counting all territories[29] with which the EU is in a treaty relationship – including in large multilateral fora[30] – the number of the EU's treaty partners amounts to 152.

However, also content-wise, the scope of the EU's international agreements is far-reaching. In the EU's treaty database, the agreements were divided into 33 subject matters. While lengthy, only a listing of these can provide an accurate impression of the scale of the EU's international relations and what is potentially at risk for Member States upon EU withdrawal. At the time of Brexit, the EU (partly together with its Member States) had concluded international agreements relating to:

Agriculture; Audiovisual and Media; Commercial Policy; Competition; Consumers; Culture; Customs; Development; Economic and Monetary

---

following information is based on data download by the author prior to the removal of the database. The table including all international agreements listed in the database in January 2018 is on file with the author.

27 This number does not include the EU-only agreements concluded by the EU with international organisations on their mutual cooperation. These were not included in the database.

28 An example of this is the Protocol on Integrated Coastal Zone Management in the Mediterranean (4 February 2009) OJ L34/19 to which besides the EU itself only those Member States are a party that border the Mediterranean Sea (Croatia, France, Greece, Italy, Malta, Slovenia, and Spain).

29 This includes agreements with entities such as Hong Kong and Kosovo, which are not independent states or have not globally been recognised as such.

30 With many states, the EU has concluded international agreements dealing with specific issues in their bilateral relations. With some states, however, the EU only has treaty relations via (universal) multilateral agreements to which both are parties. Examples for such agreements are the Agreement Establishing the Common Fund for Commodities (adopted on 27 June 1980, entered into force 19 June 1989) 1538 UNTS 3 [Commodities Agreement], the International Tropical Timber Agreement (adopted on 27 January 2006, entered into force 7 December 2011) 2797 UNTS 75 [Timber Agreement], and the International Cocoa Agreement (adopted on 25 June 2010, provisionally applied since 1 October 2012) 2871 UNTS 3.

Affairs; Education, Training, Youth; Education; Employment and Social Policy; Energy; Enlargement; Enterprise; Environment; External Relations; Fisheries; Foreign and Security Policy; Fraud; Human Rights; Humanitarian Aid; Information Society; Internal Market; Justice, Freedom and Security; Monetary Policy; Public Health; Research and Innovation; Tax Fraud; Taxation; Trade; Transport; World Trade Organization.[31]

The question if and how post-Brexit UK still participates in international agreements concluded by the EU and often by the UK itself during its EU membership is thus not only relevant for the UK in many respects, ranging from air transport to fishing quotas and trade; for the same reasons, it is also relevant for a large number of states worldwide.

For a Member State leaving the EU, the task of gaining an overview of the (possibly affected) international agreements is further complicated by the fact that the EU database may not be the sole point of reference. In fact, the EU's treaty partners may approach the question coming from entirely different numbers. In the context of Brexit, Larik demonstrated how difficult even a first inventory can be, describing the challenge of simply attempting to determine the number of agreements in force between the EU and the United States of America (USA).[32] While he counted 21 bilateral agreements between the EU and the USA in the official US database, the EU's database listed 52.[33]

In comparison to the sheer mass of international agreements with non-EU states and the issues that they cover, one may be tempted to disregard the importance of the EU Member States' *inter se* agreements. Being agreements only between EU Member States, these are, by their very nature, not global. In the case of the UK, moreover, the number of concluded *inter se* agreements is vanishingly small.[34] Of what relevance can these agreements be in the overall context of EU withdrawal? In fact, however, the three *inter se* agreements to which the UK had become a party as an EU Member State demonstrate in a particularly illustrative way what –

---

31 Subject areas as taken from the EU's treaty database, see (n 26).
32 J Larik, 'Brexit and the Transatlantic Trouble of Counting Treaties' (*EJIL:Talk!*, 6.12.2017) <https://www.ejiltalk.org/brexit-and-the-transatlantic-trouble-of-counting-treaties/>.
33 Ibid. The US treaty database can be accessed at https://www.state.gov/treaties-in-force/.
34 While the UK initially ratified a fourth *inter se* agreement, the Agreement on a Unified Patent Court (20 June 2013) OJ C175/1 [UPC Agreement]), this agreement did not enter into force before Brexit. Meanwhile, the UK has withdrawn its ratification.

in case of EU withdrawal – may be at risk and which (legal) problems could arise therefrom.

The first *inter se* agreement is the *Convention Defining the Statute of the European Schools*[35] (ES Convention). Having initially been concluded in 1957 between the Member States, the Convention was reformed in 1994 and has since counted the EU itself as a contracting party.[36] Its aim is the establishment of schools in EU Member States for the children of the Union's employees.[37] In 1978, one such school was founded in Culham in the UK.[38] Besides the financing and functioning of European Schools, the ES Convention also regulates the recognition of degrees obtained at these schools.[39] The second *inter se* agreement is the *Convention Setting up a European University Institute*[40] (EUI Convention), an international agreement concluded only between the EU Member States. It established the European University Institute (EUI), a Florence-based research institute for international postgraduate and post-doctoral teaching and studies.[41] Both educational institutions – the European Schools and the EUI – are financed by the EU and its Member States.[42] Although the European Schools and the EUI do exceptionally admit non-EU nationals, they are primarily aimed at pupils and students coming from EU Member States.[43]

The third *inter se* agreement differs from the previous two in that it does not establish a common educational institution. Instead, the *Internal*

---

35 Convention Defining the Statute of the European Schools (17 August 1994) OJ L212/3 [ES Convention].
36 On the history of the ES Convention, see J Heesen (n 15) 29. On the European Schools, see also J Gruber, 'Europäische Schulen: Ein in die EG integriertes Völkerrechtssubjekt' (2005) 65 *Zeitschrift für ausländisches öffentliches Recht und Völkerrecht* 1015.
37 Art. 1 ES Convention.
38 See the former website of the school, Office of the Secretary-General of the European Schools, 'United Kingdom – Culham' <https://www.eursc.eu/en/European-Schools/locations/Culham>.
39 Art. 5 ES Convention.
40 Convention Setting up a European University Institute (9 February 1976) OJ C29/1 [EUI Convention]. On the history of the EUI, see J Heesen (n 15) 30–31. On the EUI, see also S Kaufmann, *Das Europäische Hochschulinstitut: Die Florentiner »Europa-Universität« im Gefüge des europäischen und internationalen Rechts* (Duncker & Humblot 2003).
41 Arts. 1, 2 EUI Convention.
42 Art. 25 ES Convention, Art. 19 EUI Convention.
43 Art. 1 ES Convention, Art. 16(2) EUI Convention.

§ 1 Setting the Scene: Brexit and EU Treaty Practice

Agreement on the Financing of European Union Aid[44] (EDF Agreement) set up the European Development Fund (EDF), 'the EU's main instrument to finance development cooperation with African, Caribbean and Pacific (APC) countries and overseas countries and territories (OCTs)'[45]. In a mixed agreement between the EU and its Member States, on the one hand, and ACP states, on the other hand, the former have committed themselves to the payment of development aid.[46] The extent to which each Member State contributes to that sum is, in turn, agreed upon *inter se* in the EDF Agreement.[47]

On whether the UK remains a party to these agreements post-Brexit thus hinges, first, the continued financing of the two educational institutions and the EDF. Where the Member States (and the EU) agreed to contribute certain shares to a fixed (annual) budget, this may be to the detriment of the remaining treaty parties. Alternatively, the institutions' and the EDF's budgets would need to be decreased. Apart from many practical problems, in the case of the EDF, this could result in the EU and its remaining Member States incurring international responsibility *vis-à-vis* the ACP states. Secondly, the example of the European Schools and the EUI shows how Brexit – also via its impact on international agreements – may very tangibly affect individuals: if a European School is suddenly in a non-EU state; if a withdrawing state's national suddenly no longer fulfils the criteria for admission to educational institutions; and if the recognition of their degrees previously obtained at these institutions is suddenly in question.

What is at stake when considering the effect of a state's withdrawal from the EU on international agreements is thus, on the one hand, a geographically and content-wise broad network of international relations with states

---

44 Internal Agreement between the Representatives of the Governments of the Member States of the European Union meeting within the Council, on the Financing of European Union Aid under the Multiannual Financial Framework for the Period 2014 to 2020, in Accordance with the ACP-EU Partnership Agreement, and on the Allocation of Financial Assistance for the Overseas Countries and Territories to which Part Four of the Treaty on the Functioning of the European Union applies (6 August 2013) OJ L210/1 [EDF Agreement].

45 EU, 'European Development Fund' <https://eur-lex.europa.eu/EN/legal-content/glossary/european-development-fund.html>.

46 Partnership Agreement between the Members of the African, Caribbean and Pacific Group of States of the one part, and the European Community and its Member States, of the other part (15 December 2000) OJ L317/3 [EU-ACP PCA].

47 On the history and role of the EDF Agreement and its predecessors, see J Heesen (n 15) 37–39.

outside the EU and, on the other hand, common institutions aiming to deepen European integration but set outside the EU legal order. Against this backdrop, what role did the issue of international agreements play in the wake of Brexit? Furthermore, how were the questions surrounding these agreements addressed by the EU, its Member States, the UK and their non-EU treaty partners?

II. Brexit Practice: Out Means (Almost Always) Out

'Out means out' was a catchphrase often used on both sides of the Channel during the EU and the UK's Brexit talks.[48] On the EU side, this motto was based primarily on the conviction that 'cherry picking'[49] must be avoided at all costs. A Member State that decides to leave the EU should bear the full consequences of this decision and not be able to cherry-pick those aspects of European cooperation that it considers most advantageous. On the British side, 'out means out' stood above all for the idea of 'taking back control'[50], the complete regaining and exercise of supposedly lost sovereignty, that in future, the UK Parliament – or government, depending on political preferences – alone should decide on all British matters.

Very early on in the Brexit negotiations, both the UK (A.) and the EU (B.) settled on an 'out means out' approach also with regard to most international agreements concluded by the EU or its Member States in the context of their EU membership. Accordingly, the withdrawal agreement

---

48 In the UK, Prime Minister David Cameron already used the phrase pre-referendum, warning the British public that following the referendum no further negotiations with the EU would take place (see G Parker, 'Out means out in EU vote, warns David Cameron' (*Financial Times*, 25.10.2015) <https://www.ft.com/content/b52f1b0a-7aee-11e5-a1fe-567b37f80b64>). It was also employed to rally against a possible revocation of the Art. 50 TEU notification (see UK Government, 'Archived Petition: Respect the majority vote on the EU-out means out!' (08.03.2017) <https://petition.parliament.uk/archived/petitions/189340>) and later adapted by Prime Minister Theresa May to describe her Brexit politics (see N Allen, 'Brexit Means Brexit: Theresa May and post-referendum British Politics' (2018) 13 *British Politics* 105). But see also A Rinke, '"Out means out", German lawmakers warn Britain on Brexit' (*Reuters*, 26.04.2016) <https://www.reuters.com/article/britain-eu-germany/out-means-out-german-lawmakers-warn-britain-on-brexit-idINKCN0XN26Z>.

49 See eg European Economic and Social Committee, 'There is no cherry-picking on Brexit' (*Press Release*, 06.07.2017) <https://www.eesc.europa.eu/en/news-media/press-releases/there-no-cherry-picking-brexit>.

50 UK Government, 'EU Exit' Taking back control of our borders, money and laws while protecting our economy, security and Union (November 2018) Cm 9741.

concluded between the EU and the UK mirrored said approach, addressing the issue of international agreements under a withdrawal and a transition perspective (C.). With the UK setting out to establish its own international treaty network, non-EU states were also finally confronted with the Brexit repercussions (D.).

A. The UK Position: From Continuity to 'Global Britain'

The UK gave a first indicator of its position towards international agreements concluded by the EU (with or without the Member States) post-Brexit prior to the EU referendum. In a booklet, the UK government explained why it 'believe[d] that voting to remain in the European Union is the best decision for the UK'[51]. In describing the consequences of leaving the EU, the booklet stated that this 'could result in 10 years or more of uncertainty as the UK unpicks [its] relationship with the EU and *renegotiates new arrangements* with the EU and *over 50 other countries around the world*'[52]. The following footnote referred to the 'European Commission, DG Trade's World map of trade agreements in force giv[ing] a list of the markets covered by EU Trade Agreements'[53]. The statement is somewhat ambiguous. *R*enegotiations can take place where a previous agreement still exists but is no longer suitable. The negotiation of *new arrangements* could, at the same time, suggest that previous ones are no longer in place.

Following the referendum but prior to the UK's Art. 50 TEU notification, the UK government issued a white paper to Parliament. The white paper, *inter alia*, informed the parliamentarians of possible adverse Brexit effects on trade and investment relations with non-EU partners. While the paper was silent on the exact consequences of Brexit on EU trade agreements, it stated the government's aim to 'achieve continuity in our trade and investment relationships with third countries, including those covered by

---

51 UK Government, 'Why the Government believes that Voting to Remain in the EU is the Best Decision for the UK' Booklet Providing Important Information about the EU Referendum on 23 June 2016 (6 April 2016) 1.
52 Ibid 8 (emphasis added).
53 Ibid. For a more recent map of EU trade agreements, see EU Council, 'Infographic: EU Trade Map' (25.11.2021) <https://www.consilium.europa.eu/en/infographics/eu-trade-map/>.

existing EU free trade agreements or EU preferential arrangements'[54]. The government was in the process of 'exploring with [its] trading partners ways to achieve this'[55].

During the course of the Brexit negotiations with the EU, however, the tone in the UK very much changed. The government started to pursue a strategy of 'Global Britain', aiming to take advantage of the (perceived) freedoms it gained when no longer being an EU Member State.[56] The primary goal was, thus, no longer to 'achieve continuity'[57], but to negotiate new and better trade agreements.[58] Nevertheless, what did the government believe would happen to the EU's trade agreements which, being mostly mixed agreements, it had often co-concluded? Moreover, apart from trade agreements – what was the UK's general stance on international agreements post-Brexit?

In detail, the UK government commented on the issue of international agreements post-Brexit in a guidance note on its website. According to this note, '[a]s the UK leaves the EU, it will leave international agreements to which it is currently party by virtue of EU membership'[59]. Further on, this is specified as follows:

> If the UK leaves the EU without a deal, it will no longer be covered by EU-only international agreements, or by 'mixed' bilateral agreements between the EU and its Member States on one hand, and a third party on the other, unless the UK and the third party agree to transition the agreement, or agree to other measures to ensure the continuity of the effect(s) of the agreement.
>
> The UK will remain a party to most mixed multilateral agreements after exit day, where it is already a party in its own right. [...] Whether or

---

54 UK Government, 'The United Kingdom's Exit from and New Partnership with the European Union' White Paper (2 February 2017) Cm 9417 55.
55 Ibid.
56 For a comprehensive report on this strategy, see UK House of Commons, 'Global Britain' Sixth Report of Session 2017–19 (6 March 2018) HC 780.
57 'UK Brexit White Paper' (n 54) 55.
58 On the UK government's mixed record so far, see P Foster, 'UK has failed to demonstrate benefit of post-Brexit trade deals, MPs warn' (*Financial Times,* 18 March 2022) <https://www.ft.com/content/af1ef504-ee32-43c0-b7d5-81d045714618>.
59 UK Government, 'International Agreements if the UK leaves the EU without a Deal', Guidance Note (5 November 2019) 1.

§ 1 Setting the Scene: Brexit and EU Treaty Practice

not the UK will remain a party to mixed agreements after exit day will depend on the terms and structure of the agreement in question.[60]

Thus, the UK differentiated between EU-only and bilateral mixed agreements, on the one hand, and multilateral mixed agreements, on the other hand. From an international law perspective, this differentiation is surprising, given that the UK had become a party to *both* bilateral and multilateral mixed agreements. Moreover, the guidance note provided no explanation as to *why* two categories of international agreements would no longer cover the UK, while it remained a party to another. The agreements' 'terms and structure' are relevant to identify which mixed agreement is structured bilaterally and which multilaterally. However, reference to an agreement's terms and structure alone fails to explain why this – in the view of the UK government – is legally relevant.

B. The EU Position: Of Guidelines and Directives

The EU first addressed the issue of Brexit and international agreements following the UK's Art. 50 TEU notification. At a special meeting on occasion of the notification, the European Council adopted a first set of guidelines which were to 'set out the overall positions and principles that the Union [would] pursue throughout the negotiation'[61] with the UK. In 'defin[ing] the framework for negotiations under Art 50 TEU'[62], the guidelines aimed to set the tone for the talks with the UK, both as regards the sequencing and the content of the negotiations. The guidelines already included a 'phased approach to negotiations'[63] – separating the withdrawal from the future relationship negotiations – as well as the EU's core substantive points to be included in an 'agreement on arrangements for an orderly withdrawal'[64].

However, the EU's Brexit guidelines were also of relevance for an external audience. Not only do they acknowledge that the withdrawal negotiations should 'aim to provide as much clarity and legal certainty as possible *to* [...]

---

60 Ibid 2.
61 European Council, 'Guidelines following the United Kingdom's Notification under Article 50 TEU' (29 April 2017) EUCO XT 20004/17 2.
62 Ibid.
63 Ibid 4.
64 Ibid 5.

II. Brexit Practice: Out Means (Almost Always) Out

international partners on the immediate effects of the United Kingdom's withdrawal from the Union'[65]. The section on withdrawal also states the EU's position on the effect of Brexit on international agreements:

> Following the withdrawal, the United Kingdom will no longer be covered by agreements concluded by the Union or by Member States acting on its behalf or by the Union and its Member States acting jointly. The Union will continue to have its rights and obligations in relation to international agreements. In this respect, the European Council expects the United Kingdom to honour its share of all international commitments contracted in the context of its EU membership. In such instances, a constructive dialogue with the United Kingdom on a possible common approach towards third country partners, international organisations and conventions concerned should be engaged.[66]

Just as the UK's guidance note, the EU's statement is somewhat ambiguous.[67] On the one hand, the first sentence claims that the UK 'will no longer be covered' by certain agreements, which itself raises the question what is meant by 'covered'.[68] Does this refer to the UK no longer being bound by international agreements via Art. 216 TFEU or also under international law, where the UK is a party itself? On the other hand, expecting the UK to 'honour its share of all international commitments' suggests at least a certain continuity of international obligations. In any event, the fact that the EU reminded the UK of its commitments and recognised the necessity to engage with the non-EU treaty partners indicates two things: First, the EU seemed to acknowledge that its own formal status with regard to these international agreements does not change with the UK's exit, and, secondly, that Brexit will nevertheless have an effect on these agreements.

The EU's negotiating directives did not provide further clarity. Instead, they reiterated the necessity to seek solutions in dialogue with the UK and the affected treaty partners, this time, however, with a view to obligations for which the EU seemed to assume continuity. The directives stated that

---

65 Ibid 4 (emphasis added).
66 Ibid 6.
67 On this, see also M Cremona, 'The Withdrawal Agreement and the EU's International Agreements' (2020) 45(2) *European Law Review* 237, 243–244.
68 The same can be said of the formulation in the UK's guidance note, see above at § 1 section II.A.

§ 1 Setting the Scene: Brexit and EU Treaty Practice

a constructive dialogue should be engaged as early as practicable with the United Kingdom during the first phase of the negotiation on a possible common approach towards third country partners, international organisations and conventions in relation to the international commitments contracted before the withdrawal date, *by which the United Kingdom remains bound*, as well as on the method to ensure that the United Kingdom honours these commitments.[69]

What then were international agreements to which the UK would, in the view of the EU, remain bound and by which would it 'no longer be covered'[70]? The Brexit guidelines had referred to three types of international agreements, all of which would cease to apply to the UK: 'agreements concluded by the Union', that is EU-only agreements; agreements concluded by 'Member States acting on behalf of the Union', meaning agreements to which the EU could not itself become a party, although being competent to conclude them; and agreements concluded by 'the Union and its Member States acting jointly', which appeared to refer to mixed agreements. By which agreements concluded with 'third country partners'[71] or international organisations would the UK then remain bound, as stated in the negotiating directive?

The EU's approach was finally refined in an internal preparatory document prepared by the Commission's Task Force for the Preparation and Conduct of the Negotiations with the United Kingdom under Article 50 TEU. On January 31, 2018, the Art. 50 Task Force presented slides on 'Internal EU27 preparatory discussions on the framework for the future relationship: "International Agreements"' to the Art. 50 Working Party of the Council laying out the consequences of withdrawal concerning international agreements and the types of agreements to which they were thought to apply.[72] According to this document, the phrase 'the United Kingdom will no longer be covered' used in the Brexit guidelines was to be understood

---

69 Council of the European Union, 'Directives for the Negotiation of an Agreement with the United Kingdom of Great Britain and Northern Ireland setting out the Arrangements for its Withdrawal from the European Union' (22 May 2017) XT 21016/17 ADD 1 REV 2 7 (emphasis added).
70 'EU Brexit Guidelines' (n 61) 6.
71 'EU Brexit Directives' (n 69) 7.
72 EU Commission, 'Internal EU27 Preparatory Discussions on the Framework for the Future Relationship' International Agreements and Trade Policy (6 February 2018) TF50(2018) 29.

in the sense that 'the agreement no longer applies to the *territory* of the UK; *the UK* loses the benefits and is no longer bound by the obligations; *automatic*, from the day of withdrawal'[73]. These consequences were thought to apply to

> 'EU only' agreements: agreements concluded by the EU (and/or Euratom); or by the Member States on its behalf; Bilateral 'mixed' agreements: concluded on the one hand by the Union and its Member States, and on the other hand by the third country partner (e.g. Association agreements; Aviation agreements; European Economic Area).[74]

In contrast, the 'UK [would] remain party to multilateral agreements to which the EU is also a party, to the extent that UK is party in its own right (eg WTO agreements, Paris climate).'[75] Here, the UK would 'recover the full competence'[76].

C. The UK-EU Withdrawal Agreement: Transitioning International Agreements

It was on this basis that the EU and the UK proceeded to negotiate an agreement on withdrawal arrangements. The outcome of these negotiations, the *Agreement on the Withdrawal of the United Kingdom of Great Britain and Northern Ireland from the European Union and the Atomic Energy Community*[77] (UK-EU WA), served two main goals: on the one hand, it aims to permanently settle issues arising as an immediate consequence of the UK's withdrawal[78] and, on the other hand, it provides for a transition period during which the UK is no longer a Member State but continues to be treated as such in certain respects[79]. The Withdrawal Agreement deals with the effect of Brexit on international agreements – as approached by

---

73 Ibid 4 (emphasis in original).
74 Ibid 5.
75 Ibid.
76 Ibid.
77 Agreement on the Withdrawal of the United Kingdom of Great Britain and Northern Ireland from the European Union and the European Atomic Energy Community (12 November 2019) OJ C384 I/1 [UK-EU WA].
78 See in the UK-EU WA: Part Two – Citizens' Rights, Part Three – Separation Provisions, and Part Five – Financial Provisions.
79 See in the UK-EU WA: Part Four – Transition.

the EU and the UK – both under the aspect of separation issues as well as regarding to a transition phase.

The first mention of international agreements features very early on in the agreement's text. Art. 2(a) UK-EU WA defines 'Union law' for the purposes of the agreement as, *inter alia*,

> (iv) the international agreements to which the Union is a party and the international agreements concluded by the Member States acting on behalf of the Union
>
> (v) the agreements between Member States entered into in their capacity as Member States of the Union.

Thus, whenever a provision in the Withdrawal Agreement refers to Union law, this encompasses EU-only and *inter se* agreements. This is especially notable in the context of the transition phase. According to Art. 126 UK-EU WA, '[t]here shall be a transition or implementation period, which shall start on the date of entry into force of this Agreement and end on 31 December 2020.' Pursuant to Art. 127 UK-EU WA, '[u]nless otherwise provided in this Agreement, Union law shall be applicable to and in the United Kingdom during the transition period.' Considering the definition of Union law in Art. 2 UK-EU WA, the continued application was thus thought to encompass EU-only and *inter se* agreements.

In addition, Art. 129 UK-EU WA provides for '[s]pecific arrangements relating to the Union's external action'. In so doing, the article, on the one hand, broadens the transitional arrangements with regard to international agreements even further, by also addressing mixed agreements. According to Art. 129(1) UK-EU WA, 'the United Kingdom shall be bound by the obligations stemming from the international agreements concluded by the Union, by Member States acting on its behalf, *or by the Union and its Member States acting jointly*'[80]. Thus, while the EU and the UK took the position that certain international agreements would no longer be binding for the UK (under EU, respectively international law), they sought to provide for temporary continuity for the duration of the transition period. On the other hand, Art. 129(2) UK-EU WA severely limits the UK's institutional rights with regard to these agreements:

> During the transition period, representatives of the United Kingdom shall not participate in the work of any bodies set up by international

---

80 Emphasis added.

agreements concluded by the Union, or by Member States acting on its behalf, or by the Union and its Member States acting jointly [...].

An exception was only made for those international agreements in which 'the United Kingdom participates in its own right'[81]. Considering the EU and the UK's previous statements, this most likely refers to multilateral mixed agreements, where the EU and its Member States are not treated as one party. Moreover, the UK could participate in treaty bodies if and when the EU considered the UK's presence necessary and 'exceptionally invite[s]'[82] it to attend.

There are two further aspects of Art. 129 UK-EU WA which warrant attention in the context of international agreements. The first is a footnote to Art. 129(1). Here, the EU and the UK specify the method by which they sought to achieve the temporary continuity of international agreements envisaged in that article. After all, all the agreements mentioned in Art. 129(1) were international agreements concluded with *external* partners. Thus, the EU and the UK intended to 'notify the other parties to these agreements that during the transition period the United Kingdom is to be treated as a Member State for the purposes of these agreements'[83]. And indeed, following the signing of the Withdrawal Agreement, the EU sent a *note verbale* – explicitly 'endorsed by [...] the United Kingdom'[84] – to its treaty partners and the depositaries of multilateral agreements. In this *note*, the EU and the UK informed the recipients of the factual circumstances of Brexit and of their position as regards EU-only and bilateral mixed agreements: 'During the transition period, the United Kingdom is treated as a Member State of the Union [...] for the purposes of these international agreements'[85]. At the same time, the *note* also informed treaty partners that, thereafter, 'the

---

[81] Art. 129(2)(a) UK-EU WA.
[82] Art. 129(2)(b) UK-EU WA. The full text reads: '(b) the Union exceptionally invites the United Kingdom to attend, as part of the Union's delegation, meetings or parts of meetings of such bodies, where the Union considers that the presence of the United Kingdom is necessary and in the interest of the Union, in particular for the effective implementation of those agreements during the transition period; such presence shall only be allowed where Member States participation is permitted under the applicable agreements.'
[83] See Art. 129(1) Withdrawal Agreement, footnote.
[84] EU Commission, 'Cover Letter and Note Verbale on the Agreement on the Withdrawal of the United Kingdom of Great Britain and Northern' (5 December 2018) COM(2018) 841 final 1.
[85] Ibid 2.

United Kingdom will no longer be covered by [these] international agreements [...]. This is without prejudice to the status of the United Kingdom in relation to multilateral agreements to which it is a party in its own right.'[86]

The second noteworthy aspect of Art. 129 UK-EU WA is its fourth paragraph. In contrast to the previous paragraphs, Art. 129(4) does not deal with international agreements concluded prior to Brexit. Instead, it aims to regulate the UK's treaty-making *after* withdrawal from the EU. Considering that during the transition phase, the UK was to be treated like a Member State, paragraph 4 provides that

> the United Kingdom may negotiate, sign and ratify international agreements entered into in its own capacity in the areas of exclusive competence of the Union, provided those agreements do not enter into force or apply during the transition period, unless so authorised by the Union.

Thus, during the transition phase, the UK was not only banned from participating in treaty bodies pursuant to Art. 129(2) UK-EU WA. It was also prohibited from establishing through the conclusion of new agreements alternative fora for international cooperation in areas covered by EU agreements.

Besides these general provisions with regard to international agreements, two agreements find explicit mention in the UK-EU WA. These are, remarkably, two *inter se* agreements, a category of international agreements which had so far not been mentioned in EU or UK position papers on international agreements.[87] However, the way in which the Withdrawal Agreement approaches two of the three *inter se* agreements that the UK had concluded as a Member State demonstrates their approach rather clearly.

The first *inter se* agreement addressed in the UK-EU WA is the ES Convention. Regarding the European Schools, Art. 125 UK-EU WA not only contains a transitional provision, similar to that of Art. 129(1) with regard to other international agreements, but subject to a different time limit. It also seeks to provide a permanent solution as regards the recognition of degrees. Art. 125(1) provides that '[t]he United Kingdom shall be bound

---

86 Ibid 3.
87 The EDF had been mentioned in the EU's Negotiating Directives. However, these addressed the EDF only in the context of aiming for a 'single financial settlement' regarding different EU institutions/instruments such as the European Investment Bank, the European Central Bank and the EDF. The directives did not refer to the nature of the EDF as an international agreement (see 'EU Brexit Directives' (n 69) 10).

by the Convention defining the Statute of the European Schools [...] until the end of the school year that is ongoing at the end of the transition period.' Thus, the UK-EU WA aims to prevent larger disruptions in school operations in the immediate aftermath of Brexit. However, the need for such a transitional arrangement exists only where the two parties to the withdrawal agreement – the EU and the UK – are of the view that the UK will no longer be bound by the ES Convention following Brexit. This view is also reflected in Art. 125(2), which contains an obligation for the UK to continue to recognise – as provided for in Art. 5(2) ES Convention – the degrees of pupils previously, or by a certain cut-off date, enrolled at a European School.

The second *inter se* agreement explicitly mentioned in the UK-EU WA is the EDF Agreement. With regard to this agreement, Art. 152(1) UK-EU WA stipulates a similar solution as in the case of the European Schools. It provides that

> [t]he United Kingdom shall remain party to the European Development Fund ('EDF') until the closure of the 11th EDF and all previous unclosed EDFs, and shall in this respect assume the same obligations as the Member States under the Internal Agreement by which it was set up.

At the same time, Art. 152(2) UK-EU WA limits the continued participation of the UK in the EDF. While it 'may participate [...] in the EDF Committee as established in accordance with Article 8 of the [EDF Agreement]', it may do so only 'as an observer without voting rights'.

Finally, there is one *inter se* agreement which had not been dealt with in the UK-EU WA. Following the approach of the EU and the UK, the UK's membership in the EUI Convention also ended with Brexit. As with the other *inter se* agreements, however, the UK and the EUI treaty parties did not immediately agree on a permanent solution, but only settled on a transitional arrangement. Thus, since Brexit, '[t]he UK [had] been operating under the terms of an interim arrangement with the EUI [...], while discussion took place to explore the possibilities for future UK participation.'[88]

---

88 UK Government, 'Written Questions, Answers and Statements' European University Institute (tabled on 22 September 2022; answered on 11 October 2022) UIN 54450.

§ 1 Setting the Scene: Brexit and EU Treaty Practice

However, this interim arrangement ended on 31 December 2022.[89] Since then, the UK no longer participates in the EUI.[90]

The transitional arrangements put in place in the UK-EU WA confirm what the EU and the UK's individual position papers suggested. Both distinguished among different, EU-specific categories of international agreements – EU-only, bilateral and multilateral mixed, and *inter se* agreements. Furthermore, they both attached certain legal consequences of Brexit to the respective categories. In their view, for EU-only, bilateral mixed and *inter se* agreements, being out of the EU meant being out of these agreements. Continued participation was only assumed for multilateral mixed agreements. In numbers, this means that post-Brexit UK is left with only 108 of the 1262 international agreements previously applicable to the UK.

D. Rolling Over: The UK's (Re)Conclusion of International Agreements

The UK was well aware of the extent to which its international treaty relations with non-EU states would suffer if the approach of considering most international agreements as ceasing to apply to the UK was carried through. In its guidance note on international agreements, the UK government confirmed that '[t]he UK greatly values its relationship with partners across the globe and is seeking to preserve and strengthen these as we leave the European Union'[91]. However, it also acknowledged that the EU Treaty Database listed over 1000 agreements 'that the UK is covered by via membership of the EU' and that, following Brexit, action was thus required if the UK's international relations were to be indeed preserved and strengthened.[92]

As a first step, the UK sought to identify those international agreements which in its view did *not* require action. These were, primarily[93], inter-

---

89 European University Institute, 'United Kingdom' (10.11.2022) <https://www.eui.eu/en/services/academic-service/doctoral-programme/funding-information/united-kingdom>.
90 The European University Institute (EU Exit) Regulations 2022 (25 November 2022) 2022 No. 1231.
91 'UK Guidance Note' (n 59) 1.
92 Ibid 2.
93 The UK also noted that in some cases re-conclusion was not necessary because the EU treaty database was partially outdated, listing international agreements that had already been superseded by more recent (see ibid).

48

national agreements that because of their subject matter were not of relevance or interest to the UK,[94] and agreements to which it still considered itself to be a party, because they were of a multilateral mixed character.[95] For the remaining international agreements, the UK suggested two different methods of future cooperation. One possibility was to opt for non-legal instruments where cooperation through 'dialogues and Memoranda of Understanding'[96] would – in the UK's view – suffice. The other possibility was, of course, the conclusion of new international agreements. Where the UK aimed at securing a continued legal relationship, its treaty practice specifically depended on the type of agreement to be replaced.

First, the UK sought to replace multilateral EU-only agreements, ie multilateral agreements which had been concluded with several non-EU states by the EU alone and where, accordingly, the UK was not a party 'in its own right'[97]. Depending on the provisions in the respective multilateral agreement, the UK acceded to them either by depositing an instrument of accession or by concluding an accession agreement with the existing treaty parties.[98] However, even where the UK chose this path of accession, it was often acknowledged by the treaty parties that the UK was not entirely new to these agreements, but had already participated in them prior to leaving the EU. An example of such an EU-only multilateral agreement to which the UK acceded is the *Government Procurement Agreement*[99] (GPA).[100] In its decision on the UK's intended accession, the GPA Committee 'acknowledged that the United Kingdom [had been] covered by the Agreement on

---

94 As examples, the UK referred to 'agreements relating to the use of the Euro or the accession of new EU Member States' and those agreements in which '[t]he UK does not have any commercial interest', such as 'the Fisheries Partnership Agreement with the Republic of Kiribati' (see ibid).
95 Ibid.
96 Ibid.
97 Ibid.
98 Cp Art. 15 VCLT whereby the consent to be bound by an agreement can be 'expressed by accession when: (a) the treaty provides that such consent may be expressed [...] by means of accession; (b) it is otherwise established that the negotiating States were agreed that such consent may be expressed by that State by means of accession; or (c) all the parties have subsequently agreed that such consent may be expressed by that State by means of accession'.
99 Agreement on Government Procurement (signed on 12 April 1979, entered into force 1 January 1981) 1235 UNTS 258 [GPA].
100 Suggesting that the UK could by unilateral notification succeed in the GPA, see L Bartels, 'The UK's Status in the WTO Post-Brexit' in R Schütze and S Tierney (eds), *The United Kingdom and the Federal Idea* (Hart Publishing 2018) 244–248.

Government Procurement, as a member State of the European Union, until the date of its withdrawal from the European Union' and now 'may accede to the Agreement on Government Procurement in its own right'[101]. The UK itself referred to its accession to the GPA as now participating 'in its own right' and 'as a full party'[102].

Secondly, the UK approached states worldwide to (re)establish bilateral treaty relations which had previously been based on bilateral EU-only or mixed agreements. Initially, the UK's 'Global Britain' strategy had envisaged a realignment of the UK's (trade) treaty relations. Soon, however, it became clear that the UK would not be able to negotiate agreements on withdrawal and future relations with the EU and simultaneously strike (more) beneficial (trade) agreements with non-EU states. Thus, the UK ultimately reversed its course and sought a consensual solution to continue many EU-only and mixed bilateral agreements at least for as long as no new agreement had been reached. Illustrative of the UK's practice are the results achieved in the context of trade agreements. Here, the UK settled on a practice of 'rolling over'[103] many agreements that had previously been concluded by the EU, the majority of cases jointly with its Member States. Many of these rollover agreements are essentially a simple continuation, as in some instances the titles, such as *Agreement on Trade Continuity*[104], already make clear. Here, the UK and the other treaty partners either copy-pasted the text of the EU agreements[105] or even merely incorporated the EU agreement's provisions into their rollover agreements by way of reference.

---

101 WTO, 'Accession of the United Kingdom to the Agreement on Government Procurement in its own Right' Decision of the Committee on Government Procurement of 27 February 2019 (28 February 2019) GPA/CD/2 1.
102 See UK Government, 'UK Statement to the WTO Committee on Government Procurement' (07.10.2020) <https://www.gov.uk/government/speeches/uk-statement-to-the-wto-committee-on-government-procurement>.
103 A term frequently used by the UK to refer to its post-Brexit practice of re-concluding international agreements by which it had been covered during its EU membership, see eg D Webb, 'UK Progress in Rolling over EU Trade Agreements', Briefing Paper (13 December 2019) Number 7792.
104 See eg Trade Continuity Agreement between the United Kingdom of Great Britain and Northern Ireland and the United Mexican States (15 December 2020) CS Mexico No.1/2021 [UK-Mexico Trade Continuity Agreement].
105 See eg Partnership and Cooperation Agreement Establishing a Partnership between the United Kingdom of Great Britain and Northern Ireland, of the one part, and the Republic of Uzbekistan, of the other part (31 October 2019) CS Uzbekistan No. 1/2019 [PCA UK-UZB].

An example of the latter case is the *Agreement establishing an Association between the United Kingdom of Great Britain and Northern Ireland and the Republic of Chile*[106] (UK-Chile AA), which the UK and Chile signed in January 2019 and which rolled over the *Association Agreement between Chile, on the one side, and the EU and its Member States, on the other side*[107] (EU-Chile AA). In the UK-Chile AA's preamble, the UK and Chile

> recogniz[e] that the Agreement establishing an association between the European Community and its Member States, of the one part, and the Republic of Chile, of the other part, [...] will cease to apply to the United Kingdom when it ceases to be a Member State of the European Union.

Subsequently, they expressed their desire 'that the rights and obligations between them as provided for by the EU-Chile Agreement should continue after the United Kingdom has left the European Union'. Thus, the 'overriding objective of this [UK-Chile] Agreement is to preserve the links between the Parties established by the association created in Article 2 of the EU-Chile Agreement'. To achieve this, '[t]he provisions of the EU-Chile Agreement [...] in effect immediately before they cease to apply to the United Kingdom are incorporated into and made part of this Agreement, mutatis mutandis, subject to the provisions of this Instrument'. The 'subject to' caveat relates to the Annex of the UK-Chile AA, which contains modifications to the wording of certain provisions in the EU-Chile AA, adapting them to the new treaty relationship between the UK and Chile.

In some instances, the conclusion of a rollover agreement could not be achieved fast enough. The UK-Canada *Agreement on Trade Continuity*[108], for example, was signed on December 9, 2020, incorporating the EU-Canada *Comprehensive and Economic Trade Agreement*[109] (CETA). However, domestic procedures hampered it from entering into force or

---

106 Agreement establishing an Association between the United Kingdom of Great Britain and Northern Ireland and the Republic of Chile (30 January 2019) CS Chile No. 2/2019 [UK-Chile AA].
107 Agreement establishing an association between the European Community and its Member States, of the one part, and the Republic of Chile, of the other part (30 December 2002) OJ L352/3 [EU-Chile AA].
108 Agreement on Trade Continuity between the United Kingdom of Great Britain and Northern Ireland and Canada (9 December 2020) CS Canada No.1/2020 [UK-Canada Trade Continuity Agreement].
109 Comprehensive Economic and Trade Agreement between Canada, of the one part, and the European Union and its Member States, of the other part (14 January 2017) OJ L11/23 [CETA].

being provisionally applied before the end of the transition period on December 31, 2020. Thus, the UK and Canada signed a 'Memorandum of Understanding [...] concerning temporary arrangements to continue certain benefits of [CETA] pending the entry into force or provisional application of the Canada-United Kingdom Trade Continuity Agreement'[110]. Based on this non-legally binding Memorandum of Understanding[111], the UK and Canada '[desired] [...] to continue the benefits of CETA [...] to the extent possible, as between them, without interruption, once CETA ceases to apply to the United Kingdom'[112].

Primarily thanks to this method, three years after Brexit, the UK had put in place trade agreements with 67 states worldwide, with most of which it had previously conducted trade under EU trade agreements.[113] Even though the majority of these agreements have been rolled over, this is a remarkably high number considering that the responsible Department for International Trade had not even existed prior to Brexit. However, the UK's treaty practice of (re)concluding international agreements in the wake of Brexit becomes even more noteworthy when shifting the focus to its treaty partners. The UK's rolling over practice is an expression of the fact that many states accepted the UK's position on international agreements post-Brexit. While it is unclear whether they shared it from a legal standpoint, to the author's knowledge, no state openly opposed it. Instead of insisting on the fulfilment of pre-Brexit agreements, many states not only accepted the (renewed) conclusion of agreements with the UK as the sole treaty partner; in the case of rollover agreements, they also did so on very similar – if not identical – terms, thus granting the UK the same rights and benefits as during its EU membership.

---

110 Canadian Government, 'Memorandum of Understanding between the United Kingdom of Great Britain and Northern Ireland and Canada' (22 December 2020) <https://www.international.gc.ca/trade-commerce/trade-agreements-accords-commerciaux/agr-acc/cuktca-acccru/mou-pe.aspx?lang=eng>.
111 See Section 7: 'This Memorandum is not legally binding and records the understanding between the Participants on the matters referred to in this Memorandum.'
112 See Introduction, last indent.
113 UK Government, 'UK Trade Agreements in Effect' (03.02.2023) <https://www.gov.uk/guidance/uk-trade-agreements-in-effect>. Note that the number of 67 states includes a trade agreement with Palestine whose statehood is controversial under international law.

III. The Research Question: What's International Law Got to Do with It?

From a practical standpoint, the output of the UK's treaty-making efforts since Brexit is remarkable. For Brexit watchers, moreover, it is noteworthy that the question of the effect of Brexit on international agreements was not only one of the few on which the EU and the UK seemed to be in agreement, but that their approach was also accepted by their treaty partners. For an international lawyer, finally, this acceptance is even more astounding. Neither the EU nor the UK has yet provided any legal justification for its position.[114] However, from an international law perspective, the sweeping manner in which the UK announced termination of participation in different categories of international agreements – despite the variety of treaty constellations – appears problematic. This applies all the more against the background of the basic principle of *pacta sunt servanda* under international law. So, from a legal perspective: does out really (almost always) mean out?

On the one hand, the impulse to resort to the specifics of Union law in search of a legal explanation for the actions of the EU and the UK is almost reflexive. After all, not only do all agreements in question have the EU context in common. Their categorisation in EU-only, bi- and multilateral mixed and *inter se* agreements, along which the dividing line between 'out means out' and continued participation following Brexit was drawn, originates solely from EU internal necessities. On the other hand, a Union law perspective (alone) can never suffice as a rationale. After all, the UK is, except in the case of EU-only agreements, bound by these agreements under international law. Nevertheless, the specifics of the EU legal order and the EU's external action cannot be disregarded, even when taking the viewpoint of international law.

That this can lead to problems, especially in the area of mixed agreements, is demonstrated by the abundance of literature published on these agreements. For a long time, the focus of (scholarly) interest primarily lay on the intra-European distribution of competences and their external

---

114 In its internal slides on Brexit and international agreements, the EU's Task Force 50 simply referred back to the EU's Brexit Guidelines (see 'EU Internal Preparatory Discussions' (n 72) 4–5). In the UK, neither the Guidance Note nor further reports presented to Parliament offered any legal explanation (see 'UK Guidance Note' (n 59); V Miller, 'Legislating for Brexit' EU External Agreements, Briefing Paper (5 January 2017) Number 7850).

effects.¹¹⁵ More recent scholarship has also started to engage more intensely with the reception of the EU's characteristic in the international legal order.¹¹⁶ Still, the termination of mixed agreements has only been discussed sporadically and limited to classic denunciation.¹¹⁷ This is most probably due to the – until Brexit – lack of practical and legal relevance. So long as a state is an EU member, the principle of sincere cooperation under Art. 4(3) TEU would apply in the case of both a Member State's and the EU's intention to terminate an agreement. There therefore seems to be a consensus that the right of termination in the case of mixed agreements would have to be exercised jointly in all cases.¹¹⁸ In the case of Brexit, however, two particularities come together. First, the UK is no longer bound by Art. 4 TEU when it leaves the EU. Secondly, it regains its full competence to act under international treaty law.¹¹⁹

When it became clear that the UK would withdraw from the EU, scholarship began to engage with the question of what effect this would have on international agreements concluded by the EU or its Member States in the context of EU membership. The opinions expressed varied. Few legal

---

115 On the development of the EU's external competences, see eg Cremona, Evolution of EU Law (n 17). On the reception of the EU's division of competences in mixed agreements, see eg J Heliskoski, *Mixed Agreements as a Technique for Organizing the International Relations of the European Community and its Member States* (Kluwer Law International 2001).

116 For a recent monograph, see Odermatt, *International Law and the EU* (n 14). See also, eg, RA Wessel and J Odermatt (eds), *Research Handbook on the European Union and International Organizations* (Edward Elgar Publishing 2019) placing the EU in the context of international organisations. On the responsibility of the EU under international law, see PJ Kuijper, 'International Responsibility for EU Mixed Agreements' in C Hillion and P Koutrakos (eds) (n 10); PJ Kuijper and E Paasivirta, 'EU International Responsibility and its Attribution: From the Inside Looking Out' in MD Evans and P Koutrakos (eds) (n 19).

117 Mentioned, eg, in CD Ehlermann, 'Mixed Agreements: A List of Problems' in D O'Keeffe and HG Schermers (eds) (n 10) 16. See also R Mögele, 'Article 218' in R Streinz (ed), *EUV/AEUV: Vertrag über die Europäische Union, Vertrag über die Arbeitsweise der Europäischen Union, Charta der Grundrechte der Europäischen Union* (3rd edn, CH Beck 2018) paras 24–26; O Dörr, 'Article 47 TEU' in E Grabitz, M Hilf and M Nettesheim (eds), *Das Recht der Europäischen Union* (82nd supplement, CH Beck 2024) para 35. On denunciation provisions in the EU's mixed trade agreements, see S Schaefer and J Odermatt, 'Nomen est Omen?: The Relevance of "EU Party" In International Law' in N Levrat and others (eds) (n 10) 147–149.

118 KD Stein, *Der gemischte Vertrag im Recht der Außenbeziehungen der Europäischen Wirtschaftsgemeinschaft* (Duncker & Humblot 1986) 183.

119 See ibid 78.

III. The Research Question: What's International Law Got to Do with It?

evaluations corresponded in their result with the position (later) adopted by the EU and the UK.[120] The majority of scholars came to conclusions contrary to that of the EU and the UK and the practice that would later enfold.[121] Against this background, it is all the more remarkable that ever since Brexit took place, scholars have remained largely silent. Scholarship that does continue to engage with the issue of Brexit and international agreements generally focuses on the questions *following* Brexit, looking, for example, at the UK's practice of rollover agreements.[122] Thus, there exists a body of pre-Brexit scholarship arguing how dealing with international agreements *should* be done and some post-Brexit writing summarising how it *was* done and otherwise focusing on post-Brexit issues. What is missing, however, is a critical debate on what happened and what to make of it.

However, this is not the only reason why the question was put aside prematurely as having been conclusively treated. Most writing on the topic of Brexit and international agreements has also been limited to one single explanatory approach. It has analysed the effect of Brexit on international

---

120 See eg C Herrmann, 'Brexit, WTO und EU-Handelspolitik' (2017) 24 Europäische Zeitschrift für Wirtschaftsrecht 961, 966; JWJ Kim, 'Is the United Kingdom Still a Party to the EU-Korea FTA after Brexit?' in JA Hillman and GN Horlick (eds), *Legal Aspects of Brexit: Implications of the United Kingdom's decision to withdraw from the European Union* (Georgetown Law 2017); P Koutrakos, 'Managing Brexit: Trade Agreements Binding on the UK pursuant to its EU Membership' in J Santos Vara, RA Wessel and PR Polak (eds), *The Routledge Handbook on the International Dimension of Brexit* (Routledge 2020).

121 See eg RA Wessel, 'Consequences of Brexit for International Agreements Concluded by the EU and its Member States' (2018) 55 (Special Issue) *Common Market Law Review* 101; S Silvereke, 'Withdrawal from the EU and Bilateral Free Trade Agreements: Being Divorced is Worse?' (2018) 15(2) *International Organizations Law Review* 321; T Voland, 'Auswirkungen des Brexit auf die völkervertraglichen Beziehungen des Vereinigten Königreichs und der EU' (2019) 79(1) *Zeitschrift für ausländisches öffentliches Recht und Völkerrecht* 1; J Odermatt, 'Brexit and International Legal Sovereignty' in J Santos Vara, RA Wessel and PR Polak (eds) (n 120); C Kaddous and HB Touré, 'The Status of the United Kingdom Regarding EU Mixed Agreements after Brexit' in N Levrat and others (eds) (n 10); Y Kaspiarovich and N Levrat, 'European Union Mixed Agreements in International Law under the Stress of Brexit' (2021) 13(2) *European Journal of Legal Studies* 121.

122 See eg P Koutrakos, 'Negotiating International Trade Treaties After Brexit' (2016) 41(4) *European Law Review* 475; Koutrakos, Routledge Handbook Brexit (n 120); A Łazowski, 'Copy-Pasting or Negotiating?: Post-Brexit Trade Agreements between the UK and non-EU Countries' in J Santos Vara, RA Wessel and PR Polak (eds) (n 120); P Koutrakos, 'Three Narratives on the United Kingdom's Trade Agreements post-Brexit' in A Łazowski and AJ Cygan (eds), *Research Handbook on Legal Aspects of Brexit* (Edward Elgar Publishing 2022).

agreements from the viewpoint of international treaty law and international institutional law: how does Brexit compare to the withdrawal of Member States from (other) international organisations?[123] Do the international agreements concluded in the context of EU membership – explicitly or implicitly – provide for the withdrawal of a Member State?[124] Is a denunciation in line with the grounds for treaty termination provided for in the *Vienna Convention on the Law of Treaties*[125] (VCLT) possible in the case of Brexit?[126]

While these appear like the natural questions to ask, there is a risk to analysing Brexit only from the perspective of international organisations: what if such comparisons prove futile? What if the answers to these questions do not match with the practice that unfolded during Brexit negotiations and which is now, nearly three years after the UK's withdrawal, very much settled? An approach that has so far been very much underexplored is to change perspective on the EU as the object of study. When considering '[t]he UK's Status in the WTO Post-Brexit'[127], Bartels

> submitted that on leaving the EU, the UK is entitled to succeed to the [Government Procurement Agreement] in its own right, in accordance with rules of customary international law on the succession of states to treaties, and practice under the GATT 1947 […].[128]

Thus, instead of comparing Brexit to prior withdrawals from international organisations, Bartels compared Brexit to the 'succession of states from unions and federations'[129]. The rules applied to the disintegration of such entities differ from treaty law as codified in the VCLT and generally referred

---

123 See eg in A Schwerdtfeger, 'Austritt und Ausschluss aus Internationalen Organisationen: Zwischen staatlicher Souveränität und zwischenstaatlicher Kooperation' (2018) 56(1) *Archiv des Völkerrechts* 96; CM Brölmann and others, 'Exiting International Organizations: A Brief Introduction' (2018) 15(2) *International Organizations Law Review* 243.
124 See eg in Kim (n 120); A Kent, 'Brexit and the East African Community (EAC)-European Union Economic Partnership Agreement (EPA)' in JA Hillman and GN Horlick (eds) (n 120); I Fressynet, 'The Legal Impact of Brexit on the Comprehensive Economic Trade Agreement (CETA) Between the European Union and Canada' in JA Hillman and GN Horlick (eds) (n 120).
125 Vienna Convention on the Law of Treaties (adopted 23 May 1969, entered into force 27 January 1980) 1155 UNTS 331 [VCLT].
126 See eg Voland (n 121).
127 Bartels (n 100) 227.
128 Ibid 244.
129 Ibid 245.

III. The Research Question: What's International Law Got to Do with It?

to in the context of Brexit. The question would then be whether the outcome of applying the law of treaty succession would, in turn, accord with actual Brexit practice. However, the few authors who have subsequently addressed this line of reasoning have not only approached it with a good amount of scepticism but also treated it rather curtly.[130] Their main argument is based again on their perspective on the EU as an international organisation to which the law of *state* succession does not apply.[131] There are, however, two ways of approaching Bartel's argument.

The first is to revisit the debate on the nature of the EU. Is the EU an international organisation, a state, state-like or an entity *sui generis*? Discussions regarding the nature of the EU are sometimes considered 'academic' or purely 'semantic'.[132] But as Odermatt argues,

> [a]s the EU seeks to play a greater role in the international legal order, and as one of its Member States seeks to extricate itself from the EU legal order, the Union, its Member States, and third states will be faced with legal questions that touch upon the EU's legal order.[133]

Where the EU presents itself on the global stage, its characterisation matters. 'While it may be possible to create special rules for *sui generis* entities', international law as a legal system 'only works when it is applied across the board for certain categories of international actors'[134]. Yet, determining the nature of the EU as an international actor is not only about international law functioning as a legal system. The qualification of a legal actor also

---

130 J Odermatt, 'Brexit and International Law: Disentangling Legal Orders' (2017) 31 *Emory International Law Review Recent Developments* 1051, 1057–1059; Wessel, *Consequences of Brexit* (n 121) 116.
131 Odermatt, *Disentangling Legal Orders* (n 130) 1059; Wessel, *Consequences of Brexit* (n 121) 116.
132 For an overview of the different notions, see B De Witte, 'EU Law: Is it International Law?' in C Barnard and S Peers (eds), *European Union Law* (3rd edn, Oxford University Press 2020).
133 J Odermatt, 'Unidentified Legal Object: Conceptualizing the European Union in International Law' (2018) 33(2) *Connecticut Journal of International Law* 215, 216. See also J Crawford, 'The Current Political Discourse Concerning International Law' (2018) 81(1) *The Modern Law Review* 1, 16: 'There is considerable tension within the EU legal order between the underlying international law framework of treaties, and the internal law of the EU, which is not international law in any straightforward sense. But when negotiating within the EU for a situation outside it, the hybrid character of the EU is very much in issue.'
134 RA Wessel, 'Close Encounters of the Third Kind: The Interface between the EU and International Law after the Treaty of Lisbon' (2013) 8 *SIEPS Reports*, 16–17.

§ 1 Setting the Scene: Brexit and EU Treaty Practice

impacts its reception under international law. International organisations have long been accepted as subjects of international law in addition to states.[135] Nevertheless, in many fields, different international legal regimes apply to states than to international organisations.[136]

For the EU, such a categorisation does not always appear clear-cut. As Eckes and Wessel have shown, at least since the *Treaty of Lisbon*, 'the EU has been taking up 'state-like functions' in more areas than before'[137]. In doing so, the EU's growing international role is often accepted by the international community at large and many non-EU Member States in particular. This is also mirrored in the EU's treaty-making practice, with its international agreements appearing 'much more "state-like" in nature'[138]. At the same time, in the context of multilateral treaty-making, the EU's participation has repeatedly failed at provisions in multilateral agreements limiting accession to states. This again has led to a special qualification of the EU as a 'regional economic integration organization'[139].

Thus, the EU's nature may be discussed controversially. Against this background, however, it is more than unlikely that it would be recognised internationally as a predecessor *state*. There is, however, a second way of approaching Bartel's argument. The EU does not necessarily need to *be* a state to apply the rules on *state* succession to it. It may suffice, if the nature of its treaty practice is sufficiently similar to that of a state. Legal reasoning could then present an alternative to direct application of a rule. A method that has been used before to transfer rules for states to other subjects of international law is reasoning by analogy.[140]

The following two parts, each divided into three chapters, will offer two alternative viewings of the EU and accordingly Brexit and analyse their

---

135 See eg the seminal case of ICJ *Reparation for Injuries Suffered in the Service of the United Nations* (Advisory Opinion) [1949] ICJ Rep 1949, p 174.
136 See eg in the law of treaties the 1969 VCLT and the 1986 VCLT-IO, even though the rules contained therein are only marginally different. See also on the issue of responsibility the ILC, 'Articles on the Responsibility of States for Internationally Wrongful Acts', YBILC (2001) Vol. II(2) and the ILC, 'Draft Articles on the Responsibility of International Organizations' UN Doc A/66/10, YBILC (2011) Vol. II(2).
137 C Eckes and RA Wessel, 'An International Perspective' in R Schütze and T Tridimas (eds), *The Oxford Principles of European Union Law: The European Union Legal Order* (Oxford University Press 2018) 74.
138 Odermatt, *International Law and the EU* (n 14) 62.
139 Ibid 18.
140 On the use of analogies in international law, see below Part II § 5 section II.

III. The Research Question: What's International Law Got to Do with It?

respective effects on the international agreements concluded by the EU and its Member States. *Part I* will analyse Brexit from the viewpoint of international institutional and treaty law. Characterising the European Treaties as founding treaties of an international organisation, withdrawal from the EU must be perceived as a member state's exit from this organisation. The question is, then, which consequences arise from the termination of membership for agreements concluded by or within the framework of an international organisation and how this compares to the Brexit practice.

Part II will focus on those aspects of the EU that differentiate it from (other) international organisations and have earned it 'state-like'[141] attributes. The EU has been positioned in the context of (con)federations and federalism[142] and Art. 50 TEU has been referred to as a 'secession clause'[143]; here, recourse to international institutional and treaty law potentially lacks adequacy. Instead, drawing an analogy to the law of state successions could, indeed, offer a more suitable approach. Rather than directly discarding the comparison between unions and federations because of the EU's lack of direct correspondence, it therefore seems sensible to take a closer look at their similarities and the rules on state succession to be analogically applied.

---

141 See eg Odermatt, *International Law and the EU* (n 14) 62. See also Eckes and Wessel (n 137) 76–80 and, more generally, RA Wessel, 'Can the EU Replace its Member States in International Affairs?: An International Law Perspective' in I Govaere and others (eds), *The European Union in the World: Essays in Honour of Professor Marc Maresceau* (Martinus Nijhoff Publishers 2014).

142 See with further references in RA Wessel, 'Studying International and European Law: Confronting Perspectives and Combining Interests' in I Govaere and S Garben (eds), *The Interface Between EU and International Law: Contemporary Reflections* (Hart Publishing 2019) 83. On the EU and federalism, see, eg, M Burgess, *Federalism and European Union: The Building of Europe, 1950–2000* (Routledge 2000). On the EU as an actor on 'federal middle ground', see R Schütze, 'On "Federal Ground": The European Union as an (Inter)national Phenomenon' in R Schütze (ed), *Foreign Affairs and the EU Constitution: Selected Essays* (Cambridge University Press 2014).

143 See eg M Gatti, 'Art. 50 TEU: A Well-Designed Secession Clause' (2017) 2(1) *European Papers – A Journal on Law and Integration* 159.

Part I: Brexit and the Law of Treaties

The starting point for any legal analysis is the determination of the relevant parameters: what is the subject of the study and what rules apply? What is the EU and what rules apply to the situation of a state leaving it? As Isiksel once pointedly remarked, '[t]he debate over whether the EU is a state, federation, international organization or flying saucer is as old as European integration itself'[1], and still its final outcome remains uncertain.[2] Instead, a certain acceptance appears to have developed that the answer may well depend on one's perspective as well as the respective context.[3] As a result, a bouquet of designations for the EU exists, illustrating the breadth of the discussion. In contrast to the terms Isiksel references (state,

---

1 T Isiksel, 'European Exceptionalism and the EU's Accession to the ECHR' (2016) 27(3) *European Journal of International Law* 565, 571.
2 Cp eg the many different opinions expressed in commentaries on the EU Treaties alone: R Geiger and Kirchmair, 'Article 1 TEU' in R Geiger, D-E Khan, M Kotzur and Kirchmair L (eds), *EUV/AEUV: Vertrag über die Europäische Union und Vertrag über die Arbeitsweise der Europäischen Union* (7th edn, CH Beck 2023) para 12 ('es handelt sich um die Neuschöpfung einer Rechtsordnung "eigener Art"'); M Pechstein, 'Article 1 TEU' in R Streinz (ed), *EUV/AEUV: Vertrag über die Europäische Union, Vertrag über die Arbeitsweise der Europäischen Union, Charta der Grundrechte der Europäischen Union* (3rd edn, CH Beck 2018) para 13 ('Die Diskussionen, ob die EU [...] als internationale Organisation angesehen werden konnte [...] sind nunmehr überholt: Die EU ist nunmehr als solche zu klassifizieren.'); M Nettesheim, 'Article 1 TEU' in E Grabitz, M Hilf and M Nettesheim (eds), *Das Recht der Europäischen Union* (82nd supplement, CH Beck 2024) para 63 ('Bezeichnung des Verbundes von EU und Mitgliedstaaten als konsoziativem Föderalismus'); C Calliess, 'Article 1 TEU' in C Calliess and M Ruffert (eds), *EUV/AEUV: Das Verfassungsrecht der Europäischen Union mit Europäischer Grundrechtecharta* (6th edn, CH Beck 2022) para 45 ('der so verstandene – notwendig föderale – Staaten- und Verfassungsbund'). For a recent contribution to the debate, see J Hoeksma, 'The Identification of the EU as a New Kind of International Organisation' (*Opinio Juris*, 19.11.2022) <http://opiniojuris.org/2022/11/19/the-identification-of-the-eu-as-a-new-kind-of-international-organisation/>.
3 Explaining the 'diverging views' in detail, J Odermatt, *International Law and the European Union* (Cambridge University Press 2021) 22–28. See C Binder and JA Hofbauer, 'The Perception of the EU Legal Order in International Law: An In- and Outside View' in M Bungenberg and others (eds), *European Yearbook of International Economic Law 2017* (Springer 2017) 147–155 on the 'self-representation' and 'self-assessment' of different EU institutions.

federation, international organisation) many others (*Staatenverbund*[4], *sui generis*) escape traditional categories. Sometimes creating new categories is preferable to pigeonholing. Rather than cramming the EU into an existing legal drawer, it may be helpful to create a new one; however, problems arise if it does not fit into the existing chest.

International law is such a chest. It is 'the legal order which is meant to structure the interaction between entities participating in and shaping international relations'[5]. These entities are no longer just states, but today encompass a broader range of actors such as international organisations, belligerent groups and individuals, all 'capable of possessing international rights and duties'[6]. Which concrete rights and obligations these refer to, in turn, largely depends on the kind of subject. Some rules of international law apply only to states and others specifically to international organisations.[7] If the EU is now understood as an entity *sui generis*, this may allow it a more dynamic process of integration, free(r) from traditional thought patterns.[8] But where the EU is 'participating in and shaping international relations'[9] – as it has the competence to do[10] – *sui generis* is a drawer that does not fit. So, what rules of international law apply to an entity that purports to be different from all others?

---

4 First used by the German Constitutional Court in its judgement on the Maastricht Treaty (German Federal Constitutional Court, 2 BvR 2134/92, 2 BvR 2159/92 *Maastricht* [1993] BVerfGE 89, 155, [90]).
5 R Wolfrum, 'International Law' in R Wolfrum (ed), *The Max Planck Encyclopedia of Public International Law* (Oxford University Press 2012) para 1.
6 C Walter, 'Subjects of International Law' in R Wolfrum (ed) (n 5) para 1.
7 Although these rules are sometimes very similar, if not partly identical. See the two conventions on the law of treaties, one limited to states (Vienna Convention on the Law of Treaties (adopted 23 May 1969, entered into force 27 January 1980) 1155 UNTS 331 [VCLT]) and one applicable to agreements between international organisations and between states and international organisation (Vienna Convention on the Law of Treaties between States and International Organizations or between International Organizations (adopted and opened for signature 21 March 1986) UN Doc A/CONF.129/15 [VCLT-IO]).
8 See also J Odermatt (n 3) 12.
9 Wolfrum (n 5) para 1.
10 Cp Art. 3(5) TEU according to which the EU 'shall contribute [...] to the strict observance and the development of international law'. Moreover, Art. 216 TFEU allows the EU the conclusion of international agreements 'with one or more third countries or international organisations where the Treaties so provide or where the conclusion of an agreement is necessary in order to achieve, within the framework of the Union's policies, one of the objectives referred to in the Treaties, or is provided for in a legally binding Union act or is likely to affect common rules or alter their scope.'

It is important to note that the assumption underlying this question is one seldomly shared by international lawyers.[11] As Schütze argues, not only is 'the *sui generis* "theory" [...] historically unfounded'[12], it also 'only views the Union in *negative* terms', making any analysis impossible.[13] Thus, for many international lawyers, the most natural approach to viewing the EU is from an international institutional law perspective:[14] while the EU is undoubtedly the most integrated international organisation, its foundations are nevertheless international treaties concluded, revised and acceded to by its Member States.[15] With the UK withdrawing from these treaties, Brexit thus presents itself as a case of termination of membership in an international organisation (§ 2).

Regarded as such, Brexit is no new phenomenon. While rising scepticism among states towards international cooperation has led to recent renewed scholarly attention on the topic, withdrawals from international organisations have occurred throughout their history.[16] Moreover, many international organisations regularly engage in international treaty-making. While the EU is an especially 'active treaty-maker'[17], most international organisations possess the legal personality, capacity and competence necessary to conclude international agreements with states and other inter-

---

11   P Hay, *Federalism and Supranational Organizations: Patterns for New Legal Structures* (Illinois University Press 1966) 44; E Denza, *The Intergovernmental Pillars of the European Union* (Oxford University Press 2005) 1.
12   R Schütze, *European Constitutional Law*, 2nd edn (Cambridge University Press 2015) 67.
13   R Schütze, 'On "Federal Ground": The European Union as an (Inter)national Phenomenon' in R Schütze (ed), *Foreign Affairs and the EU Constitution: Selected Essays* (Cambridge University Press 2014) 34.
14   RA Wessel, 'Studying International and European Law: Confronting Perspectives and Combining Interests' in I Govaere and S Garben (eds), *The Interface Between EU and International Law: Contemporary Reflections* (Hart Publishing 2019) 83.
15   See in detail, B De Witte, 'EU Law: Is it International Law?' in C Barnard and S Peers (eds), *European Union Law* (3rd edn, Oxford University Press 2020).
16   CM Brölmann and others, 'Exiting International Organizations: A Brief Introduction' (2018) 15(2) *International Organizations Law Review* 243, 243–244. On the issue generally, see N Singh, *Termination of Membership of International Organisations* (Praeger 1958) and more recently, A Schwerdtfeger, 'Austritt und Ausschluss aus Internationalen Organisationen: Zwischen staatlicher Souveränität und zwischenstaatlicher Kooperation' (2018) 56(1) *Archiv des Völkerrechts* 96.
17   J Larik, 'Instruments of EU External Action' in RA Wessel and J Larik (eds), *EU External Relations Law: Text, Cases and Materials* (Bloomsbury Publishing 2020) 109–110 with a graph demonstrating the increase in activity until the early 2000s and a slowing down in the years since then.

national organisations.[18] If both withdrawal and treaty-making are known phenomena in the law of international organisations, the question of the effect of the former on the latter should not be considered a Brexit novelty. What then are the rules generally applicable in the case of member withdrawal and what is the practice as regards its effect on international agreements? Can these rules or prior practice explain EU and UK claims that EU-only, bilateral mixed and *inter se* agreements cease to bind the UK, even where – as in the latter two cases – it became a party itself?

To answer these questions, two situations must be distinguished: firstly, exiting an international organisation entails direct legal consequences, in some cases also for international agreements (§ 3). Considering the possible effect on international agreements as a legal consequence of Brexit could provide a direct cause-and-effect nexus, speaking to the EU and UK's claim of *automatic* termination. At the same time, while the UK is leaving the EU, Brexit is still an EU internal process. Especially with regard to international agreements concluded with non-EU states, the *external* legal consequences of such an *internal* process are limited.

Secondly, withdrawal from an international organisation results in factually changed circumstances which can have an effect on international agreements (§ 4). Thus, while Brexit can be considered as a process entailing legal consequences, the UK's loss of EU membership is also a fact and as such may be invoked as grounds for denouncing international agreements. Consideration of Brexit with the rules for treaty denunciation appears reasonable given that the UK became party to many international agreements itself. At the same time, this questions the narrative of *automatic* termination. While treaty law generally acknowledges treaty termination as a corollary of state sovereignty, it also aims to strike a balance with the core principle of treaty stability.[19] In doing so, the procedural

---

18 See only the work of the International Law Commission on the VCLT-IO (ILC, 'Analytical Guide to the Work of the International Law Commission: Questions of Treaties concluded between States and International Organizations or between two or more International Organizations' (7.2.2022) <https://legal.un.org/ilc/guide/1_2.shtml>). On treaty-making by international organisations in general, see HG Schermers and N Blokker, *International Institutional Law: Unity within Diversity* (5th edn, Martinus Nijhoff Publishers 2011) 1262 and J Klabbers, *An Introduction to International Institutional Law* (2nd edn, Cambridge University Press 2009) 251 ff.
19 H Krieger, 'Article 65' in O Dörr and K Schmalenbach (eds), *Vienna Convention on the Law of Treaties: A Commentary* (2nd edn, Springer 2018) para 2.

hurdles, such as notifications, negotiations in good faith and waiting periods, *prima facie* seem to speak against any automatic effect of Brexit.

§ 2 EU Withdrawal: Exiting an International Organisation

Depending on the characterisation of a process – in this case, the UK leaving the EU – different rules of international law may apply. In the case of Brexit, the preliminary question is how the EU itself should be classified. The answer underlying the vast majority of studies on the effect of Brexit is that the EU must be characterised as an international organisation.[1] This is supported by the fact that the EU fulfils all the typical characteristics of an international organisation (I.). Moreover, in the past, the hypothetical scenario of a state leaving the EU long played a role in the debate: what did the absence of a withdrawal provision mean for the determination of the EU's legal nature? Would the question of whether a state could leave the Union have to be answered from an international or constitutional law background? The introduction of Art. 50 TEU with the *Treaty of Lisbon* resolved the question whether a Member State may withdraw, granting a clear right to do so. Its design, moreover, very much resembles the exit clauses of other international organisations (II.). Brexit being the first case of Art. 50 TEU's application, it thus presents itself as the exit from an international organisation (III.).

---

1 The question is rarely explicitly addressed (for an exception, see D Steiger and W Günther, 'Brexit: What's Public International Law Got to Do with it' in KA Prinz von Sachsen Gessaphe, JJ Garcia-Blesa and N Szuka (eds), *Legal Implications of Brexit* (MV Wissenschaft 2018) 95–97), but the classification shows in the comparisons drawn (see eg RA Wessel, 'You Can Check out Any Time You like, but Can You Really Leave?' (2016) 13(2) *International Organizations Law Review* 197, 197 and A Schwerdtfeger, 'Austritt und Ausschluss aus Internationalen Organisationen: Zwischen staatlicher Souveränität und zwischenstaatlicher Kooperation' (2018) 56(1) *Archiv des Völkerrechts* 96, 1 both referring to Brexit as a withdrawal from an international organisation) or the rules of international law applied (see eg S Silvereke, 'Withdrawal from the EU and Bilateral Free Trade Agreements: Being Divorced is Worse?' (2018) 15(2) *International Organizations Law Review* 321, 321 referring to Art. 70 VCLT; on the relevance of Art. 70 VCLT in the context of Brexit, see below Part I § 3).

§ 2 EU Withdrawal: Exiting an International Organisation

I. (Un)Identified Legal Object[2]? The EU as an International Organisation

In international institutional law, definitions of the term 'international organisation' vary in detail but range around two main overlapping criteria: cooperation that is, firstly, founded on an international agreement and, secondly, features an organ with a *volonté distincte* from its Member States.[3] Considering the EU Treaties (and their predecessors) and the institutional structure of the EU[4], the Union undoubtedly falls within this definition or, as De Witte puts it, can 'tick all the boxes'[5]. Thus, the debates regarding the nature of the EU do not purport that it does not meet these criteria. Rather, the EU is considered to have outgrown them by featuring characteristics surpassing international organisations' basic attributes. While there seems to be consensus regarding the origins of the EU being international agreements between Member States, proponents of non-organisational concepts

---

2 Cp J Odermatt, 'Unidentified Legal Object: Conceptualizing the European Union in International Law' (2018) 33(2) *Connecticut Journal of International Law* 215.
3 See eg J Klabbers, *An Introduction to International Institutional Law* (2nd edn, Cambridge University Press 2009) 6–12 defines an international organisation as 'created between states', 'on the basis of a treaty' and having 'an organ with a distinct will'; HG Schermers and N Blokker, *International Institutional Law: Unity within Diversity* (5th edn, Martinus Nijhoff Publishers 2011) para 33: 'forms of cooperation (1) founded on an international agreement; (2) having at least one organ with a will of its own; (3) established under international law'. After refraining from a clear definition in previous works (cp Art. 2(1)(i) VCLT-IO: '"international organization" means an intergovernmental organization'), Art. 2(a) of the International Law Commission's (ILC) Draft Articles on Responsibility of International Organizations defines the term as 'an organization established by a treaty or other instrument governed by international law and possessing its own legal personality. International organizations may include as members, in addition to states, other entities' (ILC, 'Draft Articles on the Responsibility of International Organizations' UN Doc A/66/10, YBILC (2011) Vol. II(2)). On the drafting history of this definition, see HG Schermers and N Blokker (n 3) para 29A.
4 For the different legal instruments of the EU institutions, see Art. 288 TFEU.
5 B De Witte, 'EU Law: Is it International Law?' in C Barnard and S Peers (eds), *European Union Law* (3rd edn, Oxford University Press 2020) 179. International institutional law literature, thus, regularly treats the EU as one of their subjects of study, see eg the seminal works by J Klabbers (n 3) and HG Schermers and N Blokker (n 3). See also RA Wessel and J Odermatt (eds), *Research Handbook on the European Union and International Organizations* (Edward Elgar Publishing 2019).

I. (Un)Identified Legal Object? The EU as an International Organisation

question the *continued* nature of the founding Treaties as 'ordinary international agreements'.[6],[7]

In arguing in favour of the Union's 'organisationhood'[8], De Witte makes the case that the EU has been and is 'still situated *within* international law'[9] by essentially relying on three arguments.[10] Firstly, considering the history and subsequent development of the EU's foundational Treaties, he concludes that Member States never intended for the EU to depart from its international law origins. During the post-World War II rebuilding of Europe, governments resorted to the classical means of international cooperation by concluding treaties on the establishment of a variety of international organisations – the Organisation for European Economic Cooperation[11] (OEEC), the Council of Europe[12] (CoE), and the European Coal and Steel Community[13] (ECSC).[14] Although the ECSC differed from the previous two in that it encompassed supranational elements,[15] neither the *Treaty Establishing the European Economic Community*[16] (EEC Treaty) nor any of its successors evidence any intention of the Member States to

---

6 A notion repeatedly employed by the ECJ, see rather recently in ECJ, Opinion 2/13 *Accession to the ECHR* [2014] ECLI:EU:C:2014:2454, 157: 'the founding treaties of the EU, unlike *ordinary international treaties*, established a new legal order' (emphasis added).

7 On the EU Treaties as 'Europe's "constitutional treat(ies)"', see R Schütze, 'On "Federal Ground": The European Union as an (Inter)national Phenomenon' in R Schütze (ed), *Foreign Affairs and the EU Constitution: Selected Essays* (Cambridge University Press 2014) 22–26.

8 The term is used in contrast to FG Mancini, 'Europe: The Case for Statehood' (1998) 4(1) *European Law Journal* 29. In response JH Weiler, 'Europe: The Case Against the Case for Statehood' (1998) 4(1) *European Law Journal* 43.

9 De Witte (n 5) 178 (emphasis in the original).

10 Ibid 179–184. See also B de Witte, 'The European Union as an International Legal Experiment' in G de Búrca and JH Weiler (eds), *The Worlds of European Constitutionalism* (Cambridge University Press 2012).

11 Convention for European Economic Cooperation (adopted on 16 April 1948, entered into force 28 July 1948) 888 UNTS 141 [EEC Convention].

12 Statute of the Council of Europe (signed on 5 May 1949, entered into force 3 August 1949) 87 UNTS 103 [CoE Statute].

13 Treaty establishing the European Coal and Steel Community (adopted 18 April 1951, entered into force 23 July 1952) 261 UNTS 140 [ECSC Treaty].

14 De Witte (n 5) 179.

15 Ibid 180. Cp ECSC Treaty, Art. 9 referring to the 'supranational character' of the High Authority.

16 Treaty establishing the European Economic Community (adopted on 25 March 1957, entered into force 1 January 1958) 294 UNTS 3 [EEC Treaty].

§ 2 EU Withdrawal: Exiting an International Organisation

depart from this 'treaty path'[17]. Instead, in external relations with non-EU states, and especially in the context of multilateral fora, the EU and its Member States have repeatedly accepted the EU's qualification as an international organisation.[18]

Secondly, De Witte argues that the features distinguishing the EU from (most) other international organisations neither contradict said intention nor, as such, change the legal character of the EU. While he acknowledges that features such as the EU's 'constant stream of new legislation in a broad range of policy areas'[19], vested with primacy[20] and enforced through broad judicial enforcement mechanism,[21] are not typical for international organisations, De Witte views them as exemplifying the flexibility of international law to encompass new developments.[22]

Finally, De Witte points to – what he considers – objective evidence of the continuing international character of the EU. Formally speaking, the EU's founding treaties have all availed themselves of treaty law's traditional forms and language.[23] Not only have attempts to 'constitutionalise'[24] the language of the Treaties failed with the rejection of the *Constitution of Europe*.[25] Even in the two instances that most prominently stand for a

---

17 De Witte (n 5) 180.
18 An example for this is the practice of including so-called REIO clauses in multilateral agreements, so as to open them for participation by the EU. These clauses allow for and regulate the participation of regional (economic) integration organisations (R(E)IOs). On the practice of REIO clauses, see J Odermatt, *International Law and the European Union* (Cambridge University Press 2021) 69–75. On the problems these can cause under international law, see E Paasivirta and PJ Kuijper, 'Does one Size fit All?: The European Community and the Responsibility of International Organizations' (2005) 36 *Netherlands Yearbook of International Law* 169, 204–212.
19 De Witte (n 5) 186.
20 Ibid 187–190.
21 Ibid 186–187.
22 Ibid 178.
23 Besides the two most prominent examples of treaty language referred to by De Witte (ibid 181) in Art. 1 TEU (use of the term 'Treaty' and reference to the Member States as 'HIGH CONTRACTING PARTIES', capital letters in the original), typical treaty elements include the preamble, comprising the enumeration of state representatives, the listing of the plenipotentiaries as well as the final provisions (Arts. 47–55) followed by the list of signatories.
24 For the expression, cp T Christiansen and C Reh, *Constitutionalizing the European Union* (Bloomsbury Publishing 2017).
25 For the draft text of the Constitution, see Draft Treaty Establishing a Constitution for Europe (18 July 2003) OJ C169/1. On the use of 'constitutional terminology', see De Witte (n 5) 192–194.

I. (Un)Identified Legal Object? The EU as an International Organisation

'deepening' and 'widening'[26] of European integration – revisions of and accessions to the EU Treaties – the Member States make use of the traditional means of international law.[27] The respective articles on amendment and accession procedures in the EU Treaties are not only modelled along those provided for in the *Vienna Convention on the Law of Treaties*[28] (VCLT), they are also more rigid than those included in other founding treaties of less integrated organisations.[29] Even after having introduced participation of the EU Parliament and two simplified revisions procedures, the basis for any treaty amendment and accession is still consent by all Member States.[30]

Though Member States thus remain the *Herren der Verträge* concerning amendments and accessions, for decades this was questioned regarding the termination of membership.[31] With all pre-Lisbon Treaties being silent on the issue of withdrawal from the Union, especially scholars continuously discussed the possibility of and potential conditions for an exit.[32] In con-

---

26 De Witte (n 5) 183.
27 Ibid.
28 Vienna Convention on the Law of Treaties (adopted 23 May 1969, entered into force 27 January 1980) 1155 UNTS 331 [VCLT].
29 De Witte (n 5) 183–185.
30 For amendments, Art. 48(4) sentence 2 TEU provides: 'The amendments shall enter into force after being ratified by all the member States in accordance with their respective constitutional requirements.' For accessions, Art. 49 sentence 5 and 6 TEU provide: 'The conditions of admission and the adjustments to the Treaties on which the Union is founded, which such admission entails, shall be subject of an agreement between the Member States and the applicant State. This agreement shall be submitted for ratification by all the contracting States in accordance with their respective constitutional requirements.' On the balancing of the intergovernmental character of accession and the EU institutions influence, see C Hillion, 'Accession and Withdrawal in the Law of the European Union' in A Arnull and D Chalmers (eds), *The Oxford Handbook of European Union Law* (Oxford University Press 2017) 129–134.
31 Cp U Everling, 'Sind die Mitgliedstaaten der Europäischen Gemeinschaft noch Herren der Verträge?: Zum Verhältnis von Europäischem Gemeinschaftsrecht und Völkerrecht' in R Bernhardt and others (eds), *Völkerrecht als Rechtsordnung, Internationale Gerichtsbarkeit, Menschenrechte: Festschrift für Hermann Mosler* (Springer 1983) 183–185.
32 For an overview of past instances where the question gained relevance, see A Waltemathe, *Austritt aus der EU: Sind die Mitgliedstaaten noch souverän?* (Lang 2000) 22–28. For two further examples of monographs from different decades addressing the question, see H Steiger, *Staatlichkeit und Überstaatlichkeit: Eine Untersuchung zur rechtlichen und politischen Stellung der Europäischen Gemeinschaften* (Duncker & Humblot 1966) 138–143; F Götting-Biwer, *Die Beendigung der Mitgliedschaft in der Europäischen Union* (Nomos 2000). For the history of Art. 50 TEU, see KA Armstrong, *Brexit Time: Leaving the EU – Why, How and When?* (Cambridge University

trast to the prescribed amendment and accession procedures, termination of membership – in the absence of any withdrawal procedure or practice – did not inform the debate on the EU's legal nature. Rather, the different perceptions of the EU provided a point of departure from which to argue for or against an (unconditional) possibility of withdrawal.[33] With the different qualifications of the EU being the baseline, the discussion (again) revolved around the applicability of general international law to the Union. While supporters of organisationhood referred to international treaty law, advocates of supranational, federal and constitutional concepts rejected such recourse, accepting withdrawal, if at all, only under the condition of consensus among all Member States.[34]

From the vantage point of international institutional law, the absence of a withdrawal clause by no means disqualified the EU from being considered an international organisation. In contrast, discussions on member state withdrawals without a respective withdrawal provision in the founding treaty are well-known in the field.[35] While the founding treaties of many international organisations address the issue, this is far from uniform practice.[36] Recourse is then taken to the VCLT's rules on treaty denunciation.[37] Art. 56(1) VCLT sets out that '[a] treaty which contains no provision regarding its termination and which does not provide for denunciation or withdrawal is not subject to denunciation or withdrawal'. This general rule, however, is subject to two qualifications.

Firstly, Art. 56(1) VCLT provides for exemptions where either an initial intention of the parties to allow for unilateral withdrawal is established

---

Press 2017), chapter 15 and M Dougan, *The UK's Withdrawal from the EU: A Legal Analysis* (Oxford University Press 2021) 21–25.

33 O Dörr, 'Article 50 TEU' in E Grabitz, M Hilf and M Nettesheim (eds), *Das Recht der Europäischen Union* (82nd supplement, CH Beck 2024) para 1.

34 A Thiele, 'Der Austritt aus der EU: Hintergründe und rechtliche Rahmenbedingungen eines „Brexit"' (2016) 51(3) *Europarecht* 281, 289–290 with further references.

35 For a summary of the main arguments, see HG Schermers and N Blokker (n 3) paras 134–135.

36 While according to Schermers and Blokker '[m]ost constitutions of international organizations expressly provide that membership may be brought to an end by (unilateral) withdrawal' (see ibid para 120), Klabbers considers silence of the founding treaties on withdrawal to be the standard (J Klabbers (n 3) 85).

37 According to Art. 5 VCLT, the VCLT's provisions are applicable to the founding treaties of international organisations. On the 'intersection' between international institutional law and the law of treaties in case of member state withdrawal, see CM Brölmann and others, 'Exiting International Organizations: A Brief Introduction' (2018) 15(2) *International Organizations Law Review* 243, 247–251.

(lit. a) or the nature of the treaty implies such a right (lit. b). Secondly, withdrawal may take place in accordance with the provisions of the VCLT.[38] Thus, Arts. 60–62 VCLT allow for denunciation of an international agreement in certain extraordinary circumstances.[39] On this basis, many examples of states' notifications of withdrawal and subsequent non-participation in international organisations have been analysed regarding their legality.[40]

Most importantly, however, recourse to international treaty law does not preclude arriving at the same results as those of proponents of other concepts. When trying to establish the initial intention of the parties or the nature of the EU Treaties, one must necessarily come across the 'unlimited duration'[41] of the Treaties aimed at creating an 'ever closer union'[42].[43] Moreover, as observed by Hillion regarding Art. 62 VCLT,

> [i]t has particularly been questioned whether the strict conditions for termination based on a change of circumstances could ever be met by a Member State in view of the original 'ever closer union' purpose of the Treaties to which all had to subscribe, and considering that any significant modifications, for example of the treaties, requires unanimous approval.[44]

When, however, the conditions of Arts. 56 and 60–62 VCLT are not met, withdrawal of a treaty party may take place only based on mutual consent.[45]

---

38 Art. 42(2) VCLT: 'The termination of a treaty, its denunciation or the withdrawal of a party may take place only as a result of the application of the provisions of the treaty or of the present Convention.'
39 Art. 60 VCLT provides for termination as a consequence of a material breach by another party, Art. 61 VCLT because of a supervening impossibility of performance, and Art. 62 VCLT as a consequence of a fundamental change of circumstances.
40 For a discussion of some pertinent examples, see HG Schermers and N Blokker (n 3) paras 125–133.
41 Art. 53 TEU and Art. 356 TFEU.
42 Preamble of the TEU, recital 13.
43 Cf Hillion, Oxford Handbook EU Law (n 30) 148.
44 Ibid with references to J Herbst, 'Observations on the Right to Withdraw from the European Union: Who are the "Masters of the Treaties"?' (2005) 6(11) *German Law Journal* 1755, 1755 and J-P Jacqué, *Droit institutionnel de l'Union Européenne* (4th edn, Editions Dalloz 2006) 115.
45 Art. 54 VCLT: 'The termination of a treaty or the withdrawal of a party may take place: (a) in conformity with the provisions of the treaty; or (b) at any time by consent of all the parties after consultations with the other contracting States.'

So, while differing perceptions of the EU formed the basis of the debate on the possibility of withdrawal, this offered no definite answers: allowing only consensual withdrawal was compatible both with a claim to organisation- or (emerging) statehood. However, since its introduction with the Treaty of Lisbon, Art. 50 TEU provides an additional layer to De Witte's argument. While the absence of a withdrawal clause arguably worked both ways – and was certainly nothing unique from the perspective of the 'intergovernmentalists'[46] – its inclusion and content now can be seen as speaking in favour of the Union's organisationhood.

II. Art. 50 TEU: A Regular Withdrawal Clause

By introducing Art. 50 TEU, the EU's founding Treaties now include the possibility of withdrawal as envisaged in Art. 42(2) VCLT: the EU's Member States may terminate their EU membership in accordance with the EU's founding Treaties. While Art. 50(1) TEU pronounces the right to denunciation itself, paragraphs 2 and 4 concern procedural issues and paragraphs 3 and 5 touch upon the legal consequences of withdrawal. In its *Wightman* judgement, the European Court of Justice (ECJ) summarised Art. 50 TEU as 'pursu[ing] two objectives, namely, first, enshrining the sovereign right of a Member State to withdraw from the European Union and, secondly, establishing a procedure to enable such a withdrawal to take place in an orderly fashion'[47].

Art. 50 TEU not only puts an end to the debates on the possibility of withdrawal from the EU, its design also appears to firmly place the EU itself and the process of withdrawal in the realm of international institutional and treaty law. Art. 50 TEU mirrors the typical elements of a treaty withdrawal clause (A.), and the features of Art. 50 TEU that seem to 'unionalise'[48] the withdrawal process are also not so exceptional as to distinguish withdrawal from the EU from withdrawal from any other international organisation (B.).

---

46 Cp Thiele (n 34), 290.
47 ECJ, C-621/18 *Wightman* [2018] ECLI:EU:C:2018:999, 56.
48 The term is used to describe those aspects of the withdrawal process that are less 'state-centred' and 'provide for a significant input from EU institutions [...] and for the application of EU rules' (cp Hillion, Oxford Handbook EU Law (n 30) 142).

A. The International Law Template and Art. 50 TEU

Art. 42(2) VCLT explicitly envisages the possibility of withdrawal from a treaty based either on a provision in the treaty or as an application of the VCLT's provisions on treaty termination. The latter set high bars for withdrawal: Arts. 60–62 VCLT lay out strict conditions under which a state may invoke a unilateral right to withdrawal. Additionally, where such a right exists, its enactment is subject to several procedural hurdles.[49] Where, however, states include a withdrawal provision in their treaty, the VCLT makes no specifications on the design of such a clause, granting the parties full autonomy to decide on the terms of withdrawal. States make use of this freedom in varying degrees. While many treaties simply state the right to withdraw, some make withdrawal conditional on certain circumstances.[50]

First and foremost, Art. 50 TEU positively states an EU Member State's right to *unilateral* withdrawal. Most prominently, Art. 50(1) TEU reads that '[a]ny Member State may decide to withdraw from the Union in accordance with its own constitutional requirements'. According to Art. 50(3) TEU, such withdrawal takes effect either on the date that a withdrawal agreement enters into force or 'failing that', two years after the withdrawing state notified its intention of withdrawal. Therefore, Art. 50 TEU not only rejects the idea of consensually agreed exit among the Member States as propagated by non-intergovernmentalists,[51] read together with Art. 50(3) TEU, it also confirms the unilateral character of the right in relation to the EU itself.

Although Art. 50(2) TEU provides for treaty negotiations between the EU and the departing state, termination of membership is not dependent on the conclusion of a withdrawal agreement between them. The legal grounds for the termination of membership, thus, remain the Member State's sovereign declaration of intent.[52] In addition to being unilateral,

---

49 Cp Arts. 65–68 VCLT.
50 Such as a minimum period of participation, see eg Art. 25(1) United Nations Framework Convention on Climate Change (adopted on 9 May 1992, entered into force 21 March 1994) 1771 UNTS 107 [UNFCCC]: 'At any time after three years from the date on which the Convention has entered into force for a Party, that Party may withdraw from the Convention by giving written notification to the Depositary.'
51 To the contrary, by introducing a unilateral right to withdrawal, recourse to a consensually agreed withdrawal has arguably been taken off the table, see eg Dörr (n 33) para 45 who concludes that a multilateral termination agreement between the Member States is excluded by EU law but would probably be valid under international law.
52 Ibid 17.

Art. 50 TEU moreover provides for *unconditional* withdrawal.[53] To invoke its right to withdraw, a Member State must not meet any substantive requirements. Reference to the Member State's 'own constitutional requirements'[54] in particular cannot be viewed as restricting a state's decision to withdraw.[55] Thus, while the EU may be the most integrated international organisation, the possibility of withdrawal from which was long highly disputed, the EU Treaties now provide Member States with the broadest possible right of denunciation.

Instead of introducing substantive conditions for withdrawal, Art. 50 TEU opts for a proceduralisation of withdrawal. In international treaty law, the procedural requirements for treaty withdrawal are relatively complex. For withdrawals based on the VCLT's grounds for termination,[56] Arts. 65–68 VCLT set out a rather elaborate procedure.[57] According to Arts. 65(1), 67(1) VCLT, a state must communicate its intention and reasons for withdrawal through written notification to the other parties. The notification takes effect at the earliest three months after its issuance,[58] except where another treaty party raises objections (Art. 65(2) VCLT) or the noti-

---

53 In doing so, Art. 50 TEU does not only positively introduce a right to withdrawal. The right even goes far beyond the withdrawal rights that, in the view of 'intergovernmentalists' so far existed in accordance with the VCLT's provisions on treaty termination, see ibid 4.
54 Art. 50(1) TEU.
55 Dörr (n 33) para 19. Arguing in favour of conditionality, see Hillion, Oxford Handbook EU Law (n 30) 136–137.
56 Art. 65(1) VCLT: 'A party which, *under the provisions of the present Convention*, invokes either a defect in its consent to be bound by a treaty or a ground for impeaching the validity of a treaty, terminating it, withdrawing from it or suspending its operation, must notify the other parties of its claim' (emphasis added). Art. 66–67(1) VCLT refer to Art. 65 VCLT.
57 While the ECJ has held that 'the *specific* procedural requirements there laid down do not form part of customary international law' (ECJ, C-162/96 *A. Racke GmbH & Co. v. Hauptzollamt Mainz* [1998] ECLI:EU:C:1998:293, [59] (emphasis added)), the International Court of Justice (ICJ) at least considers some of the underlying procedural principles to constitute customary international law (see eg ICJ *Interpretation of the Agreement of 25 March 1951 between the WHO and Egypt* (Advisory Opinion) [1980] ICJ Rep 1980, p 96, [49]; ICJ *Case Concerning the Gabčíkovo-Nagymaros Project (Hungary v Slovakia)* (Judgement) [1997] ICJ Rep 1997, p 7, [109]).
58 Where a party withdraws from a treaty on the basis of Art. 56(1)(a) or (b) (ie withdrawal from a treaty containing no withdrawal provision but from which the parties intended to admit withdrawal or whose nature implies it), Art. 56(2) requires that the 'party shall give no less than twelve month's notice of its intention to denounce or withdraw'.

fication is revoked (Art. 68 VCLT). In the case of objections, these must be addressed through consultations and, ultimately, through dispute settlement mechanisms provided for in Arts. 65(3), 66 VCLT. In contrast, for cases of termination pursuant to a treaty's withdrawal provision, Art. 67(2) only establishes a minimum requirement of notification to the other parties – without requiring the denouncing party to give reasons or even do so in written form.[59]

In practice, while treaty negotiators make use of their wide discretion,[60] the VCLT's core procedural elements, such as prior notification followed by a waiting period, are frequently found in international agreements as well as the founding treaties of international organisations.[61] With regard to Art. 50 TEU, explicit reference to the VCLT's withdrawal procedure can even be found in its drafting history.[62] Accordingly, the basic features of Arts. 65–67 VCLT are reflected in Art. 50 TEU. A case in point, Art. 50(2) TEU requires that '[a] Member State which decides to withdraw shall notify the European Council of its intention'. Pursuant to Art. 50(3) TEU, this

---

59 Art. 67(2) VCLT: 'Any act of declaring invalid, terminating, withdrawing from, or suspending the operation of a treaty *pursuant to the provisions of the treaty* or of paragraphs 2 or 3 of article 65 shall be carried out through an instrument communicated to the other parties. If the instrument is not signed by the Head of State, Head of Government or Minister for Foreign Affairs, the representative of the State communicating it may be called upon to produce full powers' (emphasis added). For these instruments, the right of revocation as per Art. 68 VCLT also applies.

60 For an overview of typical withdrawal clauses in multilateral agreements, see United Nations, 'Summary of Practice of the Secretary-General as Depositary of Multilateral Treaties' (UN Doc. ST/LEG/7/Rev.l) 77–79 and United Nations, 'Final Clauses of Multilateral Treaties: Handbook' (2nd edn, United Nations Publications 2005) 109–111. For references to a wide variety of withdrawal clauses in founding treaties, see HG Schermers and N Blokker paras 120–122 with footnotes.

61 See eg A Aust, *Modern Treaty Law and Practice* (2nd edn, Cambridge University Press 2007) 278 according to whom withdrawal clauses usually provide 'for both duration and denunciation or withdrawal [...]. This is so whether the treaty is bilateral or multilateral.' With regard to founding treaties of international organisation, HG Schermers and N Blokker (n 3) para 120 moreover find that '[p]rior notice is usually required, and after a certain period the withdrawal takes effect.'

62 Art. 50 TEU is based on the identically worded Article 46 of the failed Constitution for Europe. When the text of Art. 46 was introduced, it was stated that the 'withdrawal procedure is partly inspired by the one provided for in the Vienna Convention on the Law of Treaties' (see Praesidium de la Convention européenne, 'Titre X: L'appartenance à l'Union' CONV 648/03 (2 April 2003) 3 ('La procédure de retrait s'inspire en partie de celle prévue dans la Convention de Vienne sur le droit des traités [...].' (Translated by the author)). On Art. 50 TEU's drafting history, see KA Armstrong (n 32), chapter 15.

notification – which the ECJ has found to be revocable[63] – takes effect, at the latest, after the expiry of a two-year waiting period. Beyond that, Art. 50 TEU makes no explicit mention of which form the notification has to take nor does it require the withdrawing Member State to give reasons for its decision. Thus, as with the substantive right of withdrawal, the procedure of withdrawal as provided for in Art. 50 TEU, too, is even wider than that provided for in the VCLT.

B. Unionalisation of the Withdrawal Procedure?

At the same time, Art. 50(2) TEU stipulates an elaborate procedure for negotiations on and the conclusion of a withdrawal agreement between the withdrawing Member State and the EU. Once the Member State has notified the EU Council of its intention to withdraw, the Council shall provide guidelines on the basis of which and in accordance with Art. 218(3) TFEU the Union shall negotiate an agreement 'setting out the arrangements for [the] withdrawal, taking account of the framework for its future relationship with the Union'[64]. Before conclusion by the EU Council, the European Parliament must also consent to the agreement.[65] This has led to claims that 'the EU's withdrawal clause presents major differences from standard withdrawal mechanisms' which 'do not set up full-blown procedures aimed at securing a negotiated and orderly withdrawal' – especially as between the Member State and the respective international organisation.[66]

While it is true that the EU internal procedure for the negotiation and conclusion of a withdrawal agreement is 'firmly embedded in EU constitutional law'[67], this does not change the legal character of Art. 50 TEU. As Art. 50(3) TEU clearly demonstrates, withdrawal from the EU takes effect regardless of the conclusion of a withdrawal agreement with the departing

---

63 See ECJ, *Wightman* (n 47).
64 Art. 50(2) TEU, sentence 1.
65 Art. 50(2) TEU, sentence 2.
66 PR Polak, 'EU Withdrawal Law After Brexit: The Emergence of a Unique Legal Procedure' in J Santos Vara, RA Wessel and PR Polak (eds), *The Routledge Handbook on the International Dimension of Brexit* (Routledge 2020) 58. See also Hillion, Oxford Handbook EU Law (n 30) 136–142 and C Hillion, 'Withdrawal under Article 50 TEU: An Integration-Friendly Process' (2018) 55 (Special Issue) *Common Market Law Review* 29.
67 Hillion, *Withdrawal under Art. 50* (n 66) 30.

II. Art. 50 TEU: A Regular Withdrawal Clause

Member State. Art. 50(2) TEU, thus, constitutes a mere *pactum de negotiando*,[68] positively stating an obligation to negotiate that may even emanate from the general principles of international law.[69] In any case, the idea of guaranteeing an orderly withdrawal from an international agreement through the conclusion of a new agreement – a withdrawal agreement – was also considered by Fitzmaurice, the International Law Commission's (ILC) third Special Rapporteur (SR) on the law of treaties. In his Second Report, SR Fitzmaurice considered that

> [t]he termination of a treaty, or of any particular obligation under it, or of the participation of a particular party, may give rise to a number of consequential issues. These will, despite the termination, be governed by the treaty itself if it provides for them, and if not, *must be the subject of a separate agreement between the parties*.[70]

While this notion was not included in the ILC's drafts articles, Art. 70(1) VCLT at least mentions the possibility of settling the consequences of treaty withdrawal by subsequent agreement between the parties.[71]

In practice, the founding treaties of some international organisations even impose an obligation to conclude an agreement upon withdrawal (*pactum de contrahendo*). Art. 53 of the *Convention establishing the Multilateral Investment Guarantee Agency*[72], determining the rights and duties of

---

68 See Dörr (n 33) paras 15, 17.
69 Ascencio in his commentary on Art. 70 VCLT argues in this direction, based on an example from practice. Following the denunciation of the 1878 Monetary Convention by Switzerland, leading to the dissolution of the Latin Monetary Union, the Member States in 1885 adopted an agreement to settle unresolved issues. Based on statements made by France requesting a mutual settlement among the parties, Ascencio draws the conclusion that 'in complex situations, new negotiations and technical agreements may [not only] prove necessary to determine in detail the consequences of a treaty's termination', '[t]he conclusion [...] could even emerge as a legal obligation, resulting from the principles of legal security and good faith' (see H Ascencio, 'Article 70' in O Corten and P Klein (eds), *The Vienna Conventions on the Law of Treaties* (vol II, Oxford University Press 2011)). For the French statement, see AC Kiss, 'L'extinction des traités dans la pratique francaise' (1959) 5 *Annuaire Français de Droit International* 784, 784–785.
70 ILC, 'Second Report on the Law of Treaties, by Gerald Fitzmaurice, Special Rapporteur' UN Doc A/CN.4/107, YBILC (1957) Vol. II 35 (emphasis added).
71 Art. 70(1) VCLT: 'Unless the treaty otherwise provides or *the parties otherwise agree* [...]' (emphasis added). On Art. 70 VCLT, see below Part I § 3.
72 Convention establishing the Multilateral Investment Guarantee Agency (adopted on 11 October 1985, entered into force 12 April 1988) 1508 UNTS 99 [MIGA Convention].

states ceasing to be members, provides that 'the Agency *shall* enter into an arrangement with such State for the settlement of their respective claims and obligations. Any such arrangement shall be approved by the Board.'[73] Here, as in the case of Art. 50 TEU, the treaty puts the obligation on the organisation,[74] not the Member States, to address withdrawal issues with the departing state. Art. 50(2) TEU awards the EU with explicit treaty-making powers[75] and sets out a specific treaty-making procedure, validating the EU's international legal personality but also its functional limitation. Thus, as Dörr summarises, Art. 50 TEU

> confirms the continuing sovereignty of the Member States and anchors it palpably in the treaty text. The Member States are not only the often quoted 'Masters of the Treaties', something that especially Art. 48 and 54 TEU express [...], they are also the 'Masters' of their own membership. Just like the aforementioned provisions, Art. 50 thus underlines the continuing international legal basis of the Union and its special legal system.[76]

III. Brexit as Treaty Withdrawal

Being founded on treaties between its Member States and endowed with independently acting organs, the EU meets the criteria of organisationhood. And while it may display additional features unique to it, '[b]eing a supranational organization means also being an international organization'[77]. If the EU is thus considered an international organisation, Brexit must be

---

73 Emphasis added.
74 Art. 50(2) sentence 2 provides that 'the Union shall negotiate and conclude an agreement with that State'.
75 Dörr (n 33) para 9. On the wide scope of Art. 50(2) TEU as a treaty basis, see ECJ, C-479/21 PPU *Governor of Cloverhill Prison and Others* (Opinion of the Advocate General Kokott) [2021] ECLI:EU:C:2021:899, 45–63.
76 Dörr (n 33) para 7 („Sie [die Vorschrift, ie Art. 50 TEU] bestätigt die fortbestehende Souveränität der Mitgliedstaaten und verankert sie augenfällig im Vertragstext. Die Mitgliedstaaten sind also nicht nur die vielzitierten „Herren der Verträge", was vor allem in den Art. 48 und 54 EUV deutlich zum Ausdruck kommt [...], sie sind auch die „Herren" über ihre eigene Mitgliedschaft. Ebenso wie die genannten Bestimmungen unterstreicht Art. 50 damit die fortbestehende völkerrechtliche Geltungsgrundlage der Union und ihrer speziellen Rechtsordnung.' (Emphasis omitted, translated by the author)).
77 A Orakhelashvili, 'The Idea of European International Law' (2006) 17(2) *European Journal of International Law* 315, 343.

III. Brexit as Treaty Withdrawal

treated as the UK's termination of membership in that organisation. Or translated into treaty law terms: Brexit means that the UK unilaterally withdrew from a multilateral agreement. Thus, consideration of Brexit's effect on international agreements means looking at the effect of the denunciation of *one* international agreement on several *other* international agreements.

This effect can play out in two ways: on the one hand, '[t]he situation may arise where denunciation of a treaty produces effects on other treaties on the strength of convention provisions included in the latter.'[78] In that case, termination of membership in the founding treaties triggers, so to speak, termination provisions included in other international agreements. Analysing the effect of Brexit on international agreements would thus mean scouring every single one of these agreements for such a trigger provision.[79] On the other hand, 'the denunciation of a basic treaty can [also] bring consequences upon a group of related treaties'[80], making agreement-by-agreement scrutiny unnecessary. When and under which conditions this is the case will be analysed in the next chapter (§ 3).

---

78 Ascensio (n 69) para 6.
79 See below Part I § 4.
80 Ascensio (n 69) para 6.

§ 3 Automatic Treaty Termination: A Legal Consequence of EU Withdrawal?

In many regards, the Brexit constituted an absolute novelty. Never before had a state terminated its membership in this highly integrated organisation. At the same time, where one follows the proposition that even a supranational organisation remains an international organisation,[1] the same must hold true with regard to termination of membership in that organisation. Thus, even an exit from a supranational organisation remains a withdrawal from a multilateral agreement. Viewed from that perspective, Brexit – like any other withdrawal from an international organisation – 'moves at the cutting face of the law of treaties and institutional law'[2]. For while '[g]enerally, legal thinking about international organizations proceeds from an institutional (law) perspective', 'the scenario of a member state leaving the organization leads back to the preliminary level, that of "contractual" relations between states'[3].

What then are the rules applicable to withdrawal from a multilateral agreement? In general, the law of treaties is codified in the *Vienna Convention on the Law of Treaties*[4] (VCLT), which, according to Art. 5 VCLT, also applies to the founding treaties of an international organisation.[5] In particular, Art. 70 VCLT sets out the consequences of such a withdrawal (I.). With the article being of customary nature,[6] its provisions are applicable, even if an organisation's member state is not a party to the VCLT.

---

1 A Orakhelashvili, 'The Idea of European International Law' (2006) 17(2) *European Journal of International Law* 315, 343.
2 CM Brölmann and others, 'Exiting International Organizations: A Brief Introduction' (2018) 15(2) *International Organizations Law Review* 243, 248 (emphasis omitted).
3 Ibid 247 (emphasis omitted).
4 Vienna Convention on the Law of Treaties (adopted 23 May 1969, entered into force 27 January 1980) 1155 UNTS 331 [VCLT].
5 Art. 5 VCLT: 'The present Convention applies to any treaty which is the constituent instrument of an international organization […] without prejudice to any relevant rules of the organization.'
6 On Art. 70 VCLT's customary status, see eg PCA *Difference between New Zealand and France Concerning the Interpretation or Application of Two Agreements Concluded on 9 July 1986 between the Two States and Which Related to the Problems Arising from the "Rainbow Warrior" Affair (New Zealand v France)* [1990] 20 RIAA 217, [75]: '[…]

§ 3 Automatic Treaty Termination: A Legal Consequence of EU Withdrawal?

At the same time, both Art. 5 and Art. 70 VCLT explicitly acknowledge the contractual freedom of the parties to an international agreement to deviate from the VCLT's rules. Thus, according to Art. 5 VCLT application of the VCLT's provisions to an international organisation's founding treaties is 'without prejudice to any relevant rules of the organization' and Art. 70 VCLT begins with the caveat 'unless the treaty otherwise provides'. In some instances, the member states of international organisations have made use of this contractual freedom and modified the consequences of leaving to also apply to other international agreements. The practice of these member states not only shows what is possible; it also illustrates the limits of such *lex specialis* arrangements (II.). When applying Art. 70 VCLT and the practice of previous exits from international organisations, what conclusions can be drawn for the question of the consequences of an EU exit on international agreements (III.)? As this chapter shows, the automatic consequences are, in fact, rather limited (IV.).

I. Lex generalis: Legal Consequences of Exiting an International Organisation

Just as the VCLT regulates the grounds and procedure for treaty denunciation, it also provides for the consequences of withdrawal from an international agreement. According to Art. 70(1)(a) VCLT 'the termination of a treaty [...] releases the parties from any obligation further to perform the treaty'. Subparagraph (b), however, clarifies that this 'does not affect any right, obligation or legal situation of the parties created through the execution of the treaty prior to its termination'. Where a party withdraws from a multilateral agreement, such as in the case of exiting an international organisation, this applies to the relationship between the withdrawing and the remaining states.[7] While subparagraph (a), thus, refers to the rather obvious consequence that a party withdrawing from an agreement is no longer

---

certain specific provisions of customary law in the Vienna Convention are relevant in the case, such as Article 60 [...] and Article 70, which deals with the legal consequences of the expiry of a treaty'. See also S Wittich, 'Article 70' in O Dörr and K Schmalenbach (eds), *Vienna Convention on the Law of Treaties: A Commentary* (2nd edn, Springer 2018) paras 38–39 with further references.

7 Art. 70(2) VCLT: 'If a State denounces or withdraws from a multilateral treaty, paragraph 1 applies in the relations between that Sate and each of the parties to the treaty from the date when such denunciation or withdrawal takes effect.'

bound by this agreement and thus exempted from any further performance, subparagraph (b) highlights the non-retroactivity of termination.[8] As such

> the termination does not affect the validity of the acts of the parties performed during the treaty's existence and prior to its termination; *a fortiori* it will not dissolve rights previously acquired under the treaty. The validity of these acts persists, although the treaty which gave them life no longer does.[9]

As regards the founding treaty of an international organisation – a multilateral agreement between all member states – the consequences of withdrawal are, thus, twofold: the exiting state is exempted from any further performance provided for in the treaty, such as continued participation in the activities of the organisation or any future financial obligations.[10] At the same time, any obligations already executed – such as the payment of previous membership fees – remain valid. In addition, however, the question arises as to the continued validity of rights and obligations that do not arise *directly* from the founding treaties. What consequences occur from the withdrawal with regards to any acts of the organisation or of the withdrawing state undertaken in the context of its membership? Here, a distinction must be made as regards the legal basis and the legal effects of any such instrument.

Firstly, international organisations can take unilateral decisions binding on the member states.[11] Such decisions may concern the functioning of the organisation or impose substantive rules on the member states in the organisation's field of activity. Binding decisions are dependent on the organisation's founding treaty, their 'enactment and binding force […]

---

8   Especially in comparison to invalidity, see Art. 69 VCLT.
9   ME Villiger, 'Article 70' in ME Villiger (ed), *Commentary on the 1969 Vienna Convention on the Law of Treaties* (Martinus Nijhoff Publishers 2008) para 9.
10 On the UK's financial obligations post-Brexit, see M Waibel, 'The Brexit Bill and the Law of Treaties' (*EJIL:Talk!*, 4 May 2017) <https://www.ejiltalk.org/the-brexit-bill-and-the-law-of-treaties/>.
11 While it is generally recognised that international organisations may make internal rules, they may only make external rules where their founding treaties so provide (see with further references HG Schermers and N Blokker, *International Institutional Law: Unity within Diversity* (5th edn, Martinus Nijhoff Publishers 2011) paras 1196, 1320).

derive from this treaty'[12]. Thus, where the founding treaty terminates for a member state as provided for in Art. 70(1)(a) VCLT, so does the binding force of the organisation's decisions.[13]

Secondly, in creating internal rules, international organisations can also take recourse to traditional international treaty-making. In contrast to unilateral decisions, such 'conventions'[14] are negotiated within the framework of the organisation but acquire legal force through ratification by the member states.[15] Their legal basis, thus, is not the organisation's founding treaty. Instead, by concluding conventions the member states create a legal situation based in and binding on them through international law. As per Art. 70(1)(b) VCLT, conventions, thus, generally continue to apply to a withdrawing state and, if desired, must be terminated in accordance with the general rules of treaty law.[16]

Thirdly, to fulfil their functions, international organisations can conclude international agreements with other organisations or non-member states. But with only the organisation becoming a party,[17] what is the legal position of its member states under international law with regard to these external international agreements? Do the member states acquire a quasi-party status or must they be considered as third states[18]? When drafting the *Vienna Convention on the Law of Treaties between States and International Organizations or between International Organizations*[19] (VCLT-IO), the Special Rapporteur (SR) of the International Law Commission (ILC), Paul Reuter, proposed the inclusion of Art. 36*bis* to address this question. According to the proposed article, member states would have been considered

---

12 R Bernhardt, 'International Organizations: Internal Law and Rules' in R Bernhardt (ed), *International Organizations in General: Universal International Organizations and Cooperation* (Elsevier Science Publishers 1983) 144.
13 Cp M Ruffert and C Walter, *Institutionalisiertes Völkerrecht: Das Recht der Internationalen Organisationen und seine wichtigsten Anwendungsfelder* (2nd edn, CH Beck 2015) 99.
14 HG Schermers and N Blokker (n 11) para 1262.
15 Ibid paras 1281–1294.
16 A Schwerdtfeger, 'Austritt und Ausschluss aus Internationalen Organisationen: Zwischen staatlicher Souveränität und zwischenstaatlicher Kooperation' (2018) 56(1) *Archiv des Völkerrechts* 96, 122.
17 For the special case of mixed agreements, see below Part I § 3 section III.C.2.
18 Art. 2(1)(h) VCLT defines a 'third State' as 'a State not a party to the treaty'.
19 Vienna Convention on the Law of Treaties between States and International Organizations or between International Organizations (adopted and opened for signature 21 March 1986) UN Doc A/CONF.129/15 [VCLT-IO].

I. Lex generalis: Legal Consequences of Exiting an International Organisation

as third states to the international agreements of their organisation. However, this general rule was not thought to apply if the agreement intended to establish rights and obligations *also* for the organisation's member states, if the member states had 'unanimously agreed to be bound' by the agreement, and if their 'assent [...] [had] been duly brought to the knowledge of' the organisation's treaty partners.[20]

In the end, Art. 36*bis* did not make it into the final text of the VCLT-IO.[21] According to Klabbers, '[w]hat it indicated, though, was that, at least within the International Law Commission, there were some strong opinions generally favouring the view of member states as legally distinct from their organizations'[22]. This view seemed to rest on the premise that states should only be bound if and when they have expressed their consent.[23] The only accepted exception appears to be if the organisation's founding treaty binds the member states to the rights and obligations stemming from external agreements of the organisation.[24] This tie would then, however, be one stemming from the organisation's rules and not bind the member states as parties under international law. Thus, as in the case of conventions, the legal basis of an organisation's external international agreements is international law. Therefore, withdrawal by a member state *per se* does not affect the validity of the agreements themselves.[25] However, as in the case of unilateral decisions, the binding force of these agreements on the member

---

20 ILC, 'Report of the International Law Commission on the Work of its 34th Session (3 May-23 July 1982)' UN Doc A/37/10, YBILC (1982) Vol. II(2) 43.
21 On the history of Art. 36*bis*, see CM Brölmann, 'The 1986 Vienna Convention on the Law of Treaties: The History of Draft Article 36*bis*' in J Klabbers and R Lefeber (eds), *Essays on the Law of Treaties: A Collection of Essays in Honour of Bert Vierdag* (Brill Nijhoff 1998).
22 J Klabbers, *An Introduction to International Institutional Law* (2nd edn, Cambridge University Press 2009) 261.
23 ILC, 'Tenth Report on the Question of Treaties concluded between States and International Organizations or between two or more International Organizations, by Paul Reuter, Special Rapporteur' UN Doc A/CN.4/341 and Add.1 & Corr.1, YBILC (1981) Vol. II(1) ('The real question which may be dealt with in article 36 *bis* is how *direct* relationships can evolve between States members of an organization and parties other than the organization to a treaty concluded by the organization. The ultimate source of such direct relationships is clear: it can only be the consent of all interested parties.', (emphasis in original)).
24 Note, however, that, according to Klabbers, the EU is the only organisation with a respective provision in its founding treaties (Klabbers, *International Institutional Law* (n 22) 262). On Art. 216(2) TFEU, Part I § 3 section III.C.1.
25 On the possibility of denunciation following the withdrawal of a member state, see below at Part I § 4.

§ 3 Automatic Treaty Termination: A Legal Consequence of EU Withdrawal?

states (if at all) stems from and ceases with the application of the founding treaty to the member states.

II. Lex specialis: Arrangements between Member States

Applying the general rules as set out in Art. 70(1) VCLT, withdrawal terminates the application of the founding treaty and any secondary law of the organisation for the exiting state. At the same time, based on Art. 70(1)(b) VCLT, it does not affect the validity of any international agreements concluded by the organisation or the member states during the course of membership. However, Art. 70(1) VCLT provides the parties to an international agreement with twofold autonomy: to modify the provision's specifications either by defining legal consequences of withdrawal in the agreement itself or by (subsequent) agreement between the parties. While a limited practice in that regard exists in some founding treaties (A.), general principles of international law set strict limits on any such special arrangements (B.).

A. The Practice: Conventions Concluded between Member States

Not many founding treaties include special arrangements for the consequences of a member state's withdrawal, much less on the effect of such withdrawal on other international agreements. Nevertheless, a limited practice to that effect can be observed in founding treaties that explicitly envisage the established international organisation to promote convention-making.

One rare – and early – example is provided by the *Constitution of the International Labour Organization*[26] (ILO Constitution). Besides being the first founding treaty to expressly refer to conventions as instruments that give binding force to organisations' proposals,[27] Art. 1(5) sentence 3 ILO Constitution also provides that '[w]hen a Member has ratified any inter-

---

26 Constitution of the International Labour Organisation (adopted on 1 April 1919, entered into force 28 June 1919) 15 UNTS 40 [ILO Constitution].
27 Art. 19 ILO Constitution: 'When the Conference has decided on the adoption of proposals with regard to an item on the agenda, it will rest with the Conference to determine whether these proposals should take the form: (a) of an international Convention, or (b) of a Recommendation [...].' Cp HG Schermers and N Blokker (n 11) para 1271.

II. Lex specialis: Arrangements between Member States

national labour Conventions, [its] withdrawal [from the ILO Constitution] shall not affect the continued validity' of these conventions. A similar provision can be found in the *Agreement Establishing the World Trade Organization*[28] (WTO Agreement) regarding the so-called Plurilateral Trade Agreements. Although included in Annex 4 of the WTO Agreement,[29] these conventions constitute separate international agreements that are only binding to those member states who have ratified them. In relation to the denunciation of a Plurilateral Trade Agreement, Art. XV(2) WTO Agreements provides that '[w]ithdrawal [...] shall be governed by the provisions of that Agreement'. Thus, while both the ILO's and the WTO's founding treaties expressly address the consequences of a member state withdrawal for the organisations' conventions, Art. 1(5) ILO Constitution and Art. XV(2) WTO Agreement are of a mere declaratory nature. They confirm the continued validity of the agreements as per Art. 70(1)(b) VCLT.

A contrary example is provided by Art. 25(3) of the *United Nations Framework Convention on Climate Change*[30] (UNFCCC). According to Art. 17 UNFCCC, UNFCCC's primary organ – the Conference of the Parties (COP) – 'may, at any ordinary session, adopt protocols to the Convention' that shall then be communicated to UNFCCC's parties and enter into force in accordance with the respective protocol's final provisions. While entry into force of the protocols is, thus, independent from the UNFCCC, their termination is not: Art. 25(3) UNFCCC provides that '[a]ny Party that withdraws from the [UNFCCC] shall be considered as also having withdrawn from any protocol to which it is a Party'. Art. 25(3) UNFCCC thus provides for legal consequences of withdrawal from UNFCCC going beyond those provided for in Art. 70 VCLT.

From these cases, two constellations must be distinguished that only appear to be referring to Art. 70(1)(b) VCLT. For both of them, the WTO provides instructive examples. Firstly, besides including a declaratory statement on the continued validity of the Plurilateral Trade Agreements, Art. XV WTO Agreement also addresses the Multilateral Trade Agreements. Contrary to Art. XV(2), paragraph 1 provides that any withdrawal from the WTO Agreement shall also apply to the Multilateral Trade Agreements.

---

28 Agreement Establishing the World Trade Organization (adopted on 15 April 1994, entered into force 1 January 1995) 1867 UNTS 4 [WTO Agreement].
29 Art. II(3) WTO Agreement.
30 United Nations Framework Convention on Climate Change (adopted on 9 May 1992, entered into force 21 March 1994) 1771 UNTS 107 [UNFCCC].

§ 3 Automatic Treaty Termination: A Legal Consequence of EU Withdrawal?

While this appears to mirror the constellation in the UNFCCC, in contrast to Art. 25(3) UNFCCC, Art. XV(1) WTO Agreement does not amend the legal consequences provided for in Art. 70(1)(b) VCLT. This is due to the different status of the Multilateral Trade Agreements compared to their plurilateral siblings and the protocols to the UNFCCC. While the latter two are independent from their respective organisation's founding treaty,[31] the Multilateral Trade Agreements constitute 'integral parts of [the WTO] Agreement'[32]. As such, withdrawal from the founding treaty inevitably means withdrawal from the Multilateral Trade Agreements. Thus, instead of modifying the legal consequence of treaty withdrawal as per Art. 70(1)(b) VCLT, Art. XV(2) WTO Agreement only clarifies the scope of Art. 70(1)(a) VCLT.

Secondly, while Art. XV WTO Agreement confirms the validity of the Plurilateral Trade Agreements, some of these agreements themselves address the effect of a party's withdrawal from the WTO on its continued status as a party to these Plurilateral Trade Agreements. Art. XXII(13) of the *Agreement on Government Procurement*[33] (GPA), for example, states that '[w]here a Party to this Agreement ceases to be a Member of the WTO, it shall cease to be a Party to this Agreement with effect on the date on which it ceases to be a Member of the WTO'. However, in doing so, the GPA does not adapt Art. 70(1)(b) VCLT with regards to the *direct* consequences of withdrawal from the WTO Agreement. Instead, in Art. XXII(13) GPA, the parties to the GPA have set out the terms for termination of membership in the GPA as envisaged in Art. 54(a) VCLT.[34]

---

31 Art. 16(1), sentence 1 UNFCCC provides that only the '[a]nnexes to the Convention shall form an integral part thereof'. According to Art. 16(1), sentence 2 'annexes shall be restricted to lists, forms and any other material of a descriptive nature that is of a scientific, technical, procedural or administrative character.' Thus, protocols, as provided for in Art. 17 UNFCCC, are not part of the annexes.
32 Art. II(2) WTO Agreement.
33 Agreement on Government Procurement (signed on 12 April 1979, entered into force 1 January 1981) 1235 UNTS 258 [GPA].
34 Art. XXII(13) GPA is thus an example for the first scenario described by Ascencio, ie that 'denunciation of a treaty produces effects on other treaties *on the strength of convention provisions included in the latter*' (H Ascensio, 'Article 70' in O Corten and P Klein (eds), *The Vienna Conventions on the Law of Treaties* (vol II, Oxford University Press 2011) para 6 (emphasis added)). On (explicit or implicit) termination provisions in international agreements of the EU and its Member States, see below at Part I § 4.

B. The Limits: Agreements Concluded with Non-Member States

All of the previous examples have two characteristics in common: firstly, all provisions in founding treaties addressing the legal consequences of withdrawal on other international agreements do so only with regard to conventions. They do not refer to, let alone modify, the legal consequences for international agreements concluded by the organisation with non-member states. Secondly, in all of the above examples, participation in the conventions is linked to membership in the organisation in the first place. Art. 17(4) UNFCCC, for example, expressly states that '[o]nly Parties to the [UNFCCC] may be Parties to a protocol'. Besides demonstrating the practice surrounding modifications to Art. 70 VCLT, the examples thus also illustrate the limit of the contractual freedom it allows: the customary principle of *pacta tertiis nec nocent nec prosunt*.[35]

According to the *pacta tertiis* principle, 'a treaty only creates law as between States which are parties to it'[36]; it may not create rights or obligations for third states.[37] Thus, the members of an international organisations may agree on legal consequences of withdrawal from the founding treaty for any further agreements *between themselves*. Such a provision of the founding treaty cannot, however, have any legal effect on *non*-member states and thus has no effect with regards to any agreements to which non-member states are parties. First and foremost, this precludes the member states of an international organisation from stipulating legal consequences in the event of withdrawal that relate to the organisation's international agreements with non-members. In addition, the *pacta tertiis* principle can

---

35 The rule was repeatedly applied by the Permanent Court of International Justice (PCIJ), eg in PCIJ *Certain German Interests in Polish Upper Silesia* (Judgement) [1926] Series A No. 7 Series A No 7, 27–29; PCIJ *Free Zones Case of Upper Savoy and the District of Gex* (Judgement) [1932] Series A/B No. 146 Series A/B No 146, 141, and confirmed by the ICJ in ICJ *Case Concerning the Aerial Incident of July 27th, 1955 (Israel/Bulgaria)* (Preliminary Objections) [1959] ICJ Rep 1959, p 127, 138; ICJ *North Sea Continental Shelf Cases (Federal Republic of Germany/Denmark; Federal Republic of Germany/Netherlands)* (Judgement) [1969] ICJ Rep 1969, p 3, [28]. On the *pacta tertiis* principle, see also AD McNair, *The Law of Treaties* (Clarendon Press 1961) 309.
36 PCIJ, *Certain German Interests* (n 35) 30.
37 Cp Art. 34 VCLT ('A treaty does not create either obligations or rights for a third State without its consent.') which codifies the principle. See ILC, 'Reports of the International Law Commission on the Work of its 18th Session (4 May-19 July 1966)' UN Doc A/CN.4/191, YBILC (1966) Vol. II 226: 'There is abundant evidence of the recognition of the rule in State practice and in the decisions of international tribunals as well as in the writings of jurists.'

§ 3 Automatic Treaty Termination: A Legal Consequence of EU Withdrawal?

also set limits with regard to conventions. A case in point is the convention practice of the Council of Europe (CoE).

While conventions are regularly only open to members of the international organisation in whose framework they were negotiated, some exceptions exist. A pertinent example is the practice of the CoE which is very active in the sponsoring of conventions.[38] Initially, only member states of the CoE could become parties to these agreements. However, over the years, the CoE also started inviting non-member states to accede to certain conventions.[39] In light of this change in practice, is has proven useful that the *Statute of the Council of Europe*[40] is silent on the consequences of withdrawal from the CoE on any of its conventions. With non-CoE members becoming parties to the conventions, any provision in this regard would violate the *pacta tertiis* principle. Instead, conventions that are intended to remain limited to CoE member states now deal with the question themselves. As in the example of the GPA, linking its parties' continued participation in the agreement to membership in the WTO, these conventions now address the effect of a party's CoE withdrawal themselves.[41]

Finally, the practice and its limits of modifying Art. 70 VCLT with regard to the consequences of treaty withdrawal for other international agreements is an expression of and is underpinned by the overarching principle of *pacta sunt servanda*, whereby '[e]very treaty in force is binding upon the parties to it and must be performed by them in good faith.'[42] To release a party from said binding force requires either the consent of the treaty parties or the existence of the narrow conditions for treaty termination as provided for in the VCLT. The member states party to a convention can express their consent that the binding force of conventions is terminated for a member state withdrawing by means of a provision in the founding

---

38 Including additional protocols, the CoE's database lists 226 conventions (CoE, 'Complete list of the Council of Europe's treaties' (*Treaty Office*, 22.02.2023) <https://www.coe.int/en/web/conventions/full-list>).

39 See HG Schermers and N Blokker (n 11) para 1300.

40 Statute of the Council of Europe (signed on 5 May 1949, entered into force 3 August 1949) 87 UNTS 103 [CoE Statute].

41 See eg Art. 15(3) of the European Convention on the Suppression of Terrorism (adopted on 10 November 1976, entered into force 27 January 1977) CoE No. 090 [ECST]: 'This Convention ceases to have effect in respect of any Contracting State which withdraws from or ceases to be a member of the Council of Europe.' On (explicit or implicit) termination provisions in international agreements of the EU and its Member States, see below Part I § 4.

42 Art. 26 VCLT.

treaty of their organisation. Non-member states party to a convention or international agreement with the organisation, however, cannot do so.

III. EU Withdrawal: Applying the Treaty Law Template

Based on the previous analysis, three findings follow: firstly, the parties to an agreement have the autonomy to regulate the legal consequences of treaty withdrawal. The member states of some international organisations have made use of this in the respective founding treaties also with regard to international agreements. Secondly, regarding the consequences for international agreements, this autonomy is limited to agreements among member states. The principles of *pacta tertiis* and *pacta sunt servanda* prevent any determination of the consequences for international agreements including a non-member state as a contracting party. Thirdly, where no special arrangement has been made, recourse must be taken to Art. 70(1)(b) VCLT. Based in international law, the international agreements concluded by or within the framework of an international organisation constitute a legal situation created outside the international organisation's founding treaty and thus remain valid following withdrawal.

It is against this background that one must evaluate whether Brexit had any direct legal consequences for international agreements concluded by the EU or its Member States. In that context, the first question that arises is whether the Member States have made any arrangements regarding the consequences of EU withdrawal deviating from those set out in Art. 70 VCLT. The obvious place to look – Art. 50 TEU – makes no reference to international agreements (A.). In contrast, the *UK-EU Withdrawal Agreement*[43] (UK-EU WA) does make mention of some international agreements concluded by the EU and its Member States. However, the extent to which it does so – and can serve as *lex specialis* at all – differs between the EU Member States' *inter se* agreements (B.) and international agreements concluded by the EU (and its Member States) with non-EU states (C.).

---

43 Agreement on the Withdrawal of the United Kingdom of Great Britain and Northern Ireland from the European Union and the European Atomic Energy Community (12 November 2019) OJ C384 I/1 [UK-EU WA].

§ 3 Automatic Treaty Termination: A Legal Consequence of EU Withdrawal?

A. Art. 50 TEU: *Lex specialis* Arrangements for International Agreements?

Besides providing for a right to withdraw and the respective procedure, Art. 50 TEU also addresses the most apparent legal consequence of an exit from the EU: according to Art. 50(3) TEU, '[t]he Treaties shall cease to apply to the State in question'. In doing so, Art. 50 TEU mirrors the general rule of Art. 70(1)(a) VCLT. As in the example of the WTO Agreement provided above, this consequence of withdrawal is not restricted solely to the TEU itself. The term 'Treaties' by definition also includes the TFEU[44] and encompasses the Protocols and Annexes that 'form an integral part' of the Treaties.[45] However, in contrast to the WTO Agreement, Art. 50 TEU does not address the legal consequences of EU withdrawal for any other international agreement, be it EU-only, mixed or *inter se* agreements. Art. 50 TEU does not explicitly refer to them nor can the term 'Treaties' be interpreted to encompass them.[46]

Does Art. 70 VCLT then function as a default rule for questions – such as the effect on international agreements – for which Art. 50 TEU does not provide any answers? Recourse to Art. 70 VCLT may be questionable for two reasons. While the VCLT applies to the founding treaties of an international organisation, not all Member States of the EU are parties to the VCLT.[47] Thus, its rules – including Art. 70 VCLT – are not directly applicable to those states' international agreements, such as the EU Treaties. However, Art. 70 VCLT is an expression of principles of customary international law, such as *pacta sunt servanda*, and is itself accepted as custom.[48] As such, Art. 70 VCLT can be applied to the EU Treaties. Secondly, it has been argued that while the VCLT *in general* applies to founding treaties,

---

44 Art. 1(3) TEU: 'The Union shall be founded on the present Treaty and on the [TFEU] (hereinafter referred to as "the Treaties").'
45 Art. 51 TEU: 'The Protocols and Annexes to the Treaties shall form an integral part thereof.'
46 To differentiate between the 'Treaties' as defined by Arts. 1(3), 51 TEU, international treaties concluded by the EU are generally referred to as 'agreements', cp Art. 216(1): 'The Union may conclude an agreement with one or more third countries or international organisations'.
47 France and Romania are not parties to the VCLT. A list of all parties is provided on the UN's depositary page, see United Nations Treaty Collection, 'Vienna Convention on the Law of Treaties' (*Chapter XXIII*, 22.02.2023) <https://treaties.un.org/pages/ViewDetailsIII.aspx?src=TREATY&mtdsg_no=XXIII-1&chapter=23&Temp=mtdsg3&clang=_en>.
48 See above Part I § 3 fn. 6.

III. EU Withdrawal: Applying the Treaty Law Template

it does not do so with regard to the *EU's* founding treaties.[49] However, any attempt to deny recourse to Art. 70 VCLT is unconvincing. Where the founding treaties of international organisations leave an issue unregulated, international treaty law fills the gaps.[50] This is true also for the TEU and TFEU.[51] Moreover, as regards the legal consequences of withdrawal for international agreements, it is not Art. 70 VCLT that brings about the continuity of the agreements. Rather, Art. 70(1)(b) is an expression of the principle *pacta sunt servanda* applicable to all international agreements – including those concluded by the EU and its Member States.

Accordingly, as an immediate consequence of EU withdrawal, the validity of international agreements – whether concluded by the EU (with or without its Member States) with external treaty partners or by its Member States *inter se* – remains unaffected. However, something different could apply in the event of an orderly, that is treaty-based, exit from the EU. While Art. 50 TEU does not address any consequences of withdrawal beyond the general rule of Art. 70(1)(a) VCLT, they both provide for the possibility of agreement by the parties on further consequences of EU withdrawal. Art. 50(2) TEU envisages an agreement, *inter alia*, 'setting out the arrangements for […] withdrawal'.[52] Although the negotiations between the EU and the UK often hung in the balance, the UK's withdrawal was ultimately effected through a withdrawal agreement. In contrast to Art. 50 TEU, the UK-EU WA makes reference to international agreements. But to what extent can it be considered a *lex specialis* arrangement?

---

49 It is noteworthy that this position was, *inter alia*, presented at a hearing of the UK House of Lords' European Union Committee in a session on Brexit and the EU budget. See UK House of Lords, 'Brexit and the EU budget' European Union Committee – 15th Report of Session 2016–17 (4 March 2017) HL Paper 125 33–37.

50 Brölmann and others (n 2), 249–251.

51 Discussing and rejecting the position presented in the House of Lords (see above n 49), Waibel (n 10) and CM Brölmann, 'Brexit en bestaande verdragsverplichtingen' (2017) 95(25) *Nederlands Juristenblad* 1748. On the EU Courts approach to the VCLT and the EU Treaties, see the analysis of case law by PJ Kuijper, 'The European Courts and the Law of Treaties: The Continuing Story' in E Cannizzaro (ed), *The Law of Treaties Beyond the Vienna Convention* (Oxford University Press 2011).

52 Besides withdrawal arrangements, the withdrawal agreement should also 'tak[e] account of the framework for [a] future relationship with the Union' (Art. 50(2) TEU). On the two-phased approach – first, withdrawal negotiations, and only then negotiations on the future relationship – see eg PR Polak, 'EU Withdrawal Law After Brexit: The Emergence of a Unique Legal Procedure' in J Santos Vara, RA Wessel and PR Polak (eds), *The Routledge Handbook on the International Dimension of Brexit* (Routledge 2020) 60.

§ 3 Automatic Treaty Termination: A Legal Consequence of EU Withdrawal?

B. *Inter se* Agreements: The UK-EU Withdrawal Agreement as *lex specialis*?

In the context of its EU membership, the UK became a party to three *inter se* agreements.[53] While the *Internal Agreement on Financing of European Union Aid*[54] (EDF Agreement) and the *Convention Setting Up A European University Institute*[55] (EUI Convention) are agreements solely between Member States, the EU is a co-contracting party to the *Convention Defining the Statute of the European Schools*[56] (ES Convention). All three agreements have in common that membership in the EU is a prerequisite for becoming a party.[57] Nevertheless, given their nature as international agreements, withdrawal from the EU as such – in the absence of a contravening provision in Art. 50 TEU – does not terminate the UK's status as a party to these agreements. At the same time, as the practice of other international organisations shows, silence in the TEU, at least with regard to *inter se* agreements, was not legally required.

If the EU Treaties could theoretically provide for automatic termination of participation in *inter se* agreements as a consequence of withdrawal from the EU, in principle, *ad hoc* arrangements should also be able to address the question. And indeed, the UK-EU WA explicitly mentions two *inter se* agreements. As regards the European Schools, Art. 125(1) UK-EU WA provides that

> [t]he United Kingdom shall be bound by the Convention defining the Statute of the European Schools, as well as by the Regulations on Accredited European Schools adopted by the Board of Governors of the

---

53 On these three *inter se* agreements, see above § 1 section I.B.
54 Internal Agreement between the Representatives of the Governments of the Member States of the European Union meeting within the Council, on the Financing of European Union Aid under the Multiannual Financial Framework for the Period 2014 to 2020, in Accordance with the ACP-EU Partnership Agreement, and on the Allocation of Financial Assistance for the Overseas Countries and Territories to which Part Four of the Treaty on the Functioning of the European Union applies (6 August 2013) OJ L210/1 [EDF Agreement].
55 Convention Setting up a European University Institute (9 February 1976) OJ C29/1 [EUI Convention].
56 Convention Defining the Statute of the European Schools (17 August 1994) OJ L212/3 [ES Convention].
57 Art. 32 EUI Convention, Art. 32 ES Convention. The EDF Agreement does not include an explicit provision in this regard. Being concluded as an 'Internal Agreement between the *Representatives of the Governments of the Member States* of the European Union *meeting within the Council*', it is inherently limited to EU Member States.

European Schools, until the end of the school year that is ongoing at the end of the transition period.

In a very similar manner, Art. 152(1) UK-EU WA addresses the EDF, stipulating that

> [t]he United Kingdom shall remain party to the European Development Fund until the closure of the 11th EDF and all previous unclosed EDFs, and shall in this respect assume the same obligations as the Member States under the Internal Agreement by which it was set up ('the 11th EDF Internal Agreement').

At first sight, the two provisions seem declaratory, confirming that the UK – as envisaged by Art. 70(1)(b) VCLT – remains a party to these agreements and thus continues to enjoy the rights and remains bound by the obligations. However, the provisions limit the UK's continued participation in the agreements to a specific date.

Thus, one way of reading Arts. 125(1), 152(1) UK-EU WA is that as a consequence of the withdrawal agreement, the UK would eventually cease to be a party to these two *inter se* agreements. However, such a reading of the UK-EU WA is incompatible with the *pacta tertiis* principle as discussed above. Regarding international agreements concluded by the EU and its Member States, any withdrawal agreement again faces limits when addressing legal consequences. *Pacta tertiis* prohibits arrangements from affecting non-EU states. Additionally, with the UK-EU WA concluded only between the exiting state and the EU – thus without the Member States becoming parties – the same applies to the *inter se* agreements. A withdrawal agreement between the EU and the UK cannot set out the consequences of such withdrawal for an international agreement concluded between the Member States, even where the EU itself is a party to said agreement.

However, there is an alternative reading of Arts. 125(1) and 152(1) UK-EU WA. According to the position taken by the EU and the UK, the UK, upon leaving the EU, automatically ceased to be a party to *inter se* agreements. Starting from this position, it would have been possible for the EU to agree with the UK on a continued performance of the obligations included in the *inter se* agreements for a further, pre-defined period.[58] The obligation is then one stemming from the UK-EU WA and not the *inter se* agreements

---

58 See on this also M Cremona, 'The Withdrawal Agreement and the EU's International Agreements' (2020) 45(2) *European Law Review* 237, 245–247.

themselves. Such an interpretation of Arts. 125(1) and 152(1) UK-EU WA is more in line with the *pacta tertiis* principle. While an agreement – here, the UK-EU WA – may *not* create obligations for third states – here, the Member States parties to the *inter se* agreements – it *can* accord rights to them.[59] However, this would, of course, still presuppose finding a justification for the EU and the UK's 'out means out' position with regard to the UK's participation in *inter se* agreements. For in the absence of a *lex specialis* arrangement, Art. 70(1)(b) VCLT applies and the UK's status as a party to the *inter se* agreements does not end as a consequence of Brexit.

C. The EU's External International Agreements

The number of international agreements concluded by the EU with non-EU states and international organisations by far exceeds the number of *inter se* agreements concluded between the Member States. Correspondingly, the practical consequences would be far more severe if withdrawal of a Member State from the EU were to have direct legal consequences for these agreements. Legally, it is excluded that EU Member States regulate the legal consequences of a withdrawal from the EU in deviation from Art. 70 VCLT: Both EU-only and mixed agreements are concluded with at least one non-EU state or international organisation. Hence, any such regulation with regard to international agreements with non-EU states – whether in Art. 50 TEU or the UK-EU WA – would run contrary to the *pacta tertiis* principle.

Thus, with no *lex specialis* arrangement possible, in principle, the lack of legal consequences of withdrawal would be applicable to the external agreements of the EU just as to those of other international organisations – except that the EU's treaty practice differs from that of other international organisations in two ways. First, its Member States (indirectly) participate in the EU's international agreements by way of Art. 216(2) TFEU (1.). Secondly, Member States may also participate as co-contracting parties where the EU does not have the exclusive competence to conclude agreements (2.).

---

59 Cp Art. 36(1) VCLT: 'A right arises for a third State from a provision of a treaty if the parties to the treaty intend the provision to accord that right either to the third State, or to a group of States to which it belongs, or to all States, and the third State assents thereto. Its assent shall be presumed so long as the contrary is not indicated, unless the treaty otherwise provides.'

III. EU Withdrawal: Applying the Treaty Law Template

1. The EU's International Agreements and Art. 216(2) TFEU

While the EU's external agreements with non-EU Member States or international organisations are clearly *international* agreements, the ECJ has nevertheless referred to them as 'an integral part of EU law'[60]. This classification does not intend to negate their basis in international law but derives from their internal effects on the EU's legal order.[61] While international agreements of international organisations are generally only binding on the organisation itself,[62] the EU is the only international organisation to explicitly include a provision on the relationship of its Member States to its international agreements. As per Art. 216(1) TFEU, '[a]greements concluded by the Union are binding upon the institutions of the Union *and on its Member States*'[63]. As Klabbers writes, '[i]t is important to realize, though, that the binding force stems from [EU] law'[64]. Thus, even where the Member States are not contracting parties themselves – as in the case of EU-only agreements – they are nevertheless bound by the EU's external agreements via EU law. And where the Member States are parties themselves – as in the case of mixed agreements – this EU law tie supplements the international law tie.

Thus, at first glance, the withdrawal of a state from the EU does not have any direct legal consequences for the EU's external agreements. Under international law, the non-EU state and the EU – and in the case of mixed agreements, the (present and former) Member States – remain bound by the agreements.[65] At second glance, however, withdrawal from the EU does have consequences for these agreements which concern all parties. With the EU Treaties ceasing to apply as per Art. 50(3) TEU, Art. 216(2) TFEU no longer applies to the withdrawing Member State. Accordingly,

---

60 See eg ECJ, C-181/73 *R. & V. Haegeman v Belgian State* [1974] ECLI:EU:C:1974:41, [5].
61 See in detail RA Wessel, 'International Agreements as an Integral Part of EU Law: Haegeman' in G Butler and RA Wessel (eds), *EU External Relations Law: The Cases in Context* (Hart Publishing 2022).
62 Cp Brölmann, Essays on the Law of Treaties (n 21); J Klabbers, 'The European Union in the Law of International Organizations: Misfit or Model?' in RA Wessel and J Odermatt (eds), *Research Handbook on the European Union and International Organizations* (Edward Elgar Publishing 2019) 39–40. On the discussion surrounding Art. 36*bis* VCLT-IO, see above at Part I § 3 section I.
63 Emphasis added.
64 Klabbers, *International Institutional Law* (n 22) 262–263.
65 On (explicit or implicit) termination provisions in international agreements of the EU and its Member States, see below at Part I § 4.

the withdrawing Member State no longer enjoys the rights and participates in fulfilling the obligations as it did by way of EU law. Moreover, the EU must fulfil its international obligations towards its treaty partners without the contribution of the leaving Member State. And, finally, for the non-EU treaty partners the scope of application of their agreements with the EU has been reduced by – depending on the withdrawing Member State – a sizeable portion. The practical implications of this have been discussed particularly with regard to the WTO at length.[66] Pre-Brexit, the EU's tariff quotas – negotiated by the EU with WTO members for all its Member States – applied to the UK. Which quotas would apply to the UK post-Brexit? How would or should this affect the EU's quotas?

In the case of EU-only agreements, this consequence occurs inevitably and for the entirety of rights and obligations stemming from these agreements. Here, only the EU is a treaty party under international law and the Member States' participation is based on EU law – Art. 216(2) TFEU – alone. With regard to mixed agreements, however, Art. 216(2) TFEU also binds the Member States internally. At the same time, the agreements being mixed, the Member States are also parties to the agreements themselves and thus bound by way of international law. Whether and to what extent the discontinuation of the binding effect under Art. 216 TFEU has an effect on a withdrawing state's status as regards mixed agreements, therefore, depends on the extent to which the Member States are parties to these agreements themselves.

2. *Lex mixity*? The Status of EU Member States in Mixed Agreements

The reason for the EU's practice of concluding mixed agreements is the division of competences between the EU and its Member States. Where the EU does not possess the competences to conclude an agreement alone, it is joined by its Member States.[67] Thus, undisputedly, the Member States be-

---

66 C Herrmann, 'Brexit, WTO und EU-Handelspolitik' (2017) 24 Europäische Zeitschrift für Wirtschaftsrecht 961; L Bartels, 'The UK's Status in the WTO Post-Brexit' in R Schütze and S Tierney (eds), *The United Kingdom and the Federal Idea* (Hart Publishing 2018); G Messenger, 'EU-UK Relations at the WTO: Towards Constructive Creative Competition' in J Santos Vara, RA Wessel and PR Polak (eds) (n 52).
67 On the EU and its Member States' division of competences as regards external action, see above at § 1 section I.A.

come formal parties to these agreements as defined in Art. 2(1)(g) VCLT.[68] With the Member States being parties themselves, withdrawal from the EU as such cannot change that status. Unless the mixed agreements contain an (implicit) termination clause for the event of a Member State leaving the EU, the withdrawing state remains a party to these agreements.[69] At the same time, the division of competences also means that both the EU and Member States become parties to an agreement for the content of which neither are fully competent. It has thus been argued that the extent of both the EU and its Member States' party status to those agreements is limited to only those parts for which they are competent.[70] In that case, following withdrawal, the Member State parts of a mixed agreement would continue to bind the withdrawing state under international law, while the EU parts – previously binding on that state under Art. 216(2) TFEU – would cease to apply to it.

The practical difficulties of this approach are obvious. Practitioners and scholars alike have long commented on the lack of transparency of the EU and its Member States' division of competences in the context of

---

[68] Art. 2(1)(g) VCLT: '"party" means a State which has consented to be bound by the treaty and for which the treaty is in force'. On the Member States' formal status as a treaty party, see S Schaefer and J Odermatt, 'Nomen est Omen?: The Relevance of "EU Party" In International Law' in N Levrat and others (eds), *The EU and its Member States' Joint Participation in International Agreements* (Hart Publishing 2021) 132–134. See also with regard to the Member States' party status in mixed agreements and the implications of Brexit, C Kaddous and HB Touré, 'The Status of the United Kingdom Regarding EU Mixed Agreements after Brexit' in N Levrat and others (eds) (n 68) 273–274; Y Kaspiarovich and N Levrat, 'European Union Mixed Agreements in International Law under the Stress of Brexit' (2021) 13(2) *European Journal of Legal Studies* 121, 136–139.

[69] On this question, see below at Part I § 4.

[70] A view which Advocate General Tesauro seemed to corroborate when referring to 'the provisions to which the EEC may possibly subscribe' (see ECJ, C-53/96 *Hermès International v FHT Marketing Choice BV* (Opinion of the Advocate General Tesauro) [1998] ECLI:EU:C:1997:539, [14]). See in detail, KD Stein, *Der gemischte Vertrag im Recht der Außenbeziehungen der Europäischen Wirtschaftsgemeinschaft* (Duncker & Humblot 1986) 93–107. Using the examples of mixed agreements in the area of international environmental law, V Rodenhoff, *Die EG und ihre Mitgliedstaaten als völkerrechtliche Einheit bei umweltvölkerrechtlichen Übereinkommen* (Nomos 2008) 229–255.

§ 3 Automatic Treaty Termination: A Legal Consequence of EU Withdrawal?

mixed agreements.[71] It is arguably impossible[72], or at least unreasonable[73], to expect a non-EU treaty partner to know where the competence of the EU starts and that of the Member States ends. Attempts to achieve more clarity and legal certainty for treaty partners failed in the past: the so-called Declarations of Competence (DoCs) submitted by the EU, especially in the context of multilateral fora, are generally considered to be 'imprecise, incomplete and open-ended'[74].[75] Additionally, internal disputes between the EU and its Member States on the exact scope of their competences remain.[76] Against this background, withdrawal from the EU would then not only mean 'disentangling'[77] different legal orders, it would also become the ultimate test for 'unmixing'[78] mixed agreements.

Moreover, from a legal perspective, the approach of considering the EU and its Member States each as 'partial parties'[79] is highly questionable. Under international law, the default rule is that a party's consent covers the

---

71 As pointedly put by Olson from the US perspective: 'When a sovereign State becomes party to a treaty, it is clear what it has committed itself to. It has typically accepted the same package of rights and obligations as every other party – and, as a general proposition, if a party understands its own rights and obligations, it also understands those of every other party. It is clear, as a matter of international law, who bears operational and legal responsibility for addressing any problems that may arise. This clarity largely disappears, however, in the context of mixed agreements.' (see P Olson, 'Mixity from the Outside: The Perspective of a Treaty Partner' in C Hillion and P Koutrakos (eds), *Mixed Agreements Revisited: The EU and its Member States in the World* (Hart Publishing 2010) 333). See also AD Casteleiro, 'EU Declarations of Competence to Multilateral Agreements: A Useful Reference Base?' (2012) 17(4) *European Foreign Affairs Review* 491 and Y Kaspiarovich and RA Wessel, 'Unmixing Mixed Agreements: Challenges and Solutions for Separating the EU and its Member States in Existing International Agreements' in N Levrat and others (eds) (n 68).
72 P Allot, 'Adherence to and Withdrawal from Mixed Agreements' in D O'Keeffe and HG Schermers (eds), *Mixed Agreements* (Kluwer 1983) 105.
73 C Tomuschat, 'Liability for Mixed Agreements' in D O'Keeffe and HG Schermers (eds) (n 72) 130.
74 J Heliskoski, 'EU Declarations of Competence and International Responsibility' in MD Evans and P Koutrakos (eds), *The International Responsibility of the European Union: European and International Perspectives* (Hart Publishing 2013) 202.
75 On DoCs in general, see Casteleiro (n 71); Heliskoski (n 74).
76 For a rather recent ECJ judgement on the division of competences in the EU's Free Trade Agreements, see ECJ, Case 2/15 *FTA Singapore* [2015] EU:C:2017:376.
77 Cp J Odermatt, 'Brexit and International Law: Disentangling Legal Orders' (2017) 31 *Emory International Law Review Recent Developments* 1051.
78 Cp Kaspiarovich and Wessel (n 71).
79 Schaefer and Odermatt (n 68) 134.

entire agreement.⁸⁰ The division of competences between the EU and its Member States, being a *res inter alios acta* for their treaty partners, cannot change this.⁸¹ An exception to the default rule is only possible under narrow circumstances. According to Art. 17(1) VCLT, 'the consent of a State to be bound *by part of a treaty* is effective only if the treaty so permits or the other contracting States so agree.'⁸²

To the knowledge of the author, no explicit agreement on the limitation of the EU and its Member States' consent exists for any mixed agreement. In the absence of any agreement on partial consent, the question is whether (some) mixed agreements nevertheless (implicitly) provide for it. Naturally, it is impossible to consider all mixed agreements here. However, two instruments of the EU's treaty practice come to mind that could potentially serve as implicit permission: the DoCs in multilateral mixed agreements and the definition of the parties in bilateral mixed agreements. While the DoCs usually list some of the EU's competences relevant to the subject matter of the respective agreement, they also regularly include a dynamic reference to the EU's evolving division of competences. The definitions of the parties in bilateral mixed agreements, in turn, are limited from the outset to a general reference to the EU's internal division of competences. A typical example is Art. 1.1(c) CETA Canada, according to which

> Parties means on the one hand, the European Union or its Member States or the European Union and its Member States within their respective areas of competences as derived from the [TEU] and the [TFEU] [...], and on the other hand, Canada.⁸³

While both the DoCs and the definition clauses explicitly point the non-EU treaty partners to the EU's division of competences, neither fulfil the

---

80 ILC, 'First Report on the Law of Treaties, by Sir Humphrey Waldock, Special Rapporteur' UN Doc A/CN.4/144 and Add. 1, YBILC (1962) Vol. II 53; Draft Convention on the Law of Treaties (adopted 20 February 1928) 1935 (29) AJIL 657 [Harvard Draft], Art. 20.
81 A Bleckmann, 'The Mixed Agreements of the EEC in Public International Law' in D O'Keeffe and HG Schermers (eds) (n 72) 161. Rather, a lack of internal competence may lead to the treaty being voidable; something neither the EU nor the Member States have so far invoked, see, eg E Steinberger, 'The WTO Treaty as a Mixed Agreement: Problems with the EC's and the EC Member States' Membership of the WTO' (2006) 17(4) *European Journal of International Law* 837, 844ff.
82 Emphasis added.
83 Emphasis omitted.

§ 3 Automatic Treaty Termination: A Legal Consequence of EU Withdrawal?

requirements of Art. 17 VCLT. In particular, they cannot be considered as granting permission to partial consent.

'So permit'[84], read according to its ordinary meaning,[85] generally means 'to consent to expressly or formally'[86]. This is supported by Art. 17 VCLT's drafting history.[87] In its commentaries on Art. 17 VCLT, the ILC held that '[s]ome treaties *expressly* authorize States to consent to a part or parts only of the treaty [...] and then, of course, partial ratification [...] is admissible'[88]. In international agreements that served the ILC as state practice, the 'express' condition had been fulfilled in two ways: the respective clauses *explicitly* referred to the act of expressing consent and *precisely* named the parts that would be included or excluded by a party's consent.[89] In contrast, neither the DoCs nor the definition clauses expressly refer to a limitation of consent or precisely delimit the EU or Member States' competences.

Finally, any precise delimitation of competence – as Art. 17 VCLT requires – would, in any case, be contrary to the EU's interest. This is not only due to the precise scope of its competences often being contested even internally, but also because the scope evolves dynamically. Over the duration of an international agreement, the EU can gain competences that still lay with the Member States at the time of treaty conclusion. Only partly consenting to an international agreement based on the competence lines at the time of conclusion, would thus 'freeze'[90] the division of competences externally.[91]

---

84 Art. 17(1) VCLT.
85 Cp Art. 31(1) VCLT: 'A treaty shall be interpreted in good faith in accordance with the ordinary meaning to be given to the terms of the treaty in their context and in the light of its object and purpose.'
86 'Definition of 'permit'' (*Merriam-Webster Dictionary*) <www.merriam-webster.com/dictionary/permit>.
87 According to Art. 32 VCLT, an agreement's *travaux préparatoires* can be used as a supplementary means of interpretation. On the drafting history of Art. 17 VCLT in more detail, see Schaefer and Odermatt (n 68) 134–135.
88 'Reports 18th Session' (n 37) 201–202 (emphasis added); see also 'SR Waldock First Report' (n 80) 53. The drafting of Art. 17 VCLT-IO is based on the drafting of Art. 17 VCLT ('Report 34th Session' (n 20) 32).
89 For an overview of the state practice cited by the ILC, see Schaefer and Odermatt (n 68) 135. For the ILC's analysis of it, see ILC, 'Summary Records of its 14th Session (24 April-29 June 1962)' UN Doc A/CN.4/SR.647, YBILC (1962) Vol. I 112.
90 JH Weiler, 'The External Legal Relations of Non-Unitary Actors: Mixity and the Federal Principle' in D O'Keeffe and HG Schermers (eds) (n 72) 181.
91 See in detail, Schaefer and Odermatt (n 68) 136–138.

Upon withdrawal from the EU, Art. 216(2) TFEU ceases to apply to a former Member State, thereby freeing it from its obligation under EU law to perform international agreements concluded by the EU. In the case of mixed agreements, however, this consequence is absorbed by the state's status as a party to these agreements in their entirety. Following withdrawal, the former Member State is thus not only bound by all provisions of a mixed agreement, it has also regained its competence to perform them.

IV. Brexit and its (Limited) Automatic Consequences

When treating the EU as an international organisation, Brexit – like any previous exit from an international organisation – lies at the 'intersection of the law of treaties and the law of the organization'[92]. How the meeting of the two plays out with regard to international agreements concluded by the EU or its Member States in the context of their membership is demonstrated by the practice of other organisations. While some founding treaties address the issue of termination of membership and its consequence for agreements between their Member States, most are silent on the issue. The same is true for the EU's founding treaties. Moreover, while Art. 50 TEU even provides for an *ad hoc* agreement on the consequences of withdrawal, the party constellation of the UK-EU WA – concluded between the EU and the withdrawing state – impedes it from addressing the consequences for international agreements. Any arrangement between the EU and the withdrawing state on the question would constitute a *pacta tertiis* for non-EU states as parties to EU-only and mixed agreements and for the remaining Member States as parties to the *inter se* agreements.

Where no *lex specialis* arrangement exists, recourse must be taken to international treaty law, which spells out the consequences of withdrawal from an international agreement in Art. 70 VCLT. Based hereon, withdrawal from an international organisation does not impact the validity of any international agreements – whether concluded with an external treaty partner or between Member States – nor does it affect the withdrawing state's participation in international agreements to which it is itself a party. An EU Member State's participation in EU-only agreements ceasing as a consequence of withdrawal is solely owed to its previous participation being one under EU law only. Where the EU Treaties cease to apply to a state –

---

92 Brölmann and others (n 2), 247.

as envisaged by Art. 70(1)(a) VCLT – so does Art. 216(2) TFEU, establishing the obligation for Member States to respect the EU's international agreements.

The preliminary result that a state does not lose its status as a party to mixed and *inter se* agreements as a consequence of withdrawal from the EU is, however, only half the story. To understand it in its entirety, one must shift the approach from *considering* Brexit as a legal act to *accepting* it as a legal fact. Factual circumstances – such as the loss of membership in an organisation – can have effects on international agreements, potentially even leading to a party's (automatic) withdrawal.

§ 4 EU Withdrawal: Grounds for Treaty Termination?

It seems almost banal to state that when a state leaves the EU, the EU Treaties are no longer binding. Anything but banal, on the other hand, is the statement that this has consequences – albeit indirectly – for other international agreements. EU-only agreements are, as their name clearly states, concluded with non-EU states by the EU alone, its Member States' participation being a matter of EU law. Thus, in the case of an EU withdrawal, these agreements continue to bind the EU and its non-EU treaty partner under international law but cease to apply to the withdrawing state. However, where the withdrawing state is a party itself under international law – as in the case of mixed and *inter se* agreements – this status is not automatically terminated as a legal consequence of Brexit. From the perspective of international treaty law, there is, however, a second possibility: withdrawal from the EU may present a legal ground for termination of the withdrawing state's party status.[1]

The *Vienna Convention on the Law of Treaties*[2] (VCLT) regulates when and how international agreements may be denounced, providing the substantive reasons under which states have the right to denounce and the procedure to be followed. Concerning the legal grounds for ending a treaty relationship, the VCLT knows two alternatives: firstly, a party may denounce an agreement where the agreement itself – explicitly[3] or implicitly[4]

---

1 Note that the same question could be asked with regard to the EU-only agreements and their treaty parties. The EU-only agreements, of course, continue to bind the EU and its treaty partners after Brexit. Nevertheless, Brexit has an effect on these agreements by, *inter alia*, reducing their scope of application (see above at Part I § 3 section III.C.1). Following Brexit, the EU or its treaty partners could thus consider invoking these changed circumstances to denounce these agreements.
2 Vienna Convention on the Law of Treaties (adopted 23 May 1969, entered into force 27 January 1980) 1155 UNTS 331 [VCLT].
3 Cp Art. 54 VCLT: 'The termination of a treaty or the withdrawal of a party may take place: (a) in conformity with the provisions of the treaty.'
4 Cp Art. 56(1) VCLT: 'A treaty which contains no provision regarding its termination and which does not provide for denunciation or withdrawal is not subject to denunciation or withdrawal unless: (a) it is established that the parties intended to admit possibility of denunciation or withdrawal; or (b) a right of denunciation or withdrawal may be implied by the nature of the treaty.'

§ 4 EU Withdrawal: Grounds for Treaty Termination?

– allows for denunciation. Where an agreement provides for denunciation, the respective provisions can also modify or completely discard the procedural requirements of the VCLT. Secondly, the parties to an international agreement can invoke legal grounds for termination as provided for in the VCLT.[5] However, in so doing, they must respect the procedure as envisaged in the VCLT.

One possibility is, thus, that the EU's mixed agreements and the Member States' *inter se* agreements themselves provide for the termination of a Member State's party status once it leaves the EU (I.). Alternatively, EU withdrawal, or the circumstances created through the state's loss of membership, could potentially fulfil the requirements of one of the VCLT's grounds for treaty termination (II.).

Before looking at these two alternatives, two preliminary remarks are necessary. Firstly, to fully answer the questions raised, this chapter – in contrast to the previous one – would essentially require a case-by-case examination of all mixed and *inter se* international agreements. A closer look is, thus, taken at the three *inter se* agreements to which the UK became a party as an EU Member State before withdrawing from the EU. With regard to mixed agreements, this is – for obvious quantitative reasons – impossible. Thus, the aim of this chapter is to draw some generalisable conclusions where possible and, where better suited, provide some guidance as to what to look for in international agreements when assessing the effect of withdrawal from the EU.

Secondly, the VCLT's provisions cited are often not directly applicable. Not only are not all Member States of the EU parties to the VCLT.[6] But the VCLT's scope of application is also limited to international agreements concluded between states.[7] In relation to the EU, the VCLT's successor, the *Vienna Convention on the Law of Treaties between States and International*

---

5 Cp Art. 42(2) sentence 1 VCLT: 'The termination of a treaty, its denunciation or the withdrawal of a party, may take place only as a result of the application of the provisions of the treaty or of the present Convention.'
6 France and Romania are not parties to the VCLT. For a full list of VCLT treaty parties, see United Nations Treaty Collection, 'Vienna Convention on the Law of Treaties' (*Chapter XXIII*, 22.02.2023) <https://treaties.un.org/pages/ViewDetailsIII.aspx?src=TREATY&mtdsg_no=XXIII-1&chapter=23&Temp=mtdsg3&clang=_en>.
7 Art. 1 VCLT: 'The present Convention applies to treaties between States.'

Organizations or between International Organizations[8] (VCLT-IO) would thus be better suited. However, so far the VCLT-IO still lacks the number of ratifications required for its entry into force.[9] Thus, the European Court of Justice (ECJ) regularly applies the VCLT, even to mixed agreements where the EU is one of the contracting parties.[10] The VCLT's provisions are often of a customary law character. The VCLT-IO's provisions, for example as regards treaty withdrawal, are, moreover, largely identical to those of the VCLT.[11] Where these two conditions are met, this chapter will thus follow the approach taken by the ECJ.

I. Termination by Design: EU Membership as a Resolutory Condition?

Arts. 42(2), 54(a) VCLT acknowledge that the termination of or withdrawal from an international agreement is always possible if it takes place 'in conformity with the provisions of the treaty'.[12] Put differently, the VCLT limits the possibility of termination to several reasons provided for in the Convention,[13] but leaves it to the contractual freedom of an agreement's parties to decide under which circumstances they are willing to allow for it.

---

8 Vienna Convention on the Law of Treaties between States and International Organizations or between International Organizations (adopted and opened for signature 21 March 1986) UN Doc A/CONF.129/15 [VCLT-IO].

9 For a full list of all contracting states and international organisations, see United Nations Treaty Collection, 'Vienna Convention on the Law of Treaties between States and International Organizations or between International Organizations' (*Chapter XXIII*, 22.02.2023) <https://treaties.un.org/Pages/ViewDetails.aspx?src=IND&mtdsg_no=XXIII-3&chapter=23&clang=_en#1>.

10 At least in the application between the Member States and the non-EU treaty partners, this corresponds with Art. 3 VCLT: 'The fact that the present Convention does not apply to international agreements concluded between States and other subjects of international law […] shall not affect: […] (c) the application of the Convention to the relations of States as between themselves under international agreements to which other subjects of international law are also parties.' On the ECJ's application of the VCLT, see also PJ Kuijper, 'The European Courts and the Law of Treaties: The Continuing Story' in E Cannizzaro (ed), *The Law of Treaties Beyond the Vienna Convention* (Oxford University Press 2011) and J Odermatt, *International Law and the European Union* (Cambridge University Press 2021) 63–66.

11 On the method behind the drafting of the VCLT-IO, see below Part II Concluding Remarks. In detail FL Bordin, *The Analogy between States and International Organizations* (Cambridge University Press 2019) 39–43.

12 Art. 54(a) VCLT.

13 Cp Arts. 56, 59–64 VCLT.

§ 4 EU Withdrawal: Grounds for Treaty Termination?

In doing so, the parties to an international agreement may not only decide on the substantive preconditions for a valid denunciation (if any), but also on the procedure to be adhered to. The procedural provisions in Arts. 65–68 VCLT and many withdrawal clauses in international agreements regularly provide for a certain waiting period between notification and when denunciation takes effect.[14] Parties are, however, also free to include denunciation clauses providing for immediate termination or termination upon the occurrence of certain conditions or a certain event.

In the case of international agreements concluded together with the EU or in the context of EU membership, such an event could be the withdrawal of a Member State from the EU. For this to be the case, the mixed or *inter se* agreements would have to provide for the termination of a Member State's party status on account of its withdrawal from the EU. The obvious instrument to do so would be an explicit provision to this effect (A.). However, where no such explicit provision exists, an implicit link between a state's participation in a certain agreement and its continued EU membership may suffice (B.).

A. Explicit Termination and Withdrawal Clause

The founding treaties of some international organisations explicitly provide for the effect of terminating the membership in said organisation for the continued participation in international agreements concluded under its auspices. Such provisions adapt the legal consequences of treaty termination – the withdrawal from the organisation's founding treaty – as provided for in Art. 70 VCLT.[15] Where the legal consequences for international agreements concluded in the framework of membership in an international organisation are not addressed in the founding treaties, these agreements may, nevertheless, automatically end with a state's membership if the agreements themselves include a termination clause in this regard. Or, as put by Ascensio, 'the situation may arise where denunciation of a treaty produces effects on other treaties on strength of convention provisions included in

---

14 According to Art. 65(2) VCLT a minimum waiting period of three months is required. Art. 56 VCLT, which allows for denunciation based on the established intention of the parties or the nature of the agreement, even provides for twelve months notice period.
15 See above Part I § 3 section II.

I. Termination by Design: EU Membership as a Resolutory Condition?

the latter.'[16] In practice, this is a method regularly used in the agreements concluded within the framework of an international organisation. By linking the termination of the party status in an international agreement to the withdrawal from another international agreement – an international organisation's founding treaty – membership in said organisation, in effect, becomes a resolutory condition. If and when a state loses its membership in a specified international organisation, this automatically triggers a withdrawal clause of another international agreement.

An example of such a provision is Art. 58(3) of the *European Convention on Human Rights*[17] (ECHR), according to which '[a]ny High Contracting Party which shall cease to be a member of the Council of Europe shall cease to be a Party to this Convention under the same conditions'. In contrast to the previous examples, it is thus not the organisation's founding treaty – the *Statute of the Council of Europe*[18] – which provides for the termination of a state's party status in an international agreement – the ECHR – concluded in its context. Instead, the ECHR itself provides for the loss of a state's party status where that state ceases to be a member of the Council of Europe. A veritable cascade of treaty withdrawals can be triggered by a state's exit from the International Monetary Fund[19] (IMF): loss of IMF membership functions as a resolutory condition for membership in the International Bank for Reconstruction and Development[20] (IBRD), loss of IBRD membership in turn as a resolutory condition for membership in the International Finance Cooperation (IFC)[21] and in the International

---

16 Cp H Ascensio, 'Article 70' in O Corten and P Klein (eds), *The Vienna Conventions on the Law of Treaties* (vol II, Oxford University Press 2011) para 6.
17 Convention for the Protection of Human Rights and Fundamental Freedoms (adopted 4 November 1950, entered into force 3 September 1953) 213 UNTS 221 [ECHR].
18 Statute of the Council of Europe (signed on 5 May 1949, entered into force 3 August 1949) 87 UNTS 103 [CoE Statute].
19 Articles of Agreement of the International Monetary Fund (adopted 27 December 1945, entered into force 27 December 1945) 2 UNTS 39 [IMF Agreement].
20 Articles of Agreement of the International Bank for Reconstruction and Development (adopted 27 December 1945, entered into force 27 December 1945) 2 UNTS 134 [IBRD Agreement], Art. VI Sec. 3: 'Any member which ceases to be a member of the International Monetary Fund shall automatically cease after three months to be a member of the Bank unless the Bank by three-fourths of the total voting power has agreed to allow it to remain a member.'
21 Articles of Agreement of the International Finance Corporation (adopted 25 May 1955, entered into force 20 July 1956) 264 UNTS 117 [IFC Agreement], Art. V Sec. 3: 'Any member which is suspended from membership in, or ceases to be a member

§ 4 EU Withdrawal: Grounds for Treaty Termination?

Development Association[22] (IDA). In each case, it is not the agreement from which the state actually withdraws that provides for this cascade: it is the respective agreement itself that provides for this domino effect.

The advantage of including a termination provision in the agreement itself instead of in the organisation's founding treaty is that this constellation could also work in those cases where international agreements are open to states not members of a given international organisation. Where all parties consent to the fact that the participation of some states in the agreement is linked to their membership in an international organisation, termination of said membership would not constitute a *res inter alios acta*, incapable of having any effect on other international agreements. Both the EU's *inter se* (1.) and its mixed agreements (2.) could, thus, include provisions explicitly terminating the UK's participation as a party upon its withdrawal from the EU.

1. The EU's *inter se* Agreements

At the time of Brexit, the UK had been a party to three *inter se* agreements: the *Internal Agreement on the Financing of European Union Aid*[23] (EDF Agreement), the *Convention Setting Up a European University Institute*[24] (EUI Convention) and the *Convention Defining the Statute of the European Schools*[25] (ES Convention). Do these agreements include provisions on their termination or the possibility of withdrawal of a treaty party? And, if

---

of, the Bank shall automatically be suspended from membership in, or cease to be a member of, the Corporation, as the case may be.'

22 Articles of Agreement of the International Development Association (adopted 29 January 1960, entered into force 24 September 1960) 439 UNTS 249 [IDA Agreement] Art. VII Sec. 3: 'Any member which is suspended from membership in, or ceases to be a member of, the Bank shall automatically be suspended from membership in, or cease to be a member of, the Association, as the case may be.'

23 Internal Agreement between the Representatives of the Governments of the Member States of the European Union meeting within the Council, on the Financing of European Union Aid under the Multiannual Financial Framework for the Period 2014 to 2020, in Accordance with the ACP-EU Partnership Agreement, and on the Allocation of Financial Assistance for the Overseas Countries and Territories to which Part Four of the Treaty on the Functioning of the European Union applies (6 August 2013) OJ L210/1 [EDF Agreement].

24 Convention Setting up a European University Institute (9 February 1976) OJ C29/1 [EUI Convention].

25 Convention Defining the Statute of the European Schools (17 August 1994) OJ L212/3 [ES Convention].

I. Termination by Design: EU Membership as a Resolutory Condition?

so, do these provisions explicitly address the situation of a Member State withdrawing from the EU?

The EDF Agreement does not envisage the possibility of withdrawal by any of its treaty parties. Instead, Art. 14(2) EDF Agreement provides for a limited duration of the agreement. It is 'concluded for the same duration as the multiannual financial framework for the period 2014 to 2020' and is thus intended to automatically expire after six years. Theoretically, the EDF Agreement would thus have terminated in the year of Brexit regardless. However, the second sentence of Art. 14(2) includes an exception whereby the agreement 'shall remain in force for as long as is necessary for all the operations financed under the ACP-EU Partnership Agreement, the Overseas Association Decision and the multi-annual financial framework to be fully executed'[26]. Based hereon, the EDF Agreement remains in force until today,[27] with no possibility for the UK to withdraw – let alone automatically terminate the agreement based on its exit from the EU – provided for by the agreement. The same holds true for the EUI Convention. While it is concluded with an unlimited duration, it does not provide for any withdrawal provision. Quite independently of EU withdrawal, a state's membership in the EDF Agreement and the EUI Convention can thus be terminated only based on a reason provided for in the VCLT.

The ES Convention, finally, does provide for a withdrawal provision. According to Art. 31(1) ES Convention, '[a]ny Contracting Party may denounce this Convention by written notification [...]. Denunciation shall be notified by 1 September of any year in order to take effect on 1 September the following year.' With the article not containing any material conditions for denouncing the agreement, the UK could have withdrawn from the ES Convention anytime subsequent to announcing its decision to withdraw from the EU. At the same time, since Art. 31(1) does not link denunciation to any substantive requirements, withdrawal from the EU as such does not simultaneously end the UK's participation in the European School system. Thus, none of the *inter se* agreements to which the UK became a party

---

26 The 'ACP-EU Partnership Agreement' refers to a mixed agreement with several African, Caribbean and Pacific states, see Partnership Agreement between the Members of the African, Caribbean and Pacific Group of States, of the one part, and the European Community and its Member States, of the other part (23 June 2000) OJ L317/3 [Cotonou Agreement].
27 See EUR-Lex, 'Document 42013A0806(01): EDF Agreement' (*Official Journal*, 23.02.2023) <https://eur-lex.europa.eu/legal-content/EN/TXT/?uri=uriserv%3A OJ.L_.2013.210.01.0001.01.ENG>.

§ 4 EU Withdrawal: Grounds for Treaty Termination?

during its EU membership includes a termination clause explicitly linking the continued participation as a party to the agreement to a continued membership in the EU.

2. The EU's Mixed Agreements

In examining the EU's mixed agreements and their final clauses, the differences in the design of these agreements make it necessary to distinguish between two types. The first type consists of bilateral mixed agreements in which the EU and its Member States are said to form a 'single contracting party'[28] and which create a reciprocal relationship between this 'single contracting party' and one or more non-EU states. The second type consists of the multilateral mixed agreements, where the EU and its Member States are both parties but the structure of the treaty creates a truly multilateral setting with a larger number of non-EU states. While the former is negotiated by the EU to specifically fit its needs, the latter is usually less adapted to the EU and its special features.[29] The inclusion of a withdrawal clause explicitly accommodating the withdrawal of a Member State from the EU thus, if at all, appears more likely in bilateral mixed agreements.

Since the conclusion of the first bilateral mixed agreement with Greece in 1963,[30] the EU and its Member States have developed an impressively stringent treaty practice. While varying in content, the contractual design of most bilateral mixed agreements follows a template tailored to accommodate the EU and its Member States as a 'single contracting party' rather than as independent parties of the same agreement.[31] Thus, not only do many mixed agreements define the EU and its Member States as one 'EU

---

28 ECJ, C-53/96 *Hermès International v FHT Marketing Choice BV* (Opinion of the Advocate General Tesauro) [1998] ECLI:EU:C:1997:539, [15].

29 Although many multilateral mixed agreements still include some EU specificities, such as 'regional economic integration organisation' clauses (on these see also further down in this section) or Declarations of Competence (on these see also Part I § 3 section III.C.2). See in detail, J Heliskoski, *Mixed Agreements as a Technique for Organizing the International Relations of the European Community and its Member States* (Kluwer Law International 2001).

30 Agreement establishing an Association between the European Economic Community and Greece (18 February 1963) OJ L26/294 [AA Greece].

31 On this treaty design, see S Schaefer and J Odermatt, 'Nomen est Omen?: The Relevance of "EU Party" In International Law' in N Levrat and others (eds), *The EU and its Member States' Joint Participation in International Agreements* (Hart Publishing 2021).

I. Termination by Design: EU Membership as a Resolutory Condition?

Party'[32]. Their connectedness also becomes visible in bilateral mixed agreements' final provisions which regularly contain a termination provision. The EU's bilateral mixed trade agreements present a good example.[33] These typically provide that '[e]ither Party may give written notice to the other of its intention to denounce this Agreement. Denunciation takes effect six months after notification by the other Party.'[34] 'Either Party' in that context is defined as the EU Party or the non-EU treaty partner.[35] Not a single one of these provisions, however, ties the possibility of denouncing the agreement to withdrawal from the EU, let alone provide for the automatic termination of an EU Member State's participation as a party on account of its withdrawal from the EU.

This is especially striking given the denunciation provisions' close proximity – content-wise but often also as regards the sequencing in the agreements – to accession provisions. Besides providing for denunciation, most of the bilateral mixed trade agreements also include a provision addressing the effects of a new Member State acceding to the EU. Some of these accession provisions simply set out the procedure to be followed for the new Member State to also become a party to the bilateral mixed agreement.[36] Others, however, even allow for automatic accession, providing that '[a]ny new Member State of the EU shall accede to this Agreement from the date of its accession to the EU by means of a clause to that effect in the act of

---

32 See in detail below Part I § 4 section I.B.1.
33 For a thorough analysis of denunciation provisions, see Schaefer and Odermatt (n 31) 147–149.
34 Stepping Stone Economic Partnership Agreement between Ghana, of the one part, and the European Community and its Member States, of the other part (21 October 2016) OJ L278/3 [EPA Ghana], Art. 75(7).
35 See eg EPA Ghana, Art. 72: '1. The Contracting Parties of this Agreement shall be the Republic of Ghana, referred to as the "Ghanaian Party" or "Ghana", of the one part, and the European Community or its Member States or the European Community and its Member States, within their respective areas of competence as derived from the Treaty establishing the European Community, referred to as the "EC Party" or the European Community, of the other part. 2. For the purpose of this Agreement, the term "Party" shall refer to the Ghanaian Party or to the EC Party as the case may be. The term "Parties" shall refer to the Ghanaian Party and the EC Party.'
36 See eg Strategic Partnership Agreement between the European Union and its Member States, of the one part, and Japan, of the other part (24 August 2018) OJ L216/4 [SPA Japan], Art. 49 which stipulates that the EU shall inform Japan of any accession requests, the process of EU accession negotiations and the signing and entry into force of the accession agreement with the new Member State.

accession.'³⁷ The term '[a]ct of accession' refers to the accession agreement between existing EU Member States and the new Member State. Thus, for the situation of accession, the EU accession agreement – usually a *res inter alios acta* for a non-EU state – is referenced in the mixed agreement with the non-EU state consenting to it developing a legal effect in its treaty relationship with the EU. While the parties to bilateral mixed agreements are thus aware of the possibility of changes to the composition of the EU Party, they have only explicitly acknowledged and provided for the situation of accession in their agreements.

Like many bilateral agreements, most multilateral agreements today include denunciation provisions.³⁸ While these generally stipulate a notification period of at least several months, they only rarely provide for substantive prerequisites for exercising the right to denunciation.³⁹ Moreover, the structure and formulations used in multilateral agreements are – in general – less adapted to the needs of specific parties. Accordingly, the membership of (one of) its parties in the EU or any other international organisation is generally irrelevant for multilateral agreements and is not specifically addressed in their denunciation clauses.

An exemption to this is multilateral agreements with so-called 'REIO clauses'.⁴⁰ Their treaty text has been designed to accommodate the participation of regional economic integration organisations (REIOs; also known as regional integration organisations, RIOs) as parties. In so doing, one could say that these multilateral agreements have, in fact, been designed to accommodate the EU as a treaty party (besides its Member States). In general, the REIO clauses in multilateral agreements not only address the conditions under which a REIO may become a party (among its Member States) to the agreement, but also the relationship between the REIO and its Member States in the exercise of rights and fulfilment of obligations under these agreements.⁴¹ Thus, presumably, if any multilateral agreement addresses the effect of a state withdrawing from a (regional economic integration) organisation for that state's continued participation as a party

---

37 Art. 77(2) sentence 1 EPA Ghana.
38 LR Helfer, 'Part VI Avoiding or Exiting Treaty Commitments: Terminating Treaties' in DB Hollis (ed), *The Oxford Guide to Treaties* (2nd edn, Oxford University Press 2020) 633.
39 See LR Helfer, 'Exiting Treaties' (2005) 91(7) *Virginia Law Review* 1579, 1596–1599 providing an overview of the different variations of denunciation clauses.
40 On these clauses, see J Odermatt (n 10) 69–77.
41 For a discussion of different variations of REIO clauses, see ibid.

it will be those including specific clauses on the participation of (regional integration) organisations.

The first multilateral agreement to introduce elaborate provisions on accession of international organisations was the *United Nations Convention on the Law of the Sea*[42] (UNCLOS). According to Art. 305(1)(f) UNCLOS, the Convention 'shall be open for signature by: [...] international organizations, in accordance with Annex IX'. The annex, in turn, provides for the conditions under which international organisations can become a party and the extent to which they can participate and exercise rights and fulfil obligations under the Convention. Moreover, Art. 8 of Annex IX also addresses the applicability of the Convention's final provisions – including its withdrawal provision – to international organisations.

For withdrawals in general, Art. 317(1) UNCLOS stipulates that

[a] State Party may [...] denounce this Convention and may indicate its reasons. Failure to indicate reasons shall not affect the validity of the denunciation. The denunciation shall take effect one year after the date of receipt of the notification, unless the notification specifies a later date.

Art. 8(c) of Annex IX, however, adapts this for international organisations:

(i) an international organization may not denounce this Convention in accordance with article 317 if any of its member States is a State Party and if it continues to fulfil the qualifications specified in article 1 of this Annex;

(ii) an international organization shall denounce this Convention when none of its member States is a State Party or if the international organization no longer fulfils the qualifications specified in article 1 of this Annex. Such denunciation shall take effect immediately.

Thus, in a sense, Art. 8(c) of UNCLOS' Annex IX does, in fact, deal with the possible effects of member States withdrawing from an international organisation which is a party to UNCLOS: the withdrawal of member States from an international organisation could, theoretically, lead to a situation where the international organisation consists only of member States that are themselves not parties to UNCLOS.[43] In that case, Art. 8(c)(ii) would

---

42 United Nations Convention on the Law of the Sea (adopted 10 December 1982, entered into force 16 November 1994) 1836 UNTS 3 [UNCLOS].
43 According to Art. 2 UNCLOS '[a]n international organization may sign this Convention if a majority of its member States are signatories of this Convention'. It is

§ 4 EU Withdrawal: Grounds for Treaty Termination?

require the international organisation to withdraw from UNCLOS with immediate effect. Hence, UNCLOS is one of the few multilateral agreements with a REIO-specific denunciation provision and, additionally, the result is exactly the opposite of that discussed in connection with Brexit. As concerns UNCLOS, withdrawal from an international organisation party to UNCLOS does not affect the withdrawing state's participation in UN-CLOS; rather, withdrawal of a member State may affect the organisation's status as a party to UNCLOS.

B. Implicit Termination Clauses

Neither the EU's mixed agreements nor its Member States' *inter se* agreements explicitly provide for the effect of a Member State's EU withdrawal on that state's status as a party to these agreements. While this has generally been acknowledged, reference has been made in practice and in scholarship to treaty provisions that could implicitly establish such a link. In this context, two provisions have attracted particular attention: the definition of the parties regularly included in bilateral mixed and *inter se* agreements (1.), and the territorial scope of application as defined in bilateral mixed agreements (2.).[44] Moreover, it has been argued that where mixed or *inter se* agreements are substantively linked to the EU and its institutions, or to the

---

thus possible for an international organisation to have members who are parties to UNCLOS and others that are not. If those who are parties to UNCLOS besides the organisation terminate their membership in the organisation, the preconditions of Art. 8(c)(ii) Annex IX are fulfilled.

44 See eg JWJ Kim, 'Is the United Kingdom Still a Party to the EU-Korea FTA after Brexit?' in JA Hillman and GN Horlick (eds), *Legal Aspects of Brexit: Implications of the United Kingdom's decision to withdraw from the European Union* (Georgetown Law 2017); A Kent, 'Brexit and the East African Community (EAC)-European Union Economic Partnership Agreement (EPA)' in JA Hillman and GN Horlick (eds) (n 44); RA Wessel, 'Consequences of Brexit for International Agreements Concluded by the EU and its Member States' (2018) 55 (Special Issue) *Common Market Law Review* 101, 119–124; T Voland, 'Auswirkungen des Brexit auf die völkervertraglichen Beziehungen des Vereinigten Königreichs und der EU' (2019) 79(1) *Zeitschrift für ausländisches öffentliches Recht und Völkerrecht* 1, 14–17; P Koutrakos, 'Managing Brexit: Trade Agreements Binding on the UK pursuant to its EU Membership' in J Santos Vara, RA Wessel and PR Polak (eds), *The Routledge Handbook on the International Dimension of Brexit* (Routledge 2020) 77; C Kaddous and HB Touré, 'The Status of the United Kingdom Regarding EU Mixed Agreements after Brexit' in N Levrat and others (eds) (n 31) 282–283.

I. Termination by Design: EU Membership as a Resolutory Condition?

Member States' capacity as *Member* States, loss of that quality may put into question the agreement as such (3.).[45] All of these arguments have a certain merit to them. To a varying degree, the contractual design of mixed and *inter se* agreements creates a link between being an EU Member State and being a party to these agreements. But while loss of EU membership thus certainly has practical implications for these agreements, the question still remains what would – or could – legally follow from this link (4.).

1. Definition of Parties: EU Member State Status in International Agreements

Undeniably, the EU and its Member States are respectively parties to mixed and *inter se* agreements in the sense of Art. 2(1)(g) VCLT[46].[47] As put by ECJ Advocate General (AG) Sharpston with regard to mixed agreements, a Member State's 'participation in the agreement is, after all, as a sovereign State Party, not as a mere appendage of the European Union'[48]. Nevertheless, in the debate surrounding the effect of Brexit on international agreements, the party status of the Member States has repeatedly been questioned. Depending on the circumstances of conclusion and especially the text of the respective agreements, the argument has been made that the EU Member States have become parties only in their capacity as EU Member States.[49] This connection between status as a treaty party to international agreements and being an EU Member State comes in two different shapes: the less EU-specific one in *inter se* agreements and the distinctly EU-specific one in the context of bilateral mixed agreements.

In the three *inter se* agreements which the UK concluded during its time as an EU Member State, participation as a party is clearly linked to EU membership. The text of these agreements explicitly refers to the parties as EU Member States. Art. 1 EUI Convention provides that '[b]y this Convention, *the Member States of the European Communities* (hereinafter called the "Contracting States") jointly set up the European University Institute

---

45 See eg Wessel (n 44), 122–123.
46 Respectively Art. 2(1)(g) VCLT-IO.
47 See also above Part I § 3 section III.C.2.
48 ECJ, Opinion 2/15 *FTA Singapore* (Opinion of the Advocate General Sharpston) [2017] EU:C:2016:992, [77].
49 See eg Wessel (n 44), 121–122; Kaddous and Touré (n 44) 275–277.

[...]'⁵⁰. Similarly, the preamble of the ES Convention defines the parties as 'the High Contracting Parties, *Members of the European Communities*, and the European Communities'⁵¹. While lacking an explicit definition of the parties, the EDF Agreement is titled 'Internal Agreement between the Representatives of the Governments *of the Member States of the European Union*'⁵² and refers to its parties simply as 'the Member States'⁵³. Moreover, at least for the EUI and the ES Convention, EU membership is also an explicit precondition for becoming a party. According to Art. 32(1) EUI Convention, '[a]ny Member State of the European Communities besides the Contracting States may accede to this Convention [...]'. And for the ES Convention, Art. 31(1) limits '[a]pplications for the accession to this Convention' to 'any State becoming a member of the Community'.

In internal agreements between the member states of an international organisation, this is a regular practice. The participation in most conventions adopted within the framework of international organisations is restricted to the organisation's member states, leading to accordingly formulated accession clauses.⁵⁴ But linking the party status of its Member States to their EU membership is a technique that the EU also successfully applies in its external agreements. In fact, the definition of parties in many mixed agreements is the reason why these are – despite the number of treaty parties – often referred to as bilateral. While mixed agreements are, formally speaking, necessarily multilateral agreements because they encompass the EU, its Member States and at least one non-EU Member State as treaty parties, some agreements create the impression of a bilateral relationship:

> [...] a treaty with a multitude of signatories may be bilaterally structured if it is concluded between one or more States on the one side and two or more States on the other side, creating rights and obligations only between the mutually facing sides (formal reciprocity).⁵⁵

---

50 Emphasis added.
51 Emphasis added.
52 Emphasis added.
53 See eg Art. 1(1): 'The *Member States* hereby set up an eleventh European Development Fund [...].' (Emphasis added).
54 HG Schermers and N Blokker, *International Institutional Law: Unity within Diversity* (5th edn, Martinus Nijhoff Publishers 2011) paras 1298–1305.
55 K Schmalenbach, 'Article 2' in O Dörr and K Schmalenbach (eds), *Vienna Convention on the Law of Treaties: A Commentary* (, 2nd edn, Springer 2018) para 9 with reference to the EU's Second ACP-Convention as an example. See AD McNair, *The*

I. Termination by Design: EU Membership as a Resolutory Condition?

A prominent example is Art. 1.1 of the *Comprehensive Economic and Trade Agreement*[56] (CETA) between Canada, the EU and its Member States, according to which

> Parties means, on the one hand, the European Union or its Member States or the European Union and its Member States within their respective areas of competence as derived from the Treaty on European Union and the Treaty on the Functioning of the European Union (hereinafter referred to as the 'EU Party'), and on the other hand, Canada.[57]

A near identical definition of the parties is contained in all bilateral mixed trade agreements.[58] In most cases it is supplemented by the introduction of the 'EU Party' as a collective reference to the EU and its Member States.[59] Where treaty provisions are reciprocal between, for example, Canada, on the one side, and the EU and its Member States, on the other side, reference is made to the 'Parties'.[60] Where a provision is intended to address solely the EU and/or its Member States, reference is made to the 'EU Party'.[61] In so doing, it remains for the EU and its Member States to fulfil their treaty obligations in accordance with the (changing) division of competences between them.

> Having consented to and being bound by the whole agreement, the term 'EU Party' [and the definition of the parties] is open to interpretation and a dynamic division of competences. Defined as 'the EU or its Member States or the EU and its Member States according to their respective competences', the term avoids direct reference, especially where compe-

---

Law of Treaties (Clarendon Press 1961) 29 who preferred 'bipartite' for agreements with two and 'multipartite' for agreements with several parties.

56 Comprehensive Economic and Trade Agreement between Canada, of the one part, and the European Union and its Member States, of the other part (14 January 2017) OJ L11/23 [CETA].
57 Emphasis omitted.
58 Based on an analysis of these agreements by the author; full analysis of typical treaty provisions in bilateral mixed (trade) agreements on file with the author.
59 On the use of the term 'EU Party' in bilateral mixed trade agreements, see Schaefer and Odermatt (n 31).
60 See eg Art. 1.4 CETA: 'The Parties hereby establish a free trade area [...].' See in detail, ibid 143–149.
61 See eg Art. 8.2 paragraph 3 CETA: 'For the EU Party, Section B and C do not apply [...].'

tence is controversial, and provides for a joint or alternative performance of treaty obligations.[62]

Thus, while Member States become parties to these agreements under international law, it has been argued that '[t]he Member States should not be considered as having an independent and autonomous status as states parties to these mixed agreements'[63] and consequently 'do not enjoy the autonomy that is attached to this status under international law'[64].

But what does it mean for a state to lose its capacity as an *EU Member State* if membership is a precondition for accession, as in the case of *inter se* agreements? And where '[t]he contracting party "the Union and its Member States" has a composite character that implies prior membership'[65] as in the case of bilateral mixed agreements? For some authors, the consequence is the automatic termination of the former Member State's participation as a party to those agreements.[66] As Koutrakos states with regard to Brexit, '[...] once the UK left the EU and lost its status as a Member State, it would also cease to be a party to such Agreements [...]'[67].

In essence, this mirrors what Schermers and Blokker argue with regard to membership in international organisations, claiming that '[i]n all international organizations it should be possible to declare that membership is terminated if a state has ceased to fulfil the conditions for the *existence* of membership. [...] Membership will end *ipso jure* if the member [...] changes in such a way that it loses essential qualifications for membership'[68]. Thus, for example, '[i]f the organization unites a well defined group of states such as oil exporting states (OPEC), a state will no longer qualify for membership when it ceases to export such products'[69]. Based hereon, it could be argued that the EUI Convention, the ES Convention and the EDF Agreement, respectively, unite a well defined group of states – EU Member

---

62 Schaefer and Odermatt (n 31) 144. On the extent to which the EU and its Member States are bound by mixed agreements, see above Part I § 3 section III.C.2. On the joint and alternative treaty performance of mixed agreements, cp in detail J Heliskoski (n 29) chapter 4.
63 Kaddous and Touré (n 44) 275.
64 Ibid 276.
65 Ibid.
66 See eg C Herrmann, 'Brexit, WTO und EU-Handelspolitik' (2017) 24 Europäische Zeitschrift für Wirtschaftsrecht 961, 966; Kim (n 44) 44–50; Kent (n 44) 62; Koutrakos (n 44) 77.
67 Koutrakos (n 44) 77.
68 HG Schermers and N Blokker (n 54) para 149.
69 Ibid para 152.

States – in running two common institutions – a *European* University Institute and a system of *European* schools – and financing a common *European* development fund.

Moreover, in the debate over the effect of EU withdrawal on international agreements, a link is created between termination and accession: what is considered a condition for accession to *inter se* agreements must also serve as a reason for resolution of the treaty relationship. For the fact that membership in the EU is a prerequisite for accession demonstrates the intent of the parties to limit the agreement to EU Member States. A similar argument is also made for bilateral mixed agreements, although here the circle of treaty parties is obviously not limited to Member States. In general, new Member States accede to mixed agreements by concluding an accession protocol with the non-EU treaty partner(s) and the EU.[70] However, some more-recent bilateral mixed agreements also provide for the possibility of *automatic* accession of new EU Member States if such accession is agreed upon in the EU Act of Accession.[71] Where an agreement provides for automatic accession of new EU Member States, for exiting Member States

> an analogous analysis could be proposed. It would lead to the conclusion that when a state withdraws from the EU, it may lose its participation to the mixed agreements if the Withdrawal Agreement provides for an automatic termination of the participation of that state to the mixed agreements.[72]

Where the automatic termination of the former Member State's party status in bilateral mixed agreements is justified with the definition of the parties, another typical treaty clause in the EU's bilateral mixed agreements – the territorial scope of application – is also regularly mentioned.

---

70 On accession clauses in bilateral mixed trade agreements, see Schaefer and Odermatt (n 31) 146–147.
71 See eg Art. 30.9(5) CETA: 'Any new Member State of the European Union shall accede to this Agreement from the date of its accession to the European Union by means of a clause to that effect in the act of accession to the European Union. If the act of accession to the European Union does not provide for the automatic accession of the European Union Member State to this Agreement the European Union Member State concerned shall accede to this Agreement by depositing an act of accession to this Agreement [...].'
72 Kaddous and Touré (n 44) 281.

2. Territorial Scope of Application

In early bilateral mixed agreements, the territorial scope of application was defined with reference to the territory of the Member States. Art. 73(1) of the former AA Greece, for example, provided that

> [t]his Agreement shall apply to the European territories of the Kingdom of Belgium, of the Federal Republic of Germany, of the French Republic, of the Italian Republic, of the Grand Duchy of Luxembourg and of the Kingdom of the Netherlands on the one hand, and to the Kingdom of Greece on the other.

The disadvantage of this becomes obvious when considering the number of Member State accessions that the EU has experienced since. With every new accession to the EU, the provisions on territorial application in these bilateral mixed agreements had to be supplemented accordingly. In all current bilateral mixed trade agreements, the territorial scope of application is thus defined by reference to the TEU and TFEU's scope of application.[73] According to Art. 1.3(b) CETA Canada, for example, the agreement applies 'for the European Union, to the territories in which the Treaty on European Union and the Treaty on the Functioning of the European Union are applied and under the conditions laid down in those Treaties'.

This formula not only accommodates accessions to EU membership without requiring amending: it also allows for constitutional changes within Member States, affecting the application of EU law. An example is Greenland, still part of the territory of Denmark but to which the TEU and TFEU and accordingly bilateral mixed agreements do not apply.[74] Based hereon, the articles on the territorial scope of application in the EU's external agreements are often described as establishing a so-called moving treaty frontier that flexibly widens and narrows with the increasing or decreasing

---

73 Based on an analysis of these agreements by the author; full analysis of typical treaty provisions in bilateral mixed (trade) agreements on file with the author.
74 On Greenland and further constitutional or territorial changes to EU Member States, see below Part II § 5 section I.C.2. On state succession and the EU legal order in general, see A Zimmermann, *Staatennachfolge in völkerrechtliche Verträge: Zugleich ein Beitrag zu den Möglichkeiten und Grenzen völkerrechtlicher Kodifikation*, (Springer 2000) 673 ff.

I. Termination by Design: EU Membership as a Resolutory Condition?

reach of the EU Treaties.⁷⁵ And accordingly, the conclusion that withdrawal from the EU *automatically* leads to the termination of that state's status as a party to bilateral mixed agreements 'is also borne out by a clause in a large number of mixed agreements on their territorial application'⁷⁶. For where a moving treaty frontier allows for the application of an agreement to a new Member State, it must, arguably, also work the other way around: when a Member State withdraws from the EU, the TEU and TFEU are necessarily no longer applicable to it;⁷⁷ and where the TEU and TFEU cease to apply to a state, so do the bilateral mixed agreements whose scope of application is linked to the EU Treaties.

3. Frustration of the Object and Purpose

Finally, the debate about the effect of EU withdrawal on international agreements is not only conducted on the basis of two rather formal treaty clauses: the content of these agreements also plays a role. The question that explicitly or implicitly resonates in most contributions on the topic is whether and what role a former EU Member State can play in these agreements.⁷⁸ It is a question that can again be raised with regard to *inter se* and bilateral mixed agreements that both establish this close link between EU membership and being a party to the agreement. And it again requires a differentiated consideration: in *inter se* agreements, a continued party status of a former EU Member State would transform the agreements from internal agreements, restricted solely to EU Member States, to external agreements, encompassing a non-EU state. The question here is, thus, whether participation of a non-EU Member State in a circle of EU Member States is compatible with an agreement's object and purpose. Bilateral mixed agreements, on the one hand, already encompass at least one non-EU state as a

---

75 Ibid 698–701; 711. See also PJ Kuijper, 'The Community and State Succession in Respect of Treaties' in D Curtin and T Heukels (eds), *Institutional Dynamics of European Integration* (Martinus Nijhoff Publishers 1994) 624.
76 Koutrakos (n 44) 77.
77 Cp Art. 50 TEU.
78 See eg Wessel (n 44), 122 who cautions that 'it would be difficult to force third States to continue to accept the UK as a partner to an agreement even if this were possible. After all, the very reason that the signature of the UK was accepted may have been its EU membership.' Where continued UK participation is accepted, this could lead to 'unforeseen practical problems' and 'change the nature of a bilateral agreement to a multilateral agreement.'

§ 4 EU Withdrawal: Grounds for Treaty Termination?

party. On the other hand, these agreements present the EU and its Member States as a 'team'[79] *vis-à-vis* a pre-defined (group of) non-EU state(s). Is a former Member State's participation – belonging neither to the former nor the latter – compatible with the agreements' aims?[80]

As regards *inter se* agreements, it has been stated that

> [w]ithout the inclusion of primary or secondary [EU] law, the agreements often cannot be understood at all. In this sense, the agreements, regardless of their legal nature under international law, are part of the law of the European association between the Union and the Member States. They form its horizontal dimension.[81]

Nevertheless, there are significant differences in the degree to which their content and structure are linked to EU membership.[82] Of the three *inter se* agreements concluded by the UK, the EUI Convention has the weakest connection to the EU legal order. The purpose of the EUI Convention is to set up the European University Institute, the aim of which

> shall be to contribute, by its activities in the field of higher education and research to the development of the cultural and scientific heritage of Europe, as a whole and in its constituent parts. Its work shall also be concerned with the great movements and institutions which characterize the history and development of Europe. It shall take into account relations with cultures outside Europe.[83]

---

79 Ibid 119.
80 Ibid 122.
81 J Heesen, *Interne Abkommen: Völkerrechtliche Verträge zwischen den Mitgliedstaaten der Europäischen Union*, (Springer 2015) 187 ('Ohne Einbeziehung des [EU-] Primär- oder Sekundärrechts sind die Abkommen häufig gar nicht zu verstehen. In diesem Sinne sind die Abkommen, ungeachtet ihrer völkerrechtlichen Rechtsnatur, Bestandteil des Rechts des europäischen Verbundes aus Union und Mitgliedstaaten. Sie bilden seine horizontale Dimension.', translated by the author).
82 But see Heesen who warns of a fragmentation of the integration process through permanently established further 'integration tracks' such as the EUI Convention and the ES Convention (ibid 206: 'Das Problem einer Aufspaltung des Integrationsprozesses stellt sich bei solchen internen Abkommen verschärft, die nicht auf eine spätere Integration in das Unionsrecht angelegt sind, sondern die dauerhaft als zusätzliche Integrationsschienen bestehen bleiben sollen, wie die Gründungsabkommen über die Europäischen Schulen und das Europäische Hochschulinstitut. [...] Das Problem der Fragmentierung, mit dem das Völkerrecht kämpft, wird durch den Abschluss monothematischer interner Abkommen in das Unionsrecht re-importiert.').
83 Art. 2(1) EUI Convention.

I. Termination by Design: EU Membership as a Resolutory Condition?

Thus, while the parties are limited to Member States of the *European Union*, the Institute's research shall be concerned with *Europe* (as a whole). Moreover, while the agreement makes mention of the EU and its institutions, it only does so in very limited instances and without attributing any active role to them[84].

In contrast, the ES Convention more closely links the European Schools to the EU. According to Art. 1 ES Convention, '[t]he purpose of the Schools is to educate together children of the staff of the European Communities'. To do so, 'in the territory of a Member State' schools may be set up at which children of EU staff may acquire the European baccalaureate or other 'diplomas and certificates' which 'shall be recognized in the territory of the Member States'. The EU – itself being a party to the ES Convention – is represented by a member of the Commission in the Board of Governors and the Administrative Board and contributes to the schools' budgets.

But these interrelations between an international agreement and the EU legal order are even more striking in the case of the EDF Agreement. An 'internal agreement', the EDF Agreement, is concluded 'between the Representatives of the Governments of the Member States of the European Union meeting within the Council' to finance European development aid agreed upon with the African, Caribbean and Pacific Group of States (ACP States) in a bilateral mixed agreement.[85] In so doing, it delegates tasks to EU institutions, makes use of their legislative and decision-making functions and closely links the agreement with EU secondary law instruments and the EU's multiannual financial framework.[86] It is because of these close connections that the EDF in 2021 itself became an integral part of the EU's multi-annual financial framework, thereby being funded through the EU budget and no longer via an international agreement between Member States.[87]

---

84 According to Art. 6(3), representatives of the EU may take part in meetings of the Institute's High Council but without a right to vote. Art. 17(3) acknowledges the possibility of the EU awarding grants to researchers at the Institute. Art. 29 tasks the President of the CJEU with determining an arbitration body in case of a dispute between the parties to the Convention.
85 Cotonou Agreement (n 26).
86 See eg Art. 1 on allocation of funds by the Council and the Commission, Arts. 4 and 5 on the role of the European Investment Bank, Art. 7 on the Commission's contributions.
87 EU, 'European Development Fund' <https://eur-lex.europa.eu/EN/legal-content/glossary/european-development-fund.html>; EU Commission, 'EU and EDF Annual

§ 4 EU Withdrawal: Grounds for Treaty Termination?

Similarly, there are also differences in the content of bilateral mixed agreements, with some being rather general in nature and others distinctly EU-specific. Bilateral mixed agreements spread a whole range of topics. Thus, as Eeckhout has noted, it is, in general, 'preferable to look at the practice on its own merits and not to base oneself on a pre-conceived typology'[88]. Indeed, to determine the exact content and accordingly the object and purpose, it would be necessary to consider each bilateral mixed agreement on a case-by-case basis. While this goes well beyond the scope of this study, considering a rough classification of typical bilateral mixed agreements should suffice to give an impression of the differences.

Often, mixed agreements are typologised based on formal criteria, such as the distribution of competences (mandatory, facultative or false mixity) or the number of parties (complete and incomplete, bilateral or multilateral mixed agreements).[89] In contrast, Maresceau attempted a classification along four more substantive categories, dividing bilateral mixed agreements into association agreements, cooperation agreements of a general nature, mixed trade and cooperation agreements with political dialogue, and mixed sectoral agreements without political dialogue.[90] How far is participation by a former Member State compatible with the objects and purposes of these agreements?

Association agreements have, for example, often been concluded with a 'genuine pre-accession nature'[91] with the treaty partners 'aspir[ing] to become members of the EU'[92]. A rather recent example of this is the Association Agreement with Ukraine[93], the aims of which are, *inter alia*, 'increas-

---

Accounts' (*Directorate-General for Budget*, 23.07.2021) <https://commission.europa.eu/publications/eu-and-edf-annual-accounts_en>.

88 P Eeckhout, *External Relations of the European Union: Legal and Constitutional Foundations* (Oxford University Press 2004) 191.

89 See J Heliskoski and G Kübek, 'A Typology of EU Mixed Agreements Revisited' in N Levrat and others (eds) (n 31). Along the same lines, HG Schermers, 'A Typology of Mixed Agreements' in D O'Keeffe and HG Schermers (eds), *Mixed Agreements* (Kluwer 1983).

90 M Maresceau, 'A Typology of Mixed Bilateral Agreements' in C Hillion and P Koutrakos (eds), *Mixed Agreements Revisited: The EU and its Member States in the World* (Hart Publishing 2010) 17 ff.

91 Ibid 17.

92 Ibid 18.

93 Association Agreement between the European Union and the European Atomic Energy Community and their Member States, of the one part, and Ukraine, of the other part (29 May 2014) OJ L161/3 [AA Ukraine].

ing *Ukraine's association with EU policies* and participation in programmes and agencies'[94] and 'to establish conditions for enhanced economic and trade relations leading towards *Ukraine's gradual integration in the EU Internal Market*'[95]. It is easy to see how continued participation of a withdrawing EU Member State may be questionable here. Which role should or could a former Member State play in the rapprochement of another state to the EU? At the same time, throughout the decades, the EU has also increasingly concluded association agreements 'totally disconnected from the enlargement question'[96], rather 'symboliz[ing] the EU's political and economic interest'[97] in a certain region. The differences are distinctly visible as can be seen, for example, in the objective and scope of the EU-Chile Association Agreement[98]: 'This Agreement establishes a Political and Economic Association between the Parties, based on *reciprocity* [...]. The Association is a process that will lead to a growing relationship and cooperation between the Parties structured around *the bodies created in this Agreement*'[99]. Here, a distinct interest – and purpose – in the former Member State's continued participation appears less far-fetched.

Similar differences as regards agreements' substantive relation to the EU – its institutions and legal order – exist between but also within the further subcategories of bilateral mixed agreements. For example, Partnership and Cooperation Agreements (PCAs), forming a subcategory of the cooperation agreements of a general nature, have been described as 'meagre' with 'the concrete substantive scope of the provisions of the PCAs [being] limited'[100]. An example for this is the 2016 PCA with Cuba[101] in which Cuba and the EU Party commit to cooperation and dialogue in generally held subject areas such as human rights promotion, the modernisation of the Cuban economy and the development of joint responses to global

---

94 Art. 1(2)(a) (emphasis added).
95 Art. 1(2)(e) (emphasis added).
96 Maresceau (n 90) 17.
97 Ibid 20.
98 Agreement establishing an association between the European Community and its Member States, of the one part, and the Republic of Chile, of the other part (30 December 2002) OJ L352/3 [EU-Chile AA].
99 Art. 2(1) and (2) (emphasis added).
100 Maresceau (n 90) 21.
101 Political Dialogue and Cooperation Agreement between the European Union and its Member States, of the one part, and the Republic of Cuba, of the other part (13 December 2016) OJ L337I/3 [PCA Cuba].

§ 4 EU Withdrawal: Grounds for Treaty Termination?

challenges.[102] Discussing these broad issues of international cooperation is certainly something possible for former EU Member States.

Mixed sectoral agreements on the other hand are – as the category suggests – thematically much more specific. Some of them are part of the so-called Bilaterals I and II, EU-only and mixed agreements concluded between the EU and Switzerland.[103] Content-wise, Swiss-EU treaty relations have been described as 'integration without membership'[104], with 'the agreements [being] based on European law' and '[dealing] with cooperation between Switzerland and the EU within the framework of EU agencies and programmes'[105]. Other sectoral agreements exclusively address the participation of non-EU Member States in EU projects, such as the agreements on participation in the EU's Civil Global Navigation Satellite System (Galileo System).[106] And yet others are thematically not *per se* EU-specific, such as, for example, the *EU-China Maritime Transport Agreement*[107] or the different EU Air Transport Agreements[108]. While these agreements are, of course, tailored to the circumstances of transport and air services specif-

---

102 For the general objectives, see Art. 2 PCA Cuba. Part II provides for political dialogue, *inter alia*, on human rights (Art. 5), illicit arms and weapons trade (Art. 6), disarmament and non-proliferation (Art. 7), fight against terrorism (Art. 8) as well as serious crimes (Art. 9), combating trafficking and smuggling (Arts. 11, 12) and sustainable development (Art. 14).
103 The Bilaterals I and II were drawn up to shape the EU-Swiss relations following the Swiss referendum on the European Economic Area in which majority voted against a Swiss accession. Cp Swiss Federal Department of Foreign Affairs/Federal Department of Economic Affairs, 'Bilateral Agreements Switzerland-EU' (August 2009) 4. On the Bilaterals I, see also Maresceau (n 90) 24–25.
104 See M Vahl and N Grolimund, 'Integration without Membership' Switzerland's Bilateral Agreements with the European Union, CEPS (2006).
105 'Bilateral Agreements Switzerland-EU' (n 103) 5.
106 Maresceau (n 90) 25–26. See eg Cooperation Agreement on a Civil Global Navigation Satellite System (GNSS) between the European Community and its Member States, of the one part, and the Republic of Korea, of the other part (19 October 2006) OJ L288/31.
107 Agreement on Maritime Transport between the European Community and its Member States, of the one part, and the government of the People's Republic of China, of the other part (21 February 2008) OJ L46/25 [EU-China Maritime Agreement].
108 See eg Air Transport Agreement between the United States of America, of the one part, and the European Community and its Member States, of the other part (25 May 2007) OJ L134/5 [EU-US Open Skies].

I. Termination by Design: EU Membership as a Resolutory Condition?

ically between the EU and its treaty partners, the subject matter of these agreements is not limited to this relationship.[109]

4. Legal Consequences of Changes to An International Agreement

It has been argued that the agreements concluded by a Member State in connection with its membership in the EU are 'package deals, and part of the package is the status of the [withdrawing state] as a Member State of the EU'[110]. This becomes visible in the content, structure and formulation of individual treaty provisions of *inter se* and bilateral mixed agreements. These agreements – as any international agreement – have undeniably been adapted to the specific situation and needs of the treaty parties. This unquestionably leads to problems where this specific situations change, here because of the withdrawal of a state from the EU. At the same time, the question still remains as to how far this change not only creates practical problems but is indeed *legally* relevant. Can the definition of the parties, the agreements' territorial scope of application or their object and purpose really lead to the termination of the former Member State's status *as a party* to these agreements? Several factors speak against this.

Firstly, the practice concerning conventions concluded within the framework of other international organisations does not support the argument that the loss of membership in an international organisation *automatically* leads to the termination of conventions for the respective state. In contrast, the legal consequences of termination of a state's membership in an organisation for any other international agreements concluded in the context of said membership is regularly either spelt out in the organisation's founding treaty or in the conventions themselves.[111] Even where membership in a certain organisation is an explicit accession criterion, conventions inextricably linked to membership still include a corresponding cessation provision. Thus, if the disappearance of an accession criterion would suffice as a

---

109 A good example is the EU-US Open Skies Agreement. Before a ruling of the CJEU, many Member States had individual air transport agreements with the United States. The EU-US Open Skies Agreement did not only replace them. It also adapted these classic bilateral air transport agreements between two states to the situation of a European Common Aviation Area. On the EU-US Open Skies Agreement, see Maresceau (n 90) 26. On Brexit and air transport, see W Douma, 'Come Fly With Me?: Brexit and Air Transport' in J Santos Vara, RA Wessel and PR Polak (eds) (n 44).
110 Koutrakos (n 44) 77.
111 See above Part I § 3 section II.A.

resolutive condition, why would states deem it necessary to additionally include provisions on the agreements' termination?

Despite this practice, Schermers and Blokker nevertheless seem to advocate exactly this: that a state's party status in an agreement terminates *ipso jure* where it loses an essential quality such as its membership in an international organisation. But while the authors include illustrations where they deem such a condition fulfilled – an OPEC state that ceases to export oil or a Member State of the World Meteorological Organization that no longer has a meteorological service – they do not point to any actual example to corroborate their claim. Instead, they go on to explain that '[s]ome international organizations restrict their membership to members of specific organizations. States will then no longer qualify for membership when they lose their membership of these specific organizations'. But the examples used to substantiate this proposition include precisely conventions that *explicitly* regulate the loss of the party status where a party withdraws from a certain international organisation, such as the IMF, the World Bank, the IFC and the IDA.[112]

Secondly, practice also speaks against reading the provisions on the bilateral mixed agreements' territorial scope of application as implicit termination clauses. Reference to the territorial application of the TEU and the TFEU is made in the respective provisions of many EU-only and mixed bilateral agreements. In the case of EU-only agreements, the provisions on territorial application may truly be considered as an expression of the moving treaty frontier rule. The EU gains more or loses parts of its territory and thus the scope of its EU-only agreements changes accordingly. In the case of bilateral mixed agreements, however, the treaty frontier does not, in fact, move automatically, the difference to EU-only agreements being their co-conclusion by the EU *and* its Member States. Practice shows that new EU Member States do not automatically also become parties to bilateral mixed agreements simply because they fall under the scope of application of the TEU and the TFEU. Instead, they must conclude accession agreements with the EU (usually representing its existing Member States) and the non-EU treaty partner(s). The lesson to be learned from joining the EU is, thus, not one of moving treaty frontiers but rather that with regard to mixed agreements a formal act of accession is required. Transferred to the withdrawal situation, the *actus contrarius* would thus be a formal denunciation of the mixed agreements.

---

112 See above Part I § 3 section II.A.

I. Termination by Design: EU Membership as a Resolutory Condition?

Even where more recent bilateral mixed agreements include a clause allowing for the automatic accession of new EU Member States,[113] these cannot by an 'analogous analysis'[114] be applied to the reverse situation. An automatic accession clause still does not introduce the moving treaty frontier principle into the mixed agreement. Instead, it expresses the anticipated consent of all parties to the mixed agreement to the accession of a new EU Member State. The new EU Member State, in turn, would have to express its consent to be bound by these mixed agreements in the EU Act of Accession.[115] The analogy to be drawn from automatic accession clauses would thus be that automatic termination is possible with the previous consent of all parties. However, in proposing the analogy, Kaddous and Touré themselves admit that the EU's bilateral mixed agreements do not contain such an automatic withdrawal provision. Accordingly, nowhere have the EU's treaty partners consented to an automatic cessation of a state's party status following withdrawal from the EU – or to the resulting loss of their rights *vis-à-vis* that state.

Thirdly, understanding the bilateral mixed agreements' territorial scope as implicitly providing for a withdrawing Member State's loss of its party status is incompatible with the wording of Art. 29 VCLT[116] and the Convention's systematicity. Art. 29 VCLT addresses the issue of an agreement's territorial scope: 'Unless a different intention appears from the treaty or is otherwise established, a treaty is binding upon each party in respect of its entire territory.' The parties to bilateral mixed agreements are, therefore, free to determine the territorial scope of their agreement. However, in

---

113 For an example, see above Part I § 4 section I.B.1.
114 Kaddous and Touré (n 44) 281.
115 See eg the automatic accession clause in Art. 77(2) EPA Ghana that provides: 'Any new Member State of the EU shall accede to this Agreement from the date of its accession to the EU by means of a clause to that effect in the act of accession. If the act of accession to the Union does not provide for such automatic accession of the EU Member State to this Agreement, the EU Member State concerned shall accede by depositing an act of accession with the General Secretariat of the Council of the European Union, which shall send certified copies to the Ghanaian Party.'
116 On the customary status of Art. 29 VCLT, see K Odendahl, 'Article 29' in O Dörr and K Schmalenbach (eds), *Vienna Convention on the Law of Treaties: A Commentary* (2nd edn, Springer 2018) para 3. Art. 29 VCLT-IO has an identical wording; in particular, it does not define the territorial scope of international agreements for international organisations. Nevertheless, Art. 29 VCLT can be applied in the case at hand as the extent to which the mixed agreements bind the UK – not the EU – is in question. The UK is not only a state, but it is also a party to the VCLT.

so doing, the exact formulation is crucial: there is a difference between the 'geographical application of the relevant treaty and the geographical reach of its binding force'[117]. Thus, where an agreement '*applies* [...] for the European Union, to the territories in which the Treaty on European Union and the Treaty on the Functioning of the European Union are applied'[118], following withdrawal from the EU, that agreement's geographical application may no longer cover the leaving Member State. However, the agreement may, according to Art. 29 VCLT, nevertheless continue to be '*binding* upon each party in respect of its entire territory'[119].

Moreover, while Art. 29 VCLT encompasses the moving treaty frontier rule,[120] that rule has never been understood in the sense of terminating a state's participation *as a party* to an international agreement. It does not deal with the status of a state with regard to an agreement. Instead, it is designed to address the effect of changes to one state's *territory* either because part of that territory separates or because more territory is incorporated. Thus, the rule has been described as

> stat[ing] that any territorial change affecting a States Parties after the entry into force of a treaty alters the treaty frontiers. Neither the treaty regime itself *nor the number* or identity of the States Parties is affected. Only the territorial scope of the treaty changes, since it depends on the geographical expansion of the States Parties.[121]

This description accords with the VCLT's systematicity. Art. 29 VCLT is included in Part III of the Convention dealing with the 'observance, application and interpretation of treaties'. It is neither included nor referred to in Part V, addressing the 'invalidity, termination and suspension of the operation of treaties'. Thus, a territorial change as such does not relieve a party of its obligations under an agreement.[122] Rather, where the change

---

117 Ibid para 18.
118 Art. 1.3 CETA Canada.
119 Emphasis added.
120 Odendahl (n 116) para 28.
121 Ibid para 29 (emphasis omitted, emphasis in italics added).
122 'Draft Convention on the Law of Treaties (Harvard Draft)' (1935) 29 (Supplement: Research in International Law) *American Journal of International Law* 635, Art. 26: 'A change in the territorial domain of a State, whether by addition or loss of territory, does not, in general, deprive the State of rights or relieve it of obligations under a treaty, unless the execution of the treaty becomes impossible as a result of the change.'

I. Termination by Design: EU Membership as a Resolutory Condition?

leads to a disruption of the treaty relation, the State concerned may invoke a corresponding right of treaty termination.[123] This may specifically be the right to withdraw in the case of the impossibility of performance[124] or in the case of a fundamental change of circumstances. The former does not apply in the case of Brexit for it requires the disappearances or destruction of an indispensable object – not to be mistaken with the impossibility to realise the treaty's objective.[125] The latter ground for withdrawal, however, leads over to the final argument on implicit automatic termination.

The latter ground for treaty withdrawal – a fundamental change of circumstances – is addressed in detail below. The reason for that is that this ground for treaty termination is designed precisely to deal with the situations described above. It allows a party to withdraw from a treaty where its 'stipulations come to place an undue burden on one of the parties as a result of a fundamental change of circumstances'[126]. This is, *inter alia*, the case where 'changes in the factual basis of the parties' consent'[127] occur, such as the extent of a party's territory but also the loss of an essential qualification.[128] Where these changes come to frustrate the agreement's object and purpose, the threshold of an undue burden is reached.[129] Thus, if it is, for example, established that a state's EU membership is a quality essential to a particular agreement and loss of that quality puts into question the achievement of the agreement's object and purpose, this does not *ipso facto* terminate that state's status as a party to the agreement. Rather, where a state has lost an essential qualification, or a change to an agreement's

---

123 Odendahl (n 116) para 31.
124 Art. 61 VCLT: '1. A party may invoke the impossibility of performing a treaty as a ground for terminating or withdrawing from it if the impossibility results from the permanent disappearance or destruction of an object indispensable for the execution of the treaty. If the impossibility is temporary, it may be invoked only as a ground for suspending the operation of the treaty. 2. Impossibility of performance may not be invoked by a party as a ground for terminating, withdrawing from or suspending the operation of a treaty if the impossibility is the result of a breach by that party either of an obligation under the treaty or of any other international obligation owed to any other party to the treaty.'
125 T Giegerich, 'Article 61' in O Dörr and K Schmalenbach (eds), *Vienna Convention on the Law of Treaties: A Commentary* (2nd edn, Springer 2018) para 13.
126 ILC, 'Reports of the International Law Commission on the Work of its 18th Session (4 May-19 July 1966)' UN Doc A/CN.4/191, YBILC (1966) Vol. II 258.
127 T Giegerich, 'Article 62' in O Dörr and K Schmalenbach (eds), *Vienna Convention on the Law of Treaties: A Commentary* (2nd edn, Springer 2018) para 40.
128 Ibid paras 34–44.
129 See in detail below Part I § 4 section II.B.2.

§ 4 EU Withdrawal: Grounds for Treaty Termination?

scope of application has occurred, and that changed situation puts into question the attainment of an agreement's object and purpose, this is generally considered under the terms of Art. 62 VCLT providing for the possibility of treaty withdrawal – not *automatic* termination. The answer to the question if the interaction between the definition of the parties, the agreements' territorial scope of application, their object and purpose and EU withdrawal are *legally* relevant is yes, but only if the cumulative conditions of a fundamental change of circumstances as per Art. 62 VCLT are fulfilled.

II. Termination by Invocation: EU Withdrawal as a Fundamental Change of Circumstances

An infamous exception to the principle of *pacta sunt servanda* is the so-called *clausula rebus sic stantibus*, allowing for the unilateral denunciation of an international agreement where its 'stipulations come to place an undue burden on one of the parties as a result of a fundamental change of circumstances'[130]. To limit the disruptive potential of the *clausula* for the stability of international treaty relations, its codification in Art. 62 VCLT[131] is formulated in the negative, with Art. 62(1) VCLT providing that a 'fundamental change of circumstances [...] *may not be invoked* as a ground for terminating or withdrawing from the treaty *unless* [...]'[132] certain very narrow, cumulative conditions are met. Moreover, it also provides for two exceptions which render invocation of Art. 62 VCLT inapplicable altogether.[133]

Despite its exceptional character and strict requirements, Art. 62 VCLT received considerable attention in the context of Brexit.[134] Neither the EU

---

130 'Reports 18th Session' (n 126) 258.
131 On the customary nature of Art. 62 VCLT, see ICJ *Fisheries Jurisdiction Case (Federal Republic of Germany v Iceland)* (Jurisdiction) [1973] ICJ Rep 1973, p 3, [36]; ICJ *Case Concerning the Gabčíkovo-Nagymaros Project (Hungary v Slovakia)* (Judgement) [1997] ICJ Rep 1997, p 7, [38]; ECJ, C-162/96 *A. Racke GmbH & Co. v. Hauptzollamt Mainz* [1998] ECLI:EU:C:1998:293, [55].
132 Emphasis added.
133 On the conditions, see below Part I § 4 section II.B.2. On the exceptions, see below Part I § 4 section II.B.1.a.
134 Scholarly contributions discuss Art. 62 VCLT when analysing the possible consequences of EU withdrawal on international agreements, see eg Voland (n 44), 25–28. Moreover, after conclusion of the withdrawal agreement, the UK contemplated

II. Termination by Invocation: EU Withdrawal as a Change of Circumstances

nor the UK explicitly invoked a fundamental change of circumstances in justifying their 'out means out' approach. This is rather unsurprising given that they claimed an *automatic* termination of the UK's status as a party to all bilateral mixed and *inter se* agreements (A.). However, where a former Member State remains a party to these agreements, the question arises as to whether or not the parties to these agreements – the EU, Member States, a former Member State or non-EU states – can invoke Art. 62 VCLT *post*-withdrawal (B.).

A. Automatic Termination: The Inappropriateness of Art. 62 VCLT

With regard to the effects of Brexit on international agreements, the EU, its Member States and the UK took the same approach: the UK would cease to be a party to bilateral mixed and *inter se* agreements, while remaining one in multilateral mixed agreements. Two things are noteworthy about this positioning: the categorisation of these international agreements based solely on their structure (bilateral or multilateral) and the constellation of the parties (with a non-EU treaty partner or without); and the blanket assignment of legal consequences based on these categorisations. In assessing whether the EU and the UK approaches to Brexit and international agreements can be justified in terms of a fundamental change of circumstances, both of these points are highly relevant.

The question of whether or not EU withdrawal constitutes a legal ground for treaty denunciation can only be truly answered when individually analysing every single international agreement. The need for such a case-by-case analysis is reemphasised by the exceptional character of Art. 62 VCLT, which prohibits any generalising statements. This is all the truer for a generalising categorisation – based on treaty structure or the treaty parties – as done in the case of Brexit. Assessing whether the circumstances surrounding an agreement have fundamentally changed so as to affect its continued performance also necessarily involves considering its content. Moreover, even where agreements with a certain structure all contain similar provi-

---

the invocation of Art. 62 VCLT to relieve itself of the withdrawal agreement's provisions on trade between its main island and Northern Ireland, see eg M Milanovic, 'Brexit, the Northern Irish Backstop, and Fundamental Change of Circumstances' (*EJIL:Talk!*, 2019) <https://www.ejiltalk.org/brexit-the-northern-irish-backstop-and-fundamental-change-of-circumstances/>.

sions as, for instance, the definition of the parties and the territorial scope of application, it is impossible to make a general statement on the circumstances surrounding and the parties' intentions upon conclusion of these agreements.[135] Thus, the question of whether EU withdrawal constitutes an invokable fundamental change of circumstances as per Art. 62 VCLT for *any* of the EU and its Member States' international agreements cannot be exhaustively analysed here; nor is it possible to apply Art. 62 VCLT in a manner that would justify the EU and the UK's generalised approach with regard to certain categories of agreements.

Moreover, the consequence of a successful invocation of Art. 62 VCLT is not an *automatic* termination of treaty relations. Rather, where the requirements of Art. 62 VCLT are fulfilled, the parties have a right to invoke the fundamental change of circumstances to denounce the agreement or to suspend its operation. To make use of this right, they must follow the procedural steps set out in Arts. 65–67 VCLT. This encompasses, *inter alia*, a written notification communicated to the other parties that 'shall indicate the measure proposed to be taken with respect to the treaty and the reasons therefor'[136]. While it is unclear whether the procedural requirements of Arts. 65–67 VCLT – especially with their technical character and great level of detail[137] – can be considered customary, at least certain parts of its procedural standards already derive from the principle of good faith.[138] The parties may thus not be obliged to provide as detailed a notification as Art. 65(1) VCLT demands. However, good faith – and practicability – will

---

135 On this point, see further below Part I § 4 section II.B.2.
136 Cp Art. 65(1), 67 VCLT.
137 S Wittich, 'Article 70' in O Dörr and K Schmalenbach (eds), *Vienna Convention on the Law of Treaties: A Commentary* (2nd edn, Springer 2018) para 7.
138 See ICJ, *Gabčíkovo-Nagymaros Project* (n 131) [109] noting that Arts. 65–67 VCLT 'if not codifying customary international law, at least generally reflect customary international law and contain certain procedural principles which are based on an obligation to act in good faith.' Notably, the UK has repeatedly relied on Arts. 65–68 VCLT, even before entry into force of the VCLT. In ICJ *Fisheries Jurisdiction (United Kingdom v Iceland)* (Jurisdiction) [1973] ICJ Rep 1973, p 3, [44] The Court noted: 'In the United Kingdom Memorial it is asserted that there is a flaw in the Icelandic contention of change of circumstances: that the doctrine never operates so as to extinguish a treaty automatically or to allow an unchallengeable unilateral denunciation by one Party; it only operates to confer a right to call for termination and, if that call is disputed, to submit the dispute to some organ or body with power to determine whether the conditions for the operation of the doctrine are present. In this connection the Applicant alludes to Articles 65 and 66 of the Vienna Convention on the Law of Treaties.'

II. Termination by Invocation: EU Withdrawal as a Change of Circumstances

at least require a denouncing party to provide the other party/parties with some form of notification and information.

Before the UK withdrew from the EU, the EU indeed sent a *note verbale* to non-EU states and other international organisations and requested those governments and organs acting as depositaries for international agreements to which the EU is a party to circulate said *note* among the other parties.[139] The content of the *note verbale*, however, is of a purely informative character. It informs the recipients of the signing of a withdrawal agreement between the EU and the UK and the transition period agreed therein. As regards international agreements, the EU notifies the other parties 'that, during the transition period, the United Kingdom is treated as a Member State of the Union [...] for the purposes of these international agreements'[140]. However, 'at the end of the transition period, the United Kingdom will no longer be covered by the international agreements [...]', this being 'without prejudice to the status of the United Kingdom in relation to multilateral agreements to which it is a party in its own right'[141]. Thus, the *note* does not indicate the measures – in the sense of 'a step or legal act performed with respect to the treaty'[142] – that the EU intends to take, nor is it, being sent by the EU, an invocation of grounds for treaty termination or withdrawal by the UK, the party deemed to leave the agreements.

Based on these considerations, it is consistent that neither the EU – effectively as a proxy for the UK – nor the UK itself invoked Art. 62 VCLT. Recourse to the *clausula* does not and cannot justify the approach taken by the EU, its Member States or the UK with regard to the effects of Brexit on international agreements. Considering their structure and the constellation of parties, the categorisation into mixed and *inter se* agreements and the distinction between bilateral and multilateral mixed agreements is comprehensible. However, international treaty law does not provide for specific termination rules for (EU-)specific categories of agreements. In particular, a change in the composition of parties neither blankly amounts to a fundamental change of circumstances nor does it lead to an *automatic* loss of party status.

---

139 EU Commission, 'Cover Letter and Note Verbale on the Agreement on the Withdrawal of the United Kingdom of Great Britain and Northern' (5 December 2018) COM(2018) 841 final 1.
140 Ibid 2.
141 Ibid 3.
142 ILC, 'Summary Records of the 18th Session (4 May – 19 July 1966)' UN Doc. A/CN.4/Ser.A/1966, YBILC (1966) Vol. I(2) 150.

§ 4 EU Withdrawal: Grounds for Treaty Termination?

B. Invoking Art. 62 VCLT: Terminating International Agreements Post-Withdrawal

The EU and the UK's 'out means out' approach with regard to the UK's status as a party to bilateral mixed and *inter se* agreements cannot be justified with reference to a fundamental change of circumstances. Still, Art. 62 VCLT may nevertheless play a role in the context of EU withdrawal as a regular ground for treaty denunciation invoked *following* withdrawal by *any* state or international organisation party to an agreement affected by the withdrawal. Thus, many authors critical of the EU and the UK's position point to Art. 62 VCLT. Where the UK is a party under international law, it remains a party also following Brexit; if this leads to disruptions reaching the threshold of Art. 62 VCLT, the article provides the parties with a possibility to free themselves of burdensome treaty obligations.

However, given the necessary case-by-case analysis and the hundreds of international agreements concerned, most authors indicate only a general tendency as regards the actual possibility of invoking Art. 62 VCLT, often without closer examination of its requirements.[143] Yet there are some general obstacles that would have to be overcome with regard to *all* concerned international agreements (1.), before one could even consider whether in the case of a *particular* agreement the narrow criteria of Art. 62 VCLT may be satisfied (2.).

1. Possible Obstacles in the Case of EU Withdrawal

The substantive requirements of Art. 62 VCLT demand a thorough analysis of each international agreement for which a party intends to invoke a fundamental change of circumstances. When considering invoking Art. 62 VCLT in the context of EU withdrawal, there are, however, also some general issues which states would have to consider. The first two are the

---

[143] G van der Loo and S Blockmans, 'The Impact of Brexit on the EU's International Agreements' (*CEPS Commentary*, 2016) <https://www.ceps.eu/ceps-publications/impact-brexit-eus-international-agreements/> Fn. 9; Wessel (n 44), 122; Koutrakos (n 44) 77; Kaddous and Touré (n 44) 281; Y Kaspiarovich and N Levrat, 'European Union Mixed Agreements in International Law under the Stress of Brexit' (2021) 13(2) *European Journal of Legal Studies* 121, 141. More in detail, see S Silvereke, 'Withdrawal from the EU and Bilateral Free Trade Agreements: Being Divorced is Worse?' (2018) 15(2) *International Organizations Law Review* 321, 333–335; Voland (n 44), 25–28.

II. Termination by Invocation: EU Withdrawal as a Change of Circumstances

questions of whether a fundamental change of circumstances may be invoked by (all) states party to international agreements affected by Brexit at all or if an (implicit) exception applies (a.). The third preliminary question concerns the consequences of Art. 62 VCLT, which does not differentiate between bilateral and multilateral agreements (b.), something that could especially cause difficulties in the case of bilateral mixed agreements (c.).

a. The Applicability of Art. 62 VCLT

In practice, states rarely invoke a fundamental change of circumstances to denounce their international treaty commitments. Instead, they turn to the regular termination provisions often included in international agreements. On the one hand, these usually provide for far less strict conditions for denunciation; often, no substantive requirements must be met, only procedural aspects complied with. On the other hand, the narrow conditions of Art. 62 VCLT not only make invocation of a fundamental change less attractive – in many cases, recourse to Art. 62 VCLT is also legally impossible.

The application of the *clausula* is subject to exceptions. Two explicit ones are specified in Art. 62(2) VCLT:

> A fundamental change of circumstances may not be invoked as a ground for terminating or withdrawing from a treaty:
> (a) if the treaty establishes a boundary; or
> (b) if the fundamental change is the result of a breach by the party invoking it either of an obligation under the treaty or of any other international obligation owed to any other party to the treaty.

Before the introduction of Art. 50 TEU, one could have debated whether exiting the EU may – in the absence of a right to withdraw – be considered a breach of international obligations owed to the remaining EU Member States under the EU Treaties. In that case, Art. 62(2)(b) VCLT would have barred the UK from invoking a fundamental change of circumstances with regard to mixed and *inter se* agreements where the EU's Member States are all parties. However, with Art. 50 TEU now explicitly providing for a right to EU withdrawal, neither of the two exceptions mentioned in Art. 62 VCLT apply.

There are, however, potentially two further exceptions to Art. 62 VCLT that are unwritten but could be relevant in the case of EU withdrawal.

The first is advocated for by Villiger. In his view, 'from the principle of good faith it follows [...] that a fundamental change of circumstances may not be invoked by a party which *by its own acts or omissions caused* the fundamental change of circumstances'[144]. At first sight, such an exception is not only supported by Art. 62 VCLT's drafting history: in their first reports, the International Law Commission's (ILC) Special Rapporteurs (SR) Fitzmaurice and Waldock even included an explicit exception to that effect.[145] This also appears reasonable considering the object and purpose of Art. 62 VCLT.

> For the sake of equity and justice, the concept of *rebus sic stantibus* codified in Art. 62 is intended to offer relief to *an innocent party* which *unexpectedly* faces intolerable burdens *imposed on it* by an unforeseeable fundamental change of circumstances.[146]

Art. 62 VCLT thus aims to protect the 'innocent party' by providing it the possibility of escaping burdensome treaty obligations. Where a party has, however, contributed to its situation, it shall not profit from the same right. Against this background, can a state withdrawing from the EU be considered 'innocent'? A Member State leaving the EU does so of its own free will and in the knowledge that this may affect the treaty relations created in the context of its membership. The change may thus have been unforeseen, in the sense that the state did not know at the time of concluding these agreements that it would someday withdraw from the EU. However, when

---

144 ME Villiger, 'Article 62' in ME Villiger (ed), *Commentary on the 1969 Vienna Convention on the Law of Treaties* (Martinus Nijhoff Publishers 2008) para 23 (emphasis added). But see Giegerich, 'Art. 62 VCLT' (n 127) para 84 who claims that Villiger 'goes too far in qualifying any failure to prevent the change as a breach of good faith' (Fn. 168).

145 ILC, 'Second Report on the Law of Treaties, by Gerald Fitzmaurice, Special Rapporteur' UN Doc A/CN.4/107, YBILC (1957) Vol. II 33: 'Even where the character of the change of circumstances itself is such as to conform to the foregoing conditions, it may not be invoked: [...] (iii) If the change of circumstances has been caused, brought about, or directly or proximately contributed to, by the act or omission of the party invoking it.' See ILC, 'Second Report on the Law of Treaties, by Sir Humphrey Waldock, Special Rapporteur' UN Doc. A/CN.4/156 and Add.1 – 3, YBILC (1963) Vol. II 80: '4. An essential change in the circumstances forming the basis of a treaty may not be invoked for the purpose of denouncing or withdrawing from a treaty if – (a) it was caused, or substantially contributed to, by the acts or omissions of the party invoking it [...]'.

146 Giegerich, 'Art. 62 VCLT' (n 127) para 46 (emphasis added).

II. Termination by Invocation: EU Withdrawal as a Change of Circumstances

deciding to leave the EU, the exit's consequences are neither unexpected nor imposed on the withdrawing state.[147]

In any event, reading an implicit good faith exception into Art. 62 VCLT is unconvincing when considered in the context of the explicit exception in Art. 62(2)(b) VCLT. During the VCLT's drafting process, the initially proposed exception based on *any* act or omission causing a change was replaced with an exception limited to *unlawful* acts or omissions. Why should Art. 62(2)(b) VCLT provide for an exception for unlawfully caused changes if Art. 62 implicitly (still) provides for an exception even in the case of the lawful conduct of a state? Art. 62(2)(b) would be unnecessary, if *any* self-inflicted change of circumstances would bar the responsible state from invoking Art. 62 VCLT. Thus, in general, a state withdrawing from the EU would not be excepted from invoking Art. 62 VCLT with regard to any international agreements affected by the exit. Interestingly in the case of Brexit, though, is the British delegation (of all) keeping to the original understanding of the exception even after it had been amended to today's version. The delegation expressed its understanding at the Vienna Conference on the ILC's VCLT draft that 'no State was entitled to invoke its own act or omissions as amounting to a fundamental change of circumstances giving rise to the operation of article 59 [now 62]'[148]. Thus, at least when holding the UK to its own understanding, it would not be able to invoke a fundamental change to free itself from treaty obligations post-Brexit.

The second implicit exception to Art. 62 VCLT is not only by far less controversial; it is also highly relevant for a large number of international agreements affected by an EU withdrawal and concerns the possibility of all treaty parties to invoke Art. 62 VCLT, not just that of the withdrawing state. This involves the relationship of Art. 62 VCLT to other grounds for termination. On this question, SR Fitzmaurice held in his Second Report on the Law of Treaties that

---

147 And indeed, discussion, *inter alia*, in the UK Parliament show that the UK was well aware of the fact that Brexit would not only terminate their EU membership, but also affect many of its treaty relations with non-EU states, see eg the expert hearing with Prof Alan Dashwood and Prof Panos Koutrakos (UK House of Commons, 'Oral Evidence' Costs and Benefits of EU Membership for the UK's Role in the World (8 December 2015) HC 545 27–28.).

148 UN Conference on the Law of Treaties, 'Official Records of the UN Conference on the Law of Treaties (Summary Records of the Plenary Meetings and of the Meetings of the Committee of the Whole)' First Session, 26 March – 24 May 1968 369.

[e]ven where the character of the change of circumstances itself is such as to conform to the foregoing conditions, it may not be invoked: (i) Unless the treaty is of indefinite duration, *and contains no provisions,* express or implied, *for its expiry or termination* on giving notice [...].[149]

Just as the previously discussed good faith exception, a subsidiarity exception had thus also been explicitly included in early drafts of the *clausula*; in contrast to the former, however, it continues to enjoy wide support in spite of its deletion from the article's text. Today, 'given the exceptional nature of the invocation of a fundamental change of circumstances' the view is still widely shared 'that Article 62 is subsidiary to Articles 54–60 and Articles 63 and 64'[150]. With Art. 62 VCLT being of a subsidiary character, however, it could only be invoked where the termination of an agreement is not possible 'in conformity with the provisions of the treaty'[151]. With most *inter se* and mixed agreements including an explicit right to denunciation[152], recourse to Art. 62 VCLT – for example to avoid long notification periods provided for in the agreement itself – is thus barred.

b. The Consequences of Invoking Art. 62 VCLT

In contrast to the first two, the third obstacle is not *prima facie* a legal one. Instead, it concerns the question of in whose interest it would be to invoke a fundamental change of circumstances at all. Art. 62 VCLT provides the parties to a treaty with three possibilities: to invoke the fundamental change as grounds for terminating a bilateral agreement, to invoke it to withdraw from a multilateral agreement or to invoke it in order to suspend the operation of an agreement. Thus, for an EU Member State (in the case of an *inter se* agreement) or a non-EU treaty party (in the case of a mixed agreement), the changed circumstances due to another state's EU withdrawal may cause a real dilemma: on the one hand, it is possible that these parties become overly burdened as a result of the other state's EU exit.

---

149 'SR Fitzmaurice Second Report' (n 145) 33 (emphasis added).
150 Villiger (n 144) para 28 (emphasis omitted). See also W Heintschel von Heinegg, 'Treaties, Fundamental Change of Circumstances' in R Wolfrum (ed), *The Max Planck Encyclopedia of Public International Law* (Oxford University Press 2012) para 29; Giegerich, 'Art. 62 VCLT' (n 127) para 110.
151 Cp Art. 54(a) VCLT.
152 See above Part I § 4 section I.A.

II. Termination by Invocation: EU Withdrawal as a Change of Circumstances

On the other hand, invoking Art. 62 VCLT would – most likely – not lead to the desired outcome.

Were a Member State to invoke another state's EU withdrawal as constituting a fundamental change of circumstances in the context of an *inter se* agreement, this would *prima facie* lead to *its* withdrawal from the agreement, while the former Member State would remain a party. Likewise in the context of mixed agreements, invocation by a non-EU treaty party would affect *that state's* status as a party to the agreement, not that of the former Member State. Most probably, however, the remaining Member States will want to continue their *inter se* agreements, albeit without the former Member State. Similarly, in the case of mixed agreements, it is probably in the non-EU treaty partner's interest to continue its treaty relations with the EU and its Member States, only its relationship with the *former* EU Member State being strained by the withdrawal. However, considering its wording, Art. 62 VCLT is not designed to expel a disruptive treaty party from an agreement. Instead, it is intended as a 'safety valve'[153], offering an unduly burdened state treaty termination as an alternative 'option [to] the unlawful breach of the defective treaty'[154].

Considering the (potential) interests involved, the question is if a more accommodating legal solution can be found. Unlike Art. 60 VCLT,[155] Art. 62 does not contain elaborate specifications on if (and if so, when) the invocation of a fundamental change of circumstances necessarily affects all parties to an international agreement or if (and if so, when) it affects the treaty relations of only a limited number of parties. However, Art. 62 VCLT was not designed this way from the outset. To the contrary, SR Fitzmaurice argued that '[t]he application of the principle *rebus sic stantibus* is subject to condi-

---

153 'Reports 18th Session' (n 126) 258.
154 MN Shaw and C Fournet, 'Article 62' in O Dörr and K Schmalenbach (eds), *Vienna Convention on the Law of Treaties: A Commentary* (2nd edn, Springer 2018) para 1.
155 Cp Art. 60(2) VCLT: 'A material breach of a multilateral treaty by one of the parties entitles: (a) the other parties by unanimous agreement to suspend the operation of the treaty in whole or in part or to terminate it either: (i) in the relations between themselves and the defaulting State; or (ii) as between all parties; (b) a party specifically affected by the breach to invoke it as a ground for suspending the operation of the treaty in whole or in part in the relations between itself and the defaulting State; (c) any party other than the defaulting State to invoke the breach as a ground for suspending the operation of the treaty in whole or in part with respect to itself if the treaty is of such a character that a material breach of its provisions by one party radically changes the position of every party with respect to the further performance of its obligations under the treaty.'

tions and limitations broadly analogous, *mutatis mutandis*, to those set out in article 19 above regarding the case of termination resulting from a fundamental breach of the treaty'[156]. Thus, just as with breaches, Fitzmaurice suggested '[l]imitations arising out of the type of treaty involved'[157] to the application of the *clausula*. Parties should not be able to invoke the *clausula* at all

> [i]n the case of law-making treaties (*traités-lois*), or of system or regime creating treaties [...], or of treaties involving undertakings to conform to certain standards and conditions, or of any other treaty where the juridical force of the obligation is inherent, and not dependent on a corresponding performance by the other parties.[158]

From such multilateral law-making agreements, Fitzmaurice differentiated a multilateral 'treaty which consists in a reciprocal grant or interchange between the parties of rights, benefits, concessions or advantages'[159]. With regard to the latter, the parties were to be able to invoke a fundamental change. However, 'in the case of an essential change of circumstances affecting one or more parties only', it should not 'be invoked as a ground for the termination of the treaty itself, but only as a ground for the withdrawal, or of the suspension of the obligations of such particular party or parties'[160]. Finally, in the case of multilateral treaties where the 'performance by any party is necessarily dependent on an equal or corresponding performance by all the other parties'[161], the 'withdrawal [...] of one party, on grounds of *rebus sic stantibus*, may justify the withdrawal of the other parties'[162].

Thus, Fitzmaurice differentiated among multilateral agreements that were bilaterally structured, those of an *erga omnes partes* and those of a law-making nature. Depending on the nature of the agreement, a fundamental change of circumstances could be invoked only concerning the treaty relation affected by the change with regard to all parties, or not at all. Waldock, following Fitzmaurice as Special Rapporteur, in his first dealing with the *clausula* dropped any reference to the structure or nature of an agreement. Instead, he introduced exceptions to the *clausula* based on the

---

156 'SR Fitzmaurice Second Report' (n 145) 32.
157 Ibid.
158 Ibid 31–32.
159 Ibid 31.
160 Ibid 32.
161 Ibid 31.
162 Ibid 32.

II. Termination by Invocation: EU Withdrawal as a Change of Circumstances

agreements' content, one of which (concerning boundary agreements) is still included in Art. 62 VCLT today. This is understandable, given that neither state practice nor scholarship on the *clausula* (then or now) seem to draw a distinction between the invocation of a fundamental change of circumstances with regard to bilateral as opposed to multilateral agreements. Furthermore, it is questionable whether (all) international agreements could be classified strictly according to Fitzmaurice's categories at all.[163]

Nonetheless, there are good reasons for a more differentiated solution for multilateral treaties. Feist demonstrates the potential of a fine-tuning of the consequences of invoking Art. 62 VCLT by adapting an example originally used by Fitzmaurice:[164] states A, B, C and D conclude a multilateral agreement granting their respective merchant fleets reciprocal access to their ports. State A loses parts of its territory and is subsequently a landlocked state. With ships sailing under state A's flag still entering the ports of the other state parties to the agreement, state B invokes a fundamental change of circumstances, claiming that the fair balance of rights and obligations is disturbed. This is, however, only the case in the relation between state A and B. State B's ships are not only still traveling to any other state party's ports, but its ships will most likely also have an interest in maintaining this access. Based on a traditional understanding, invocation of Art. 62 VCLT – assuming that the conditions are fulfilled – would lead to the complete withdrawal of state B from the multilateral agreement. The interests of state B – and arguably also state C and D – would, however, be better served, if state B were able to invoke a fundamental change *only* in relation to state A.

A possible textual point of reference for such an application of Art. 62 VCLT could be paragraph 1, lit. b. For a state to be able to invoke a fundamental change of circumstances, such a change must have 'radically [...] transform[ed] the extent of obligations still to be performed under the

---

163 Schmalenbach (n 55) para 14. Criticising the distinction between law-making agreements and contractual agreements, see in more detail A Pellet, 'Article 38' in A Zimmermann and others (eds), *The Statute of the International Court of Justice: A Commentary* (2nd edn, Oxford University Press 2012) para 205: 'In reality, all treaties are 'particular' in one sense – since they only apply to the parties – and all are 'law-making' in that they create rights and obligations – still for the parties – even if there is no doubt that some treaties have an influence far beyond the circle of the parties.' (Footnotes omitted).
164 C Feist, *Kündigung, Rücktritt und Suspendierung von multilateralen Verträgen* (Duncker & Humblot 2001) 179–180 adapting the example provided in 'SR Fitzmaurice Second Report' (n 145) 61.

treaty'. Where a change has, however, only affected the obligations to be performed with regard to a *certain* treaty party, the preconditions of Art. 62 VCLT are strictly speaking only fulfilled in their bilateral relations. The already restrictive nature of Art. 62 VCLT speaks in favour of this reading: 'so as to disparage as little as possible the rule *pacta sunt servanda*'[165]. Providing states the possibility of terminating their treaty relations only *vis-à-vis* a certain state in a multilateral agreement arguably better serves the interest of the affected state and the international community's interest in treaty stability. In the port agreement example, state B will most likely want to continue its treaty relations with all parties but state A. Allowing it to do so would encourage state B to remain a party to the agreement.

What would this mean with regard to EU withdrawal and international agreements?[166] With regard to *inter se* and multilateral mixed agreements, the answer is relatively straightforward. Firstly, it would be necessary to analyse whether these create reciprocal relations between the parties or obligations owed *erga omnes partes*. In the former case, any party – the EU, its Member States, the former Member State or a non-EU party – could terminate the agreement with respect only to this party in relation to which the obligations – as a consequence of the EU withdrawal – have become overly burdensome. In the case of bilateral mixed agreements, however, the answer is more complex: it depends on one's preconception of these agreements and how this is affected by a Member State's withdrawal. The first possibility is to view them as formally multilateral agreements, based on the number of parties. In that case, it would be possible to apply a nuanced withdrawal approach. The alternative is to treat them as bilateral agreements based on their structure, in which case termination of the agreement could be the only option.

c. *Lex mixity* again? Art. 62 VCLT and Bilateral Mixed Agreements

On the one hand, being *mixed*, the bilateral mixed agreements formally encompass 30+ parties – the EU, its Member States, the UK and at least one non-EU state. This is reflected in the number of ratifications as well as

---

165 Giegerich, 'Art. 62 VCLT' (n 127) para 101.
166 Assuming that Brexit – the UK's loss of EU membership, the diminishment of the EU's internal market, etc. – would, indeed, amount to a fundamental change of circumstances. On Art. 62 VCLT's conditions, see below Part I § 4 section II.B.2.

in – to some extent – the agreement's text.¹⁶⁷ As Schmalenbach describes it, a 'bilaterally structured' multilateral agreement, '[i]n principle [...] adds up to the same legal effect as when one State concludes a number of textually identical treaties separately with two or more States except that these treaties may evolve in different ways'¹⁶⁸. Accordingly, a bilateral mixed agreement such as CETA could, in essence, be viewed as 29 bilateral agreements (of the EU, the Member States, and the UK) with one non-EU State. As Advocate General Sharpston has argued, this individual party status of the Member States also extends to denunciation.

> Finally, where an international agreement is signed by both the European Union and its Member States, each Member State remains free under international law to terminate that agreement in accordance with whatever is the appropriate termination procedure under the agreement. Its participation in the agreement is, after all, as a sovereign State Party, not as a mere appendage of the European Union [...].¹⁶⁹

Following this understanding, allowing for a 'partial' invocation of Art. 62 VCLT would provide the parties to such mixed agreements with a potentially more interest-oriented solution: the non-EU state, for example, could invoke a fundamental change of circumstances only in the bilateral relation with the UK if it feels that the UK's loss of EU membership has overly burdened their relation.

On the other hand, in bilateral mixed agreements, the EU and its Member States are often described as forming a 'single contracting party'¹⁷⁰ or even expressly defined as the 'EU Party'¹⁷¹. Provisions such as the definition of the parties create not only a linguistic connectedness between the EU and its Member States; they also enable a joint and alternative performance of the treaty obligations *vis-à-vis* their non-EU treaty partner(s).¹⁷² In that sense, the 'EU Party' differs significantly from groups of non-EU states which have jointly concluded a mixed agreement with the EU and its Member States. Although these states – like the EU and its Member States – stand on one side of the agreement, they are generally completely inde-

---

167 See above Part I § 3 section III.C.2.
168 Schmalenbach (n 55) para 9.
169 ECJ, *FTA Singapore AG Sharpston* (n 48) [77].
170 ECJ, *Hermès AG Tesauro* (n 28) [15].
171 See eg Art. 1.1 CETA. On the definition clauses, see also above Part I § 4 section I.B.1.
172 On the term 'EU Party', see Schaefer and Odermatt (n 31). On the joint and alternative performance of mixed agreements, see J Heliskoski (n 29), chapter 4.

pendent from each other, unless they explicitly commit to act collectively, for example, within the institutional framework of an agreement.[173]

An illustrative example for this is the *Trade Agreement with Colombia and Peru*[174] (TA Colombia/Peru). Here, 'the European Union or its Member States or the European Union and its Member States within their respective areas of competence' form the 'EU Party'[175]. Art. 6(1) TA Colombia/Peru provides that '"Parties" means, on the one hand, the EU Party and, on the other hand, *each* signatory Andean Country'[176]. Thus, 'for the signatory Andean Countries the terms "another party" or "the other Parties" shall mean the EU Party'[177]. This ensures that

> [t]he provisions of this Agreement apply to the bilateral trade and economic relations between, on the one part, each individual signatory Andean Country and on the other part, the EU Party; but not to the trade and economic relations between individual Andean Countries.[178]

This impression of a single 'EU Party' and two individual non-EU parties is further emphasised in the context of denunciation. Art. 331(3) TA Colombia/Peru provides that

> [w]hen a signatory Andean Country withdraws from this Agreement, this Agreement shall continue to be in force between the EU Party and the other signatory Andean Countries. This Agreement shall be terminated in case of withdrawal by the EU Party.

While the non-EU states may individually withdraw from the agreement, the individual denunciation of a Member State is not provided for. Based on the wording of the denunciation provisions, read together with the 'EU

---

173 See eg Agreement establishing an Association between the European Union and its Member States, on the one hand, and Central America on the other (15 December 2012) OJ L346/3 [AA Central America], Art. 352(3): 'For the purposes of this Agreement, the Republics of the [Central America] Party agree and commit to act collectively in the following provisions: (a) in the decision making through the bodies referred to in Title II (Institutional Framework) of Part I of this Agreement [...]'.
174 Trade Agreement between the European Union and its Member States, of the one part, and Colombia and Peru, of the other part (21 December 2012) OJ L354/3 [TA Colombia/Peru].
175 Art. 6(1).
176 Emphasis added.
177 Art. 6(3).
178 Art. 7(1).

II. Termination by Invocation: EU Withdrawal as a Change of Circumstances

Party' definition, any notification of denunciation by *one* member of the 'EU Party' would have to be counted for and against the whole 'EU Party'. Thus, in agreements such as the TA Colombia/Peru, it is questionable whether the individual EU Member States are really still in a position to denounce these agreements individually, at least – as suggested by AG Sharpston – 'in accordance with whatever is the appropriate termination procedure *under the agreement*'[179].[180]

However, based on an understanding of a single 'EU Party', invocation of Art. 62 VCLT by a non-EU party *vis-à-vis only one* Member State is inconceivable. Schmalenbach's description of a bilaterally structured but formally multilateral agreement would still fit where the agreement is concluded with two or more non-EU states: *one* EU Party has concluded *two* bilateral agreements, one with Colombia and one with Peru, both encompassed in one instrument. However, even when applying a narrow reading of Art. 62 VCLT allowing for partial withdrawal, withdrawal by Colombia or Peru would take effect with regard to the *whole* EU Party, that is the EU *and* all Member States. In contrast, with the EU and its Member States forming one EU Party, a bilateral mixed agreement concluded with *one* non-EU state, such as the CETA Canada, would no longer fall under Schmalenbach's description.[181] Instead, it would have to be treated as a bilateral agreement, the consequence of invoking Art. 62 VCLT thus being the termination of the agreement.

Whether or not withdrawal *vis-à-vis only* the UK following Brexit is a possibility then depends on how one considers Brexit to affect the 'EU Party'. Would the UK following Brexit still have to be counted as part of the 'EU Party' for the purpose of these agreements? That is, at least, how the treaty parties entered into the agreement and how the agreements continue

---

179 ECJ, *FTA Singapore AG Sharpston* (n 48) [77] (emphasis added).
180 On this question and the denunciation provisions in the EU's mixed bilateral trade agreements, see Schaefer and Odermatt (n 31) 147–149.
181 It is unclear how Schmalenbach views the EU's bilaterally structured mixed agreements. She describes an agreement as 'bilaterally structured if it is concluded between *one or more* States on one side and *two or more* States on the other side' and names the Cotonou Partnership Agreement, an agreement between a group of African, Caribbean and Pacific states, on the one side, and the EU and its Member States, on the other side, as an example (Schmalenbach (n 55) para 9 and fn. 24, emphasis omitted, emphasis in italics added). Depending on the understanding, this could be an example of an agreement between *one* party (the EU Party) and several states on the other side, or an agreement between the EU and several states, on the one side, and several non-EU states, on the other side.

to list the UK.[182] Or would it step outside the EU bloc, essentially trilateralising the bilaterally structured mixed agreements? With the Member States becoming full parties to these agreements, thus being bound by all rights and obligations,[183] this would be possible. If, however, as Wessel writes 'the changing status of the UK would change the nature of a bilateral agreement to a multilateral agreement'[184], there would again exist a separable bilateral relation between the UK and another non-EU state that the latter could terminate – independently of the mixed agreement with the EU.

2. The Substantive Conditions of Art. 62 VCLT: EU Withdrawal as a Fundamental Change of Circumstances?

Based on the above considerations, a state contemplating the invocation of Art. 62 VCLT following a (or its) withdrawal from the EU would be well advised to first consider the applicability of the article and its consequences. Where invocation of Art. 62 VCLT is possible and desired, its substantive requirements come into play. Stating the obvious, the most basic requirement for invoking Art. 62 VCLT is, of course, the occurrence of a change of circumstances. Such a change undoubtedly occurs for the international agreements concluded by a state within the context of membership in the EU when this state leaves the EU.[185] Not only does the state lose a characteristic – EU membership – to which many of these agreements expressly refer; in many cases, the territorial scope of application of the agreements is also affected. However, to be invokable as a ground for denouncing an international agreement, the change must fulfil several further criteria.

Art. 62(1) VCLT further qualifies the change: it must pertain to circumstances that existed at the time of conclusion, be unforeseen and be fundamental in nature. A change is unforeseen when it is not anticipated by the parties, even though it may have been foreseeable.[186] Whether or not a change can be deemed fundamental, in turn, seems to correlate with the additional conditions of Art. 62(1)(a) and (b) VCLT. These provide that the circumstances which have changed 'constituted an essential basis of the consent of the parties' and that 'the effect of the change is radically

---

182 See eg the preamble in CETA.
183 See above Part I § 3 section III.C.2.
184 Wessel (n 44), 122.
185 See in detail above Part I § 4 section I.B.
186 Giegerich, 'Art. 62 VCLT' (n 127) para 58.

II. Termination by Invocation: EU Withdrawal as a Change of Circumstances

to transform the extent of obligations still to be performed'. In the eyes of Giegerich, these additional requirements inform the decision on the magnitude of the change, for

> [o]ne can indeed scarcely conceive of any change which firstly affects circumstances whose existence formed an essential basis of the consent of the parties to be bound by the treaty and secondly radically transforms the extent of the remaining treaty obligations but is still not fundamental.[187]

For certain circumstances to have formed the essential basis of the parties' intent, they 'must have been the determining factor for all the parties to enter the treaty, not just the motive or inducement of one or a few of them'[188]. Such an intention of the parties is determined objectively by applying the rules of interpretation as per Arts. 31–33 VCLT. The condition of a radical transformation of obligations, in turn, has been described by the International Court of Justice (ICJ) as an increase in 'the burden of the obligations to be executed to the extent of rendering the performance something essentially different from that originally undertaken'[189]. Performance must, thus, not be impossible, but in burdening the party invoking Art. 62 VCLT must exceed a *de minimis* threshold.[190] Notably, however, this is the case where the change has led to the frustration of an agreement's object and purpose, that is in the case of an impossibility as regards its objective.[191]

At least as regards the *inter se* and bilateral mixed trade agreements, the UK's EU membership is undoubtedly a circumstance that existed upon conclusion of these agreements. While not as visible in their design and text, the same is true for multilateral mixed agreements that were concluded by the UK *after* accession to the EU.[192] Especially where the EU and its

---

187 Ibid para 49.
188 Ibid para 59 (emphasis omitted).
189 ICJ, *Fisheries Jurisdiction (Germany v Iceland) (Jurisdiction)* (n 131) [43].
190 Giegerich, 'Art. 62 VCLT' (n 127) paras 62, 66.
191 See Waldock's draft article 22 on a fundamental change of circumstances whose para. 2 lit. (c) read: 'the effect of the change in that fact or state of facts is such as – (i) in substance to frustrate the further realization of the object and purpose of the treaty; or (ii) to render the performance of the obligations contained in the treaty something essentially different from what was originally undertaken.' ('SR Waldock Second Report' (n 145) 79). See also Giegerich, 'Art. 62 VCLT' (n 127) para 65.
192 Where the UK concluded multilateral agreements and the EU later acceded to that agreement, the circumstance 'EU membership' did not exist upon conclusion of the agreement.

Member States jointly participate in the negotiations and the conclusion of these agreements, the fact that the UK was an EU Member State at that time is also abundantly clear to all non-EU treaty parties. While all treaty parties were thus aware of the same circumstances upon conclusion of the agreements, the change to them was not foreseen. Since the inclusion of Art. 50 TEU, the withdrawal of a Member State may have increasingly become foreseeable. However, the actual withdrawal of the UK could not have been foreseen by any of the concerned treaty parties. An exception is the international agreements concluded after the Brexit referendum in June 2016 or latest after the UK's Art. 50 notification. Here, not only the EU and its Member States but also non-EU states will, with all likelihood, have known of the situation of a Member State leaving the EU and could have provided for this change in the agreements.

But for all agreements prior to 2016/2017, the question is, firstly, whether the UK's loss of EU membership can be considered a *fundamental* change and, relatedly, whether the UK's EU membership lies at the heart of the parties' consent. Secondly, does the UK's EU withdrawal radically change the treaty obligations?

In the case of mixed agreements, one could argue that EU membership was essential at least for the EU and its Member States so as to form one 'team'[193], indicators of which being the definition of the parties in bilateral mixed agreements and the disconnection clauses in multilateral mixed agreements.[194] For the non-EU treaty partners, the answer is perhaps less straightforward: on the one hand, the EU membership of all (at the time of conclusion) 28 European states may have been an essential factor for a non-EU state intending to establish, for example, trade relations with the EU as an economic bloc. On the other hand, in multilateral agreements such as UNCLOS, EU membership as a determining factor for the parties' consent can almost certainly be negated. While these agreements accommodate for joint participation by the EU and its Member States, they do not build on it. Even in *inter se* agreements, the question of whether membership in the EU constitutes an essential basis is by no means answered by reference to their restrictive accession criteria. Member States certainly conclude these agreements *knowing* that all parties are EU Member States, but whether

---

193 Wessel (n 44), 119.
194 On disconnection clauses, J Odermatt (n 10) 82–87.

II. Termination by Invocation: EU Withdrawal as a Change of Circumstances

this was *essential* to them would have to be established.[195] Judging solely from the text of the agreements, this seems less likely in the case of the EUI Convention, more probable in the case of the ES Convention and quite likely in the case of the EDF Agreement.[196]

Similar considerations can be made with respect to the effect of a loss of EU membership on the contractual obligations arising from *inter se* and mixed agreements. Without doubt, following Brexit, the UK and all participating EU Member States continue to be able to pay their financial contributions to the European University Institute, the size of which is unaffected by the change from a purely *inter se* agreement to an agreement including a non-EU state.[197] Even so, Brexit may nevertheless frustrate an agreement's purpose. Debatable is, for instance, whether participation of the UK as a non-EU state would really frustrate the ES Convention's stated purpose of '[educating] together children of the staff of the European Com-

---

195 An interesting case in this regard would have been the Agreement on a Unified Patent Court (20 June 2013) OJ C175/1 [UPC Agreement]. The UK ratified this *inter se* agreement before Brexit but subsequently withdrew its ratification, before the agreement entered into force. The UPC Agreement in its current form was drawn up following an opinion by the ECJ declaring its predecessor – the Draft Agreement Creating a Unified Patent Litigation System – incompatible with the EU Treaties (ECJ, Opinion 1/09 *Creation of a Unified Patent Litigation System* [2011] ECLI:EU:C:2011:123). The first draft agreement had envisaged participation by all states parties to the Convention on the Grant of European Patents (adopted 5 October 1973, entered into force 7 October 1977) 1065 UNTS 199 [Patent Convention], thus being open to non-EU states. Following the ECJ's Opinion, the UPC Agreement is restricted to EU Member States. The shift to an *inter se* agreement was, in the eyes of the Commission, necessary to meet the Court's concerns with the first draft agreement. Here, the fact that all parties are EU Member States would, thus, arguably have to be considered essential to the consent of the parties, taking into consideration the agreement's drafting history (cp Art. 32 VCLT). On the UPC Agreement and Brexit, see T Jaeger, 'Reset and Go: The Unitary Patent System post-Brexit' (2017) 3 International Review of Intellectual Property and Competition Law 254.
196 See above Part I § 4 section I.B.3.
197 Cp Art. 19 EUI Convention which determines that '[t]he financial contributions of the Contracting States to cover the expenditure provided for in the Institute's budget shall be determined on the following scale', subsequently listing all parties and the respective fixed percentage to be borne. Likewise, the financing of the European Schools would not change as a result of Brexit. Cp Art. 25 ES Convention: 'The budget of the Schools shall be financed by: 1. contributions from the Member States through the continuing payment of the remuneration for seconded or assigned teaching staff and, where appropriate, a financial contribution decided on by the Board of Governors acting unanimously [...]'.

munities'[198], especially as Art. 1 explicitly allows children whose parents are not EU staff to attend European Schools. It is also debatable whether or not the purpose of promoting reciprocal trade relations between a non-EU state and the EU and its Member States may be frustrated by the UK leaving the EU. At the same time, rollover agreements concluded by the UK and non-EU treaty partners that simply copy and paste the content of the agreement with the EU are testimony to the fact that the UK – and the non-EU treaty partner – are able and willing to continue to comply with the obligations included in these agreements.[199] In that case, performance of the agreement does not appear overburdensome.

III. Brexit and its (Practical) Effects

The VCLT provides parties to an international agreement with two possibilities to terminate their status: 'as a result of the application of the provisions of the treaty or the present Convention'[200]. In the sweeping terms claimed by the EU and the UK, neither of these options apply in the case of Brexit. The mixed and *inter se* agreements do not explicitly provide for the loss of a Member State's party status upon withdrawal from the EU nor can the fact that the UK concluded these agreements as a Member State be understood as an implicit resolutory condition. A blanket reference to Art. 62 VCLT as a ground for the UK's loss of party status neither does justice to the provision's narrow wording and its exceptional character nor does it take into account the procedural obstacles that an invocation of Art. 62 VCLT would entail.

The EU and the UK's 'out means out' approach in the case of Brexit pertains to two categories of international agreements: Member States' *inter se* agreements and the bilateral mixed agreements concluded by the EU and its Member States with one or more non-EU states. It is true that the treaty design and wording of both of these categories of agreements often establish a close connection between the Member States' status as parties to these agreements and their capacity as EU Member States. It thus suggests itself to seek the reason for the former in the latter. However, treaty law simply does not justify such a result: a state does not simply cease to be a

---

198 Art. 1 ES Convention.
199 On the UK's rollover practice, see above § 1 section II.D.
200 Art. 42(2) VCLT.

III. Brexit and its (Practical) Effects

party to an international agreement because of how the parties are defined or because it falls outside the territorial scope of application.

That is not to say that withdrawal of a Member State from the EU does not have an effect on these international agreements. Where the parties of an international agreement are defined as EU Member States, one can argue that the agreements no longer apply to a former Member State *ratione personae*. Likewise, the territorial scope of application of an agreement linked to the application of the TEU and the TFEU will, following withdrawal from the EU, no longer cover the former Member State *ratione loci*. It would be wrong, however, to mistake an agreement's application to a state with its binding force on that state. But what would be the consequence of a state being party to an international agreement but no longer being covered by its substantive provisions? Where the consent of all parties is required, as for example in case of accessions or treaty amendments, would this still include the UK? Could the UK then – no longer being a Member State – effectively hold a veto in the EU's external actions?

From the perspective of treaty law, withdrawal from the EU may render an international agreement inapplicable – at least in relation to the withdrawing state – or to some extent even dysfunctional. It does not, however, mean that the withdrawing state ceases to be a party. Thus, with regard to Brexit many authors referred to the need for the EU and the UK to enter into negotiations with their treaty partners. Depending on the respective author's opinion on the effect of Brexit on international agreements, proposals ranged from suggesting negotiations with the aim of treaty termination to negotiations with the aim of treaty adaption to negotiations as required under Art. 62 VCLT.[201] The fact is, however, that neither the EU nor the UK negotiated with non-EU treaty partners on the agreement's termination or adaption. Instead, they assumed an *ipso facto* termination of *inter se* and bilateral mixed agreements for the UK.

---

201 See eg Wessel (n 44), 122; Silvereke (n 143), 335–336; Kaddous and Touré (n 44) 283–284. For the House of Common's hearing, Prof Alan Dashwood summarised the UK's position, using the example of the Free Trade Agreement with Korea, as follows: 'I don't believe that the UK could retain the rights and obligations that apply to it under the agreement. We would have to renegotiate and, of course, we would be renegotiating from a much less favourable position because we wouldn't be able to offer the South Koreans access to the internal market, which is the quid pro quo for the extent to which they were willing to open up their market. I think we would find that difficult, and we would probably be in a somewhat less favourable position.' (see 'UK House of Commons 2015' (n 147) 28).

Concluding Remarks: Brexit and Treaty Law – Match or Misfit?

§ 2 began with a widely shared and well-founded proposition: that the EU – despite any peculiarities – for the purposes of international law can (still) be categorised as an international organisation. This is not to say that different categorisations may not prove more fitting in other settings. While one *can* consider the EU's internal rule-making from the perspective of international institutional law, other approaches *may* be more useful. However, where the EU and its Member States enter into exchange with the international community or resort to traditional legal instruments under international law, such as the conclusion of international agreements, *sui generis* labelling is neither helpful nor appropriate: '[h]ow the EU fits within the wider system of international law [...] is legally relevant when the EU acts on the plane of international law'[1].

Attaching a label to the EU is one thing: by and large the EU at least does not reject its classification as an international organisation. However, having its conduct judged based on the consequences that this label entails is quite another thing. While the EU may exhibit the typical characteristics of an international organisation, one can question the extent to which it accepts and acts according to the rules that international law imposes on such an international legal subject. An often-cited yet legally relatively trivial example of this is the European Court of Justice's reference to rules of the 1969 *Vienna Convention on the Law of Treaties* when dealing with international agreements between non-Member States and the EU.[2] As the 1969 VCLT and 1986 *Vienna Convention on the Law of Treaties between States and International Organization and between Organizations* are nearly identical, the consequences are at most marginal. In contrast far more consequential, is the clear deviation from the rules on and practice by international organisations in case of memerbship withdrawal as witnessed in the EU's and UK's Brexit practice.

---

1 J Odermatt, *International Law and the European Union* (Cambridge University Press 2021) 9.
2 See in detail, ibid 63–66 and PJ Kuijper, 'The European Courts and the Law of Treaties: The Continuing Story' in E Cannizzaro (ed), *The Law of Treaties Beyond the Vienna Convention* (Oxford University Press 2011).

Part I: Brexit and the Law of Treaties

§ 3 and § 4 considered the effect of EU withdrawal on international agreements concluded by the EU and its Member States from the perspective of international institutional and treaty law. Art. 70 VCLT formed the starting point, although its appropriateness may well be doubted. How useful is a provision dealing with the consequence of withdrawal from one agreement – in this case, the TEU/TFEU – when looking into effects on other international agreements? Primarily, if not exclusively, Art. 70 VCLT and the principles of international law expressed therein focus on the consequences of an agreement being terminated or withdrawn from for the treaty parties. It is for this reason that reference to Art. 70 VCLT – though not tailored to the situation of interrelated agreements – is appropriate with regard to conventions. Here, a group of treaty parties to an international organisation's founding treaty is typically identical with those of the conventions concluded in the context of membership in that organisation.

In the context of their EU membership, EU Member States conclude *inter se* agreements. In all EU treaty practice, these agreements are the most comparable to those found in the context of other international organisations. Conventions concluded under the auspices of other international organisations and EU *inter se* agreements are both, subject-wise, generally linked to the aim and functioning of the respective organisation. Both create a layer of rights and obligations beyond but not separate from the organisations' founding treaties. Thus, EU Member States resort to a classic organisational method by opting for an *inter se* agreement to set common rules or establish common institutions.

Accordingly, what is applicable to the conventions of other international organisations should also apply to *inter se* agreements. EU Member States are able to determine the fate of their *inter se* agreements in case of EU withdrawal through provisions to that effect in the TEU and TFEU. Additionally, they could include a respective provision in the *inter se* agreements themselves that establishes loss of EU membership as a resolutory condition. Where neither is done, however, a withdrawing state remains a party to the *inter se* agreements. A change to the constellation of treaty parties may only be brought about by the valid invocation – by one or several of the *inter se* agreement's parties – of a right to withdraw. This did not take place in the case of the UK's withdrawal from the EU, but it is still understood that the UK ceased being a party to all *inter se* agreements. The practice of other international organisations shows that international treaty law – and specifically Art. 70 VCLT – is capable of engaging with the broader consequences of a party exiting an international organisation. It was, however, not followed in the case of Brexit.

With regard to the EU's agreements concluded with non-EU states, with or without co-conclusion by its Member States, only considering Art. 70 VCLT as a starting point is unsatisfactory. Art. 70 VCLT does not and cannot truly provide for situations where states – or other subjects of international law – beyond the parties to the agreement being denounced are affected by said denunciation. It is, of course, nevertheless possible to broadly resort to treaty law. The principles of consent and *res inter alios acta* would then lead to the conclusion that – contrary to Brexit practice – a withdrawing EU Member State does *not* automatically cease to be a party to bilateral mixed agreements. Yet the question remains – is it actually satisfactory, appropriate or even possible to treat Brexit (solely) through the lens of treaty law? While the EU 'ticks all the boxes'[3] of what defines an international organisation, its treaty practice with non-EU states does not. A general comparison to the practice of other international organisations becomes difficult, if not futile.

Firstly, the EU's external agreements differ from international agreements concluded by other international organisations as regards the constellation of how they are concluded. Mixity is a phenomenon strictly limited to the EU context. No other international organisation co-concludes international agreements with its Member States. Additionally, the construction of Art. 216 TFEU, binding Member States via EU law to EU-only agreements, is unique. Secondly, while the international agreements of international organisations generally differ content-wise from those concluded by states, this is not the case for many of the EU's external international agreements concluded with or without its Member States: 'in the case of a supranational organisation – which has taken on certain functions of the member states, mostly to the exclusion of the latter [...]' international agreements will '*in substance* be similar to state treaties'[4]. Thirdly, and related to the previous points, many EU-only and (bilateral) mixed agreements feature a reference to the territory of the EU's Member States, a characteristic rarely seen in the treaty practice of international organisation.

---

3 B De Witte, 'EU Law: Is it International Law?' in C Barnard and S Peers (eds), *European Union Law* (3rd edn, Oxford University Press 2020) 179.
4 CM Brölmann, *The Institutional Veil in Public International Law: International Organisations and the Law of Treaties* (Hart Publishing 2007) 131 (footnote omitted, emphasis in the original).

The law of treaties is premised on an important distinction. States possess full competence to enter into binding agreements on a range of issues, whereas international organizations exercise only limited powers, and may only enter into agreements in a limited capacity such as headquarter agreements. However, the agreements to which the EU is a party fall more in the first category, that is, its commitments are much more 'state-like' in nature. This practice calls into question the logic of the dichotomy between states and international organizations.[5]

In the context of states, however, one must differentiate between territorial changes that treaty law, as codified in the VCLT, is capable of dealing with and changes that fall outside of its scope. In general, changes to a state's territory may move an agreement's frontier as per Art. 29 VCLT or – in extraordinary circumstances – allow for treaty denunciation in accordance with Art. 62 VCLT. These provisions, however, 'shall not prejudice any question that may arise in regard to a treaty from a succession of States'[6]. Thus, situations of uniting and separation leading to the creation of a new state are governed not by the VCLT, but the law of state succession in respect of international agreements. This domain of international law acknowledges that the separations of states can have external repercussions and attempts to strike a balance between the interests of the states involved and the treaty partners affected. In so doing, might the law of succession be better suited to examine a case of disintegration from the EU?

---

5 J Odermatt (n 1) 62.
6 Cp Art. 73 VCLT: 'The provisions of the present Convention shall not prejudice any question that may arise in regard to a treaty from a succession of States or from the international responsibility of a State or from the outbreak of hostilities between States.' Particularly noteworthy is the VCLT-IO's equivalent. According to Art. 74(2) VCLT-IO, '[t]he provisions of the present Convention shall not prejudice any question that may arise in regard to a treaty [...] *from the termination of participation by a State in the membership of the organization*.' (Emphasis added).

Part II: Brexit and the Law of Succession

Part I has shown that the rules governing withdrawal from an international organisation inadequately capture the consequences of EU withdrawal on the treaty relations of the EU and its Member States. The sheer number of agreements affected by a Member State's withdrawal could be accepted as 'collateral damage' of disintegration. However, it is their quality that really raises questions regarding the fate of the EU's international agreements in light of other international organisations' practice. The quality of the agreements, in turn, results from the character of the EU as such. While it can be viewed as an international organisation, there are simply no other international organisations that conclude agreements comparable to those concluded by the EU (together with its Member States). Withdrawal from the EU puts into question continued effects on trade, aviation and development aid agreements – agreements generally concluded by states. Yet, where states conclude such agreements, their fate in the case of withdrawal of a state's constituent part is not governed by general treaty law. Instead, the effect of a separation of part of a state's territory on international agreements is addressed by the *Vienna Convention on Succession of States in Respect of Treaties*[1] (VCSSRT).

Based on the proposition that the EU – at least in its treaty-making – may be more 'state-like'[2] and that EU withdrawal could be more comparable to a state's territorial separation than a withdrawal from an organisation, the law of succession could present an alternative legal framework for determining the fate of international agreements post-EU exit. This part explores application of the VCSSRT to Brexit and more generally to the case of a Member State exiting the EU. While a direct application of the rules on state succession fails due to the EU's lack of statehood, a comparison between the EU and unions of states paves the way for an analogous approach (§ 5). Such an analogy is justified given the similarities

---

1 Vienna Convention on Succession of States in Respect of Treaties (adopted 23 August 1978, entered into force 6 November 1996) 1946 UNTS 3 [VCSSRT].
2 J Odermatt, *International Law and the European Union* (Cambridge University Press 2021) 62.

between the EU and unions of states and the VCSSRT's drafting history (§ 6), and it also offers an alternative perspective on actual treaty practice surrounding Brexit (§ 7).

§ 5 EU Withdrawal and Succession: The Case for an Analogy

The previous chapters examined EU withdrawal and its effect on international agreements through the lens of international treaty law. In so doing, the EU is primarily considered as an international organisation and a Member State's exit as a withdrawal therefrom. The aim of this chapter is to refocus on the character of the EU but to change the perspective: if the rules generally applied to international organisations do not provide a satisfactory answer, perhaps the law of state succession can provide an alternative legal framework. To do so, either it would have to be directly applicable to the EU or to the situation of a Member State exiting the EU, or its rules would have to be transferred through methods of legal reasoning (I.). The obvious approach in this regard – even if sometimes questioned in the public international law context – is an argument by analogy (II.). If leaving the EU is, indeed, comparable to a separation (III.), the provision of the *Vienna Convention on Succession of States in Respect of Treaties*[1] (VCSSRT) on separation may also inform the debate on the case of Brexit (IV.).

I. The Law of Succession: An Alternative Framework?

Taking recourse to the law of succession as an alternative framework under which to consider the effect of EU withdrawal on international agreements requires two preliminary considerations. Of course, the rules established therein must substance-wise indeed present an alternative. This is undoubtedly the case: the International Law Commission (ILC) specifically did not address any aspects of the effect of succession on international agreements in the *Vienna Convention on the Law of Treaties*[2] (VCLT), knowing that these questions would be addressed in a separate project. How the rules on succession in respect of international agreements would specifically play out when applied to Brexit will be addressed in detail

---

1 Vienna Convention on Succession of States in Respect of Treaties (adopted 23 August 1978, entered into force 6 November 1996) 1946 UNTS 3 [VCSSRT].
2 Vienna Convention on the Law of Treaties (adopted 23 May 1969, entered into force 27 January 1980) 1155 UNTS 331 [VCLT].

below. As a preliminary step, however, the law of succession must also be applicable to the facts under consideration.

On a formal level, the articles of an international agreement such as the VCSSRT are *prima facie* applicable to those subjects of international law who have become a party to them. To date, the VCSSRT, however, merely counts 23 state parties, with Croatia, Cyprus, Czechia, Estonia and Slovakia being the only EU Member States to have ratified the Convention.[3] Moreover, with the VCSSRT being open only to states, the EU itself cannot become a party.[4] At the same time, the VCSSRT is the result of a codification project by the ILC. It is thus conceivable that at least some of its provisions are of a customary law nature and as such bind the EU, its Member States and any non-EU treaty partner.

On a substantive level, however, the VCSSRT's provisions – even when applied as a matter of customary law – must also be applicable to the situation under consideration, here the withdrawal of a Member State from the EU. In many aspects, EU withdrawal – or specifically Brexit – could be compared to a situation dealt with in the VCSSRT, namely the separation of territory (A.). Crucially, however, the VCSSRT only regulates those instances of separation where the predecessor entity is a state, something that cannot (yet) be said of the EU (B.). There are, however, two further possibilities of applying the rules on succession in respect of international agreements to the situation of EU withdrawal (C.): if the customary law of succession is broader than what is codified in the VCSSRT, extending to subjects of international law other than states; or if the rules established for states are transferred to the situation of the EU by means of legal reasoning.

---

3 The remaining parties are Bosnia and Herzegovina, Brazil, Dominica, Ecuador, Egypt, Ethiopia, Iraq, Liberia, Montenegro, Morocco, North Macedonia, Republic of Moldova, Serbia, Seychelles, St. Vincent and the Grenadines, Tunisia, Ukraine (United Nations Treaty Collection, 'Vienna Convention on Succession of States in Respect of Treaties' (*Chapter XXIII*, 18.12.2022) <https://treaties.un.org/pages/ViewDetails.aspx?src=IND&mtdsg_no=XXIII-2&chapter=23&clang=_en>).
4 Cp Art. 48 VCSSRT: 'The present Convention shall remain open for accession by *any State*. The instruments of accession shall be deposited with the Secretary-General of the United Nations.' (Emphasis added).

I. The Law of Succession: An Alternative Framework?

A. Brexit as Separation?

When states leave an international organisation, the terminology generally employed is that of withdrawal: the state withdraws from an international organisation. Likewise, the UK is usually referred to as having 'withdrawn'[5] from the EU. By employing said terminology, however, the user does not limit herself to a factual description. Rather, the term 'withdrawal' linguistically places the Brexit process within the overall context of treaty termination as provided for in Art. 42 ff. VCLT.[6] Leaving the EU is thus characterised as the one-sided termination of a multilateral agreement the consequences of which are either regulated by the agreement itself or Art. 70 VCLT. Although technically correct, the limited usefulness of such a classification has been demonstrated in *Part I*.[7]

In writing on the possibility of a Member State leaving the EU, Friel – among others – offered an alternative framing, repeatedly referring to 'secession from the European Union'[8]. In explaining his choice of terminology, he points to the ordinary meaning given to 'withdrawal' and 'secession'.

> While the term often used with respect to departure from the Union is 'withdrawal', this Article uses the term 'secession.' The difference is important: 'Withdrawal' simply means 'the act of retreating from a place, position, or situation.' *See* BLACK'S LAW DICTIONARY 1594 (7th ed. 1999) (defining 'withdrawal'). 'Secession,' on the other hand, has particular connotations: 'the process or act of withdrawing, esp. from a religious or political association.' *See id.* at 1353 (defining 'secession').[9]

Based hereon, Friel argues that 'the term "withdrawal" does not accurately reflect the seriousness or difficulty that the action [of leaving the EU] would involve' and thus finds 'secession' to be preferable.[10]

---

5 See only the title of the Agreement on the Withdrawal of the United Kingdom of Great Britain and Northern Ireland from the European Union and the European Atomic Energy Community (12 November 2019) OJ C384 I/1 [UK-EU WA].
6 The provisions on treaty termination in the VCLT refer to 'termination' in the case of a bilateral agreement and 'withdrawal' in case of a multilateral agreement, see eg Art. 70 VCLT.
7 For a summary of the findings, see above Part I Concluding Remarks.
8 RJ Friel, 'Secession from the European Union: Checking Out of the Proverbial "Cockroach Motel"' (2003) 27(2) *Fordham International Law Journal* 590.
9 Ibid 592–593, fn. 7.
10 Ibid, fn. 7.

§ 5 EU Withdrawal and Succession: The Case for an Analogy

Considering the sheer length of the Brexit process and the complexity of the EU-UK negotiations, Friel's factual assessment was certainly correct. Brexit is not comparable to any case of withdrawal from an international organisation. As regards the seriousness of the consequences for the UK legal order, this was explicitly acknowledged by the UK Supreme Court. In its *Miller* case, the Court held that while treaty withdrawal 'in normal circumstances'[11] does not require parliamentary approval, such is necessary for exiting the EU.[12] The Court based its finding on the nature of the EU Treaties as 'unique in their legislative and constitutional implications', with the consequence that

> [a]lthough article 50 operates on the plane of international law, it is common ground that, because the EU Treaties apply as part of UK law, our domestic law will change [...], and rights enjoyed by UK residents granted through EU law will be affected.[13]

The difficulty of 'disentangling legal orders'[14] not only affects the UK's national legal order – it also becomes apparent in the question of the effect of Brexit on international agreements. The term 'withdrawal' insinuates the retreat from *one* international agreement or organisation, here the EU Treaties. However, Brexit has had practical consequences for hundreds of international agreements.

Friel may thus be right in that 'withdrawal' is not a fitting term. Moreover, 'secession' does appear like a promising alternative. It, too, is

---

11 UK Supreme Court *R (on the Application of Miller and Another) v Secretary of State for Exiting the European Union* [2017] UKSC 5, [30].
12 The UK government and the dissenting judges argued that the EU Treaties are international agreements from the viewpoint of UK law and withdrawal thus falls within the royal prerogative. See J Odermatt, 232–235 who takes these diverging views as a sign of different understandings of the EU's legal identity. On the *Miller* case and the nature of the EU legal order, see also J Crawford, 'The Current Political Discourse Concerning International Law' (2018) 81(1) *The Modern Law Review* 1, 15–16 ('There is considerable tension within the EU legal order between the underlying international law framework of the treaties, and the internal law of the EU, which is not international law in any straightforward sense. But when negotiating within the EU for a situation outside it, the hybrid character of the EU is very much in issue.')
13 UK Supreme Court, *Miller* (n 11) [69].
14 Cp J Odermatt, 'Brexit and International Law: Disentangling Legal Orders' (2017) 31 *Emory International Law Review Recent Developments* 1051. See already on the difficulty of counting the agreements affected by Brexit, J Larik, 'Brexit and the Transatlantic Trouble of Counting Treaties' (*EJIL:Talk!*, 6.12.2017) <https://www.ejiltalk.org/brexit-and-the-transatlantic-trouble-of-counting-treaties/>.

I. The Law of Succession: An Alternative Framework?

concerned with the unilateral detachment from a larger entity. Furthermore, in cases of secession, the law of succession is specifically designed to address the legal questions arising from the need of disentanglement. In doing so, the rules on succession with respect to international agreements explicitly recognise the effect that the disintegration process of one treaty party has on the agreement and the treaty partners. However, the term 'secession' also bears a connotation that reveals the difficulty of using it to refer to an exit from the EU. For, as Friel admits, '[t]he use of secession [...] implies that the Union is a State'[15]. Indeed, in international law, the term secession is defined as 'the unilateral withdrawal *from a State* of a constituent part, with its territory and its population'[16].

Where parts of a state unilaterally separate, the VCSSRT deals specifically with the effects on international agreements.[17] While its text does not itself refer to 'secession',[18] Art. 34 VCSSRT addresses the situation 'when a part or parts of the territory of a State separate to form one or more States, whether or not the predecessor State continues to exist'[19].[20] Thus, the term 'secession' presupposes the existence of a state and, furthermore, the VCSSRT is limited to dealing with the legal consequences arising from a succession *of states*.[21] This raises two questions with regard to dealing with an EU exit in the context of secessions. Firstly, while the UK is a sovereign state after Brexit, it undoubtedly also enjoyed said statehood during its EU

---

15   Friel, *Secession from the EU* (n 8) 592–593, fn. 7.
16   D Thürer and T Burri, 'Secession' in R Wolfrum (ed), *The Max Planck Encyclopedia of Public International Law* (Oxford University Press 2012) 1 (emphasis added).
17   On the background of the VCSSRT, its ratification and customary status, Part II § 6 section II.B.1.
18   A Zimmermann, 'Secession and the Law of State Succession' in MG Kohen (ed), *Secession: International Law Perspectives* (Cambridge University Press 2006) 209: '[...] with regard to the law of State succession, the term "secession" is only infrequently used. Instead, more technical terms such as "separation of parts of a State", "dismemberment" or the creation of "newly independent States" have been used in the past. All these terms describe situations, however, which at the same time might at least partially be also described as instances of secession.'
19   Art. 34(1) VCSSRT.
20   Separation is generally understood as the generic term, covering any withdrawal of parts of a territory, whereas 'the objection by the [affected] State turns separation [...] into secession', see Thürer and Burri (n 16) 1.
21   Art. 1 VCSSRT: 'The present Convention applies to the effects of a *succession of States* in respect of treaties
between States.' (Emphasis added).

membership. Does the UK then qualify as a *successor* state? And secondly, and more prominently: does the EU qualify as a predecessor *state*?

B. The EU, its Member States and Statehood

Friel and others not only use the term 'secession' as a rhetorical device, but have also discussed the possibility of exiting the EU – before and after the introduction of Art. 50 TEU – against the background of (federal) states' experience with secession.[22] But can the EU – and leaving it – truly be placed within that context? For some writers, the introduction of Art. 50 TEU enshrining a unilateral, unconditional right to withdrawal clearly speaks against any EU aspiration to statehood. Thus, as Friel summarised pre-Art. 50 TEU: 'No prohibition on departure would indicate that the Union is not a State as we currently understand that concept; prohibited or limited departure would indicate it is far closer to a State than many recognize.'[23] In fact, however, lack of an exit provision proved inconclusive as regards the EU's nature.[24] Also, inclusion of Art. 50 TEU does not provide a definite answer seeing that a number of (federal) states have explicitly allowed for secession in their constitutions or, at least, have implicitly alluded to the possibility.[25]

While the foundation of the initial European Economic Community (EEC) clearly was an international treaty between the Member States, the foundational aspiration of many was its development into a (federal) state, with the founders envisaging a United States of Europe as the ultimate –

---

[22] Friel, *Secession from the EU* (n 8); RJ Friel, 'Providing a Constitutional Framework for Withdrawal from the EU: Article 59 of the Draft European Constitution' (2004) 53(2) *International & Comparative Law Quarterly* 407; M Gatti, 'Art. 50 TEU: A Well-Designed Secession Clause' (2017) 2(1) *European Papers – A Journal on Law and Integration* 159; VF Comella, 'Does Brexit Normalize Secession' (2018) 53(2) *Texas International Law Journal* 139.

[23] Friel, *Secession from the EU* (n 8) 592–593, fn. 7.

[24] See above Part I § 2 section I.

[25] See F Harbo, 'Secession Right – An Anti-Federal Principle?: Comparative Study of Federal States and the EU' (2008) 1(3) *Journal of Politics and Law* 132, 133–137 who names 'the former USSR (1922, Art. 17 and Art. 72 in the revised Constitution from 7 October 1977 to 1991); the former Yugoslavia (1945–1946, 1963–1991); the Constitution of the Malaysian Federation (1957–1965); St. Kitts-Nevis (until 1983) and Ethiopia (1962–1993 and 1994 – present)'.

I. The Law of Succession: An Alternative Framework?

and perhaps inevitable – goal of European integration.[26] Accordingly, the institutional structure of the EEC displayed a variety of federal elements.[27] However, as early as the late 1960s and consistently during the following decades, federal and constitutional aspirations have taken the form of a more functional, intergovernmental approach.[28] As a result, from 1957 until today scholars have continuously characterised the EU as an entity on the brink of, but not (yet[29]) having crossed the threshold to statehood.

Seeking to address the 'not yet' disclaimer, scholars have repeatedly (re-)assessed the EU against the classic criteria of statehood found in international law.[30] These criteria not only serve as a 'means of determining which entities are "States"'[31] and thus enjoy the 'special position'[32] that international law accords to them: 'The criteria of statehood are [also] of a special character, in that their application conditions the application of most other international law rules'[33]. If the VCSSRT, thus, speaks of *state* succession, it *prima facie* refers to entities possessing the following criteria:[34] 'The State as a person of international law should possess the following qualifications: (a) a permanent population; (b) a defined territory;

---

26 S Oeter, 'Föderalismus und Demokratie' in A von Bogdandy and J Bast (eds), *Europäisches Verfassungsrecht: Theoretische und dogmatische Grundzüge* (2nd edn, Springer 2009) 77–78. On federalism and the origins of European integration, see eg M Burgess, *Federalism and European Union: The Building of Europe, 1950–2000* (Routledge 2000) 55–95. Programmatically see W Hallstein, *Der unvollendete Bundesstaat: Europäische Erfahrungen und Erkenntnisse* (Econ-Verlag 1969).
27 On the federal character of the EU, see below Part II § 5 section III.B.
28 Oeter (n 26) 77–78.
29 See R Grawert, 'Staatsvolk und Staatsangehörigkeit' in J Isensee and P Kirchhof (eds), *Handbuch des Staatsrechts der Bundesrepublik Deutschland* (3rd edn, CF Müller 2004) § 16 para 67 that prompts Epping to reassess the 'not yet' disclaimer for the EU post-Lisbon in the *Festschrift* for Grawert (V Epping, 'Die Europäische Union: Noch international Organisation oder schon Staat?: Zur Vision der Vereinigten Staaten von Europa' in C Brüning and J Suerbaum (eds), *Die Vermessung der Staatlichkeit: Europäische Union – Bund – Länder – Gemeinden. Symposium zu Ehren von Rolf Grawert anlässlich seines 75. Geburtstages* (Duncker & Humblot 2013).
30 See eg C Dorau, *Die Verfassungsfrage der Europäischen Union: Möglichkeiten und Grenzen der europäischen Verfassungsentwicklung nach Nizza* (Nomos 2001) 29; T Schmitz, *Integration in der Supranationalen Union: Das europäische Organisationsmodell einer prozeßhaften geo-regionalen Integration und seine rechtlichen und staatstheoretischen Implikationen* (Nomos 2001) 198; Epping (n 29).
31 J Crawford, 'State' in R Wolfrum (ed) (n 16) para 11.
32 Ibid para 8.
33 Ibid para 12.
34 Ibid para 8.

(c) government; and (d) capacity to enter into relations with the other States.'[35] According to Klabbers, the first two criteria – population and territory – are 'more or less formal in nature; a state either has them (in whatever quantity) or does not', while '[t]he two remaining criteria are more substantive'[36]. Interestingly, however, in analysing the character of the EU, it is precisely on the first two criteria that opinions vary the most, whereas state authority, underlying an (effective) government and the capacity to conduct foreign relations, is preponderantly disputed.

Where population and territory are viewed in a mere formal sense as an '[aggregate] of individuals'[37] and a (more or less) defined 'territorial entity'[38], it is easy to see how the EU may fulfil these criteria. The EU Treaties define a precise territorial scope of application and even provide for EU citizenship.[39] At the same time, both EU citizenship and the EU Treaties' territorial scope of application are dependent on the nationality and territory of the Member States. EU citizenship does not replace Member State nationality, rather it is 'additional'.[40] It grants additional rights without itself encompassing the rights and obligations usually generated by nationality.[41] With regard to territory, the EU Treaties' scope of application is subject to any territorial change to the Member States.[42]

Reference to the dependence of the EU on its Member States already hints at what becomes the decisive obstacle to EU statehood when turning to the last criterion of an (internally and externally) effective government.

---

35 Convention on the Rights and Duties of States (adopted 26 December 1933, entered into force 26 December 1934) 165 LNTS 19 [Montevideo Convention], Art. 1.
36 J Klabbers, *International Law* (3rd edn, Cambridge University Press 2021) 77.
37 J Crawford, *Creation of States in International Law* (2nd edn, Oxford University Press 2007) 52.
38 Ibid 46.
39 For EU citizenship, see Art. 9 sentence 2, 3 TEU and Art. 20 TFEU; for the territorial scope of application of EU law, see Art. 52 TEU, Art. 355 TFEU. Reference to EU citizenship and the Treaties' territorial scope of application in the context of the EU's 'statehoodness' is sometimes criticised due to its dependence on nationality and territory of the Member States, see eg M Pechstein, 'Article 1 TEU' in R Streinz (ed), *EUV/AEUV: Vertrag über die Europäische Union, Vertrag über die Arbeitsweise der Europäischen Union, Charta der Grundrechte der Europäischen Union* (3rd edn, CH Beck 2018) para 10. For a discussion on the criterium of population, see eg Epping (n 29) 15–19 and C Busse, *Die völkerrechtliche Einordnung der Europäischen Union* (C Heymanns 1999)
40 Art. 20(1) sentence 2 TFEU.
41 Epping (n 29) 15–16.
42 On previous 'exits' from the EU, see below Part II § 5 section I.C.2.

I. The Law of Succession: An Alternative Framework?

Indisputably, the EU exercises effective power with respect to a permanent population and within a defined geographical area. However, it does not do so independently. While not mentioned in the classic definitions of statehood, Crawford identifies 'independence [as] the central criterion for statehood', underlying any other criterion.[43] Referring to a definition of independence by Justice Anzilotti[44], Crawford concludes that 'the exercise of substantial governmental authority with respect to some territory and people' may suffice to create a 'State-area'[45]. To create statehood, however, 'some further element is necessary – the absence of subjection to the authority of another State or States'[46]. It is, therefore, not the principle of conferred powers as such that bars the EU from becoming a state. A division of powers in a federal state does not put into question its statehood. The EU's lack of independence is rather evidenced by its lack of *Kompetenz-Kompetenz* which hinders it from disposing of and further developing its own treaty basis.[47] After all, regarding treaty amendments, the Member States remain the often-cited 'masters of the treaties'[48].[49]

Arguably, one may consider the question of *Kompetenz-Kompetenz* as a criterium capable of grey areas.[50] With the Treaty of Lisbon, the process of treaty amendment has – to some degree – become more 'unionalized'[51].

---

43 Crawford, *Creation of States* (n 37) 62.
44 PCIJ *Customs Regime between Germany and Austria* (Individual Opinion) [1931] Series A/B No. 41 Series A/B No 41, 57–58 ('The conception of independence, regarded as the normal characteristic of States as subjects of international law, cannot be better defined than by comparing it which the exceptional and, to some extent, abnormal class of States known as "dependent States". These are States subject to the authority of one or more other States. [...] It also follows that the restrictions upon a State's liberty, whether arising out of ordinary international law or contractual engagements, do not as such in the least affect its independence. As long as these restrictions do not place the State under the legal authority of another State, the former remains an independent State however extensive and burdensome those obligations may be.')
45 Crawford, *Creation of States* (n 37) 66.
46 Ibid.
47 M Nettesheim, 'Article 1 TEU' in E Grabitz, M Hilf and M Nettesheim (eds), *Das Recht der Europäischen Union* (82nd supplement, CH Beck 2024) paras 68–71.
48 See, *inter alia*, coined in the famous *Maastricht* decision, German Federal Constitutional Court, 2 BvR 2134/92, 2 BvR 2159/92 *Maastricht* [1993] BVerfGE 89, 155.
49 On the amendment of the EU treaties, see above Part I § 2 section I.
50 Cp Nettesheim (n 47) paras 70–71 ('gradualisierbares Kriterium').
51 The term is used to describe those aspects of the withdrawal process that are less 'state-centred' and 'provide for a significant input from EU institutions [...] and for the application of EU rules' (cp C Hillion, 'Accession and Withdrawal in the Law of

§ 5 EU Withdrawal and Succession: The Case for an Analogy

Art. 48 TEU provides for the participation of Union organs in amending the Treaties[52] and Art. 355(6) TFEU even allows the European Council, after consulting the European Commission, to change the Treaties' territorial scope of application, albeit in limited circumstances.[53] Likewise, in federal states, constitutional amendments do not always fall into the exclusive realm of the federation. Nettesheim thus argues that 'the definition of the transition point [of the EU, ie from international organisation to state] requires an evaluative decision, which is to be made without any significant guidance in terms of state and integration theory'[54]. However, to date, such a decision has neither been taken by the EU itself (through its institutions) nor by its Member States.

Regarding the EU's self-assessment, both the Commission and the European Court of Justice (ECJ) seem to be hovering between an international and constitutional reading of the union. While the Court initially referred to the EU as 'a new legal order *of international law*'[55], it has since dropped the 'international law' qualifier and started referring to the

---

the European Union' in A Arnull and D Chalmers (eds), *The Oxford Handbook of European Union Law* (Oxford University Press 2017) 142).

52 See especially Art. 48(3) TEU: 'If the European Council, after consulting the European Parliament and the Commission, adopts by a simple majority a decision in favour of examining the proposed amendments, the President of the European Council shall convene a Convention composed of representatives of the national Parliaments, of the Heads of State or Government of the Member States, of the European Parliament and of the Commission. The European Central Bank shall also be consulted in the case of institutional changes in the monetary area. The Convention shall examine the proposals for amendments and shall adopt by consensus a recommendation to a conference of representatives of the governments of the Member States as provided for in paragraph 4.'

53 Art. 355(6) TFEU: 'The European Council may, on the initiative of the Member State concerned, adopt a decision amending the status, with regard to the Union, of a Danish, French or Netherlands country or territory referred to in paragraphs 1 and 2. The European Council shall act unanimously after consulting the Commission.'

54 Nettesheim (n 47) para 72 ('Die Festlegung des Umschlagpunkts bedarf insofern einer wertenden Entscheidung, die ohne wesentliche staats- und integrationstheoretische Anleitung vorzunehmen ist.' Translated by the author). See also R Schütze, *From Dual to Cooperative Federalism: The Changing Structure of European Law* (Oxford University Press 2009) 29–30 who notes that the US was initially not considered a state, but that this shifted as 'after the Civil War the emotional supremacy was gradually transferred to the American nation'. See also Schütze, *Cooperative Federalism* (n 54) 37–38 quoting Kelsen referring to sovereignty and supremacy as 'emotional questions'.

55 ECJ, C-26/62 *NV Algemene Transport- en Expeditie Onderneming van Gend & Loos v Netherlands Inland Revenue Administration* [1963] ECLI:EU:C:1963:1, 3.

I. The Law of Succession: An Alternative Framework?

Treaties as the 'constitutional charter'[56], taking 'a strong constitutionalist approach'[57].[58] Nevertheless, it has so far also '[refrained] from detaching the EU entirely from international law'[59], finding the EU's nature to be 'peculiar' but 'precluded [...] from being considered a State'[60]. As Binder and Hofbauer show with regard to self-representation in national and international judicial fora, the Commission's approach also varies. Depending on the constellation of the proceedings, the Commission either depicts the EU as an international organisation or highlights its *sui generis*, supranational character, even '[correlating] the EU with a federal system'[61].[62] Concepts such as the *Staatenverbund* introduced by national courts, in turn, have been of 'little legal explanatory value'[63].

---

56 ECJ, C-294/83 *Parti écologiste "Les Verts" v European Parliament* [1986] ECLI:EU:C:1986:166, [23]. See also ECJ, Opinion 2/13 *Accession to the ECHR* [2014] ECLI:EU:C:2014:2454, 158 : 'own constitutional framework' and ECJ, Opinion 1/91 *Draft agreement between the Community, on the one hand, and the countries of the European Free Trade Association, on the other, relating to the creation of the European Economic Area* [1991] ECLI:EU:C:1991:490, [21]: ('[T]he [EU] Treaty, albeit concluded in the form of an international agreement, none the less constitutes the constitutional charter of a Community based on the rule of law. As the Court of Justice has consistently held, the Community treaties established a new legal order for the benefit of which the States have limited their sovereign rights, in ever wider fields, and the subjects of which comprise not only Member States but also their nationals [...] The essential characteristics of the Community legal order which has thus been established are in particular its primacy over the law of the Member States and the direct effect of a whole series of provisions which are applicable to their nationals and to the Member States themselves.').
57 KS Ziegler, 'The Relationship between EU Law and International Law' in A Södersten and DM Patterson (eds), *A Companion to European Union Law and International Law* (Wiley Blackwell 2016) 1–2.
58 See in more detail C Binder and JA Hofbauer, 'The Perception of the EU Legal Order in International Law: An In- and Outside View' in M Bungenberg and others (eds), *European Yearbook of International Economic Law 2017* (Springer 2017) 151–155.
59 Ibid 151.
60 ECJ, *ECHR Accession* (n 56) [156, 158].
61 Binder and Hofbauer (n 58) 151.
62 According to Binder and Hofbauer, the Commission takes the international law approach in proceedings where the EU is not itself a party or does not exercise exclusive jurisdiction, while it relies on the more federal, constitutional approach where it does exercise exclusive jurisdiction. See in more detail ibid 148–151.
63 Pechstein (n 39) para 12 ('geringer rechtlicher Erklärungswert', translated by the author) referring to the term *Staatenverbund* as coined by the German Federal Constitutional Court since its *Maastricht* decision (German Federal Constitutional Court, *Maastricht* (n 48) 181).

§ 5 EU Withdrawal and Succession: The Case for an Analogy

Conversely, Member States have always been decidedly clear as regards their own status. In a federal state, in general both levels of governance – the federation and its constituent parts – possess the quality of a state.[64] However, only one level is considered to be sovereign.[65] Thus, the counterpart to considering the EU's state-likeness has always been the question of whether or not the Member States are still sovereign.[66] Here the answer is overwhelmingly positive and with considerably less nuances. Regardless of how authors characterise the EU, its Member States are still that: states. The Member States' own emphasis on their identity and sovereignty as individual states is not only reflected inwardly. It can also be witnessed in the EU's external affairs, one example being Member States' at times far-reaching co-conclusion of international agreements regardless of competence-related necessity.[67] As Ehlermann pointed out,

> Member States wish to continue to appear as contracting parties in order to remain visible and identifiable actors on the international scene. Individual participation is therefore seen as a way of defending and enhancing the prestige and influence of individual Member States.[68]

Where an evaluative decision as to the EU's statehood has not been taken within the EU, it can certainly not be considered as a benchmark in the EU's external relations.[69] While referring to Brexit as a case of secession might thus come closer to factually describing the extensive disintegration

---

64 W Rudolf, 'Federal States' in R Wolfrum (ed) (n 16) para 1.
65 Ibid.
66 Cp in the context of EU withdrawal, A Waltemathe, *Austritt aus der EU: Sind die Mitgliedstaaten noch souverän?* (Lang 2000).
67 See eg the practice of so-called facultative mixity where the Member States become parties to an agreement which the EU would have been competent to conclude alone under EU law. On the practice of facultative mixity and the challenges posed by it, see M Chamon and I Govaere (eds), *EU External Relations Post-Lisbon: The Law and Practice of Facultative Mixity* (Brill Nijhoff 2020).
68 CD Ehlermann, 'Mixed Agreements: A List of Problems' in D O'Keeffe and HG Schermers (eds), *Mixed Agreements* (Kluwer 1983) 6.
69 Pointing to the limited effect of the EU's self-perception on non-EU Member States, see B Simma and D Pulkowski, 'Of Planets and the Universe: Self-contained Regimes in International Law' (2006) 17(3) *European Journal of International Law* 483, 516: 'The continuous assertion of the Community's sui generis character, however, does not by itself create an "own legal order". From a public international law perspective, the EC legal system remains a subsystem of international law.' Note in this regard also the EU's labelling as a regional economic integration *organisation* in the context of multilateral fora (see above at Part I § 2 section I).

process, legally the UK's exit cannot be characterised as such. Neither has the EU acquired statehood, nor have the Member States lost theirs. Accordingly, neither does the EU qualify as a predecessor *state*, nor can the UK be considered a *successor* state. While the UK upon leaving the EU loses its characteristic as a *Member* State, it does not (re-)gain its quality as a *state*.

C. Exiting the European Union: A Legal Lacuna

With the EU not (yet) having acquired statehood, the VCSSRT applies neither directly nor as a matter of customary law. The wording of Art. 34 VCSSRT dealing with the separation of parts of a *state*'s territory does not cover the case of an EU exit. Additionally, the VCSSRT's scope of application is limited in two ways: to the 'effects of a succession *of States* in respect of treaties *between States*'.[70] As treaty law appears ill-equipped for the withdrawal of a Member State from the EU and the VCSSRT inapplicable, does Brexit as regards its effect on international agreements then fall into a legal lacuna?

Two alternatives to such a *non liquet* are conceivable: firstly, exiting the EU could be covered by rules of succession beyond the scope of the VCSSRT. Adopted in 1978, the VCSSRT is based on a codification project of the ILC, mandated by the United Nations General Assembly (UNGA).[71] As such, it does not purport to cover all international legal rules on succession with respect to international agreements.[72] To the contrary, evidence for the fact that the ILC at least considered the possibility of rules on succession existing beyond the limitations inherent to their project can be found throughout their work (1.). Moreover, the EU has been confronted with territorial changes before. Its previous practice may have thus already contributed to the formation of rules on (EU) succession (2.). Where this is not the case, alternatively, an existing lacuna could be filled through methods of legal reasoning (3.).

---

70 Art. 1 VCSSRT.
71 UNGA, 'Future Work in the Field of the Codification and Progressive Development of International Law' UN Doc. A/Res/16/1686 (18 December 1961) para 3.
72 On the discussions in the ILC concerning the projects scope, see below Part II § 5 section I and § 6 section III.A.

§ 5 EU Withdrawal and Succession: The Case for an Analogy

1. Beyond the VCSSRT: A Broader Customary Law of Succession?

From the outset, the ILC's study of succession had been tailored to *state* succession. The UNGA's explicit recommendation to consider 'the topic of succession of States and Governments' as well as substantive considerations[73] led the ILC to narrow the scope of its draft articles in two ways: as regards the subjects of succession and regarding the agreements to which the rules of succession were to apply. At the same time, the ILC's reports explicitly acknowledged the role that subjects other than states play in modern treaty relations and sought to address the relationship between these subjects and their agreements on the one hand and the articles on state succession on the other.

In his first report, the ILC's first Special Rapporteur (SR) on the topic, Sir Humphrey Waldock, touched upon the question of whether agreements between states and international organisations should fall within the scope of the draft articles. In doing so, he did not deny that succession in respect of these agreements could take place, rather he excluded them for practical reasons for he 'doubt[ed] very much that [such] succession [...] would be found not to involve any special problems'[74]. By the time of the ILC's final draft articles, however, 'the Commission recognized that the principles which they contain may in some measure also be applicable with reference to treaties to which other subjects of international law are parties'[75]. While the limitation of the Convention to inter-state agreements was nevertheless upheld, Art. 3 VCSSRT now provides a caveat relating to agreements concluded with subjects of international law other than states:

> The fact that the Convention does not apply to the effects of a succession of States in respect of international agreements concluded between States and other subjects of international law [...] shall not affect:
> (a) the application to such cases of any of the rules set forth in the present Convention to which they are subject under international law independently of the Convention; [...]

---

73 See below § 6 section III.A.
74 ILC, 'First Report on Succession of States and Governments in Respect of Treaties, by Sir Humphrey Waldock' UN Doc A/CN.4/202, YBILC (1968) Vol. II 91.
75 ILC, 'Report of the International Law Commission on the Work of its Twenty-Sixth Session, 6 May – 26 July 1974' UN Doc. A/9610/Rev.1, YBILC (1974) Vol. II(1) 174.

I. The Law of Succession: An Alternative Framework?

That states and international organisation indeed resort to the VCSSRT's rules in cases of state succession involving agreements outside the Convention's scope is demonstrated, *inter alia*, by EU practice. Any agreement to which the EU is a treaty party falls outside the scope of the Convention. Nevertheless, where a succession occurred on the side of the EU's treaty partners the rules on succession as applied to agreements *between states* were generally also applied to the agreements concluded with the EU.[76] With regard to the disintegration of the Union of Soviet Socialist Republics (USSR), Yugoslavia and Czechoslovakia,[77] all of which had maintained treaty relations with the EU, both the EU Commission's approach and that of the successor states towards agreements with the EU by and large followed Art. 34 VCSSRT.[78] Thus, as regards the *agreements* of the EU, the provisions of the VCSSRT certainly serve – at the very least – as orientation.

Another matter altogether is, however, if any rules on succession may also be applicable to successions of *other subjects* of international law in general and to the EU specifically. Do rules of succession apply (as a matter of customary law) to the situation where a state joins or leaves an entity such as the EU?

This question became pertinent in Waldock's fifth report. The introduction of two new articles dealing with the effects of the formation and a potential subsequent dissolution of a union of states on international agreements begged the question of what exactly falls under the term 'union of states'. As several ILC members pointed out, the term 'was very ambiguous'[79], having in the past been used for different subjects of international law. Thus, for the sake of his study, Waldock defined two types of unions: unions of states 'on the plane of internal constitutional law', ie, unions that

---

[76] In detail, see PJ Kuijper, 'The Community and State Succession in Respect of Treaties' in D Curtin and T Heukels (eds), *Institutional Dynamics of European Integration* (Martinus Nijhoff Publishers 1994); A Zimmermann, *Staatennachfolge in völkerrechtliche Verträge: Zugleich ein Beitrag zu den Möglichkeiten und Grenzen völkerrechtlicher Kodifikation* (Springer 2000) 673–723. This was the case where the other treaty party was a non-EU Member State (eg the case of the USSR) or an EU Member State in the constellation of a mixed agreement, eg the independence of Algeria and the German reunification.

[77] The practice surrounding these cases of succession is discussed in further detail below Part II § 7 section I.

[78] See Kuijper (n 76) 640.

[79] ILC, 'Summary records of the Twenty-Fourth Session 2 May-7 July 1972' UN Doc. A/CN.4/Ser.A/1972, YBILC (1972) Vol. I 160.

179

§ 5 EU Withdrawal and Succession: The Case for an Analogy

became states themselves, and unions 'only on the plane of international law', ie international organisations. The first naturally fell within the scope of his study. The second type, however, in Waldock's view not only fell 'completely outside' the scope of *state* succession, but outside the topic of *succession* altogether. Thus, while the Commission acknowledged the factual possibility of an international organisation (partially) succeeding a state as regards treaty-making[80], it was of the opinion that the legal consequences thereof would not be dealt with by rules on succession, but simply 'depend on the terms of the treaty establishing the organization'[81].

Since the drafting of the VCSSRT and the ILC's remarks on succession between international organisations and their member states, this question has not arisen in the context of any international organisation other than the EU. Moreover, the EU Treaties are also the only founding treaties of an international organisation explicitly addressing the effect of EU accession on its Member States' pre-accession international agreements with non-EU states.

2. *Lex EU*: A Specific Customary Law of EU Succession?

The ILC's Special Rapporteur Waldock placed the then EEC in his category of unions of states on the plane of international law. While Waldock acknowledged that the EEC is 'not generally regarded as being simply a regional international organization', he found that 'from the point of view of succession', it 'appears without any doubt to remain on the plane of intergovernmental organization'[82]. Waldock justified this by referring to two aspects of the EEC's accession practice. Firstly, the effects on a new Member State's pre-accession agreements with non-EU states were and still are set out by the EU's foundational treaties, today specifically Art. 351 TFEU.[83]

---

80 'ILC Report 1974' (n 75) 171.
81 Ibid.
82 ILC, 'Fifth Report on Succession in Respect of Treaties, by Sir Humphrey Waldock' UN Doc. A/CN.4/256 and Add.1 – 4, YBILC (1972) Vol. II 18.
83 This includes, on the one hand, the EU's approach to international agreements concluded by its Member States prior to their membership. Waldock thus referred to then Art. 234 Treaty of Rome [today Art. 351 TFEU]. On the other hand, Waldock considered the EEC's practice of obliging new Member States to *accede* to mixed agreements in their Act of Accession (referring to Art. 4 Treaty concerning the Accession of the Kingdom of Denmark, Ireland, the Kingdom of Norway and the United Kingdom of Great Britain and Northern Ireland to the European Economic

I. The Law of Succession: An Alternative Framework?

In so doing, the EEC's founding treaties, in Waldock's view, approached the question 'from the angle, not of succession or of the moving treaty frontier rule, but of the rules governing the application of successive treaties relating to the same subject matter (article 30 of the 1969 Convention on the Law of Treaties)'[84]. Moreover, as regards the international agreements concluded by the EEC and its Member States prior to an accession, ie mixed agreements, Waldock found the EEC to 'not rely on the operation of any principle of succession or of moving treaty frontiers.'[85] Instead, a Member State acceding to the EU in its EU accession treaty commits to join these agreements by way of accession.[86]

Today, opinions on the precise nature of the EU's accession practice with regard to international agreements vary. On Member States' pre-accession agreements, Art. 351(2) TFEU provides that '[t]he rights and obligations arising from [these] agreements [...] shall not be affected by the provisions of the Treaties.' However, paragraph 2 clarifies that '[t]o the extent that such agreements are not compatible with the Treaties, the Member State or States concerned shall take all appropriate steps to eliminate the incompatibilities established.' With Art. 351 TFEU not claiming to have any direct effect on the pre-accession agreements – any stipulation in that regard would violate the *res inter alios acta* principle – some authors join the ILC in viewing the EU's practice from the perspective of treaty conflicts and consider Art. 351 TFEU as an expression of Art. 30(4)(b) VCLT.[87] As articulated by Advocate General (AG) Mischo,

> [...] no one has yet seriously defended the idea that, by creating a *regional international organisation – and that is what the European Union certainly is under international law* – States could, without recourse to

---

Community and to the European Atomic Energy Community and Act concerning the Conditions of Accession and the Adjustments to the Treaties (27 March 1972) OJ L73/5 [1972 EU Accession Agreement]).
84 'SR Waldock Fifth Report' (n 82) 18–19.
85 Ibid 19.
86 See eg Art. 4 1972 EU Accession Agreement.
87 P Koutrakos, *EU International Relations Law* (Hart Publishing 2006) 301; J Klabbers, *Treaty Conflict and the European Union* (Cambridge University Press 2010) 118; P Koutrakos, 'International Agreements Concluded by Member States Prior to their EU Accession: Burgoa' in G Butler and RA Wessel (eds), *EU External Relations Law: The Cases in Context* (Hart Publishing 2022) 134.

§ 5 EU Withdrawal and Succession: The Case for an Analogy

any other procedure, release themselves from the obligation to fulfil earlier commitments to non-member countries.[88]

In contrast, other writers – especially those granting the EU a status distinct from a (regional) international organisation – view Art. 351 TFEU and the EU's accession practice with regard to international agreements as a response to gaps in general international law.[89] Attesting that '[c]lassic international law struggles with "composite" subjects'[90], these authors argue that the EU devised its own rules and methods of dealing with the effects of its formation and subsequent accessions on international agreements. Some of these do not immediately follow from Art. 351 TFEU's wording but from the ECJ's jurisprudence in this regard.

One the one hand, based on the ECJ's interpretation, Art. 351 TFEU by now goes 'beyond the ordinary international law principle of *res inter alios acta*' in establishing a hierarchy between pre-accession agreements and the EU Treaties for the benefit of the former.[91] But while paragraph 1 ostensibly still protects anterior agreements, the following paragraphs are ultimately more about balancing said protection with the safeguarding of the EU's integration process.[92] The Member States taking 'all appropriate steps'[93] to achieve this has been interpreted by the ECJ as far as encompassing an obligation to denounce pre-accession agreements incompatible with

---

88 ECJ, C-62/98 and C-84/98 *Commission of the European Communities v Portuguese Republic* (Joined opinion of Advocate General Mischo) [1999] ECLI:EU:C:1999:509, [57].
89 See eg KM Meessen, 'The Application of Rules of Public International Law within Community Law' (1976) 13(4) *Common Market Law Review* 485, 489 ('The formation of international organisations of the type of the European Community is a new phenomenon in the history of international relations. Hence, general international law is unlikely to contain any rules as regards the succession to treaty commitments of Member States by the Community.'); R Schütze, 'The "Succession Doctrine" and the European Union' in R Schütze (ed), *Foreign Affairs and the EU Constitution: Selected Essays* (Cambridge University Press 2014) 92–94.
90 Schütze, Foreign Affairs (n 89) 92.
91 Ibid 104; H Lenk, 'The Member States' Duty to Denounce Anterior Treaties: Commission v Portugal (Maritime Policies)' in G Butler and RA Wessel (eds) (n 87) 398.
92 Klabbers, *Treaty Conflict* (n 87) 118.
93 Cp Art. 351(2) TFEU: 'To the extent that such agreements are not compatible with the Treaties, the Member State or States concerned shall take all appropriate steps to eliminate the incompatibilities established. Member States shall, where necessary, assist each other to this end and shall, where appropriate, adopt a common attitude.'

I. The Law of Succession: An Alternative Framework?

the EU legal order.[94] On the other hand, where all Member States have (pre-accession) become parties to an international agreement that falls within the exclusive competence of the EU, the Court has also recognised the possibility of the EU succeeding the Member States in their treaty rights and obligations.[95]

Schütze, thus, argues that 'as a second best solution as long as international law retains its (partial) blindness toward compound international subjects', the EU has 'developed its own theory and practice of *functional succession*'.[96] But have similar rules or practices evolved as regards the situation of a state leaving the EU? Brexit is certainly the first instance of a Member State exiting the EU. Nevertheless, the Union has already previously undergone territorial reductions. How comparable were these situations to the UK's exit? And how did they affect international agreements concluded by the EU (and its Member States)?

While the cases of Greenland[97], Saint Pierre-et-Miquelon and Saint-Barthelemy[98] are regularly referred to as exits from the EU, all three are

---

94 See ECJ, C-84/98 *Commission of the European Communities v Portuguese Republic* [2000] ECLI:EU:C:2000:359, 58: 'If a Member State encounters difficulties which make adjustment of an agreement impossible, an obligation to denounce that agreement cannot therefore be excluded'. For a detailed discussion of when denunciation may be necessary, see Koutrakos, *EU International Relations Law* (n 87) 313–316. Discussing the decision and placing putting it into context, see Lenk (n 91).

95 ECJ, C-21 to 24/72 *International Fruit Company NV and others v Produktschap voor Groenten en Fruit* [1972] ECLI:EU:C:1972:115, [18]. On the judgement and its aftereffects, see A Petti and J Scott, 'International Agreements in the EU Legal Order: International Fruit' in G Butler and RA Wessel (eds) (n 87).

96 Schütze, Foreign Affairs (n 89) 119.

97 After the granting of a so-called 'home rule' in 1979, Greenland enjoyed a constitutionally autonomous status within Denmark. While this did not automatically affect the application of the EEC Treaty to Greenland, it enabled the introduction of two different regimes: 'Rest-Denmark' remained a member of the EEC, while Greenland's status under EU law was changed in 1985 to that of an associated overseas territory. On this 'Grexit', see HR Krämer, 'Greenland's European Community (EC)-Referendum: Background and Consequences' (1982) 25 *German Yearbook of International Law* 273; F Harhoff, 'Greenland's Withdrawal from the European Communities' (1983) 20(1) *Common Market Law Review* 13; F Weiss, 'Greenland's Withdrawal from the European Communities' (1985) 10 *European Law Review* 173; KK Patel, *Project Europe: A History* (Cambridge University Press 2020) 209–212.

98 Following changes to the constitutional status of Saint-Pierre-et-Miquelon and Saint-Barthelemy under the French constitution, both territories were 'downgraded' from 'outermost territories' under Art. 349 TFEU to 'overseas countries or territories associated with the EU' under Art. 355 TFEU (see for Saint-Pierre-et-Miquelon, Annex I, Council Decision (86/283/EEC) of 30 June 1986 on the association of the overseas

§ 5 EU Withdrawal and Succession: The Case for an Analogy

neither comparable with Brexit nor a helpful indicator as regards the effect on international agreements. The main difference lies in the fact that none of the three – in contrast to the UK – possesses statehood, Greenland being a constituent part of Denmark, and Saint Pierre-et-Miquelon and Saint-Barthelemy overseas collectivities of France. As such, neither of them – in contrast to the UK – had or gained the capacity to conclude international agreements that a state has.[99]

Hence, the case most comparable to Brexit appears to be the independence of Algeria in 1962, solely for the reason of it being a state and thus capable of becoming a party to international agreements. Nonetheless, this 'Algexit' factually differs from Brexit in key respects. Algeria did not – unlike the UK – become part of the then EEC as a sovereign state. Rather, what is now the Algerian territory fell under the scope of the EEC Treaty as part of France's territory. With its independence from France, the EEC Treaty's scope of application was reduced in size by the newly formed Algerian state. Therefore, with regard to the EEC, Algeria's exit was not considered a case of separation, but rather as an application of the principle of moving treaty frontiers.

Moreover, Algexit is of no real significance with regard to its effect on international agreements. Algeria's independence came only four years after the founding of the EEC and thus at a time when the EEC had made little use of this treaty-making power. The only international agreements in force at the time were agreements on inter-institutional cooperation concluded with the International Labour Organization[100] and the Central Commission

---

countries and territories with the European Economic Community (1 July 1986) OJ L175/1; for Saint-Barthelemy, see Decision of the European Council (2010/718/EU) of 29 October 2010 amending the status with regard to the European Union of the island of Saint-Barthélemy (29 October 2010) OJ L325/4). While for the former the EU Treaties in principle find full application, the special arrangements for association of Part Four TFEU apply to the latter (Art. 355(2) TFEU). On the EU's oversea territories, see D Kochenov (ed), *EU Law of the Overseas: Outermost Regions, Associated Overseas Countries and Territories, Territories sui generis* (Kluwer Law International 2011).

99 Greenland can conclude international agreements where the competence to do so has been delegated to it by Denmark, see M Ackrén and U Jakobsen, 'Greenland as a Self-Governing Sub-National Territory in International Relations: Past, Current and Future Perspectives' (2015) 51(4) *Polar Record* 404.
100 Agreement on Relations between the International Labour Organization and the European Economic Community (27 April 1959) OJ 27/521 [ILO-EEC Agreement].

for the Navigation of the Rhine[101].[102] These agreements are content-wise not comparable with those at issue in the context of Brexit. Additionally, Algeria, emerging from a process of decolonisation, vastly followed a clean-slate approach as regards international agreements.[103]

3. Filling a Legal Lacuna: Recourse to Legal Reasoning

The previous analyses show that so far no practice has emerged that would be applicable to the case of a Member States leaving the EU. At the same time, the reverse situation – accession to the EU – demonstrates that where no (adequate) rules exist, EU practice will fill the gap over time, developing an 'alternative mechanism'[104]. In doing so, there are two possible approaches. It could simply be left to the EU to devise these alternative mechanisms and tailor them to its specific perspective and needs. This, however, not only exposes the EU to accusations of 'exceptionalism'[105]; it is, in fact, problematic from the perspective of international law. Where the EU creates its own rules, there is a danger of the Union ultimately being the one to control and develop them further. An example is the EU's stance on Member States' pre-accession agreements to which

> the European legal order was originally clear and generous. Article 351 TFEU allowed Member States to fulfil their international obligations against any conflicting European law, yet it imposed a procedural European obligation to renegotiate or denounce the treaty in the future.[106]

---

101 Exchange of Letters between Mr Walter Hallstein, President of the Commission of the European Community, and Mr Jacques Fouques-Duparc, Chairman of the Central Commission for the Navigation of the Rhine, on cooperation between the EEC and the Central Commission for the Navigation of the Rhine (4 August 1961) OJ 53/1027.
102 A mixed agreement with Greece was signed on 9 July 1961 but only entered into force in 1963 after Algeria's independence.
103 Cp Part III VCSSRT.
104 Schütze, Foreign Affairs (n 89) 118.
105 On so-called European exceptionalism, see M Lickova, 'European Exceptionalism in International Law' (2008) 19(3) *European Journal of International Law* 463; G Nolte and HP Aust, 'European Exceptionalism?' (2013) 2(3) *Global Constitutionalism* 407; T Isiksel, 'European Exceptionalism and the EU's Accession to the ECHR' (2016) 27(3) *European Journal of International Law* 565.
106 Schütze, Foreign Affairs (n 89) 118.

While the EU's approach may thus have originally struck a balance between EU interests and that of non-EU treaty partners, this balance has since tipped significantly – towards the interest of the EU.

> In the last decade, the European Court has significantly lessened this tolerant stance in order to protect the autonomy and integrity of the European legal order. Not only has it set external limits to the supremacy of prior international treaties over European law to judicially safeguard the Union's 'constitutional identity'; it appears to have come to require an immediate application of Article 351(2) for all Member State treaties falling within the scope of the European legal order.[107]

In the case of accession, the EU's expanding influence still moves within the boundaries of international law. While 'all appropriate steps' as per Art. 351(2) TFEU encompasses the obligation to denounce pre-accession agreements incompatible with the EU Treaties, this obligation is restricted to instances where denunciation is legally possible, either because of a denunciation provision in the agreement or in accordance with Art. 56 VCLT.[108] In contrast, the EU's approach in the case of Brexit crosses that boundary. The claim that the UK upon withdrawal from the EU ceased to be a party to *inter se* and bilateral mixed agreements – even if accepted by the non-EU treaty parties – cannot be justified by reference to international treaty law.

Alternatively, where a gap is identified in a legal order, methods of legal reasoning often provide the means to bridge it. In order to prevent accusations of exceptionalism, when confronted with new questions such as the effect of Brexit on international agreements, the EU (and its treaty partners) could – and should – make use of such methods. The Union has done so in the past with the doctrine of functional succession whose 'rationale was borrowed from the idea of "state succession". Since the Union is not a "state", the concept had to be applied *analogously*.'[109]

The idea of applying the rationales of succession to the EU by analogy does not appear from nowhere. While dismissing the then EEC from the

---

107 Ibid 119.
108 Lenk (n 91) 404–405.
109 Schütze, Foreign Affairs (n 89) 110 (emphasis added). But see Meessen (n 89), 489 who argues that Art. 351 TFEU 'excludes any attempt on the part of the Community to have the rules of state succession concerning unions of states applied to its own formation'.

II. Methodical Excursus: Analogical Reasoning in International Law

scope of their study, the ILC's reports on state succession nevertheless present the said alternative. In rather extensively discussing the EEC as a subject for his study, Waldock addressed the character of the EEC and its similarity with unions of states: 'The direct effects in the national law of the member States of regulatory and judicial powers vested in Community organs gives to the EEC, it is said, a semblance of a federal association of States.'[110]. And where two situations bear such resemblance, analogous reasoning is 'a fast and effective way to close normative gaps'[111].

II. Methodical Excursus: Analogical Reasoning in International Law

Considering that the EU is not a state, the rules on state succession with respect to international agreements do not apply to it. At the same time, addressing the consequences of exiting the EU from a purely treaty and institutional law perspective has proven unconvincing. Waldock, the ILC's Special Rapporteur on state succession, himself termed the EU a 'hybrid' union of states, the 'precise legal character of which is a matter of discussion among jurists'[112]. Being the only hybrid union, so far, and not having experienced any exits prior to Brexit, no specific rules on succession with regard to EU international agreements have developed. On the other hand, even though Waldock dismissed the EEC as an object for his study, he nevertheless admitted that 'hybrid unions', such as the EEC then (and the EU now), 'appear to have some analogy with a union of States'[113] in the constitutional sense. Regarding the effects of Brexit for international agreements, it could thus be said that the EU, its Member States, the UK and non-EU treaty partners are operating in a legal lacuna, but the lacuna might be filled using analogical reasoning.

As a gap filling method, analogies could be particularly useful in international law.[114] Lacking both a global legislator and a global court, inter-

---

110 'SR Waldock Fifth Report' (n 82) 18.
111 S Vöneky, 'Analogy in International Law' in R Wolfrum (ed) (n 16) para 2.
112 'SR Waldock Fifth Report' (n 82) 18.
113 Ibid.
114 On the persuasiveness of analogies in legal reasoning in general, see FL Bordin, *The Analogy between States and International Organizations* (Cambridge University Press 2019) 17–26. On the broader topic of gaps in international law, see U Fastenrath, *Lücken im Völkerrecht: Zu Rechtscharakter, Quellen, Systemzusammenhang, Methodenlehre und Funktionen des Völkerrechts* (Duncker & Humblot 1991).

§ 5 EU Withdrawal and Succession: The Case for an Analogy

national law is inherently fragmentary: the scope of issues covered by treaty law is not only limited, but treaty-making has steadily been in decline.[115] Moreover, the identification of practice and *opinion iuris* establishing customary rules regularly proofs difficult.[116] At the same time, it is precisely these features of international law that put the general justifiability of using analogical reasoning into question.

Where a legal system does not address a certain situation, 'the inference is that because rule α applies to situation β, and because situation β is relevantly similar to situation γ, rule α must also apply to situation γ'[117]. Analogy is thus a type of legal reasoning based on the principles of formal justice, requiring impartiality in the application of the law, and the rule of law, addressing concerns of predictability and arbitrariness in situations of uncertainty.[118] For an analogy to be considered a 'valid tool'[119] the precondition is, thus, the existence of a legal order in which

> [f]irst, the creation of legal provisions and rules must not be exclusively subjected to other enumerated sources of law [...]. Secondly, the principle that similar cases have to be treated the same way legally has to be incorporated into or underlie the legal order in question [...]. Besides, an analogy may be drawn only if there is a lacuna in the law, ie a certain case is not covered by the existing rules of a legal order [...].[120]

Critics of applying analogies in international law point to some of its big structural questions to contest the validity of analogical reasoning: the international legal order's nature, its sources and its dependence on (state) consent.[121] As regards the first, the presumption underlying the application

---

115 J Pauwelyn, RA Wessel and J Wouters, 'When Structures Become Shackles: Stagnation and Dynamics in International Lawmaking' (2014) 25(3) *European Journal of International Law* 733, 734–738.
116 On the elements of customary international law, see ICJ *North Sea Continental Shelf Cases (Federal Republic of Germany/Denmark; Federal Republic of Germany/Netherlands)* (Judgement) [1969] ICJ Rep 1969, p 3, [70–74]. For the uncertainties regarding its identification, see eg J Kammerhofer, 'Uncertainty in the Formal Sources of International Law: Customary International Law and Some of Its Problems' (2004) 15(3) *European Journal of International Law* 523, 524–536. For the ILC's work on methods of identification, see ILC, 'Draft Conclusions on Identification of Customary International Law, with Commentaries', YBILC (2018) Vol. II(2).
117 FL Bordin (n 114) 15.
118 Ibid 22–23.
119 Vöneky (n 111) para 3.
120 Ibid paras 3–4.
121 For a detailed discussion, see FL Bordin (n 114) 26–35.

II. Methodical Excursus: Analogical Reasoning in International Law

of analogical reasoning is that international law forms a coherent legal system.[122] Debates on the fragmentation of international law have challenged this presumption.[123] But even if it is considered as such, the international rule of law underlying said order may still be more 'a political ideal' than a 'normative reality'[124,125] Secondly, the sources of international law are arguably enumerated in Art. 38 ICJ Statute[126] – and, thus, restricted to treaty law, custom and general principles.[127] Finally, while international law undoubtedly features lacunae, the principle of (state) consent calls into question whether these are involuntary. Where states have not consented to a rule, gaps in the legal order may rather be considered as voluntary – or as held by the Permanent Court of International Justice (PCJI) in the *Lotus*

---

122 Analogical reasoning requires systematicity; it is only within a coherent legal system that the idea of treating like cases alike can serve as an overall logic justifying analogy. On systematicity in analogical reasoning in general, see ibid 20–24. On the systematicity of international law, see FL Bordin (n 114) 28–31.

123 The question whether international law is indeed a coherent legal system has (meanwhile) been overwhelmingly answered in the positive. In ILC, 'Conclusions of the Study Group on the Fragmentation of International Law' Difficulties arising from the Diversification and Expansion of International Law, YBILC (2006) Vol. II the Commission confirms that '[i]nternational law is a legal system' and not just a 'random collection of [...] norms'.

124 S Chestermann, 'Rule of Law' in R Wolfrum (ed) (n 16) 46. But see Bleckmann who derives the postulate that like cases must be treated alike under international law from the prohibition of arbitrariness and the imperative to avoid contradictions which he considers to be general principles of international law (A Bleckmann, 'Analogie im Völkerrecht' (1977) 17(2) *Archiv des Völkerrechts* 161, 173–176).

125 On the systematicity of international law and the notion of an international rule of law in the context of analogical reasoning, see FL Bordin (n 114) 28–31.

126 Statute of the International Court of Justice (adopted 24 October 1945, entered into force 18 April 1946) 33 UNTS 993 [ICJ Statute], Art. 38 provides that: 'The Court, whose function is to decide in accordance with international law such disputes as are submitted to it, shall apply: a. international conventions, whether general or particular, establishing rules expressly recognized by the contesting states; b. international custom, as evidence of a general practice accepted as law; c. the general principles of law recognized by civilized nations; d. [...] judicial decisions and the teachings of the most highly qualified publicists of the various nations, as subsidiary means for the determination of rules of law.' See the list of identical sources in Statute of the Permanent Court of International Justice (adopted 13 December 1920, entered into force 8 October 1921) Serie D – No. 1 [PCIJ Statute], Art. 38.

127 But see *Bleckmann* who argues that arguments by analogy can be subsumed under Art. 38(c) or (d) ICJ Statute (Bleckmann (n 124), 167–169).

§ 5 EU Withdrawal and Succession: The Case for an Analogy

case, lacking a rule, '[r]estrictions upon the independence of States cannot [...] be presumed'[128].[129]

In practice, however, international courts and tribunals have consistently resorted to analogical reasoning, thereby rebutting some of the theoretical criticism.[130] Notably, the PCIJ and the International Court of Justice (ICJ) have used analogies despite limitations on the applicable sources of law in their Statutes and the *Lotus* 'precedent'[131].[132] A prominent example is the ICJ's 1984 *Nicaragua* judgement. Here, the Court had to determine whether the United States of America could modify with immediate effect

---

128 PCIJ *The Case of the S.S. Lotus* (Judgement) [1927] Series A No. 10 Series A No 10, 18.

129 On the completeness of the system and the *Lotus* closure rule, see FL Bordin (n 114) 31–35. See also critically Bleckmann (n 124), 169–171 and Vöneky (n 111) paras 13–15.

130 For the Permanent Court of Arbitration, see PCA *Muscat Dhows Case (France v Great Britain)* (Award) [1905] XI RIAA 83 (1961); PCA *Russian Claim for Interest on Indemnities (Damages Claimed by Russia for Delay in Payment of Compensation Owed to Russians Injured During the War of 1877–1878) (Russia v Turkey)* (Award) [1912] XI RIAA 421 (1961). For the International Tribunal on the Law of the Sea, see eg ITLOS *Responsibilities and Obligations of States Sponsoring Persons and Entities with respect to Activities in the Area* (Advisory Opinion) [2011] ITLOS Rep 10, [60]: 'The fact that these instruments are binding texts negotiated by States and adopted through a procedure similar to that used in multilateral conferences permits the Chamber to consider that the interpretation rules set out in the Vienna Convention may, *by analogy*, provide guidance as to their interpretation. In the specific case before the Chamber, the analogy is strengthened because of the close connection between these texts and the Convention.' (Emphasis added).

131 For a recent contribution on the issue of precedents, see JG Devaney, 'The Role of Precedent in the Jurisprudence of the International Court of Justice: A Constructive Interpretation' (2022) 35(3) *Leiden Journal of International Law* 641 with further references in fn. 3.

132 In PCIJ *Case of the S.S. Wimbledon (United Kingdom, France & Italy v. Germany)* (Judgement) [1923] Series A No 1, [33] the Court employs an argument *a contrario*, as special form of analogical reasoning. On this case see Bleckmann (n 124), 164. For the ICJ, see ICJ *International Status of South-West Africa* (Advisory Opinion) [1950] ICJ Rep 1950, p 128, [142]; ICJ *Case Concerning Military and Paramilitary Activities in and against Nicaragua (Nicaragua v United States of America)* (Jurisdiction and Admissibility) [1984] ICJ Rep 1984, p 392, [63]; ICJ *Case Concerning Military and Paramilitary Activities in and against Nicaragua (Nicaragua v United States of America)* (Merits) [1986] ICJ Rep 1986, p 4, [210]; ICJ *Case Concerning the Land and Maritime Boundary between Cameroon and Nigeria (Cameroon v Nigeria)* (Preliminary Objections) [1998] ICJ Rep 1998, p 275, [30, 33]; ICJ *Case Concerning the Arrest Warrant of 11 April 2000* (Judgement) [2002] ICJ Rep 2002, p 3, [52]; ICJ *Case Concerning Application of the Convention on the Prevention and Punishment of the Crime Genocide (Bosnia and Herzegovina v Serbia and Montenegro)* (Judgement) [2007] ICJ Rep 2007, p 43, [419, 420].

its unilateral declaration under Art. 36 ICJ Statute to exclude disputes with Nicaragua from the Court's jurisdiction. Being confronted with the question of terminability of unilateral declarations, the ICJ identified a legal lacuna, observing that 'the right of immediate termination of declarations with indefinite duration is far from established'[133]. It then reasoned that such unilateral declarations 'should be treated, *by analogy*, according to the law of treaties' and could thus not be revoked without a reasonable waiting period as required with regard to 'withdrawal from or termination of treaties that contain no provision regarding the duration of their validity'[134].

Admittedly, in some instances the language employed by the Court is less explicit. In the *Arrest Warrant* case, the ICJ found that the international agreements invoked by the parties did not

> contain any provision specifically defining the immunities enjoyed by Ministers for Foreign Affairs. It is consequently *on the basis of customary international law* that the Court must decide the questions relating to the immunities of such Ministers raised in the present case.[135]

But instead of examining state practice and *opinio juris*, the Court compared the position of ministers of foreign affairs to those of heads of state and found relevant similarities to grant these ministers with the same jurisdictional immunity.[136] Thus, even though the ICJ claimed to establish customary international law, *Arrest Warrant* – like *Nicaragua* – displays the typical steps of an argument by analogy: comparing a regulated and an unregulated case, identifying the similarities and inferring additional characteristics.[137]

III. EU Withdrawal and Separation: Treating Like Cases Alike

Analogical arguments are usually divided into several steps. While the precise steps may vary, the basis for every argument by analogy is an

---

133 ICJ, *Nicaragua (Jurisdiction and Admissibility)* (n 132) [63].
134 Ibid.
135 ICJ, *Arrest Warrant* (n 132) [52].
136 Ibid, [54, 55]. For its reasoning, Judge van den Wyngaert heavily criticised the Court (see ICJ *Case Concerning the Arrest Warrant of 11 April 2000* (Dissenting Opinion of Judge van den Wyngaert) [2002] ICJ Rep, p 137, [11–23]).
137 For a brief overview of the preconditions for justifying a specific analogy (and not analogical reasoning as such), see Vöneky (n 111) para 17. For the third step, see below Part II § 6 section I.

§ 5 *EU Withdrawal and Succession: The Case for an Analogy*

analogical assertion: the comparison of two items – one better known (the source) and one less well known (the target) – leads to the inference that because they share some characteristics, the target possesses an additional characteristic which the source is known to have. The general form of an argument by analogy is thus: the source A has characteristics F and G. The target B has characteristics F and G. A also has characteristic H. Therefore, B has characteristic H. Taking the example of the *Nicaragua* case, both treaties (the source) and unilateral declarations (the target) are of an indefinite duration and create legal obligations on which other states may rely (shared characteristics). The inference is that because such treaties may not be terminated without a reasonable period of notice (additional characteristic), unilateral declarations may also not be terminated with immediate effect.

As regards the EU and Member State exits, the starting point for a comparison was already laid down by the ILC: 'hybrid unions' such as the EU 'may appear to have some analogy with a union of states'[138]. The following sections will thus compare the source – unions of states (A.) – with the target – the EU (B.). In the case of a separation from a union of states, Art. 34 VCSSRT provides for the continuity of international agreements with regard to the union and the successor state. If unions of states and the EU are, in fact, similar, it may be inferred that the same rule applies to international agreements in the case of a Member State leaving (C.).

A. The Source: Unions of States

In its simplest form, unions of states may be defined as associations of states. In that sense, it has been remarked that '[t]heoretically and logically the world community as a whole can be considered as [such]'[139]. As Forsyth notes in his extensive study on the topic, based on the vagueness of the

---

138 'SR Waldock Fifth Report' (n 82) 18.
139 F Ermacora, 'Confederations and Other Unions of States' in R Bernhardt (ed), *Encyclopedia of Disputes Installment* (Elsevier Science Publishers 1987) 60. Cp also G Jellinek, *Die Lehre von den Staatenverbindungen* (Alfred Hölder 1882) 95 ('Die in der Natur gegründete und durch das Völkerrecht zur Rechtsgemeinschaft erhobene Staatengemeinschaft ist die erste und umfassendste Form einer Staatenverbindung.') and see I Kant, 'Perpetual Peace: A Philosophical Sketch' in HS Reiss (ed), *Kant: Political Writings* (2nd edn, Cambridge University Press 1991) 102–105 who proposed a worldwide 'Federation of Free States' to ultimately perpetuate peace.

definition, unions of states have 'in the past gone by a variety of names, of which confederacy, confederation, union, federal union, federal government, system of states, community, perpetual league, *république federative*, *Staatenbund*, *Bund*, and *Eidgenossenschaft* have been perhaps the most prominent'[140]. This variety has, however, not only concerned the names given to such unions, but also the 'constitutional relationships which might be considered as falling within the concept of union of States'[141]. To be able to systematically deal with his study material, SR Waldock thus deemed it 'necessary at the outset to identify what is meant by this concept for the purposes of succession of States in respect of treaties'[142]. His findings will form the starting point for comparison with the EU.

SR Waldock introduces the term 'unions of states' in the context of two draft articles – one on the effect of a union's formation on agreements previously concluded by the uniting states[143], and one on the effect of a union's (partial) dissolution on the agreements of the union.[144] Aware of the plurality of state associations that the term conveys,[145] Waldock begins by defining 'unions of states' as used for the sake of his study on succession.

> 'Union of States' means a federal or other union formed by the uniting of two or more States which thereafter constitute separate political divisions of the united State so formed, exercising within their respective territories the governmental powers prescribed by the constitution.[146]

This definition conveys three central characteristics of unions of states which Waldock further elaborates on in the commentaries to the draft articles. From these commentaries, three additional characteristics can be gleaned.

The three characteristics contained in Waldock's definition are all concerned with distinguishing the concept of 'unions of states' from other forms of state association. Firstly, it is fundamental to Waldock that a 'union of states' is a 'united *State*'[147]. The starting point in his commen-

---

140 M Forsyth, *Unions of States: The Theory and Practice of Confederation* (Leicester University Press 1981) 1 (emphasis in original).
141 'SR Waldock Fifth Report' (n 82) 18.
142 Ibid.
143 Ibid, draft article 19.
144 Ibid 35, draft article 20.
145 Ibid 18.
146 Ibid, draft article 1(h).
147 Ibid, draft article 1(h).

taries on unions of states is thus the distinction between constitutional and international unions. A union in the sense of his study is not an international organisation, but has itself acquired statehood. Secondly, this state is formed through a 'uniting of two or more States'. Waldock's second main distinction is thus between different cases *within* his study. A union of states, to which draft articles 19 and 20 applied, consists of previously sovereign states. Where territories, not previously having themselves been states, unite to form a new state or separate, Waldock suggests two separate draft articles.[148] Finally, the third characteristic encompassed in the definition distinguishes a union of states from a unitary state: the uniting states do not fully merge, but must 'constitute separate political divisions', 'exercising governmental functions'[149].

Waldock considers these characteristics leading to the 'creation of a composite international person'[150] as fulfilled by two types of unions: real and federal unions.[151] As defined by Waldock, both real and federal unions are formed by a uniting of two or more formerly independent states into one new state. Real differences only arise in the internal structure of these unions: while '[a] real union is indistinguishable for international purposes from a federal union'[152], the two usually differ in 'the extent to which func-

---

148 Ibid 32, 39, Excursus A ('States other than unions of States, which are formed from two or more territories') and draft article 21 ('Other dismemberments of a State into two or more States'). While this distinction is maintained as regards the uniting of states, it is ultimately abandoned with regard to the separation of a constituent state from a union of states, see below Part II § 6 section II.B.1.
149 Ibid 18, draft article 1(h).
150 For real unions, ibid 20; for federal unions, 'SR Waldock Fifth Report' (n 82) 26 ('composite states').
151 Waldock acknowledges that there is a third type of union, the so-called 'personal union', where two or more states, 'sometimes almost accidental', share the same person as their Head of State ('SR Waldock Fifth Report' (n 82) 20). As such, Waldock dismisses personal unions as a subject for his study. In his view, they do not represent a uniting of states but rather a uniting of functions in one person, with the states and, decisive to the issue of his study, their treaty relations remaining unaffected ('SR Waldock Fifth Report' (n 82) 20). In the same vein, G Jellinek (n 139) 85 ('Die Personalunion ist daher keine juristische, sondern eine historisch-politische Staatenverbindung. Sie ist rechtlich zufällige Gemeinschaft mehrerer Staaten durch die Person des Herrschers, welcher juristisch so viele Persönlichkeiten enthält, als er Staaten regiert.'). M Forsyth (n 140) 1 describes personal unions as a 'laxer form' of union.
152 WE Hall, *A Treatise on International Law* (8th edn, Clarendon Press 1924) 26.

III. EU Withdrawal and Separation: Treating Like Cases Alike

tions of government are concentrated in the central authorities'[153]. Their analysis by Waldock can help shed some light on the rather vague third characteristic of constituting 'separate political divisions'.

The two real unions most elaborately discussed by Waldock are the United Arab Republic (UAR) formed by Syria and Egypt in 1958 and the uniting of Tanganyika and Zanzibar in the Republic of Tanzania in 1964. In both instances, the constituent instruments provided for a common Head of State and a common legislature. While in the case of the Republic of Tanzania, Zanzibar retained a separate executive and legislature for internal matters, the UAR possessed full legislative and executory power over Egypt and Syria. Nevertheless, the UAR's Provisional Constitution provided for regional executive councils in Egypt and Syria to examine the execution of policies pertaining to the respective region. Although both deemed real unions, the degree of division of governmental powers thus varies between the two. In both cases, however, the constitution vested the treaty-making power fully with the union, not leaving any treaty-making power to the component States. Nevertheless, Egypt, Syria, Tanganyika and Zanzibar were all 'recognized as in some measure retaining their separate identity as distinct units'[154] also on the outside. This was 'encouraged'[155] by the fact that both unions applied the pre-union agreements of their constituent states within the regional limits of the constituent states' prior territories.[156]

In contrast to real unions[157], Waldock does not offer a general definition of federal unions or discusses their constitutive features. A *federal* union – as far as Waldock is concerned – is a composite state organised in a *federal* form. Waldock may have abstained from providing a more elaborate provision because '[a] uniform type of federal State with a fixed physiognomy

---

153 DP O'Connell, *State Succession in Municipal Law and International Law: International Relations* (vol II, Cambridge University Press 1967) 71.
154 'SR Waldock Fifth Report' (n 82) 20.
155 Ibid.
156 But see also MC R Craven, *The Decolonization of International Law: State Succession and the Law of Treaties* (Oxford University Press 2007) 218 who notes that Syria and Egypt are geographically separated by over 1000 miles, making it fairly easy to assert that they retained separate identities (to some degree).
157 'SR Waldock Fifth Report' (n 82) 20: 'Such a union exists when two or more States, each having a separate international personality, are united under a common constitution with a common Head of State and a common organ competent to represent them in their relations with other States.'

does not exist'[158]; but also because it is safe to say that in a federal union governmental powers are always divided and the exact division was irrelevant to his study. Instead of engaging in a discourse on the 'different gradations of federation'[159], Waldock thus opts for providing examples of such unions and discussing their practice as regards succession.[160] Nevertheless, in his further study one aspect of a federal union's physiognomy warrants his attention.

In analysing federal unions as regards succession in respect of international agreements, a feature of the federal unions that interested Waldock was the division of external competences between the federation and the component states. Here, Waldock was influenced by the work of the International Law Association (ILA), which had concluded that the component states' (degree of) competence to conclude treaties was irrelevant for the question of succession.[161] Sceptical of that result, Waldock addressed this question for all federal unions analysed, while in general ignoring the federal structure in his examples. Ultimately, he ascribed the exact division of competences ancillary importance.[162] However, Waldock's analysis shows how much the degree of centralisation of external competences varies between different federal unions. While in the case of the United States of America, for example, the federal government is solely in charge of external relations, the treaty-making competence is divided in the Swiss federation

---

158 Rudolf (n 64) para 1 with reference to ILC, 'Third Report on State responsibility, by Roberto Ago, Special Rapporteur' UN Doc. A/CN.4/246 and Add.1 – 3, YBILC (2000) Vol. II(1) 261: '[T]here is not just one single type of federal State, whose physiognomy is definitively fixed: historical reality has only specific situations, each with its own characteristics, [...] and no one can say what future situations will be like.'
159 'SR Waldock Fifth Report' (n 82) 29.
160 These are chronologically by the date of unification the admission of Texas into the United States in 1845, the formation of the Swiss federation in 1848 and the German federation in 1871, the uniting of El Salvador, Nicaragua and Honduras to form the Greater Republic of Central America in 1895, extended in 1897 to Costa Rica and Guatemala, and the formation of the Soviet Union in 1922, see ibid 27–29.
161 For the text of ILA's resolution, see ILC, 'Second Report on Succession in Respect of Treaties, by Sir Humphrey Waldock' UN Doc. A/CN.4/214 and Add. 1 & 2, YBILC (1969) Vol. II 48.
162 Waldock came to the conclusion that the extent to which succession in case of uniting of states to form a federal union 'was linked to the continued possession by the individual States of some measure of treaty-making power or international personality is not clear' ('SR Waldock Fifth Report' (n 82) 29).

III. EU Withdrawal and Separation: Treating Like Cases Alike

and some composite states of the USSR were even capable of concluding agreements alongside the union.[163]

Three additional characteristics of unions of states, surfacing throughout Waldock's report, are relevant to mention here. The first concerns the manner in which unions of states are formed. Being 'new political [entities] on the plane of internal constitutional law'[164], they are based on a constitutional document. Nevertheless, Waldock acknowledges that '[t]he constitution of a union may take the form of or be based upon, a treaty'[165], that is, an instrument of public international law.

The second additional characteristic concerns the situations in which questions of successions in respect of treaties arises. Waldock introduces and defines the term 'unions of states' in the context of a draft article addressing the effects of a union's *creation* on pre-union agreements of its component states. However, the following draft article deals also with the consequences of a union's *dissolution* for the union's agreements. As such, Waldock defines not only the complete dismemberment of the union, but also cases '[w]hen a union of States is dissolved only in respect of one of its constituent political divisions which becomes a separate State'[166].[167] While Waldock does not address *why* unions (partially) dissolve, he nevertheless recognises *that* unions of state may dissolve or parts thereof separate, giving rise to questions of succession.

The third implicit characteristic of unions of states pertains to their external relations. While the division of external competences varies for each union, the nature of their bilateral international agreements, in particular, show overlaps. Upon their dissolution, several unions had concluded, for

---

163 On treaty-making by Belarus and Ukraine before separation from the USSR, see Zimmermann, *Staatennachfolge* (n 76) 392, 397.
164 'SR Waldock Fifth Report' (n 82) 18.
165 Ibid 31 ('[t]he constitution of a union may take the form of or be based upon, a treaty').
166 Ibid 35–36, draft article 20, Alternative A, para. 3 and Alternative B, para. 2.
167 The cases of (partial) dissolution analysed by Waldock are the dissolution of the Union of Columbia (1831); the dissolution of the Union of Norway and Sweden (1905); the termination of the Austro-Hungarian Empire which is treated as a dissolution as regards Austria and Hungary (1919); the dissolution of the Icelandic-Danish (1944); the separation of Syria from the United Arab Republic (1961); the dissolution of the Mali Federation (1960) (see ibid 36–39).

§ 5 EU Withdrawal and Succession: The Case for an Analogy

example, extradition[168] and air transport agreements[169], but all unions had established trade agreements[170] which had to be considered as regards the effect of succession on them.

B. The Target: The European Union

The EU has throughout its history repeatedly been compared to or even itself been described as a union of states. Famously, Forsyth in his study on unions considers the then EEC as a new form of economic union. Placing the EEC in the tradition of the 1789 US constitution and the 1834 German customs union, for Forsyth, 'the Community represents essentially the transformation of the external economic relations between a number of states into an internal market'[171]. However, this classification – and any other – is based on the respective authors' very own understanding of 'unions'. Hence, seeing how diverse the use of the term 'unions of states' is, it seems reasonable for the current analogy to compare the EU to unions of states as studied by Waldock in his reports on state succession.[172] For it

---

168 See the UN Secretariat's study on succession in respect of extradition agreements referring, *inter alia*, to state practice regarding the following unions: the Icelandic-Danish union, the Austro-Hungarian Empire, and the Federation of Rhodesia (UN Secretariat, 'Succession of States in Respect of Bilateral Treaties – Study prepared by the Secretariat' UN Doc. A/CN.4/229, YBILC (1970) Vol. II).
169 See the UN Secretariat's study on succession in respect of air transport agreements referring, *inter alia*, to state practice regarding the following unions: the United Arab Republic and the Federation of Mali (UN Secretariat, 'Succession of States in Respect of Bilateral Treaties – Second and Third Studies prepared by the Secretariat' A/CN.4/243 and Add.1, YBILC (1971) Vol. II(2).
170 See the UN Secretariat's study on succession in respect of trade transport agreements referring, *inter alia*, to state practice regarding the following unions: the Icelandic-Danish union, the Austro-Hungarian Empire, the Federation of Rhodesia, the United Arab Republic and the Federation of Mali (ibid). In his fifth Report, Waldock further discusses the treaties of amity, navigation and *commerce* concluded by the Union of Colombia (see 'SR Waldock Fifth Report' (n 82) 36).
171 M Forsyth (n 140) 183.
172 Thus, while eg Forsyth considers the EEC to be a union of states, he equates unions of states with confederations, ie as not themselves constituting states, see ibid 1: 'First, it is a union that falls short of complete fusion or incorporation in which one or all the members lose their identity as states'. In doing so, he differs from the definition used by Waldock.

is based on their practice, that a rule as regards the effects of their (partial) dissolution on international agreements was developed.[173]

Taking Waldock's definition and commentaries as a basis, several shared characteristics and one obvious difference stand out. Both the EU and the unions of states referred to by Waldock are formed by the uniting of several independent states. Before founding – or acceding to – the EU, all Member States individually fulfilled the criteria for statehood. The basis for their uniting is international agreements, which through Art. 50 TEU recognise the possibility of withdrawal. The obvious difference, of course, is the EU's lack of statehood. Instead of creating a 'united State'[174], the Member States themselves remain states. The question then is, whether the EU and unions of states nevertheless share common characteristics in their *composition*, rather than only as regards their creation and (partial) dissolution, which mirrors any constitutional or international association of states.

What makes the EU a – as Waldock called it – 'hybrid union'[175]? In the eyes of Waldock, it was the then EEC's 'resemblance of a quasi-federal association of States'. Although the Member States retain their statehood, they (also) become 'political divisions' in the EU's system of governance, 'exercising within their respective territories the governmental powers'[176] as defined by the EU Treaties. It is here where a closer consideration of the inner life of unions of states becomes important. Both real and federal unions are defined by an *internal* division of competences between the union and the constituent states in addition to an *external* visibility of the constituent states as retaining some degree of separateness. While it was seemingly irrelevant for Waldock to specify the federal aspects of the unions analysed, it does become relevant when drawing a comparison to the EU. Besides not being a state, can the EU be compared to a federal union of states?

In general, a federal union is a system of governance which has at least two orders of government, authority being 'divided between the federation, on the one side, and the Member States on the other, both of which possess certain assigned competences and functions'[177]. Bernier defines the features of a federal polity as the following:

---

173 See below Part II § 5 section III.C.
174 Cp Waldock's definition in 'SR Waldock Fifth Report' (n 82) 18.
175 Cp ibid.
176 Cp Waldock's definition ibid.
177 Rudolf (n 64) para 1.

(1) a division of powers between a central and regional government; (2) a certain degree of independence between central and regional governments; (3) direct action on the people by central and regional governments; and (4) some means of preserving the constitutional division of powers [...].[178]

In the EU, the Member States have transferred certain competences to the EU so that power is divided between the EU and its Member States creating two levels of governance. Where the EU has competences, the enhanced possibilities of majority voting allow it to exercise them increasingly independent from any veto of the Member States. In exercising its respective competences, the EU can take direct action on the Member States' citizens with regulations[179] and decisions[180] taking direct effect on individuals. Moreover, following rulings by the ECJ, directives, in general only binding on the Member States, may also have direct vertical effects within national legal orders.[181] Finally, the ECJ serves as an arbiter between the EU and the Member States to address disputes over the allocation of competences, preserving their division as provided for by the EU Treaties. Thus, the EU has been described as a 'classic case of federalism without a federation'[182], showcasing 'federal features'[183] in its internal structure without being a federal *state* on the outside.[184]

The question is then how this affects the EU and its Member States in their external relations and how they are perceived as international actors. With regard to unions of states, Waldock repeatedly highlighted the union's and its component states' dual visibility on the international plane: while the union (largely) conducted the external relations, its component states retained a certain degree of individual identity and international visibility.

---

178 I Bernier, *International Legal Aspects of Federalism* (Longman 1973).
179 Art. 288(2) TFEU: 'A regulation shall have general application. It shall be binding in its entirety and directly applicable in all Member States.'
180 Art. 288(4): 'A decision shall be binding in its entirety. A decision which specifies those to whom it is addressed shall be binding only on them.'
181 Laying the foundation, ECJ, C-41/74 *Yvonne van Duyn v Home Office* [1974] ECLI:EU:C:1974:133, [12]. On the direct effect of directives, see in detail M Ruffert, 'Article 288 TFEU' in C Calliess and M Ruffert (eds), *EUV/AEUV: Das Verfassungsrecht der Europäischen Union mit Europäischer Grundrechtecharta* (6th edn, CH Beck 2022), paras 48–77.
182 M Burgess (n 26) 28–29.
183 Schütze, *Cooperative Federalism* (n 54) 72.
184 Cp ibid who criticises the 'federation equals state' equation with references to supporters and opponents.

The EU possesses an international legal personality with the capacity and competence to conclude international agreements on a broad range of subjects, which are in many aspects identical to the agreements studied in the ILC's reports. In addition, the EU has, in fact, used said power to become a prominent actor on the international stage. At the same time, the Member States continue to engage in treaty-making – alongside the EU, in the case of mixed agreements, and individually in the areas of their exclusive competence.

C. The Inferred Characteristic: Continuity of International Agreements

While the VCSSRT itself no longer speaks of unions of states, their formation and dissolution are still covered by its articles. Art. 31 VCSSRT addresses the effects on international agreements 'when two or more States unite and so form one successor State'. In no longer referencing the formation of a 'union of states', Art. 31 aims 'not to take into account the particular form of the internal constitutional organization adopted by the successor state'[185]. While most unions of states covered in Waldock's fifth report on the topic of succession were organised in a federal manner, Art. 31 VCSSRT now acknowledges the fact that 'uniting may lead to a wholly unitary State, to a federation or to any other form of constitutional arrangement'[186].

In the same vein, the 'form of constitutional arrangement'[187] of a state is no longer of relevance when it comes to the dissolution of a state or the separation of parts of its territory. While Waldock had originally drafted an article dealing exclusively with the effects of a (partial) dissolution of a constitutional union of states, these are now included when Arts. 34 and 35 VCSSRT more broadly take 'the concept of "the State" [...] as the starting point'[188]. While Art. 34 addresses the effects of a separation on the successor state(s), Art. 35 VCSSRT deals with the effects of separation on the predecessor state, where it continues to exist.

---

185 'ILC Report 1974' (n 75) 253.
186 Ibid.
187 Ibid.
188 Ibid 265.

Article 34. Succession of States in cases of separation of parts of a State

1. When a part or parts of the territory of a State separate to form one or more States, whether or not the predecessor State continues to exist:
   (a) any treaty in force at the date of the succession of States in respect of the entire territory of the predecessor State continues in force in respect of each successor State so formed;
   (b) any treaty in force at the date of the succession of States in respect only of that part of the territory of the predecessor State which has become a successor State continues in force in respect of that successor State alone.
2. Paragraph 1 does not apply if:
   (a) the States concerned otherwise agree; or
   (b) it appears from the treaty or is otherwise established that the application of the treaty in respect of the successor State would be incompatible with the object and purpose of the treaty or would radically change the conditions for its operation.

Article 35. Position if a State continues after separation of part of its territory

When, after separation of any part of the territory of a State, the predecessor State continues to exist, any treaty which at the date of the succession of States was in force in respect of the predecessor State continues in force in respect of its remaining territory unless:
(a) the States concerned otherwise agree;
(b) it is established that the treaty related only to the territory which has separated from the predecessor State; or
(c) it appears from the treaty or is otherwise established that the application of the treaty in respect of the predecessor State would be incompatible with the object and purpose of the treaty or would radically change the conditions for its operation.

Both articles are based on the principle of continuity: in general, the predecessor state simply continues its treaty relations and the successor states succeeds into these relations upon separation. The situation thus created means that – following succession – both the predecessor and the successor state will be parties to the multilateral agreements which the predecessor had concluded pre-separation. In contrast, in the case of a bilateral agreement 'there is no question of the treaty's being brought into force *between the successor State and its predecessor*'[189]. Instead, succession creates a 'new and purely bilateral relation'[190] between the successor state and the other treaty party.

To this principle of continuity, Arts. 34 and 35 VCSSRT contain three limitations: the agreement's previous territorial scope of application, the principle of consent and a *rebus sic stantibus*-like exception. As regards the first, succession shall not extend an international agreement beyond its pre-separation territorial scope. An agreement that related only to the territory of the predecessor or the territory of the successor state will continue in force only for the respective state.[191] Secondly, the rules on succession as provided for in Arts. 34, 35 VCSSRT are subject to any diverging agreement between the 'States concerned'[192]. Importantly, an agreement between the 'States concerned' refers to any arrangements made between the predecessor state *or* the successor state and their treaty partner(s). Thus, the continuity rule of Art. 34 VCSSRT cannot be set aside by an agreement between the predecessor and the successor state.[193] The third exception applies to situations where succession proves difficult from the viewpoint of an agreement's content, either because it collides with the object and purpose or the performance of the agreement.[194]

As has been discussed above, the EU and constitutional unions of states share a number of characteristics: both are formed through a uniting of states; during the union, these states as constituent states of the union retain a (certain degree of) separate identity; this separateness manifests itself through elements of federalism, also (or especially) with regard to foreign relations; and the conduct of foreign relations includes, *inter alia*, the conclusion of qualitatively similar international agreements. In comparison to the EU, constitutional unions of states have an additional characteristic pursuant to Arts. 34, 35 VCSSRT: the principle of continuity applies to its international agreements in the case of (partial) dissolution. Based on the similarities between unions and the EU, it could thus be inferred that

---

189 ILC, 'Fourth Report on Succession in Respect of Treaties, by Sir Humphrey Waldock' UN Doc A/CN.4/249, YBILC (1971) Vol. II(1) 146.
190 Ibid.
191 Arts. 34(1)(b), 35(b) VCSSRT.
192 Arts. 34(2)(a), 35(a) VCSSRT.
193 According to Art. 8 VCSSRT any agreements reached between a predecessor and a successor state have no effect on the other states parties and thus cannot abrogate the continuity principle in Arts. 34, 35 VCSSRT.
194 Arts. 34(2)(b), 35(c) VCSSRT.

§ 5 EU Withdrawal and Succession: The Case for an Analogy

the EU, too, must possess this characteristic. In that case, the effects of the withdrawal of a Member State on international agreements concluded by the EU would be governed by Arts. 34, 35 VCSSRT.

IV. Applying Art. 34 VCSSRT to the Case of Brexit

The previous sections have shown that it may be possible to apply the rules of succession in case of separation to the EU and Brexit, albeit by means of analogical reasoning. The EU not being a state, it is not covered by the VCSSRT's scope of application, which is limited to *state* succession and its effects on agreements *between states*. This arguably leaves a gap in the international legal order. The effect of exiting the EU on its international agreements is neither convincingly addressed by applying the VCLT, nor is it provided for in the VCSSRT. The similarities between the EU and unions of states, a non-unitary form of a state consisting of several constituent states, appears to allow for the closing of this gap. Where Art. 34 VCSSRT is applied to the situation of a separation from a union of states, it seems reasonable to infer that it may also be applied to a situation with similar circumstances: leaving the EU.

Art. 34 VCSSRT provides for a general rule of *de jure* continuity of international agreements following a separation, regardless of the survival of the predecessor state. For the separation of a constituent state from a union that does not result in its complete dissolution, this means that both the union as the predecessor (pursuant to Art. 35 VCSSRT) and the former constituent state as the successor (pursuant to Art. 35 VCSSRT) continue the union's treaty relations. Transferring this to the situation of a Member State leaving the EU, the result would be that the EU's external international agreements – meaning *all* EU-only and mixed agreements – continue to apply to the former Member State, this state becoming (or remaining) a party to these agreements. Hence, Art. 34 VCSSRT clearly presents itself as an *alternative* legal framework: the result of analogically applying it to an EU exit is a legal outcome clearly different from the one produced by applying the VCLT where withdrawal from the EU results in the discontinuation of all EU-only agreements for the withdrawing state.[195]

The question is, however, if it is also a *convincing* alternative, the persuasiveness of the analogy hinging on two aspects. Firstly, while the EU and

---

195 For a summary of the legal analysis based on international institutional and treaty law, see Part I Concluding Remarks.

IV. Applying Art. 34 VCSSRT to the Case of Brexit

unions of states have many similarities, they are also different in various aspects, the most obvious being the statehood of the latter. Thus, that two subjects share certain characteristics as such cannot suffice to establish a convincing argument by analogy. Rather, the analogical assertion – the EU and unions are similar, and thus we can infer that the rules applicable to unions in case of separation are likewise applicable to an EU exit – requires further justification. Secondly, so far neither of the legal frameworks – the VCLT or the VCSSRT – appear to be coherent with the practice as is visible in the case of Brexit. The fact that practice does not accord with a given rule does not as such make a statement about the rule's adequateness or persuasiveness. It does, however, pose a question to the whole endeavour: why go through the trouble of establishing a sound argument by analogy only to conclude that it was not followed in practice? The following two chapters will address both aspects. They will show that analogical application of the law of succession presents a justifiable alternative (§ 6), and furthermore that it did – to some extent – do so in practice (§ 7).

§ 6 EU Withdrawal and Succession: Justifying the Analogy

The first task in reasoning by analogy is the initial comparison. The EU and unions of states share certain similarities. The second task is to explore if on the basis of this comparison a *convincing* argument by analogy can be made. It is one thing to identify similarities between a source and a target case and quite another to transfer a rule applicable to one to the other. This is a well-known difficulty in legal reasoning. To tackle it, there are different approaches to coming to a 'valid'[1] analogical argument. When engaging with these approaches, not only the particularities of international law in general, but especially those of the *Vienna Convention on Succession in Respect of Treaties*[2] (VCSSRT) must be taken into account (I.).

In then proceeding to justify the analogy between the separation from a union of states, on the one hand, and withdrawal from the EU, on the other, two main questions must be answered. Firstly, of what relevance is the EU and union of states' main dissimilarity – the EU's lack of statehood – to the analogy (II.)? Secondly, what relevance do their shared characteristics have to the rule – Art. 34 VCSSRT – for analogical application to the EU (III.)? Besides the strict comparison between the EU and unions of states, further considerations may also need to be taken into account. Thus, while the drafting of Art. 34 VCSSRT was largely based on a rationale of treaty stability, this may be challenged by the reference to the principle of consent (IV.), and indeed these two principles may require careful balancing in the case of EU withdrawal (V.).

---

1 See S Brewer, 'Exemplary Reasoning: Semantics, Pragmatics, and the Rational Force of Legal Argument by Analogy' (1996) 109(5) *Harvard Law Review* 923, 943, fn. 56: '[I]n a valid deductive argument, whenever the premises are true, the conclusion is also true.' Based hereon, in general, no argument by analogy can be 'valid'. But see S Brewer, 'Indefeasible Analogical Argument' in H Kaptein and BD van der Velden (eds), *Analogy and Exemplary Reasoning in Legal Discourse* (Amsterdam University Press 2018).
2 Vienna Convention on Succession of States in Respect of Treaties (adopted 23 August 1978, entered into force 6 November 1996) 1946 UNTS 3 [VCSSRT].

§ 6 EU Withdrawal and Succession: Justifying the Analogy

I. Methodical Excursus: Valid Analogical Reasoning and International Law

The previous chapter (§ 5) amounts to what may be called the 'discovery'[3] in the scheme of analogical reasoning. Being in a situation of doubt as regards a specific case, the legal reasoner effects a rule-like sorting of the examples they are confronted with.[4] A case displays particular circumstances and is covered by a legal rule; perhaps *all* cases with similar circumstances should fall under that rule. In the case of withdrawal from the EU, the comparison between unions of states and the EU has led to the inference where the rules of succession applied to unions could also be applied to the EU. However, structured in this simplest form, 'it should readily appear that analogical reasoning does not guarantee good outcomes or truth'[5]. The fact that the source and the target share some characteristics F and G does not warrant the conclusion that they must *necessarily* also share characteristic H. An argument is valid – and thus indefeasible – 'if and only *whenever all the premises are true, the conclusion must be true*'[6].

Returning to the example of the *Nicaragua* case[7], even if we know all the premises on treaties and unilateral declarations to be true, they still do not logically entail the conclusion that unilateral declarations must *necessarily* be treated the same as treaties concerning their termination.[8] Instead, an argument by analogy can 'at best show only that the conclusions are more likely to be true than false'[9]. Achieving this requires a process of 'confirmation or disconfirmation' in which the legal reasoner tests the analogical assertion previously made by '[measuring] [it] against a separate set of explanatory and justificatory propositions'[10].

In doing so, one concern is usually the relation between the shared and the inferred characteristics. As Brewer points out,

---

3 Brewer, *Exemplary Reasoning* (n 1) 1022.
4 Ibid 962.
5 CR Sunstein, 'On Analogical Reasoning' (1993) 106(3) *Harvard Law Review* 741, 745.
6 Brewer, Analogy and Exemplary Reasoning (n 1) 45 (emphasis in original).
7 ICJ *Case Concerning Military and Paramilitary Activities in and against Nicaragua (Nicaragua v United States of America)* (Jurisdiction and Admissibility) [1984] ICJ Rep 1984, p 392.
8 On the analogy drawn in that case, see above Part II § 5 section II.
9 M Golding, 'Argument by Analogy in the Law' in H Kaptein and BD van der Velden (eds) (n 1) 126.
10 Brewer, *Exemplary Reasoning* (n 1) 962.

I. Methodical Excursus: Valid Analogical Reasoning and International Law

[...] neither the presence of 'similarities' nor the *number* of similarities between analogized items can be sufficient to make exemplary argument a rationally compelling process of *reasoning*, for everything is similar to everything else in an *infinite* number of ways, and everything is also *dissimilar* to everything else in an infinite number of ways. One needs to discern some additional constraint on this kind of argument if it is to be compelling at all.[11]

Such additional constraint can be provided by reference to the relevance of the shared characteristics to the inferred characteristic. Thus, for Golding the 'crucial question is whether the compared objects resemble (and differ from) one another in *relevant* respects, that is, respects that are relevant to possession of the inferred characteristic'[12]. Again, using the *Nicaragua* example, the shared characteristic 'being of indefinite duration' of both treaties and unilateral declarations is relevant to the inferred characteristic 'no immediate unilateral termination' because a concerned state will rely on continued performance.

Solely relying on the relevance criterion, however, would narrow the process of (dis)confirmation to the question of *how* the source and the target's shared characteristic and inferred characteristic are related. Yet, analogical reasoning not being a deductive argument,[13] the relevance of similarities may *explain* the analogy, but cannot (by itself) *justify* it. To do so, the convincing – if not even 'true' or 'correct' – argument by analogy must also address the question *why* weight should be given to this relation, that is, why 'in the "eyes of the law"', the proposed analogical assertion 'does or *should* obtain'[14].

Brewer thus suggests a more 'holistic' two-step process of (dis)confirming an argument by analogy.[15] '[Playing] the vital role'[16] in the first step are the – as Brewer calls them – 'analogy-warranting rationales'[17]. When employing an analogy, the legal reasoner endorses the rationales underlying

---

11 Ibid 932–933 (emphasis in original, footnotes omitted).
12 Golding (n 9) 124 (emphasis in original).
13 On the (in)defeasibility of an argument by analogy, see Brewer, Analogy and Exemplary Reasoning (n 1).
14 Brewer, *Exemplary Reasoning* (n 1) 965 (emphasis in original).
15 Ibid 963.
16 Ibid 965–966.
17 Ibid 962.

the legal rule to be analogically applied to the target case.[18] Thus, it is necessary to identify these rationales and to test the analogical assertion 'for a strong degree of coherence with those rationales'[19]. In *Nicaragua*, the analogical assertion (treaty rule applied to unilateral declaration) is justified by reference to the principle of good faith entailed by both a treaty and a unilateral declaration.[20] In a second step, the legal reasoner can then look to see whether the analogy 'effects an acceptable sorting'[21]. This is not the case where one can identify 'countervailing considerations of equal importance' outweighing the previously identified rationales.[22]

This chapter will combine these approaches. Firstly, it will address the obvious difference between the EU and unions of states – the EU's lack of statehood – and considers its relevance to the analogy (II.). Secondly, it will seek to identify the rationale behind the continuity rule of Art. 34 VCSSRT and question the coherence of applying it to the EU (III.). Finally, it will address any countervailing considerations (IV.).

In (dis)confirming the analogy drawn between unions of states and the EU – which would allow applying rules on the effects of a separation to an EU exit – the particularities of international law present an additional challenge. The way in which international law is created makes it (potentially) considerably more difficult to discern the underlying rationales of a given rule or identify which similarities in a drawn analogy may be relevant. 'Since provisions of international law are not created by a legislator and the drafting history of international treaties is only a subsidiary means of interpretation', Vöneky considers any 'reference to the original intent of a law-maker […] impossible and reference to the intentions of the signatories […] not convincing'[23]. These concerns only seem to intensify when one considers that while the VCSSRT is a treaty, it is based on a (partially) progressive development of international law and to date lacks a substantial number of ratifications.[24]

Nonetheless, this chapter will take the reports of the International Law Commission (ILC) on the succession of states in respect of treaties and

---

18 Golding (n 9) 127–128.
19 Brewer, *Exemplary Reasoning* (n 1) 1022.
20 ICJ, *Nicaragua (Jurisdiction and Admissibility)* (n 7) [63].
21 Brewer, *Exemplary Reasoning* (n 1) 1022–1023.
22 Golding (n 9) 134.
23 S Vöneky, 'Analogy in International Law' in R Wolfrum (ed), *The Max Planck Encyclopedia of Public International Law* (Oxford University Press 2012) para 17.
24 See below Part II § 6 section II.B.1 and § 7 Introduction.

the records of the United Nations Conference on the Succession of States in Respect of Treaties (UNCSSRT) as a starting point. While the *travaux préparatoires* are a subsidiary means of *interpreting* a treaty, the drafting history of the VCSSRT serves as a valuable basis for *understanding* the object and purpose, the rationales, behind its rules.[25] Firstly, it may be argued that the 'closest [comparison] to a legislature' that international law has to offer 'are the diplomatic conferences of States that adopt conventions laying down rules aspiring to universal acceptance'[26]. Thus, the protocols of these diplomatic conferences may also come closest to establishing an 'original intent of a law-maker'[27]. Secondly, to systematise an entire subfield of international law, it is key for the ILC to identify the underlying rationales. In carrying out its mandate, the ILC does not 'possess legislative powers'[28]. In contrast, as put by a member, it is the Commission's job 'to understand the logic of the existing rules and to develop them in the framework of this logic, not to change the underlying logic'[29].

The interaction between the ILC's work and the discussions at the ensuing diplomatic conferences becomes particularly relevant where the outcome – as in the case of the VCSSRT – combines aspects of codification with the progressive development of the law. Being confronted with a paucity or ambiguity of state practice obliges the ILC – and subsequently the diplomatic conference – to actively develop a rule and in doing so weigh and ultimately decide on certain rationales. When the ILC began drafting the VCSSRT, substantial doubts existed regarding the codificability of (any) rules on state succession with respect to treaties.[30] As regards cases of dissolution or separation, the Commission openly opted for a (partially) progressive development. In determining the rationale for Art. 34

---

25 See Vöneky who also acknowledges that 'rules of international law have an object and purpose beyond their wording' which in justifying an analogy one has to 'extract' (Vöneky (n 23) para 17).
26 FL Bordin, *The Analogy between States and International Organizations* (Cambridge University Press 2019) 36.
27 Vöneky (n 23) 17.
28 FL Bordin (n 26) 38.
29 Quoted in ibid.
30 See on criticism before codification, MC R Craven, *The Decolonization of International Law: State Succession and the Law of Treaties* (Oxford University Press 2007) 93–96. But also in hindsight, DP O'Connell, 'Reflections on the State Succession Convention' (1979) 39(4) *Zeitschrift für ausländisches öffentliches Recht und Völkerrecht* 725, 726 concluded that 'State succession is a subject altogether unsuited to the processes of codification').

§ 6 EU Withdrawal and Succession: Justifying the Analogy

VCSSRT's continuity rule, the ILC's discussion of alternative draft articles and the UNCSSRT's reception of the final draft can thus serve as a valuable basis.

II. On Dissimilarities: The Irrelevance of the EU's Lack of Statehood

It would seem superfluous to even begin thinking about the relevance of similarities between unions of states and the EU without first addressing the obvious differences: the EU's lack of statehood. In justifying the analogy between the EU and unions of states, this is reflected in two respects. Firstly, statehood may play a role with regard to the question of whether 'from the point of view of succession'[31] leaving the EU is sufficiently comparable to a case of state succession (A.). Succession is traditionally understood as a change in sovereignty, a concept deeply connected with statehood. Can EU withdrawal then even trigger the continuity rule to be analogically applied?

Secondly, statehood has also played a decisive role in defining the unions of states to which the EU is being compared. Waldock only included those unions in his study that he believed had themselves acquired statehood. But what relevance did the distinction between unions with and without statehood really have in the drafting of the continuity rule in Art. 34 VCSSRT (B.)? With respect to the formation of a union, practice seemed to vindicate Waldock's differentiation: at first sight, the EU's practice with regard to its new Member States' pre-accession agreements deviates from the practice of (other) unions. On closer examination, however, Waldock's treatment of this practice calls into questions the conclusions he derived from his analysis (C.).

A. Changing Sovereignty? Brexit and the Definition of Succession

The relevance of the concept of sovereignty to the topic of state succession was a reoccurring question throughout the ILC's work and the ensuing UN Conference. As regards unions of states, under special consideration here, the locus of sovereignty may serve as a factor in determining the

---

31 ILC, 'Fifth Report on Succession in Respect of Treaties, by Sir Humphrey Waldock' UN Doc. A/CN.4/256 and Add.1 – 4, YBILC (1972) Vol. II 18.

II. On Dissimilarities: The Irrelevance of the EU's Lack of Statehood

character of a union of states.[32] But the concept of sovereignty is, for many, also quintessential for the question of succession as such: it is traditionally understood that 'what changes hands during a state succession is sovereignty'[33]. Thus, the fact of succession (to be distinguished from the legal consequences this may ensue[34]) has often been defined in terms of a change of sovereignty over a certain territory.

However, in defining the term 'succession of States' for the purpose of their draft articles, the ILC did not opt for the seemingly obvious. Instead, Art. 2(1)(b) VCSSRT refers to the 'replacement of one State by another in the *responsibility* for the international relations of territory'[35]. In doing so, the understanding of succession underlying the VCSSRT is not one where sovereignty plays the decisive role (1.). Instead, the definition employed places relevance on characteristics such as competences and responsibility which are not only possessed by the EU (2.), but which also change from the Member States to the EU and *vice versa* in cases of EU accession or withdrawal (3.).

1. The Irrelevance of Sovereignty to a Succession of States

In his first report on state succession in respect of treaties, Special Rapporteur (SR) Waldock introduced an initial definition of the term 'succession'. As he explained, '[specifying] the sense in which the term "succession" is used' was of 'cardinal importance for the whole structure of the present draft'[36]. The significance that Waldock attached to defining succession for the purpose of his draft articles lies in the double meaning associated with the word. On the one hand, Waldock pointed to examples in state practice and municipal law, in which '"succession" is a legal term and a legal institution which connotes the devolution [...] of rights and obligations automatically *by operating of law* on the happening of an event'[37]. Such an

---

32 See below Part II § 6 section II.B.
33 L Gradoni, 'Article 2' in G Distefano, G Gaggioli and A Hêche (eds), *La Convention de Vienne de 1978 sur la Succession d'États en Matière de Traités: Commentaire Article par Article et Études Thématiques* (Bruylant 2016) para 23 ('ce qui change de main lors d'une succession d'État, c'est la souveraineté', translated by the author).
34 On this point, see below Part II § 6 section II.A.1 and MCR Craven (n 30) 64–67.
35 Emphasis added.
36 ILC, 'First Report on Succession of States and Governments in Respect of Treaties, by Sir Humphrey Waldock' UN Doc A/CN.4/202, YBILC (1968) Vol. II 91.
37 Ibid.

§ 6 EU Withdrawal and Succession: Justifying the Analogy

understanding of succession would, however, have predetermined his study regarding if and when such a devolution or transfer of treaty rights and obligations does in fact take place. On the other hand, the term 'succession' can also be related exclusively 'to the *fact*'[38] of succession – one state replacing another – without making any statement about legal consequences. It was in that latter sense that Waldock sought to refer to it.

But when does the fact of succession occur? Traditionally, succession has often been defined in terms of a change of sovereignty over a certain territory.[39] According to Waldock's first draft definition, however, succession meant 'the replacement of one State by another [...] in the *possession of the competence to conclude treaties* with respect to a given territory'[40]. But sovereignty being '[t]he doctrine of the time'[41], the absence of any reference to it unsurprisingly led to debate in the ILC.[42] In light of this, Waldock justified his choice of the phrase 'competence to conclude treaties' over 'sovereignty' in his second report. In his view, 'to formulate "succession" only in terms of change of sovereignty may be too narrow', with competence to conclude treaties, in contrast, being 'capable of covering such special cases as "mandates", trusteeships and protected States'[43].

At the same time, Waldock yielded to the dissatisfaction expressed in the Commission. 'In view [...] of the feeling of some members that change of "sovereignty" should find mention'[44], he simply included it in his previous definition. The term 'succession' now referred to 'the replacement of one State by another in the sovereignty of territory *or* in the competence to conclude treaties with respect to territory'[45]. While this introduced the

---

38 Ibid.
39 A Zimmermann, *Staatennachfolge in völkerrechtliche Verträge: Zugleich ein Beitrag zu den Möglichkeiten und Grenzen völkerrechtlicher Kodifikation* (Springer 2000) 13–16; MCR Craven (n 30) 56.
40 'SR Waldock First Report' (n 36) 90 (emphasis added). This initial definition also included the replacement of governments ('[...] of one State by another, or, as the case may be, of one Government by another [...]'). Already in his second report, however, Waldock excluded the topic of changes of government (ILC, 'Second Report on Succession in Respect of Treaties, by Sir Humphrey Waldock' UN Doc. A/CN.4/214 and Add. 1 & 2, YBILC (1969) Vol. II 47).
41 Gradoni (n 33) para 23 ('La doctrine de l'époque', translated by the author).
42 ILC, 'Report of the International Law Commission on the work of its twentieth session, 27 May–2 August 1968' UN Doc. A/7209/Rev.1, YBILC (1968) Vol. II 217.
43 'SR Waldock Second Report' (n 40) 51.
44 Ibid.
45 Ibid 50, Art. 1(a).

II. On Dissimilarities: The Irrelevance of the EU's Lack of Statehood

concept of sovereignty into the draft, the addition was merely cosmetic: succession did not require a change of sovereignty *and* competence to conclude treaties, but – given the disjunction – a change of competence still sufficed. Taken together with the fact that Waldock perceived sovereignty to be the narrower criterion, the result of the amended definition was that a succession through a change of sovereignty simply became a 'subclass'[46] of successions where the competence to conclude treaties changes hands.[47] Thus, in the end, the criterion of the Special Rapporteur – treaty-making competence – remained the decisive one.[48]

While the result of the ILC's initial debate on the definition of succession led to the inclusion of the concept of sovereignty, the ILC's first reading of the draft articles resulted in its deletion: now that sovereignty was explicitly mentioned in the definition, it had sparked too many controversies on the precise meaning of the concept in the context of succession.[49] Thus, the Drafting Committee introduced a new – and final – formula: succession as 'the replacement of one State by another in the responsibility for the international relations of territory'[50]. In the Commission's view, this definition was 'preferable' to sovereignty and treaty-making competence 'because it is a formula commonly used in State practice and more appropriate to cover in a neutral manner any specific case independently of the particular

---

46 Gradoni (n 33) para 25.
47 Ibid 102. Kearney, too, points to the doubling created, albeit in a reverse direction: 'The use of the conjunction "or" to link the two phrases "in the sovereignty of territory" and "in the competence to conclude treaties with respect to territory" appeared to suggest that the two phrases covered different ground, whereas in fact the concept of sovereignty necessarily included the power to conclude treaties with respect to the territory over which sovereignty was exercised.' (ILC, 'Summary records of the Twenty-Fourth Session 2 May-7 July 1972' UN Doc. A/CN.4/Ser.A/1972, YBILC (1972) Vol. I 40)
48 Gradoni (n 33) para 25.
49 On the discussion, see ibid 102–103.
50 Cp Art. 2(1)(b) VCSSRT. On the drafting process, see also ibid 106–109. The awareness also of states as regards the complexity of the concept of sovereignty is made clear by the Brazilian representative to the Diplomatic Conference: 'It was also an advantage that the draft defined succession as the "replacement" of one State by another. As other delegations had said, that definition was not perfect, but it should be borne in mind that behind it [...] lay the problem of sovereignty. The International Law Commission had deliberately chosen the present wording in order to avoid discussing that complex subject.' (UNCSSRT, 'Official Records'3rd meeting of the Committee of the Whole UN Doc. A/CONF.80/C.1/SR.3 32).

§ 6 EU Withdrawal and Succession: Justifying the Analogy

status of the territory in question [...]'[51]. Yet, these substantive concerns in fact related exclusively to the definition's previous reference to sovereignty and the doubts raised in this regard. Reference to the treaty-making competence, on the other hand, was never rejected for substantive reasons, but appears to have been ultimately discarded primarily for reasons of a broader applicability. With SR Bedjaoui simultaneously working on the topic of state succession in matters *other than treaties*, a formula fitting for both projects appeared more reasonable.[52]

Thus, the first main takeaway from Art. 2(1)(b)'s drafting history is what succession, in the understanding underlying the VCSSRT, is not: a circumstance narrowly defined by a change of sovereignty. Instead, it may even be said that the ILC

> [dissociated] the concept of sovereignty from the notion of State: under the Convention, a succession of *States* can take place even in the absence of a replacement in sovereignty over a given territory, i.e., between States which are not, or not completely, sovereign.[53]

The purpose of the ILC's 'setting aside of the concept of sovereignty'[54] in defining the fact of succession was not to enable a broader application of the VCSSRT's rules in the future. It merely served to 'resolve'[55] the con-

---

51 ILC, 'Report of the International Law Commission on the Work of its Twenty-Fourth Session, 2 May – 7 July 1972, Official Records of the General Assembly, Twenty-seventh session, Supplement No.10' UN Doc. A/8710/Rev.1, YBILC (1972) Vol. II 231.

52 See eg the comments by the Ukrainian and Soviet Representative to the Diplomatic Conference in this regard (ILC, 'First Report on Succession of States in Respect of Treaties, by Sir Francis Vallat, Special Rapporteur' UN Doc. A/CN.4/278 and Add.1 – 6, YBILC (1974) Vol. II(1) 24). For the ILC's work on the issue, see ILC, 'Analytical Guide to the Work of the International Law Commission: Succession of States in Respect of Matters other than Treaties' (06.04.2022) <https://legal.un.org/ilc/guide/3_3.shtml>. The project led to the adoption of the Vienna Convention on Succession of States in respect of State Property, Archives and Debts (adopted 8 April 1983, not yet in force) A/CONF.117/14 [VCSSRSAD]with a definition of 'succession' in Art. 2(1)(a) verbatim identical to that of the VCSSRT.

53 Gradoni (n 33) para 35 ('En réalité, la démarche suivie par les rédacteurs de la Convention consista non pas à refouler mais à résoudre le problème en dissociant le concept de souveraineté de la notion d'État : aux termes de la Convention, une succession d'États peut avoir lieu même en l'absence d'une substitution dans la souveraineté sur un territoire donné, soit entre États qui ne sont pas, ou ne sont pas tous, souverains.' Translated by the author).

54 Ibid 109 ('La mise à l'écart du concept de souveraineté', translated by the author).

55 Ibid ('En réalité, la démarche suivie par les rédacteurs de la Convention consista non pas à refouler mais à résoudre le problème [...]', translated by the author).

II. On Dissimilarities: The Irrelevance of the EU's Lack of Statehood

troversies surrounding the concept and those difficult cases where during the Commission's debate the question of sovereignty had remained open. But the fact that the Commission was able to exclude the issue in this way at all argues against a greater relevance of sovereignty to the factual determination of a succession situation.

Today, the definition of the VCSSRT – speaking of a replacement in the responsibility for international relations instead of sovereignty – has been broadly accepted and is said to have acquired customary status.[56] In terms of the analogy proposed, this means that sovereignty, a characteristic that constitutional unions of states and the EU do *not* share, is at least not the decisive criterion for the determination of a factual occurrence of a succession. Instead, the application of the rules on succession – such as Art. 34 VCSSRT in the case of a succession through separation – hinges upon determining a change in the responsibility for the international relations of a territory.

2. The Relevance of Competence and Responsibility to Succession

The characteristic initially chosen in the ILC's work for determining a factual succession was the competence to conclude international agreements. When considering Waldock's primary definition of succession based on the 'replacement [...] in the possession of the competence to conclude treaties with respect to a given territory' it is difficult *not* to draw parallels to the EU. Clearly, the EU has the competence – explicitly and implicitly – to conclude international agreements.[57] Such is transferred to it by its Member States upon accession and falls back to them when exiting the Union. And while the scope of application of the EU's international agreements is often first and foremost defined in terms of that of the EU Treaties, the EU still concludes them with respect to a given territory, namely that of their Member States.[58]

Although Waldock's reliance on the treaty-making competence was eventually replaced, this was not for substantive concerns but for reasons of greater general applicability. Today's Art. 2(1)(b) VCSSRT refers to succession as a change in the responsibility over a territory's international rela-

---

56 A Zimmermann (n 39) 16.
57 See Art. 216(1) TFEU.
58 On the scope of territorial application of EU-only and mixed agreements, see above Part I § 4 section I.B.2. See also Art. 216(2) TFEU.

tions. To what extent is Waldock's original definition reflected in the current one? And, by extension, how much similarity does the new definition bear to the situation of the EU and its Member States in cases of accession or withdrawal? Although resorted to because 'it is a formula commonly used in State practice'[59], the criterion of responsibility for the international relations of territory appears comparably vague and lacking nuance: when does it arise and what does it cover?

In its commentaries to the final draft articles, the ILC defines the term 'responsibility', but only in the negative: 'The word "responsibility" [...] does *not* intend to convey any notion of "State responsibility", a topic currently under study by the Commission [...]'.[60] A more instructive – albeit still limited – discussion of the definition can be found in the first report of the ILC's second Special Rapporteur for the topic, Sir Francis Vallat, who engaged with the succession definition following its redrafting by the ILC's Drafting Committee. From his comments, it is not only possible to piece together more details as regards the individual elements of the definition: the report even discusses the definition of succession with a view to its applicability to the then EEC.

SR Vallat, too, begins by defining the term 'responsibility' in the context of succession as *not* being 'responsibility in the sense of contractual or tortious liability or [...] "State responsibility"'[61]. In order to distinguish reference to responsibility in the succession definition from any unintended meaning of the word, he highlights the necessity to consider the 'expression as a whole'[62]. In so doing, the phrase 'responsibility *for the international relations*'

> covers all aspects of international relations, including the conclusion of treaties and their performance, and, without using the controversial term 'sovereignty', covers the content of that term most relevant to the aspects of international law under consideration.[63]

In that sense, Art. 2(1)(b) VCSSRT is even broader than the previously suggested drafts, covering the issue of treaty-making (competence) but not

---

59 ILC, 'Report of the International Law Commission on the Work of its Twenty-Sixth Session, 6 May – 26 July 1974' UN Doc. A/9610/Rev.1, YBILC (1974) Vol. II(1) 175.
60 Ibid 176 (emphasis added).
61 'SR Vallat First Report' (n 52) 27.
62 Ibid.
63 Ibid.

II. On Dissimilarities: The Irrelevance of the EU's Lack of Statehood

being limited to it.[64] And while the concept of sovereignty finds mention again, Vallat – as his predecessor – fails to define exactly *which* aspects of it have *what* relevance to the question of succession.[65]

Secondly, Vallat continues to narrow the understanding of 'responsibility' as such. During the ILC's debate on the definition of succession,[66] a discussion ensued as to 'how the proposed definition related to such cases as Liechtenstein, San Marino and Andorra, where the responsibility for international relations was divided'[67]. In his report, Vallat quotes Waldock's response 'that a distinction had to be made between the *conduct* of international relations and *responsibility* for international relations'[68]. This suggests that for the purpose of the definition of succession, responsibility for international relations does not necessarily belong to the state conducting them, but lies with the state *controlling* the conduct of those relations.[69] This is underscored by Vallat's example of a kind of conduct below the threshold of control: 'Cases of representation in international relations should be distinguished from cases of responsibility for international relations and the former should be left outside the scope of "succession of States"'[70]. A replacement in the actor performing external relations, where such performance was purely representative, would thus not suffice to qualify as a case of succession.

Based on these criteria, the EU again seems to meet the criteria: in conducting external relations, the EU does not merely act as a representative of its Member States. Especially with regard to treaty-making, it is widely accepted that the EU concludes EU-only agreements in its own right and not only on behalf of its Member States.[71] In that sense, it may even be

---

64 In this sense also A Zimmermann (n 39) 16 who argues that the responsibility formula is even broader than reference to treaty-making competence ('nochmals weiter formuliert').
65 Note that the way Vallat references sovereignty appears, moreover, slightly out of context: As regards the definition of succession being discussed, there are no 'aspects of international law under consideration'. Instead, the definition pertains to the mere *fact* of succession. See above Part II § 6 section II.A.
66 For the discussion, see 'Summary Records 1972' (n 47) 270–271.
67 'SR Vallat First Report' (n 52) 27.
68 Ibid (emphasis added).
69 Gradoni (n 33) para 33.
70 'SR Vallat First Report' (n 52) 28.
71 A Łazowski and RA Wessel, 'The External Dimension of Withdrawal from the European Union' (2016) 4 Revue des Affaires européennes 623; J Odermatt, 'Brexit and

said to exercise those facets of sovereignty 'most relevant to the aspects of international law under consideration'.[72] For, as Eckes and Wessel hold,

> [i]f at least the exercise of sovereign rights under public international law relates to the power to exclusively make, implement, enforce rules in a certain area, one may argue that the EU is (quasi-) sovereign in the areas of (absolute) exclusive competence.[73]

While the EU can thus be considered as an actor exercising responsibility in international relations, for succession to occur, it would have to replace its Member States in doing so or – as in the constellation of Brexit – *vice versa*. Based on the criterion of 'replacement', however, Vallat explicitly excludes the EU from the scope of the definition.

3. Replacing in Relevant Aspects

When commenting on the succession definition as redrafted by the Drafting Committee, Vallat does not separately discuss the criterion of *'replacement* in the responsibility for international relations'. The topic arises, however, with regard to a comment made by the Dutch delegation to the Sixth Committee with a view to the scope of the draft articles. The Dutch representatives had noted that in limiting the draft articles to international agreements concluded between states, the ILC

> would leave outside the scope of the draft certain cases of succession resulting from the participation of States in certain hybrid unions, like custom unions and common markets. Such unions might obtain an exclusive right to enter into trade agreements, as in the case of EEC under the Treaty of Rome.[74]

The representative went on to note that where states accede to such hybrid unions, the treaty partners of these new Member States 'might have a real interest in obtaining some legal relationship with the successor organ-

---

International Law: Disentangling Legal Orders' (2017) 31 *Emory International Law Review Recent Developments* 1051, 93.
72 'SR Vallat First Report' (n 52) 27.
73 C Eckes and RA Wessel, 'An International Perspective' in R Schütze and T Tridimas (eds), *The Oxford Principles of European Union Law: The European Union Legal Order* (Oxford University Press 2018) 95.
74 'SR Vallat First Report' (n 52) 12.

ization'[75]. In addressing this comment in his report, Vallat first points to the general approval by governments as regards the limited scope of the VCSSRT and the decision to maintain coherence with the VCLT, which, too, is limited to states and their agreements.[76] In a second step, however, he also refers to the draft definition, noting that '[t]he kind of "succession" contemplated would be different in character from the kind of "succession" contemplated in the draft articles'[77]. In his view, the difference lies in the fact that

> 'Replacement' seems to contemplate complete replacement and not partial transfer or conferment of powers to conclude treaties. The fact of succession by replacement is one thing: the conferment of exclusive powers in a limited field is something quite different.[78]

A similar argument is made by Zimmermann against even an analogical application of the rules of succession to the EU. In his view, the difference between an accession to the EU – the constellation under his consideration – and a uniting of states is that the Member States 'in principle have retained their full capacity to act under international law even in those areas for which the Community has internal competence'[79]. In contrast to instances of state succession, the EU does not replace, ie substitute, its Member States for they are still capable of concluding treaties themselves. Neither Vallat nor Zimmermann considered the reverse situation of a state exiting the EU (then EEC). But the same logic could likewise be applied to the situation of withdrawal: the exiting Member State does not replace, ie substitute, the EU for it was always capable of concluding agreements itself. There appear to be two nuances to this argument which shall be discussed: the first concerning the *kind* of replacement, the second the *extent* of replacement.

As regards the kind of replacement, the argument seems to suggest that a 'conferment of exclusive powers', ie a change in treaty-making competence,

---

75 Ibid.
76 Ibid. On this point, see above Part II § 5 section I.C.1 and below Part II § 6 section III.A.
77 Ibid.
78 Ibid.
79 A Zimmermann (n 39) 713 ('[...] grundsätzlich ihre volle völkerrechtliche Handlungsfähigkeit auch in den Bereichen behalten haben, für welche im Innenverhältnis die Gemeinschaft zuständig ist.' Translated by the author).

§ 6 EU Withdrawal and Succession: Justifying the Analogy

does not suffice to constitute 'the fact of succession by replacement'.[80] Instead, Zimmermann, at least, explicitly claims that there is no replacement where the treaty-making capacity remains unaffected. This argument, however, qualitatively charges the criterion of 'replacement'. A replacement is merely 'the act or process of replacing or of being replaced';[81] it does not in itself cover any meaning as regards the object to be replaced.

Furthermore, it also runs contrary to previous considerations by the ILC. The initial draft definition of succession explicitly referred to the treaty-making *competence*, which is generally understood as the internal power to conclude treaties as opposed to external capacity.[82] Similarly, the formula of '*responsibility* for international relations' – understood as control over conduct[83] – implies more of a power to act than an ability to do so. In any case, to the extent that the final definition is considered broader than – and not substantially different from – its predecessor, it must also encompass the previously relied upon treaty-making competence. Finally, equating 'replacement in the responsibility for international relations' with 'replacement in the treaty-making capacity' would be inconsistent with practice. As Waldock discussed in his fifth report, some constituent states of constitutional unions continued to conclude international agreements alongside the unions.[84] To do so requires them to have retained (some) treaty-making capacity.

---

80 'SR Vallat First Report' (n 52) 12.
81 'Definition of 'Replacement'' (*Black's Law Dictionary*) <https://thelawdictionary.org/replacement/>.
82 And while the terms capacity and competence are sometimes confused (see eg the French version of Waldock's first report that defined state succession as 'désigne la substitution d'un État à un autre [...] dans la possession de la capacité de conclure des traités concernant un territoire donné'), it is difficult to imagine that Waldock – being the former Special Rapporteur for the law of treaties – would not have intentionally chosen one over the other. The VCLT clearly distinguishes between the external capacity to conclude international agreements that every state possesses (Art. 6 VCLT) and the internal competence (Art. 46 VCLT). That the ILC was indeed aware of the difference between the terms seems to be corroborated by a statement made by the ILC's Chairman who, as an alternative to Waldock's definition, suggested that 'the term "capacity" might be used, as in article 6 of the Vienna Convention on the Law of Treaties' ('Summary Records 1972' (n 47) 40).
Cp Art. 6 VCLT: 'Every State possesses the capacity to conclude treaties.'
83 Cp 'SR Vallat First Report' (n 52) 27 (emphasis added).
84 See eg Waldock's example of the Swiss Confederation where the cantons had 'a concurrent, if subordinate, power to make treaties with foreign-States' ('SR Waldock Fifth Report' (n 31) 28). Another striking example is the USSR whose constituent

II. On Dissimilarities: The Irrelevance of the EU's Lack of Statehood

As regards the *extent* of replacement, Vallat and Zimmermann's argument refers to the fact that acceding to and withdrawing from the EEC, respectively today the EU, only constitute *partial* replacements rather than *complete* replacements. It is unclear where Vallat draws his statement from that '"replacement" seems to contemplate *complete* replacement'. There is nothing in the term's ordinary meaning nor in the ILC's previous reports that would suggest so. To the contrary, as Gradoni argues, 'it is indeed difficult to see why the Convention should have been limited to cases of [...] "full" succession, since identical problems can obviously arise [...]'[85]. Moreover, practice again points in a different direction: the discussion on Liechtenstein, San Marino and Andorra in the ILC revolved around the fact that in these cases 'responsibility for international relations was divided'[86]. All three 'exercise[d] only *partial* control over their own international relations'[87]. Finally, where a union's component states continue to conclude international agreements, albeit in limited areas, their competence to do so can also only have been *partially* replaced. Despite this, both the formation and the dissolution of such unions were considered 'successions' as defined in Art. 2(1)(b) VCSSRT.

The aspect of replacement in the definition of succession is not directly linked to the question of sovereignty. For a succession to take place, a replacement between two entities has to occur – whether in the sovereignty over territory or the responsibility for the international relations of territory. But while sovereignty was removed from the succession definition, it sometimes nevertheless appears to resonate in the understanding of replacement. Vallat and Zimmermann's rejection of the notion of replacement with regard to the EU (then EEC) appears to be based on a belief that whatever changes hands in the case of EU accession and withdrawal does not qualitatively suffice. Yet, concentrating on the fact of replacement itself, the EU *does* in fact replace its Member States in cases of accession and a leaving Member States *does* replace the EU in cases of withdrawal. Precisely

---

republics of Belarus and Ukraine concluded certain international agreements before separation, see A Zimmermann (n 39) 392, 397.
85 Gradoni (n 33) para 30 ('Il est en effet difficile de voir pour quelle raison la Convention n'aurait dû viser que les cas de succession [...] "intégrale", étant donné que des problèmes identiques peuvent évidemment se poser même en dehors ces cas [...].' Translated by the author).
86 'SR Vallat First Report' (n 52) 27.
87 Gradoni (n 33) para 33 ('n'exercent qu'une emprise partielle sur leurs propres relations internationales', translated by the author, emphasis added).

§ 6 EU Withdrawal and Succession: Justifying the Analogy

said replacement distinguishes the EU's treaty practice from that of other international organisations.

The EU does not simply have competences to conclude agreements or yield some responsibility to conduct international relations. Instead, it does so in areas and on subjects that were previously the competences and responsibilities of its Member States. It is in this regard that the EU differs from traditional international organisations. These are generally created to serve a certain function and part of that function includes concluding international agreements.[88] Of course, the EU, too, serves certain functions, the difference being, however, that many of these functions were previously performed by its Member States themselves and transferred upon the Union. *Because* the EU replaces its Member States in the conclusion of certain international agreements, such as, for example, trade agreements, the EU's treaty practice is referred to as 'state-like'[89]. And when leaving the EU, an exiting Member State will, in turn, replace the EU. It is only in this constellation that the effect of acceding to or withdrawing from a union becomes a situation where the question of succession is relevant.

In the end, the EU must not and does not have to fall under the definition of succession provided for in the VCSSRT, which after all still refers to the replacement of *one state by another*. That is precisely why the rules found in Art. 34 VCSSRT are to be applied by analogy. However, to do so means questioning the similarity of the situations involved. If the characteristics of a succession – as the fact triggering legal consequences – considerably differed from the situation of a Member State leaving the EU, upholding the analogy would appear doubtful. Against this background, it is all the more significant to see that even in Waldock's reports and subsequently in the final text of the Convention, the topic of sovereignty – typically associated with states and regularly used to define succession – was deliberately left out. While the omission's aim was to avoid discussions on the locus – and thus potential change of sovereignty – in contested constellations, it does go to show that succession between territorial entities which may feature elements of a state, but *not* state sovereignty, is conceivable. But where sovereignty is not the decisive criterion, the question of its locus, for example in the context of unions, may require further

---

88 HG Schermers and N Blokker, *International Institutional Law: Unity within Diversity* (5th edn, Martinus Nijhoff Publishers 2011) para 1772.
89 J Odermatt, *International Law and the European Union* (Cambridge University Press 2021) 62.

consideration. After all, if a union is dismissed from the study as not having acquired statehood, this appears strangely at odds with a 'setting aside of the concept of sovereignty'[90] when it comes to the question of succession.

B. Locating Sovereignty: Unions of States and the EU

From the drafting history of the VCSSRT's definition of succession, it becomes clear that a change in sovereignty is not – or is no longer – the decisive criterion establishing that a succession has taken place. Thus, for the fact of succession, the dissimilarity between the unions of states and the EU – the latter's lack of statehood – does not play a relevant role. If no change of sovereignty is needed, the next question that ensues is whether sovereignty or statehood are a relevant criterion at all. What is the relevance of an entity's possessing statehood to the applicable rules in the case succession takes place? Or more poignantly: do the rules on treaty succession indeed presuppose a predecessor *state*?

Instead of comparing the EU to a state in general, the comparison at the heart of the proposed analogy is between the EU and unions of states. That these bear a whole series of similarities – without doubt more than the EU with a unitary state – is a truism and was also recognised by the ILC. But what is the value of this comparison to the analogical application of Art. 34 VCSSRT to the EU? After all, Art. 34 VCSSRT provides for the effects on international agreements of a separation from a *state*. Its text makes no reference whatsoever to unions of states. What relevance can the similarities – and dissimilarities – between the EU and unions of states have to the inferred characteristic, the continuity rule in Art. 34 VCSSRT, if said characteristic is seemingly also shared by a unitary state?

Looking into its drafting history, the role of unions of states in the development of Art. 34 VCSSRT in its current form becomes very clear (1.). It is mainly the practice with regard to the dissolution of unions on which the ILC relied in its drafting of the current article. What is less clear, however, is the role that statehood played in that practice (2.). Not only can Waldock's theoretical distinction between unions on the plane of international law and unions on the plane of constitutional law be questioned; but also his selection of study objects based on that distinction.

---

90 Gradoni (n 33) para 36 ('La mise à l'écart du concept de souveraineté', translated by the author).

§ 6 EU Withdrawal and Succession: Justifying the Analogy

1. The Relevance of Unions of States to Art. 34 VCSSRT

The ILC took up the task of codifying the law of state succession following – and to some extent still amidst – a process of decolonisation that had started in the late 1940s and continued beyond the Commission's work on the topic.[91] The ILC's Sub-Committee – reinforced by the United Nations General Assembly (UNGA)[92] – urged the ILC to 'pay special attention'[93] to the problems and practice of succession arising from the process of decolonisation. Thus, large parts of Waldock's first reports concentrated on the practice of 'new states' or later 'newly independent states'[94].[95] Finally, in his fifth report, the Special Rapporteur turned to 'particular categories of

---

91 For an overview, see MCR Craven (n 30) 96. Suriname, Mozambique, and Angola (1975), Djibouti (1977), and Dominica (1978) gained independence after the ILC had adopted the final draft articles in 1974 ('ILC Report 1974' (n 59) 174) and before the VCSSRT was adopted on 22 August 1978 by the United Nations Conference on the Succession of States in respect of Treaties and initially opened for signature at Vienna from 23 August 1978 to 28 February 1979. Namibia (1990) gained independence after the VCSSRT's adoption and East Timor (2002) after its entry into force on 6 November 1996.

92 UNGA, 'Future Work in the Field of the Codification and Progressive Development of International Law' UN Doc. A/Res/16/1686 (18 December 1961) para 3 ('*Recommends* that the Commission should: [...] (c) continue its work on the succession of States and Governments, taking into account the views expressed at the eighteenth session of the General Assembly, the report of the Sub-Committee on the Succession of States and Governments and the comments which may be submitted by Governments, with appropriate reference to the views of States which have achieved their independence since the Second World War.').

93 Rosenne, ILC, 'Report by Manfred Lachs, Chairman of the Sub-Committee on Succession of States and Governments' UN Doc. A/CN.4/160 and Corr.1, YBILC (1963) Vol. II 268.

94 Art. 2(1)(f) VCSSRT: '"newly independent State" means a successor State the territory of which immediately before the date of the succession of States was a dependent territory for the international relations of which the predecessor State was responsible'. Originally, Waldock had referred to these states as 'New States' (Draft Art. 1(e): '[...] means a succession where a territory which previously formed part of an existing State has become an independent State', see ILC, 'Third Report on Succession in Respect of Treaties, by Sir Humphrey Waldock' UN Doc. A/CN.4/244 and Add. 1, YBILC (1970) Vol. II 28).

95 See especially ibid and ILC, 'Fourth Report on Succession in Respect of Treaties, by Sir Humphrey Waldock' UN Doc A/CN.4/249, YBILC (1971) Vol. II(1). In his first and second report, Waldock discussed issues of a more preliminary or general nature such as definitions and the scope of the draft articles. He proposed, *inter alia*, draft articles on the question of constituent instruments of international organisations, succession to boundaries, cession of territory and the status of devolution agreements and unilateral declarations.

II. On Dissimilarities: The Irrelevance of the EU's Lack of Statehood

succession', including '(1) dependent territories, [...]; (2) a union of States; and (3) a separation of a State into two or more States.'[96] Regarding unions of states, Waldock's draft tackled the two situations in which succession could arise: their formation (draft article 19) and their dissolution (draft article 20).

Draft article 20 deals with cases of succession where the predecessor is a union of states and addressed two scenarios: paragraph 1 pertains to a complete dissolution of the union, following which 'one or more of its constituent political divisions become separate States'[97]. Paragraph 3 envisages a partial dissolution where the 'union of States is dissolved only in respect of one of its constituent political divisions which becomes a separate State'[98], while the rest of the union continues to exist. For both scenarios – complete and partial dissolution – Waldock presented two alternative draft articles. Draft article 20 Alternative A provided for *ipso jure* continuity of international agreements for the successor state and, where still existent, for the union.[99] In contrast, draft article 20 Alternative B worked on the assumption of a clean slate as regards the successor states to the union. While they would not be bound by any international agreements of the union, they could novate them through notification in the case of multilateral agreements and through (implicit) agreement with the treaty partners in the case of bilateral agreements.[100]

---

96 'SR Waldock Fifth Report' (n 31) 3.
97 Ibid 35.
98 Ibid 36.
99 See ibid 35, Art. 20 Alternative A: '1. When a union of States is dissolved and one or more of its constituent political divisions become separate States: (a) Any treaty concluded by the union with reference to the union as a whole continues in respect of each such States; (b) Any treaty concluded by the union with reference to any particular political division of the union which has since become a separate State continues in force in respect only of that State; (c) Any treaty binding upon the union under article 19 in relation to any particular political division of the union which has since become a separate State continues in force only in respect of that State. 2. Sub-paragraphs (a) and (b) of paragraph 1 do not apply if the object and purpose of the treaty are compatible only with the continued existence of the union of States. 3. When a union of States is dissolved only in respect of one of its constituent political divisions which becomes a separate State, the rules in paragraph 1 and 2 apply also in relation to this State.'
100 See ibid 36, Art. 20 Alternative B: '1. When a union of States is dissolved and one or more of its constituent political divisions become separate States, treaties binding upon the union at the date of its dissolution continue in force between any such successor Sate and other States parties thereto if: (a) In the case of multilateral treaties [...], the successor State notifies the other States parties that it considers

§ 6 EU Withdrawal and Succession: Justifying the Analogy

Waldock himself favoured a rule of *ipso jure* continuity. Although admitting to some 'inconsistencies'[101], he identified the dissolution of the Union of Colombia (1829–31), the Union of Norway and Sweden (1905), (to some extent) the Austro-Hungarian Empire, the union of Iceland and Denmark (1944), the United Arab Republic (1961) and the Mali Federation (1960) as giving 'general support to this thesis'[102].[103] Following lengthy discussions,[104] the ILC joined Waldock in his assessment that 'practice was sufficiently consistent'[105] as regards *ipso jure* continuity in cases of dissolutions. Nonetheless, what was initially draft article 20 Alternative A underwent substantial changes subsequent to both readings by the ILC.

The first re-drafting was largely due to the tension arising with regard to another category of succession that draft article 21 provided for: 'other dismemberments of a State into two or more States'[106]. Draft article 21 dealt with the complete dismemberment of or a separation from a state 'other than a union of states'[107]. As regards the effects on international agreements of such a succession, the draft article referred to the provisions dealing with newly independent states which provided for a clean slate approach. By introducing a definition of a union of States,[108] Waldock tried to differentiate between a succession of a union of states, as provided for in draft article 20, and a succession to a (unitary) state, as per draft article 21.

---

itself a party to the treaty; (b) In the case of other treaties, the successor State and the other States parties (i) Expressly so agree; or (ii) Must by reason of their conduct be considered as having agreed to or acquiesced in the treaty's being in force in their relations with each other. 2. When a union of States is dissolved only in respect of one of its constituent political divisions which becomes a separate State, the rules in paragraph 1 apply also in relation to this State.'

101 Ibid 39. These pertained to the approach taken by Austria following the termination of the Austro-Hungarian Empire and by Mali following the dissolution of the Mali Federation (see 'SR Waldock Fifth Report' (n 31) 38–39).
102 'SR Waldock Fifth Report' (n 31) 39.
103 Critical as regards Waldock's analysis, see MCR Craven (n 30) 167.
104 'Summary Records 1972' (n 47) 173–181.
105 'ILC Report 1972' (n 51) 295.
106 'SR Waldock Fifth Report' (n 31) 39.
107 Ibid, Art. 21(1): 'When part of a State, which is not a union of States, becomes another State either by separating from it or as a result of the division of that State [...]'.
108 Draft Article 1(h): '"Union of States" means a federal or other union formed by the uniting of two or more States which thereafter constitute separate political divisions of the united State so formed, exercising within their respective territories the governmental powers prescribed by the constitution.' (ibid 18).

II. On Dissimilarities: The Irrelevance of the EU's Lack of Statehood

However, this distinction was short-lived. Unconvinced by the differentiation, the ILC decided to omit any reference to certain types of states. Instead, taking 'the concept of "the State"'[109] as a starting point, the Commission abandoned the distinction between dissolution and dismemberment based on the prior differentiation between unions of states and states other than unions. Instead, two newly drafted articles differentiated based on the type of succession: draft article 27, referencing the practice of unions of states, provided for *ipso jure* continuity in cases of a complete dissolution of a state; draft article 28, citing secessions from unitary states, envisaged a clean slate rule in the case of a separation of parts of a state's territory.[110] As Vallat, the second Special Rapporteur, noted in his report following the ILC's first reading, 'it is clear from the discussion in the Commission' that its work

> was coloured by the traditional meaning of a 'union of States' and the implication that the component parts of the union retained a measure of individual identity during the existence of the union. This concept may have affected, perhaps imperceptibly, the view of the members of the Commission on the distinction between dissolution and separation of part of a State.[111]

During the ILC's second reading of the draft articles, criticism again arose on the precise delimitation between the two draft articles.[112] When would a territorial disintegration constitute merely a separation and when would it amount to a state's complete dissolution? A 'theoretical'[113] distinction

---

109 'SR Vallat First Report' (n 52) 70.
110 See draft articles 27 and 28, 'ILC Report 1972' (n 51) 292–295.
111 'SR Vallat First Report' (n 52) 69–70.
112 In their oral and written comments on the draft articles following the ILC's first reading, governments criticised the sharp distinction drawn between a complete dissolution of a state and the separation of parts of a state, resulting in two draft articles with differing legal consequences. In the view of many governments, such a sharp distinction – while perhaps theoretically possible – was impossible to draw in practice. See eg Belgium remarking on an 'artificial distinction between "newly independent States" and States resulting from the separation of part of an existing State, the uniting of two or more States or the dissolution of a State.' (ibid 65). The US noted that 'the distinction between the dissolution of a State (article 27) and the separation of part of a State (article 28) was quite nebulous. [...] The practice cited in the commentaries to the two articles did not provide substantial assistance in sharpening the distinction between the two situations.' ('SR Vallat First Report' (n 52) 69). Summarising the comments, see MCR Craven (n 30) 171–172.
113 'SR Vallat First Report' (n 52) 70.

§ 6 EU Withdrawal and Succession: Justifying the Analogy

offered by Vallat did not convince the Commission, leading to a second complete re-drafting. This time, however, the ILC not only abandoned any previous distinctions and combined the two kinds of succession – complete dissolution and separation – in a single draft article. In contrast to the previous versions, it also resorted to one legal consequence for both forms: *ipso jure* continuity. Besides an exception that was later removed,[114] the text of draft article 33 is identical with today's Art. 34 VCSSRT.

Art. 34 VCSSRT applies to unions of states as to any other form of state. But the drafting history of the provision shows the decisive role that unions played in the development of the provision. While the ILC eventually more broadly chose 'the concept of "the State" [...] as the starting point'[115], the practice of unions of states continued to form the heart of the draft. As noted in the Commission's final report, 'almost all of the practice relating to the disintegration of a State [...] [concern] the "dissolution" of what traditionally has been regarded as a union of States'[116]. This had not always been the case. Initially, the draft articles had reflected two competing principles: automatic continuity, introduced via the practice of unions of states, and a clean slate approach, based on the practice of unitary states. In the end, however, the former prevailed.

2. The Irrelevance of Statehood to Unions of States

Looking at the drafting history of Art. 34 VCSSRT, Waldock's consideration of unions of states not only formed the starting point of his analysis – it also shaped the drafting of the provision up until its final form. It is the practice of unions of states on which the provision's *ipso jure* continuity principle relies. It is also unions of states that Waldock compared the then

---

114 Draft article 33 paragraph 3 provided: 'Notwithstanding paragraph 1, if a part of the territory of a State separates from it and becomes a State in circumstances which are essentially of the same character as those existing in the case of the formation of a newly independent State, the successor State shall be regarded for the purpose of the present articles in all respects as a newly independent State.' ('ILC Report 1974' (n 59) 260). Vallat had tried to strike a balance between the continuity principle (originally found with regard to unions) and the idea of a territory separating to become a newly independent state. However, at the Conference of States, this exception was criticised as impractical and deleted, see below Part II § 6 section III.B.
115 'SR Vallat First Report' (n 52) 70.
116 'ILC Report 1974' (n 59) 265.

II. On Dissimilarities: The Irrelevance of the EU's Lack of Statehood

EEC to, although ultimately rejecting it as an object of study, noting that the EEC 'is not commonly viewed as a union of States'[117]. The main difference between a union of states and the EU is the latter's lack of statehood. However, a bifurcation in international (and hybrid) unions, on the one side, and constitutional unions, on the other, as done by Waldock, was in no way pre-determined. It was introduced through Waldock's definition, aiming to systematise his study material. Such a clear distinction, though, is theoretically questionable (a.) as well as unconvincing as regards practice (b.).

a. Classical Dichotomy versus Federal Middle Ground

When drafting the two articles on the formation and dissolution of unions of states, Waldock was well aware of the variety of forms of past and existent unions of states, the ensuing vagueness of the term and thus the necessity 'at the outset to identify what is meant by this concept for the purposes' of his study.[118] As *Ago* noted in discussions on the term,

> international law suffered from a paucity of legal language in that field. The term 'union of States' was to be found in all the text-books, although sometimes it was used in a looser sense to include intergovernmental, and especially economic unions.[119]

Waldock thus provided a definition of the 'ambiguous'[120] term 'unions of states', so as to ensure a common understanding in the context of his draft articles. Said definition was based on a general categorisation of unions of states, to be found in Waldock's commentaries.

The first, and for his study, most decisive, distinction concerned the legal nature of unions: in his view, they could 'create a new political entity only on the plane of international law', that is, an international organisation, or 'a new political entity on the plane of internal constitutional law'[121], that is, a state. The latter was subsequently subdivided again into two types of constitutional unions, real and federal ones. Relying on this strict dichotomy between international and constitutional unions allowed Waldock to draw

---

117 'SR Waldock Fifth Report' (n 31) 18.
118 Ibid.
119 Quoted by Waldock 'Summary Records 1972' (n 47) 169.
120 Ago, ibid 160.
121 'SR Waldock Fifth Report' (n 31) 18.

§ 6 EU Withdrawal and Succession: Justifying the Analogy

a clear line as regards the scope of his study. Being concerned with the succession of *states*, only constitutional unions formed suitable objects of study. Moreover, Waldock's distinction corresponded with a traditional understanding of state associations: the dichotomy between a *Staatenbund* (confederation) and a *Bundesstaat* (federation).

The strict distinction between these is 'theoretically of great clarity'[122]: a confederation is based on an international agreement between states, is only unanimously amendable and allows for withdrawal. It features a common organ mainly responsible for foreign and defence policy and solely acts upon the member states and not upon their citizens.[123] A federation, in contrast, may historically be based on an international agreement but has since then evolved into an independent legal subject. It derives its competence from a constitution which may be amended without the consent of all member states and which does not provide for withdrawal. The federation's organs enter into direct relations with its member states' nationals.[124]

The distinction is also theoretically necessary: for at its base lies the understanding of an indivisibility of sovereignty.[125] One of the most prominent proponents of this theory is Jellinek.[126] While acknowledging 'the differences in the legal structure and the factual position of states in a contractual community'[127], Jellinek points to the existence – or non-existence – of the constituent states' sovereignty as the sole criterion to evaluate the legal nature of their association. If sovereignty cannot be divided, its 'locus'[128] allows only two possible alternatives: where an association of states acquires sovereignty, it itself becoming a state, it does so to the detriment of the constituent states. Alternatively, where the constituent

---

122 C Schönberger, 'Die Europäische Union als Bund: Zugleich ein Beitrag zur Verabschiedung des Staatenbund-Bundesstaat-Schemas' (2004) 129(1) *Archiv des öffentlichen Rechts* 81, 88 ('[...] theoretisch von großer Klarheit').
123 Ibid.
124 Ibid 88–89.
125 See especially G Jellinek, *Die Lehre von den Staatenverbindungen* (Alfred Hölder 1882).
126 See ibid.
127 Ibid 315 ('Bei aller Verschiedenheit der juristischen Gestaltung und der factischen Stellung der in vertragsmässiger Gemeinschaft stehender Staaten, ist es die Souveränität der Glieder, welche den obersten Grundsatz für die rechtliche Beurtheilung der völkerrechtlichen Staatenverbindungen abgegeben hat.')
128 R Schütze, 'On "Federal Ground": The European Union as an (Inter)national Phenomenon' in R Schütze (ed), *Foreign Affairs and the EU Constitution: Selected Essays* (Cambridge University Press 2014) 32.

II. On Dissimilarities: The Irrelevance of the EU's Lack of Statehood

states remain sovereign, Jellinek classifies unions as a sub-category of a *Staatenbund* and thus as a purely inter-state association.[129]

While representing classical European constitutionalist thought[130], this 'conceptual polarisation into two idealised categories'[131] is far from compelling. It has been theoretically questioned and, more importantly for the question at hand, the clear categorisation of unions as constitutional or international has been criticised as historically unfounded.[132] As early as 1892, Westerkamp, in a thorough analysis of *Bundesstaaten* and *Staatenbünde* showed that the clear definitions proposed for the two did not accord with the practice he found.[133] Seeing the results of Westerkamp's study lead Robinson to poignantly ask:

> But is not the task after all of determining the characteristics which serve to distinguish a Federation from a Confederation [...], if we conscientiously consider the multifarious forms which the composite State has assumed historically in modern times, so difficult as to suggest some defect in our method of classification? Is it not after all as if we should try to classify all colors as light and dark? [...] We would soon give up in despair and adopt some other plan. For if we look at the various shades we are soon convinced that the categories, light and dark, which are very useful and often quite clear, have no scientific value. Ought we not to give up the vain hope of crowding all the varying forms of union into just *two* classes, attaching names to these classes as vague as the terms light and lighter?[134]

---

129 G Jellinek (n 125) 215.
130 See Schütze, Foreign Affairs (n 128) 32 with further references.
131 Ibid.
132 See eg S Oeter, 'Föderalismus und Demokratie' in A von Bogdandy and J Bast (eds), *Europäisches Verfassungsrecht: Theoretische und dogmatische Grundzüge* (2nd edn, Springer 2009) 84 with reference to the German *Bund* ('Nun ist die Dichotomie von „Staatenbund" und „Bundesstaat" immer schon ein theoretisches Artefakt gewesen – wies doch etwa der Deutsche Bund, an dessen Leitbild die Kategorie des Staatenbundes entwickelt worden ist, durchaus im Detail auch „supranationale", man könnte sagen: „föderale" Züge auf, während der Norddeutsche Bund von 1867 und dessen Erweiterung zum Deutschen Reich von 1871 umgekehrt in entscheidenden Grundzügen durchaus auch (noch) „staatenbündische" Züge hatte.').
133 See JB Westerkamp, *Staatenbund und Bundesstaat: Untersuchungen über die Praxis und das Recht der modernen Bünde* (Brockhaus 1892).
134 JH Robinson, 'Review: Staatenbund und Bundesstaat by J. B. Westerkamp' (1894) 4 *The Annals of the American Academy of Political and Social Science* 145, 147–148 (emphasis in original).

§ 6 EU Withdrawal and Succession: Justifying the Analogy

Interestingly, while a debate on the distinction first emerged in the late 19th century, it resurfaced and has gained increasing momentum in the context of European integration. Instead of negatively defining the EU as a creature *sui generis*, different authors have offered alternatives to the constitutional-international dichotomy, allowing accommodation of the EU as a federal system.[135]

A prominent proponent of a 'federal middle ground'[136] is Schütze. As he shows in his work, three distinct federal traditions can be identified that each influence the understanding of the legal character of a union of states. Two of them are based on the indivisibility of sovereignty and conceive of a federal union either as a purely international or a purely constitutional phenomenon. Chronologically in between these traditions, however, lies a third, 'mixed format'[137]. This mixed format of federalism emerged upon the foundation of the second US Union. The US Constitution of 1787, as Schütze argues, was 'in strictness, neither a national nor a federal [read: international] Constitution but a composition of both'[138].[139] As regards its foundational character as well as its institutional and substantive provisions, the Constitution combined national and international characteristics.[140] Based on the idea of delegation and division of sovereignty, this 'federalism implied *dual* government, *dual* sovereignty, and also *dual* citizenship'[141]. And '[i]mportantly, in the early American tradition the

---

135 See eg H Steiger, *Staatlichkeit und Überstaatlichkeit: Eine Untersuchung zur rechtlichen und politischen Stellung der Europäischen Gemeinschaften* (Duncker & Humblot 1966); M Forsyth, *Unions of States: The Theory and Practice of Confederation* (Leicester University Press 1981); O Beaud, 'La notion de pacte fédératif: Contribution à une théorie constitutionnelle de la Fédération' in J-F Kervégan and H Mohnhaupt (eds), *Gesellschaftliche Freiheit und vertragliche Bindung in Rechtsgeschichte und Philosophie* (Klostermann 1999). Building on all three, Schönberger (n 122) bases the EU within a 'Theorie des Bundes'.
136 Cp Schütze, Foreign Affairs (n 128) 31.
137 R Schütze, *From Dual to Cooperative Federalism: The Changing Structure of European Law* (Oxford University Press 2009) 15.
138 J Madison, The Federalist No 39, 187. In light of the first tradition of federalism, 'federal' here must be understood to mean international, in the sense of respect for the sovereign equality of states.
139 See in this regard also M Forsyth (n 135) 53–72, 160–166.
140 See Schütze, *Cooperative Federalism* (n 137) 23–27.
141 Ibid 29. On this political dualism, see also C Schmitt, *Verfassungslehre* (11th edn, Duncker & Humblot 2017) 371: 'In each federal union, two kinds of political bodies co-exist: the existence of the whole federation and the individual existence of each federal member. Both kinds of political existence must remain coordinate in order for the federal union to remain alive.' (translated by R Schütze).

II. On Dissimilarities: The Irrelevance of the EU's Lack of Statehood

Union was not identified with a Federal State.'[142] In the view of Schütze and others promoting a turn away from the traditional schema, they were vindicated by the difficulties that more 'classical political science'[143] had to acknowledged when applying their schema to examples of unions.[144] Thus, based on Westerkamp's analysis, Schütze concludes that '[a]ll previously existing unions of states lay between international and national law'[145].

A blurring of the traditional distinction between constitutional and international, state and non-state unions not only puts into question the clear line drawn by Waldock. Placed in the US tradition of federalism, the EU, too, may be considered a union of states located on a federal middle ground. Its founding treaties are international agreements *as well as* a 'constitutional charter'[146]; its organs act unanimously *and* by majority, representing Member States *and* being democratically elected; and, finally, the EU's powers are enumerated *but* far-reaching, targeting the Member States *and* individuals.

Can Waldock's categorisation then still be considered as a necessary sorting of his study material? Or, if a clear distinction between international and constitutional unions is impossible, does categorisation of (state) practice along this line become arbitrary? As already Westerkamp showed, the capacity to conclude international agreements is not a differentiator between constitutional and international unions.[147] The question as to the effects of their succession on these agreements can thus be posed for both. Meanwhile, Waldock's study only considers one group – though neither homogenous in itself nor clearly distinguishable from the other. The potential inaccuracy – or arbitrariness – of differentiating between constitutional and international unions becomes even more apparent when considering its practical handling.

---

142 Schütze, *Cooperative Federalism* (n 137) 29.
143 Schönberger (n 122), 92.
144 See ibid with further references.
145 Schütze, Foreign Affairs (n 128) 34 with reference to JB Westerkamp (n 133).
146 ECJ, C-294/83 *Parti écologiste "Les Verts" v European Parliament* [1986] ECLI:EU:C:1986:166, [23]. But see also ECJ, Opinion 1/91 *Draft agreement between the Community, on the one hand, and the countries of the European Free Trade Association, on the other, relating to the creation of the European Economic Area* [1991] ECLI:EU:C:1991:490, 21 and ECJ, Opinion 2/13 *Accession to the ECHR* [2014] ECLI:EU:C:2014:2454, [158].
147 JB Westerkamp (n 133) 471–473.

§ 6 EU Withdrawal and Succession: Justifying the Analogy

b. A Reasonable Systematisation of Practice?

The problem with a differentiation between constitutional and international unions that may be 'theoretically of great clarity'[148] but that is in practice potentially imprecise becomes visible in Waldock's evaluation of practice with regard to the (partial) dissolution of unions. For even among authors in support of a clear distinction between constitutional and international unions, differences in classification as regards both abstract types of unions and specific examples of unions quickly become apparent. Importantly for the question of succession to unions, this concerns one of Waldock's sub-categorisations – the classification of real unions as constitutional unions – and his (state?) practice as analysed based on said distinction.

As regards the general classification of real unions as constitutional unions, Waldock was well aware of differing views. In his commentary to draft article 19, Waldock admits that 'one well-known authority took the position that "a Real Union" is not itself a State, but merely a union of two full sovereign States which together make one single but composite "International Person"'[149]. However, instead of engaging with this differing view, Waldock merely dismissed '[t]hat somewhat mystical view of real unions' as 'not [...] universally shared' and pointed to 'another well-known authority' for confirmation.[150] But Oppenheim's, the first well-known authority referred to by Waldock, was not alone in this assessment. Jellinek, whose tradition of indivisible sovereignty Waldock appears to have followed, also came to the conclusion that real unions are only a subcategory of international unions of states for, in his view, they are based on international agreements and their members each remain sovereign.[151] While Jellinek

---

148 Schönberger (n 122), 88 ('theoretisch von großer Klarheit').
149 'SR Waldock Fifth Report' (n 31) 22 with reference to H Lauterpacht (ed), *Oppenheim's International Law: A Treatise* (vol I, 8th edn, Longmans, Green and Co. Ltd. 1955) 171.
150 'SR Waldock Fifth Report' (n 31) 22 with reference to WE Hall, *A Treatise on International Law* (8th edn, Clarendon Press 1924) 26.
151 G Jellinek (n 125) 215: 'Die Realunion ist daher nur ein Specialfall des Staatenbundes. Sie ist jene Form des Staatenbundes, welche entsteht, wenn zwei oder mehrere gegen einander selbstständige Staaten sich zu gemeinsamen Schutz derart rechtlich vereinigen, dass ein und dieselbe physische Persönlichkeit zur Trägerschaft ihrer Staatsgewalten berufen erscheint, wobei es den so vereinigten Staaten unbenommen bleibt das Bündniss auch auf andere staatliche Functionen auszudehnen.' Before establishing his own definition of a real union, Jellinek extensively engages with Juraschek's work on the issue. Both share the view that a real union does not create

II. On Dissimilarities: The Irrelevance of the EU's Lack of Statehood

acknowledges that real unions are regularly thought of as constitutional unions, he ascribes this to a mere mischaracterisation due to their perpetuality and not to their legal nature.[152] Based on Jellinek's understanding of real unions, Waldock's practice on which he based draft article 20 on the dissolution of unions – and which continues to form the basis for Art. 34 VCSSRT – is put in a different light.

While in the context of the formation of unions Waldock meticulously differentiated between different types of unions – federal and real ones – and their potentially relevant characteristics, he was less elaborate with regard to the practice analysed for their dissolution. Nevertheless, based on his previous definitions, at least four of the five examined cases of dissolution concern real unions. Thus, both Waldock and Jellinek agree in that the Union of Norway and Sweden and the Austro-Hungarian Empire can be categorised as real unions. However, in contrast to Waldock, who viewed them as constitutional unions creating a new state,[153] Jellinek treated both as mere international unions, with every participating state retaining their sovereignty.[154] As regards the Austro-Hungarian Empire, the latter's

---

a new state (see F von Juraschek, *Personal- und Realunion: Das rechtliche Verhältniss zwischen Oesterreich und Ungarn* (C Heymanns 1878) 95: 'jene Staatenvereinigung, welche besteht [...] ohne neben oder über den unierten Staaten einen neuen Staat zu errichten'). However, Juraschek considers a real union to be based on foundational constitutional laws, while Jellinek requires an international agreement ('Wenn die Realunion eine wahre Staatenverbindung sein soll, so ergibt sich aus dem Vorangehenden, dass sie nicht staatsrechtlicher, sondern nur völkerrechtliche Natur sein kann, wie alle Verbindungen souveräner oder wenigstens gegen einander selbstständiger Staaten' (p. 204).

152 G Jellinek (n 125) 218: 'Die Realunion zeigt daher eine Dauerhaftigkeit und Festigkeit, welche die aller anderen Formen des Staatenbundes bei Weitem übertrifft, und darin mag wohl der Grund zu suchen sein, weshalb man sie den staatsrechtlichen Verbindungen beizuzählen pflegt, weshalb man nur die auf die Realunion Bezug habenden Gesetze bei der Begriffsbestimmung derselben in Betracht zieht und den hinter den Gesetzen nothwendigerweise stehenden Einigungsvertrag übersieht.'

153 On the Union of Norway and Sweden, see 'SR Waldock Fifth Report' (n 31) 36–37. On the Austro-Hungarian Empire, see 'SR Waldock Fifth Report' (n 31) 37.

154 See G Jellinek (n 125) 222: 'Die Gegenwart bietet zwei hervorragende Typen der Realunion in Schweden-Norwegen und Oesterreich-Ungarn, an deren Gestaltung die Richtigkeit der entwickelten Theorien zu prüfen ist.' For the Union of Norway and Sweden, see G Jellinek (n 125) 225: 'Das gegenseitige Verhältniss Norwegens und Schwedens ist das zweier souveräner Staaten. [...] Es gibt kein Schweden-Norwegen als einheitlichen Staat, der über oder neben den Sonderstaaten bestände [...]'. For the Austro-Hungarian Empire, see G Jellinek (n 125) 234, 240.

view seems to have been shared by the Permanent Court of International Justice (PCIJ) which held that

> [t]he frontier between Hungary and Galicia was in August 1914 an *international frontier*, Galicia being then part of the Austrian Monarchy. [...] Although Austria and Hungary had common institutions based on analogous laws passed by their legislatures, they were none the less distinct international units.[155]

While the Danish-Icelandic Union and the United Arab Republic (UAR) formed after Jellinek's study, their legal nature can similarly be contested. Both are categorised by Waldock as real unions subjecting them to the same conflicting views on their statehood as the Norwegian-Swedish and Austro-Hungarian unions.[156] Moreover, the UAR serves as a prime example to illustrate not only the varying understandings of the concept of unions, but also the difficulty of bringing together the actual characteristics of an entity with any predefined categories.

For Waldock and Cotran, for example, the UAR was clearly a state, an assessment finding its basis, *inter alia*, in the express wording of the Proclamation of 1 February 1958 and the Provisional Constitution.[157] Furthermore, both acknowledged that the constitutional arrangements provided for a far-reaching 'fusion of the identities of the two States in the central organs', '[t]he separate identities of Egypt and Syria [...] [finding] only very limited expression in the Provisional Constitution'.[158] Waldock dismissed this as an 'anomaly'[159]. In his view, while the constitution *prima facie*

---

155 PCIJ *Delimitation of the Polish-Czechoslovakian Frontier (Question of Jaworzina)* (Advisory Opinion) [1923] Series B No 8, 42–43.
156 In addition, the Union between Denmark und Iceland may have even amounted only to a personal union (see eg PE Mosely, 'Iceland and Greenland: An American Problem' (1940) 18(4) *Foreign Affairs* 742, 742). A personal union, however, is unequivocally not considered a state.
157 See eg Proclamation of 1 February 1958, establishing the United Arab Republic: 'The participants declare their total agreement, complete faith and deeply rooted confidence in the necessity of uniting Egypt and Syria into *one State* to be named "The United Arab Republic".' And Part I of the Provisional Constitution of the United Arab Republic: 'The United Arab *State* is a democratic, independent, sovereign Republic, and its people are part of the Arab Nation.' (both quoted from E Cotran, 'Some Legal Aspects of the Formation of the United Arab Republic and the United Arab States' (1959) 8(2) *International & Comparative Law Quarterly* 346, 347, emphasis added).
158 'SR Waldock Fifth Report' (n 31) 22. See also Cotran (n 157), 347–349.
159 'SR Waldock Fifth Report' (n 31) 22.

II. On Dissimilarities: The Irrelevance of the EU's Lack of Statehood

pointed to a unitary state, the UAR nevertheless represented a real union as '[t]he separate identities of Egypt and Syria [...] remained a *political* fact'[160]. Cotran, on the other hand, concluded that '[i]t is clear from both these instruments that the U.A.R. is a *State* and not merely a union of States'[161]. In his view, 'both Egypt and Syria [had] lost their identities'[162].

Others did not even agree on the characterisation of the UAR as a state. In the section 'the classification of political unions' of his book 'Creation of States'[163], Crawford discusses the UAR under the heading 'Unusual formations'[164]. He comes to the conclusion that '[i]n retrospect, despite the recognition of the Republic as a unitary State, it appears to have been a loose association the existence of which was not inconsistent with the continuing international personality of its component parts'.[165] Similarly, O'Connell, author of the International Law Association's resolution on state succession, was sceptical of categorising the union at all.

> It is difficult to place the United Arab Republic within any of the traditional categories of composite States. It was not a real union because the Republic was a State; nor was it a personal union, because whatever international personality of the constituent States survived was of very limited character. At the same time it was not a federation since there was no classical distribution of legislative powers. In short, the arrangement was *sui generis* [sic!]. This however, does not necessarily invalidate analogies with other types of association.[166]

The previous examples show that the nature of real unions, whether they are constitutional or international unions, is as debatable as the strict dichotomy with regards to federal unions. Nevertheless, the practice sur-

---

160 Ibid (emphasis added).
161 Cotran (n 157), 347.
162 Ibid 349. See also R Young, 'The State of Syria: Old or New?' (1962) 56(2) *American Journal of International Law* 482 questioning the continued existence of Syria.
163 J Crawford, *Creation of States in International Law* (2nd edn, Oxford University Press 2007) 479.
164 Ibid 489.
165 Ibid. See also MCR Craven (n 30) 163: '[...] in many other respects it remained a loose federation of two separate entities' and generally, K Bühler, 'State Succession, Identity/ Continuity and Membership in the United Nations' in PM Eisemann and M Koskenniemi (eds), *State Succession: Codification Tested Against the Facts* (Martinus Nijhoff Publishers 2000) 187.
166 DP O'Connell, *State Succession in Municipal Law and International Law: International Relations* (vol II, Cambridge University Press 1967) 74.

rounding their dissolutions formed the basis for today's Art. 34 VCSSRT. From this, two possible conclusions can be drawn. On the hand, it could be argued that, based on these findings, the then EEC should have been included in Waldock's study in the first place. After all, it may not even have been the only *sui generis* union.[167] This argument, however, may just as quickly be reversed: perhaps no union should have been included if the ILC's study was to be one of *state* succession. On the other hand, one could also simply draw the conclusion that the statehood of these unions cannot have played a relevant role in the question of succession in respect of international agreements. Even with their nature being disputed, the dissolution of the unions included in Waldock's report were treated as a case of succession and the rule that crystallised was one of *ipso jure* continuity.

C. Due to Sovereignty? Differences in the Practice of Unions of States and the EU

The previous two sections (A. and B.) addressed the main aspects of why the EU did not fit into the ILC's project on the law of succession with respect to international agreements. The EU was not – and is not – considered a union of states in the sense of a *constitutional* union, meaning a union that has itself acquired statehood. Thus, the EU does not qualify as a state replacing another state or as a state being replaced by another state. Nevertheless, the previous sections have also shown that this main dissimilarity – the EU's lack of statehood – is not as relevant to the rules of succession applicable in the dissolution of a union as the ILC's apparent insistence on this characteristic may suggest. State-associated concepts such as sovereignty remained controversial throughout the ILC's work on the topic of succession, until they were eventually blended out. Furthermore, the Commission's sorting of practice along pre-defined lines of statehood proves difficult.

---

167 See eg O'Connell, who refers to the United Arab Republic as *sui generis* (ibid) but nevertheless includes it in his study on state succession (O'Connell, *State Succession* (n 166) 169–170).

II. On Dissimilarities: The Irrelevance of the EU's Lack of Statehood

Notably (or perhaps consequently[168]), however, the then EEC's lack of statehood was *not* the main reason provided in Waldock's report for excluding the EEC from its scope. Instead, Waldock – and subsequently the ILC – ultimately decided against inclusion of the EEC based on the EEC's practice with regard to its new Member State's pre-accession agreements. However, this argument is not only methodologically questionable (1.); it also falls short in the assessment of the EEC's and today EU's practice compared to the practice of (other) unions of states (2.).

1. The (Ir)Relevance of the EU's Accession Practice to Codification

A quick recapitulation helps best retrace Waldock's argument: in defining unions of states, Waldock begins with his – by now well-known – differentiation between unions on the plane of international law and such on the plane of internal constitutional law. Aside from his determination that constitutional unions are states, he does not go into detail as to how constitutional and international unions are to be differentiated or how the statehood of the former is to be determined. Subsequently, Waldock raises the issue of, what he calls, 'hybrid unions'[169] with the prominent (and to-date only actual) example being the then EEC, now the EU.

In contrast to any other union – international or constitutional – Waldock starts contemplating its 'precise legal character [...] which is a matter of discussion among jurists'[170]. While noting that the EEC is 'not commonly viewed as a union of States', he also lists those EEC characteristics that are generally cited as proving that the EEC 'is at the same time not generally regarded as being simply a regional international organization'[171]. Subsequently, however, Waldock does not form an opinion on what he considers the nature of the EEC to be based on these characteristics – possibly by comparing it to the two categories of unions previously defined. Instead, he excludes the EEC from the scope of his study based on its previous *practice* as regards the pre-accession agreements of its new Member States.

---

168 It is unclear whether Waldock was aware of the inconsistencies surrounding his treatment of unions of states. In any case, he never truly gave a clear answer as to how he viewed the EEC. It may thus have been opportune for him, to exclude the EEC from his studies on other grounds.
169 'SR Waldock Fifth Report' (n 31) 18.
170 Ibid.
171 Ibid.

§ 6 EU Withdrawal and Succession: Justifying the Analogy

In Waldock's words, the EEC's characteristics give it the 'semblance of a quasi-federal association of States', but '[b]e that as it may, from the point of view of succession, the EEC appears without any doubt to remain on the plane of intergovernmental organization'[172].

Where rules of international law for a certain category of subjects exist, the fact that an entity does not act in accordance with them usually allows two possible conclusions: either that the subject is acting in violation of international law or that the rules do not apply to it because it does not fall within that category. In a study collecting practice to identify potential rules on succession, however, such a line of argument does not hold: the rule applicable to a certain category is yet to be discovered. With this in mind, Waldock's reasoning for excluding the EEC *because of its practice* when trying to develop a rule *based on practice* becomes circular.

In codifying an area of international law, the Special Rapporteur generally collects practice falling within the scope of study and therefrom they draw conclusions as to possibly existing (or at least developing) rules of international law.[173] In considering existing practice, Waldock was confronted with a situation – accession to the EEC – that raises comparable if not identical problems to that of a uniting of states to form a constitutional union: what happens to the pre-accession agreements of the new member states with non-union states? Do existing international agreements of the union extend to the new member states? Instead of exploring whether the situations are, in fact, identical and thus require the same answer, Waldock concluded that they cannot be identical because he believed the answer given in the case of the EEC to be different from that given in the case of other unions.

However, a differing practice by no means allows for such a conclusion. This is especially so in a field such as succession, where many argue that codification was pre-dated for a lack of consistent practice.[174] One alternative is that the EEC did not qualify as a subject of study because of its

---

172 Ibid.
173 On the methodology and working methods of the ILC, see D Azaria, 'The Working Methods of the International Law Commission: Adherence to Methodology, Commentaries and Decision-Making' in United Nations, *Seventy Years of the International Law Commission: Drawing a Balance for the Future* (Brill Nijhoff 2021) and M Kamto, 'The Working Methods of the International Law Commission' in United Nations (n 173).
174 As put by Crawford: 'Suitable as it was for extended scholarly treatment [...] the topic of State succession was not self-evidently "ripe for codification" at the end of the 1960s, either intrinsically or as a matter of relative priority of importance. In

II. On Dissimilarities: The Irrelevance of the EU's Lack of Statehood

deviating characteristics; then, its practice, whether consistent with that of other unions or not, could rightly be ignored. It is irrelevant to codification. The other alternative is that the EEC qualified as an object for Waldock's study; then its practice, even if deviating, would have had to be considered alongside that of other unions, amounting to practice relevant to the identification of a rule.

2. The Practice of the EU and Unions of States: Relevantly Similar

Waldock's argument on the exclusion of the EEC from his study on state succession is, however, not only circular: his conclusion – to some extent – also amounts to a forestalling of the results of studying the practice of other examples of unions. Waldock argued that the EEC 'remained on the plane of intergovernmental organization' because it

> unmistakably approaches the question of the pre-Community treaties [...] from the angle, not of succession or of the moving treaty frontier rule, but of the rules governing the application of successive treaties relating to the same subject matter (article 30 of the 1969 Convention on the Law of Treaties).

In asserting this, however, Waldock is not only expressing his views on EEC practice; he also makes a statement about his understanding regarding the practice of (other) unions of states, namely that their practice is *not* governed by considerations of conflicting successive treaty regimes, even though constitutional unions, too, may be based on an international agreement.[175] In the eyes of Waldock, the (perceived) statehood of constitutional unions thus appears to be reflected in the international rules and principles

---

itself it is a rubric containing diverse, diffuse, and difficult issues, many of them solvable only by particular reference to the facts of individual cases. Codification was, at this time, likely to be influenced overwhelmingly by the recent experience of decolonization, an experience not necessarily typical of the cases of succession most likely to occur in future. Various administrative techniques had evolved for coping with discontinuities resulting from succession, and it was arguable that their evolution should be allowed to continue undisturbed by attempts at formulating general rules.' (J Crawford, 'The Contribution of Professor DP O'Connell to the Discipline of International Law' (1980) 51(1) *British Yearbook of International Law* 1, 31).

175 Much later in his report, Waldock does engage with the question of how Art. 30 VCLT relates to treaties establishing a union of states, see 'SR Waldock Fifth Report' (n 31) 31.

that apply: those of treaty law in the case of international unions and those of a (to be codified) law of succession in the case of constitutional unions.

Yet the differences in the practice of unions of states and the EU as well as in the considerations underlying said practice at the time of Waldock's report are not as self-evident as Waldock's reasoning suggests. The practice of unions referred to in Waldock's report suggests that upon their formation, the pre-union agreements of their constituent states with non-union states continued in force, albeit limited to the territory in respect of which they were applicable before unification.[176] The same holds true for the pre-accession agreements of new EU Member States, as confirmed by Art. 351(1) TFEU. The main difference was only introduced by Waldock himself, who opted for a progressive development, and ultimately cemented by adoption of Art. 31 VCSSRT[177]: a constitutional union of states factually replaces as well as automatically *legally* succeeds its member states, so that pre-union agreements become 'a treaty of the Union State'[178]. In contrast, while the EU *factually* replaces its Member States in some areas of their external relations, it does *not* automatically assume their international agreements, except in exceptional circumstance and with the consent of the treaty partners.[179]

---

176 Ibid 25
177 Waldock himself noted that '[a]lmost any rule formulated on this point may attract criticism from some quarter'. Nevertheless, he considered his rule of succession by the union as 'the rule most likely to meet with acceptance and most consistent with modern practice' (see ibid 30). In contrast, the International Law Association in its second resolution on state succession did not consider pre-union agreements to automatically pass to the union but linked the question of *legal* succession to the distribution of treaty-making competence between the union and its constituent states: 'In cases of unions or federations of States, treaties [...] remain in force within the regional limits prescribed at the time of their conclusion [...]. In such a case where the treaty remains in force, the question whether the union or federation becomes responsible for performance of the treaty is dependent on the extent to which the constituent governments remain competent to negotiate directly with foreign States and to become parties to arbitration proceedings therewith' (see the text of the resolution in 'SR Waldock Fifth Report' (n 31) 26).
178 'SR Waldock Fifth Report' (n 31) 30.
179 This exception refers to the rare cases of a so-called functional succession. In ECJ, C-21 to 24/72 *International Fruit Company NV and others v Produktschap voor Groenten en Fruit* [1972] ECLI:EU:C:1972:115 the ECJ first introduced a 'functional succession doctrine' whereby the EU – under certain circumstances – assumes the treaty rights and obligations of its Member States with respect to a certain international agreement, subject to the consent of the treaty partners. For a current classification of the judgement and the development of the doctrine through later

II. On Dissimilarities: The Irrelevance of the EU's Lack of Statehood

While thus today an inverse rule-exception-relationship exists for a uniting of states as per Art. 31 VCSSRT and accession to the EU, the considerations underlying both constellations very much mirror each other. The ILC spent considerable time discussing the turn away from the clean slate principle, which dominated most of the draft articles preceding Art. 31, to a principle of continuity in the case of unions of states.[180] Lacking unequivocal practice, Waldock proposed two alternative draft articles: Alternative A[181] providing for automatic continuity and Alternative B[182] based on a clean slate-approach with a possibility of continuity through notification or agreement. In debating the two alternatives, a majority of ILC members supported Alternative A, echoing Waldock's rational to preserve the 'complex of treaty relations' that, having been separate states before uniting, the constituent states of the union had created and which they 'ought not to be able completely at will to terminate [...] by joining a federal or other union'.[183] As Ustor put it, 'the Commission should not attempt to legislate

---

case law, see A Petti and J Scott, 'International Agreements in the EU Legal Order: International Fruit' in G Butler and RA Wessel (eds), *EU External Relations Law: The Cases in Context* (Hart Publishing 2022). See also R Schütze, 'The "Succession Doctrine" and the European Union' in R Schütze (ed) (n 128) 110: 'The rationale was borrowed from the idea of "state succession". Since the Union is not a "state", the concept had to be applied *analogously*.' (Emphasis added).

180 See 'Summary Records 1972' (n 47) 160.

181 See 'SR Waldock Fifth Report' (n 31) 18: '1. When two or more States form a union of States, treaties in force between any of these states and other States parties prior to the formation of the union continue in force between the union of States and such other States parties unless: (a) The object and purpose of the particular treaty are incompatible with the constituent instrument of the union; or (b) The union of States and the other States parties to the treaty otherwise agree.'

182 See ibid: '1. When two or more States form a union of States, treaties in force between any of these States and other States parties prior to the formation of the union continue in force between the union of States and such other States parties if (a) In the case of multilateral treaties other than those referred to in article 7(a), (b) and (c), the union of States notifies the other States parties that it considers itself a party to the treaty; (b) In the case of other treaties the union of States and the other States parties (i) Expressly so agree; or (ii) Must by reason of their conduct be considered as having agreed to or acquiesced in the treaty's being in force in their relations with each other.'

183 Notably, Waldock adds that '[t]oday, this argument may, perhaps, be thought to have added force in view of the growing tendency of States to group themselves in new forms of association where the line between international organizations and unions of States becomes somewhat blurred' (see ibid 29–30). At the same time, he previously spent several paragraphs on reasons excluding the so far 'blurriest' of such associations from the scope of his project.

§ 6 EU Withdrawal and Succession: Justifying the Analogy

on the basis of practice but should rely on those principles of international law which it considered useful to the international community'[184]. These were, both among the members of the ILC and the state representatives to the ensuing Diplomatic Conference, most prominently *pacta sunt servanda* and the stability of international treaty relations.[185] In confirming the Member States' obligations arising from pre-accession agreements, Art. 351(1) TFEU likewise takes account of the principle of *pacta sunt servanda* and preserves the Member States' pre-accession treaty relations.[186]

At the same time, both Art. 31 VCSSRT and Art. 351 TFEU provide for incompatibility mechanisms to safeguard the interests of the union (and its member states). In the case of the EU, Art. 351 TFEU is considered 'essentially a provision governing conflicts between treaties'[187]. And '[a]lthough it clarifies that [Member States'] obligations under international law towards third countries are being respected, the provision attempts to resolve [...] conflicts in favour of the Union legal order'[188], as a last resort, by obliging Member States to terminate pre-accession agreements in accordance with international law.[189] In the case of constitutional unions, Art. 31(1)(b) VCSSRT provides for a conflict provision in encompassing an exception to the rule of continuity in cases where 'it appears from the treaty or is otherwise established that the application of the treaty in respect of the successor State would be incompatible with the object and purpose of the treaty'.

---

184 Ustor, 'Summary Records 1972' (n 47) 166.
185 See Ustor, ibid. See eg the comments made by United Arab Emirates, UNCSSRT, 'Official Records' 37th Meeting of the Committee of the Whole (31 July 1978) UN Doc. A/CONF.80/C.1/SR.37 33; Ukraine, UNCSSRT, 'Official Records' 38th Meeting of the Committee of the Whole (1 August 1978) UN Doc. A/CONF.80/C.1/SR.38 36; Guyana, '38th Meeting of the Committee of the Whole' (n 185) 37; Chile UNCSSRT, 'Official Records' 39th Meeting of the Committee of the Whole (1 August 1978) UN Doc. A/CONF.80/C.1/SR.39 44; Egypt, '39th Meeting of the Committee of the Whole' (n 185) 44.
186 See K Schmalenbach, 'Article 351' in C Calliess and M Ruffert (eds), *EUV/AEUV: Das Verfassungsrecht der Europäischen Union mit Europäischer Grundrechtecharta* (6th edn, CH Beck 2022) para 1.
187 M Kellerbauer and M Klamert, 'Article 351 TFEU' in M Kellerbauer, M Klamert and J Tomkin (eds), *The EU Treaties and the Charter of Fundamental Rights: A Commentary* (Oxford University Press 2019) 1. See also in great detail, J Klabbers, *Treaty Conflict and the European Union* (Cambridge University Press 2010).
188 Kellerbauer and Klamert (n 187) para 1.
189 Ibid para 14.

II. On Dissimilarities: The Irrelevance of the EU's Lack of Statehood

In defending the analogy between separation from a union and exiting the EU, one could simply dismiss Waldock's argument for excluding the EEC from his study as only relating to the situation of accession. Even if Art. 351 TFEU 'excludes any attempt on the part of the Community to have the rules of state succession concerning unions of states applied to its own formation'[190], that finding would be limited to the situation of formation or accession. Neither Art. 351 TFEU nor any other provision in the EU Treaties makes any statement about the effects of leaving the EU on international agreements. However, simply dismissing Waldock's argument would overlook the lessons that can be drawn from the discussions on the effect of accession on the proposed analogy in the case of withdrawal.

As regards the formation of a union of states, the rationales underlying Art. 31 VCSSRT and those underlying Art. 351 TFEU are by far not as diametrical as sometimes presented: not only do both provisions pay tribute to the overarching importance of *pacta sunt servanda* and the maintenance of stability in international relations, they also acknowledge the necessity to adapt to new situations. In drafting Art. 31 VCSSRT, the ILC consistently referred to the possibility of further proliferation of new forms of unions and the necessity to take account of this in their work. For Waldock, this reinforced existing assumptions with regard to unions of states.

> The argument for treating unions of States as a special case is that, as sovereign States, they created a complex of treaty relations with other States and ought not to be able completely at will to terminate all those treaties by joining a federal or other union. [...] Today, this argument may, perhaps, be thought to have added force in view of the growing tendency of States to group themselves in new forms of association where the line between international organizations and unions of States becomes somewhat blurred.[191]

For others, this meant questioning the existing practice and taking recourse to considerations of principle.[192] For, as phrased by Ustor,

> [t]he Commission was legislating for the future, and the growing need to allow for unions of States was shown by the general trend towards

---

190 KM Meessen, 'The Application of Rules of Public International Law within Community Law' (1976) 13(4) *Common Market Law Review* 485, 489.
191 'SR Waldock Fifth Report' (n 31) 29.
192 Ustor, 'Summary Records 1972' (n 47) 166.

integration throughout the world today. Regional organizations, in fact, had already proved to be an economic necessity.[193]

Ironically, however, instead of doing so, the ILC simply excluded the EEC, the one union that would become synonymous with the 'trend towards integration'[194], from its study. This is all the more surprising as the principles employed by the ILC in the context of the formation of unions would have offered abundant possibilities to engage with unions other than classical constitutional unions. The EU's treatment of pre-accession agreements under Art. 351 TFEU confirms this. In the VCSSRT, the role of treaty law principles is, however, not limited to the situation of forming a union. Rather, principles of treaty law also play a fundamental role in the (partial) dissolution of a union.

III. On Similarities: The Relevance of the Concept of Treaty Stability

Given the range of similarities shared between the EU and (federal) unions of states,[195] it is unsurprising that the ILC and scholars draw a comparison between the two. This fact as such, however, does not suffice for transferring a rule applied to unions to the EU. To do so, it is not only necessary to show that the dissimilarities between the EU and unions, which inevitably also exist, are *not* relevant to that rule. The similarities must also prove relevant to, in this case, the continuity of international agreements in the case of separation. To understand the relevancy of certain characteristics, however, it is first necessary to identify the rationale underlying a rule. Only when one knows the rationale, the object and purpose of a rule, is it possible to decide whether a characteristic is relevant.

With the VCSSRT being a progressive development of international law, many rules were shaped with recourse to principles, instead of (solely) to practice. In so doing, principles from international treaty law in general (A.) and the principle of treaty stability specifically (B.) played a decisive role. The question to be answered for the purpose of drawing an analogy is thus how coherently these principles can be applied to the situation of a withdrawal from the EU (C.).

---

193 Ibid.
194 Ustor, ibid.
195 See above Part II § 5 section III.

III. On Similarities: The Relevance of the Concept of Treaty Stability

A. The Relevance of the Law of Treaties to the Law on Succession

The codification project underlying the VCSSRT arose out of a recommendation by the UNGA to include the topic of 'Succession of States and Governments' in the ILC's agenda. The topic of state succession was among the 25 possible ILC study topics identified by Lauterpacht in 1948[196] and was selected as one of 14 topics for codification at the Commission's first session in 1949[197]. Nevertheless, it only regained attention in 1961, when the UNGA, after one and a half decades of decolonisation, urged the ILC to include the topic in its 'priority list'[198]. The Commission's first steps then were to request studies on contemporary state practice from the United Nations Secretariat and to appoint a ten-member Sub-Committee tasked with making the topic more approachable.

In 1963, the Sub-Committee issued a report consisting, *inter alia*, of a set of recommendations,[199] four of which considerably shaped the ILC's subsequent work on the topic:[200] the prioritisation of *state* over *governmental* succession; the prioritisation of recent (decolonisation) practice over 'traditional rules'[201] and theories on succession; the division of the topic into three 'headings'[202] and, among them, the prioritisation of the sub-topic 'succession in respect of treaties'; and, finally, the determination that this sub-topic 'should be dealt with in the context of succession of States, rather than in that of the law of treaties'[203].[204] In 1967, following the Sub-Committee' recommendations, Sir Humphrey Waldock was finally appointed the first Special Rapporteur for the question of state succession in respect of treaties. Waldock, having just finished his work on the draft articles on the law of treaties, was certainly influenced by his previous

---

196 ILC, 'Survey of International Law in Relation to the Work of Codification of the International Law Commission' UN Doc. A/CN.4/1/Rev.1, YBILC (1949).
197 Ibid 281.
198 'UNGA Res 1686' (n 92).
199 'Report Lachs' (n 93) 260.
200 MCR Craven (n 30) 97.
201 'Report Lachs' (n 93) 293.
202 These were succession in respect of treaties, succession in respect of rights and duties resulting from other sources than treaties, and succession in respect of membership of international organisations (see ibid 261).
203 Ibid.
204 In detail on the four recommendations, see MCR Craven (n 30) 97–102.

project.[205] Despite the Sub-Committee's recommendation on the approach to be taken, it was – thus perhaps unsurprisingly – the law of treaties around which he (initially) centred his work.

Waldock shifted the starting point for his study directly in his first report, '[believing] that the solution of the problems of so-called "succession" in respect of treaties is today to be sought within the framework of the law of treaties rather than of any general law of "succession"'[206]. A main reason for this was the 'considerable diversity'[207] in state practice that Waldock was confronted with. Waldock supposed that if the Commission were to adopt 'one specific theory' on succession, this would amount to a 'strait-jacket into which the actual practice [...] could not be forced without inadmissible distortions either of the practice or the theory'[208]. Instead, it was only if 'the question of "succession" is approached from the viewpoint of the law of treaties [...] that some general rules [...] are discernible in practice'[209].[210] Waldock's approach, in turn, not only influenced the ILC's further work on the topic. It also entailed consequences relevant for the question at hand.

Following his initial decision, Waldock subsequently understood his draft articles on state succession in respect of treaties 'as a sequel'[211] to what in 1969 became the VCLT. Even as an 'autonomous instrument' the draft articles on state succession with respect to treaties were always to '[assume] the existence of the Commission's articles on the law of treaties'[212]. It was this 'link'[213], however, that so severely limited the project's scope from the outset to *state* succession in respect of treaties *between* states. Although Waldock noticed the 'enormous growth of international organizations', he acknowledged their relevance only with regards to 'the contribution which they have made both [to] the development and the publication of State and depositary practice in matters of succession to multilateral treaties'[214]. Extending the scope of his project to include international organisations or

---

205 On Waldock's background, see ibid 104–105 and, in more detail, I Brownlie, 'The Calling of the International Lawyer: Sir Humphrey Waldock and His Work' (1984) 54(7) *British Yearbook of International Law* 7.
206 'SR Waldock First Report' (n 36) 89.
207 Ibid.
208 Ibid.
209 Ibid.
210 See in more detail, MCR Craven (n 30) 113–114.
211 'SR Waldock First Report' (n 36) 89.
212 Ibid.
213 Ibid 90.
214 Ibid.

III. On Similarities: The Relevance of the Concept of Treaty Stability

their agreements, however, would have meant deviating from the VCLT's scope of application.[215] At first, Waldock could avoid this '[o]n the preliminary view' that succession with regard to agreements of other subjects of international law would likely involve 'special problems'[216]. By the time of the ILC's final draft articles, however, 'the Commission recognized that the principles which they contain may in some measure also be applicable with reference to treaties to which other subjects of international law are parties'[217].[218] Thus, the desire to maintain consistency between the two projects' scope and definitions became the main justification.[219]

Relying on the VCLT as an 'essential framework'[220] thus *prima facie* entailed a negative effect: it facilitated the limitation of the VCSSRT's scope of application, making the proposed analogy necessary in the first place. At the same time, Waldock's reliance on treaty law may also prove useful in justifying this analogy. For his approach of treating the law of succession in the context of the VCLT went beyond the verbatim copying of previously used definitions and formulations.[221] Instead, taking the law of treaties as an 'essential framework'[222] provided Waldock with central arguments for justifying his sorting of state practice. Throughout large parts of his reports and the ILC's final commentaries, principles of treaty law serve as an underlying rationale, up to a point where

---

215 Art. 1 VCLT: 'The present Convention applies to treaties between States.' Art. 2(1)(a): '"treaty" means an international agreement concluded between States [...]'. This corresponds with Art. 1 and 2(1)(a) VCSSRT.
216 'SR Waldock First Report' (n 36) 91.
217 'ILC Report 1974' (n 59) 174.
218 This led the ILC to include a new article 'analogous' to Art. 3 VCLT. Art. 3(a) VCSSRT: 'The fact that the present Convention does not apply to the effects of a succession of States in respect of international agreements concluded between States and other subjects of international law or in respect of international agreements not in written form shall not affect: (a) the application to such cases of any of the rules set forth in the present Convention to which they are subject under international law independently of the Convention [...]'.
219 'ILC Report 1974' (n 59) 174. See also Vallat's report defending the limitation when challenged by the Dutch delegation to the Sixth Committee, 'SR Vallat First Report' (n 52) 12–13.
220 'ILC Report 1974' (n 59) 168.
221 See eg the definitions in Art. 2(1) for 'treaty' (a), 'full powers' (h), 'ratification, acceptance and approval' (i), 'reservation' (j), 'contracting State' (k), 'party' (l), 'international organization' (n).
222 'ILC Report 1974' (n 59) 168.

[t]he task of codifying the law relating to succession of States in respect of treaties appears [...] to be rather one of determining within the law of treaties the impact of the occurrence of a 'succession of States' than *vice versa*.[223]

This confirms the limited relevance of succession principles, such as self-determination and sovereignty, which are genuinely linked to the understanding of a *state* actor.[224] Furthermore, treaty law principles in particular are undisputedly transferrable to situations involving subjects *other* than states. This is because under the law of treaties the nature of the actor – be it a state or not – is not all that decisive. Differences in the treatment of states and other subjects of international law in the realm of treaty law mainly pertain to the *conclusion* of international agreements.[225] However, where a subject has concluded an international agreement, treaty law awards it its own (mostly indiscriminatory) status of a 'treaty party'.[226],[227] Determining the 'impact of the occurrence of a succession' between the EU and a leaving Member State within the law of treaties – if relevantly similar – could thus involve considering the same principles and rationales as in the case of *state* succession.

B. The Relevance of Treaty Stability to the Drafting of Art. 34 VCSSRT

When the VCSSRT was adopted, Art. 34 VCSSRT did not represent customary international law, but was clearly a progressive development of the rules governing international agreements in the case of separation.[228] In comparison to all previous drafts presented by the ILC and its two Special Rapporteurs on the topic, Art. 34 VCSSRT applies to all forms of states – be they unitary, federal or a real union – and undergoing any kind of territorial disintegration – from a complete dissolution to a separation of marginal

---

223 Ibid.
224 The limits of this can be seen in the special treatment of so-called 'newly-independent states' where the principle of self-determination played a decisive role, see eg MCR Craven (n 30) 131–147.
225 Most prominently the question of the capacity and competence to conclude (certain) international agreements, see eg Arts. 6, 46 VCLT and Arts. 6, 46 VCLT-IO.
226 Cp Art. 2(1)(g) VCLT and Art. 2(1)(g) VCLT-IO.
227 See in this context also Bordin's account of the VCLT-IO's drafting history on the basis of the VCLT (FL Bordin (n 26) 39–43).
228 On this see further below in this section.

III. On Similarities: The Relevance of the Concept of Treaty Stability

parts of territory. Additionally, in contrast to all previous articles, Art. 34 VCSSRT provides a single legal consequence of such succession: *ipso jure* continuity of previously concluded international agreements in relation to the successor and, where applicable, the predecessor state. That this broad application of the continuity principle went beyond what could be justified with state practice was openly acknowledged by the ILC and the states participating at the Diplomatic Conference.[229]

Lacking sufficient practice to codify a rule on separation, the ILC had turned to 'arguments based on principles of international law, including those relating to treaties', but found them to be 'far from conclusive'[230]. Thus, the Commission eventually tried to strike a balance between the two competing approaches in their overall draft on state succession in respect of treaties: clean slate and *ipso jure* continuity.[231] While the ILC's final draft article on separation – draft article 33 – provided for *ipso jure* continuity as the general rule, paragraph 3 envisaged a clean slate exception for separations 'which are essentially of the same character as those existing in the case of the formation of a newly independent State'[232].

---

[229] See the ILC's considerations in 'ILC Report 1974' (n 59) 264–266. See also Ustor's acknowledgement of providing for the future, 'Summary Records 1972' (n 47) 166. See eg the comments made by Switzerland, UNCSSRT, 'Official Records'40th Meeting of the Committee of the Whole (2 August 1978) UN Doc. A/CONF.80/C.1/SR.40 52: 'the International Law Commission, making a bold and deliberate choice, had departed from existing international law to propose an innovative solution involving progressive development.'; United Kingdom, UNCSSRT, 'Official Records' 41st Meeting of the Committee of the Whole (2 August 1978) UN Doc. A/CONF.80/C.1/SR.41 60: 'State practice was not a wholly reliable guide and the international community must have regard to progressive development rather than codification in determining the basic rule.'; Senegal, '41st Meeting of the Committee of the Whole' (n 229) 61: 'The Commission had faithfully observed the principle of the progressive development of international law'.

[230] 'SR Vallat First Report' (n 52) 70.

[231] See eg Vallat, UNCSSRT, 'Official Records'47th Meeting of the Committee of the Whole (7 August 1978) UN Doc. A/CONF.80/C.1/SR.47 103: 'Paragraphs 1 and 2 [of Article 33] had to do with the continuity principle and exceptions to it, while paragraph 3 set aside that principle on favour of the "clean slate" principle. The essential balance in the draft convention was between those two principles [...]'. Previously, Vallat had admitted: 'In both categories of cases [ie dissolution and separation], one may argue from the principle of self-determination as applied to a new State [later defined as "newly independent State"] and from the need to maintain the stability and continuity of treaty relations.' (See 'SR Vallat First Report' (n 52) 70).

[232] Draft article 33, paragraph 3, see 'ILC Report 1974' (n 59) 260.

§ 6 EU Withdrawal and Succession: Justifying the Analogy

Ultimately, the states participating at the Diplomatic Conference had to tackle the question of whether to follow the ILC in opting for a progressive development of the law through broad application of the continuity principle. The necessity to engage with this directional decision was amplified by the fact that many states expressed discontent with the vague formulation of the clean slate exception in paragraph 3 while being hesitant of a mere deletion.[233] Additionally, France and Switzerland introduced an amendment which sought to replace the continuity rule altogether and return to a clean slate approach for all cases of separation.[234] Following lengthy discussions in the Committee of the Whole, the Franco-Swiss amendment was rejected[235], the continuity rule as drafted by the ILC approved[236] and even the clean slate-exception in paragraph 3 removed[237]. And when 'in view of the lengthy debate [...] and its importance in the convention as a whole'[238] draft article 33 was put to vote during the 13th plenary meeting of the Diplomatic Conference, 68 states voted to adopt the text as it stood.[239]

With a large majority of states deciding in favour of continuity without being able to justify this decision based on state practice[240], what was their underlying rationale? To a differing degree, the state representatives speak-

---

233 See eg Mexico, '40th Meeting of the Committee of the Whole' (n 229) 56; Pakistan, '41st Meeting of the Committee of the Whole' (n 229) 57; United States of America, '41st Meeting of the Committee of the Whole' (n 229) 58; USSR, '41st Meeting of the Committee of the Whole' (n 229) 59; Spain, '41st Meeting of the Committee of the Whole' (n 229) 59; Netherlands, '41st Meeting of the Committee of the Whole' (n 229) 60; Japan, '41st Meeting of the Committee of the Whole' (n 229) 60.
234 For the text of the amendment, see UNCSSRT, 'Official Records (Volume III)' Documents of the Conference (1979) UN Doc. A/CONF.80/16/Add.2 160 and for an explanation of the amendment and the underlying considerations, see Switzerland, '40th Meeting of the Committee of the Whole' (n 229) 52–54 and France, '40th Meeting of the Committee of the Whole' (n 229) 54–55.
235 By 69 votes to 7, with 9 abstentions (see UNCSSRT, 'Official Records' 48th Meeting of the Committee of the Whole (8 August 1978) UN Doc. A/CONF.80/C.1/SR.48 109).
236 By 77 votes to 3, with 5 abstentions (see ibid).
237 By 52 votes to 9, with 22 abstentions (see UNCSSRT, 'Official Records' 49th Meeting of the Committee of the Whole (8 August 1978) UN Doc. A/CONF.80/C.1/SR.49 110).
238 Switzerland, UNCSSRT, 'Official Records' 13th Plenary Meeting (21 August 1978) UN Doc. A/CONF.80/SR.13 11.
239 With 5 states voting against the adoption (see ibid).
240 Although some states tried to, see eg Turkey '41st Meeting of the Committee of the Whole' (n 229) 58.

III. On Similarities: The Relevance of the Concept of Treaty Stability

ing during the discussion on draft article 33 engaged with arguments based on principle rather than practice. In doing so, two main lines of argument crystalised: states advocating for a clean slate approach as proposed by the Franco-Swiss amendment referred to the principle of self-determination and called for an equal treatment of states emerging from de-colonisation and from secession.[241] As explained by the French representative,

> [a]ny separation of part of the territory of a State implied some incompatibility between that part and the territory from which it separated; it was therefore logical that the part thus separated should not be bound by the obligations applicable to the territory from which it had separated. [...] Why should a State which seceded not be considered as a newly independent State?[242]

In contrast, the majority of states favouring the ILC's continuity approach based their support on the principle of stability in international (treaty) relations.[243] As put by the Hungarian representative, the states participating at the Diplomatic Conference

---

241 See eg Mexico, '40th Meeting of the Committee of the Whole' (n 229) 56 ('[...] that the right to self-determination was applicable to all peoples and that all new States deserved equal treatment, regardless of whether they had been colonial dependencies or not'); Switzerland, UNCSSRT, 'Official Records' 42nd Meeting of the Committee of the Whole (3 August 1978) UN Doc. A/CONF.80/C.1/SR.42 69 ('The delegations of France and Switzerland had sought to remedy a paradoxical situation which consisted in attaching the "clean slate" principle to the principle of self-determination and then confining its exercise to a single category of new States.'); Sri Lanka, '42nd Meeting of the Committee of the Whole' (n 241) 70 ('[...] it would nevertheless have been logical to examine and regulate the problem of States which seceded by virtue of the principle of self-determination [...]').

242 France, '40th Meeting of the Committee of the Whole' (n 229) 54–55.

243 See eg United States of America, '41st Meeting of the Committee of the Whole' (n 229) 59; United Kingdom, '41st Meeting of the Committee of the Whole' (n 229) 60; Hungary, '41st Meeting of the Committee of the Whole' (n 229) 61; Austria, '41st Meeting of the Committee of the Whole' (n 229) 62; Romania, '41st Meeting of the Committee of the Whole' (n 229) 62; Denmark, '42nd Meeting of the Committee of the Whole' (n 241) 63; Norway, '42nd Meeting of the Committee of the Whole' (n 241) 65; Qatar, '42nd Meeting of the Committee of the Whole' (n 241) 66.
But arguing specifically against invoking treaty stability, see Switzerland, '42nd Meeting of the Committee of the Whole' (n 241) 69 ('[...] the representative of the United States had tried to justify that position by invoking the stability of international relations. But those who supported that position seemed to be attempting to bind certain new States against their will and against their interests. For the stability of treaty relations was already sufficiently safeguarded by the free play of the consent of States.').

had a duty to think of the future, and in considering the possible dissolution of States, the continuity of inter-State relations had to be safeguarded and the stability of treaty relations maintained in the interest of the community of States.[244]

Besides the principle of treaty stability, some representatives also made mention of the principle of *pacta sunt servanda* to substantiate their support of a continuity approach.[245] By deciding for treaty law principles and against the principle of self-determination, the diplomatic conference thus came to the rule as it currently stands in Art. 34 VCSSRT. But by opting for treaty continuity in cases of separation, the Convention's fourth part on 'Uniting and Separation of States' also ultimately departed from the clean slate approach followed throughout its third part dealing with newly independent states. The states opting for continuity with reference to the principle of treaty stability thus sought to justify the difference in their approach.[246]

One of the main rationales behind treaty stability is, of course, safeguarding the interests of treaty partners.[247] In arguing from the perspective of the treaty partners potentially affected by succession, several states compared the situation of separation to the uniting of states. In the case of a uniting of states, both the ILC and the states participating in the diplomatic con-

---

244 Hungary, '41st Meeting of the Committee of the Whole' (n 229) 61.
245 See eg Belarus, ibid 58; Guyana, '42nd Meeting of the Committee of the Whole' (n 241) 67.
246 The ILC seems to have viewed the matter the other way around – instead of justifying the continuity in contrast to the clean slate approach, it was the latter that needed justification. For in principle, 'consent to be bound given by the predecessor State in relation to a territory prior to the succession of States, establishes a legal nexus between the territory and the treaty [...]' ('ILC Report 1974' (n 59) 167). And as Vallat, speaking as the Expert Consultant at a meeting of the Committee of the Whole pointed out: '[...] in instances of separation, there was, in principle, always a continuation of the legal nexus between the new State and the territory which had existed prior to the succession, and that it would therefore be contrary to the doctrine of the sanctity of treaties to apply the "clean slate" principle except in special circumstances' ('47th Meeting of the Committee of the Whole' (n 231) 104).
247 See eg Turkey, '41st Meeting of the Committee of the Whole' (n 229) 58; United States of America, '41st Meeting of the Committee of the Whole' (n 229) 58; Italy, '41st Meeting of the Committee of the Whole' (n 229) 61. Several states also explicitly referred to the principle of *pacta sunt servanda*, see eg Belarus, '41st Meeting of the Committee of the Whole' (n 229) 58 and Guyana, '42nd Meeting of the Committee of the Whole' (n 241) 67. Explicitly arguing against the relevance of *pacta sunt servanda*, see Switzerland, '40th Meeting of the Committee of the Whole' (n 229) 52.

III. On Similarities: The Relevance of the Concept of Treaty Stability

ference had clearly categorised such a succession as falling under the continuity principle.[248] In their view, the interests of the treaty partners were comparable. In both instances – uniting and separating – the predecessor state(s) presumably had a 'complex of treaty relations with other States'[249] which they should not be able simply to escape: 'rights freely accorded under a treaty should not be cut off because one State united with another [...] or separated into two or more parts [...].'[250]

On the other hand, referring to the reliance on existing treaty relations still does not (in itself) explain why separation should be treated differently from emergence into independence. The predecessors of newly independence states had also entertained treaty relations which, in many cases, extended to the territories subsequently emerging into independence and on whose territorial scope of application the treaty partners may have relied. Basing continuity in cases of separation on the argument of treaty stability can thus not only be about the interest of the treaty partners but must also have something to do with the situation of a 'normal' successor state being different from a newly independent state. Why should a recently separated state cater to the interests of the other state parties in contrast to a newly independent state? Or in other words: what are the relevant characteristics of a separation that distinguish it from an emerging into independence and lead states to opt for continuity rule?

The answer given by the states participating at the Diplomatic Conference pertains – if in slightly different nuances – to the circumstances of treaty conclusion. In doing so, some states, pointed to the will of the people: in the formation of a newly independent state, 'the right to self-determination was exercised, and the will of the people of the territory which had become independent had not been consulted in the treaty-making process'[251]. In contrast, it could not

> be said of separation of part of the territory of a State, even in circumstances similar to those existing in the case of the formation of a newly

---

248 In contrast to the article on separation, the article on a uniting of states was not even voted on during the plenary meeting, see '13th Plenary Meeting' (n 238) 11.
249 'SR Waldock Fifth Report' (n 31) 29.
250 United States of America, '41st Meeting of the Committee of the Whole' (n 229) 58.
251 Pakistan, '42nd Meeting of the Committee of the Whole' (n 241) 63.

§ 6 EU Withdrawal and Succession: Justifying the Analogy

independent State, that the will of the people had never been involved when entering into treaty obligations.²⁵²

Other states referred more generally to if '[t]he part of a State which separated itself had to some extent participated in the formulation of international relations, which a newly independent State had not'²⁵³. Vallat made a similar differentiation in his report. In a non-colonial context, 'a treaty concluded by the predecessor State will have been made on behalf of the State as a whole' and '[i]t may be presumed to have been made with the consent of the people of all parts of the State'²⁵⁴. However, '[t]his is a very different situation from that of a dependent territory which, although it may be consulted about the extension of the treaty, does not normally play any part in the actual government of the State concerned'²⁵⁵. The clear bifurcation of the Convention – clean slate in the context of de-colonisation, *ipso jure* continuity in instances of uniting and separation – is thus

> grounded on a distinction between situations in which states emerged from an environment where the territory involved previously had little if any role to play in shaping its own destiny, and situations in which states emerged from an environment where they were fully able to participate in determining the destiny of the territory involved.²⁵⁶

---

252 Pakistan, '41st Meeting of the Committee of the Whole' (n 229) 57. See also Brazil, '42nd Meeting of the Committee of the Whole' (n 241) 64.
253 Senegal, '41st Meeting of the Committee of the Whole' (n 229) 61. See in the same vein, eg United Kingdom, '41st Meeting of the Committee of the Whole' (n 229) 60; Guyana, '42nd Meeting of the Committee of the Whole' (n 241) 67.
254 'SR Vallat First Report' (n 52) 71.
255 Ibid.
256 RJ Zedalis, 'An Independent Quebec: State Succession to NAFTA' (1996) 2(4) *Law and Business Review of the Americas,* 9. A similar point was made by the US representative during a discussion of the clean slate exception that draft article 33 paragraph 3 had provided for. In the view of the US, the ILC opted for the clean slate principle in situations where it considered the territory in question not to have consented to a treaty (eg newly independent States). Thus, if aiming to provide for a clean slate exception to the continuity rule in cases of separation, '[l]ogically, the circumstances in which the treaties had been concluded should have been taken into account but that would have constituted interference in the domestic affairs of States'. To avoid this, the US representative argued, the ILC 'had found itself obliged to shift the emphasis to another question, that of the circumstances in which a part of a State separated and became a State. That was an easier question but perhaps not the right one.' (see United States of America, '48th Meeting of the Committee of the Whole' (n 235) 105).

III. On Similarities: The Relevance of the Concept of Treaty Stability

With these different nuances, one could, of course, question what the participating states (and Vallat) qualified as 'involvement', 'consent' or 'participation'. That the treaty had, prior to succession, simply not been 'imposed upon'[257] the territory that had now become a successor state? Or that territories separating must have 'negotiated and accepted rights and obligations of their own free will'[258]?

The conference documents provide no definitive answer to this. What does become clear, in any case, is that when debating draft article 33, many states continued to picture the situation of a union of states. By its 1972 Report, the ILC had shifted away from attaching any importance to the internal structure of a state.[259] Nevertheless, both the 'escape' and the 'participation argument' illustrate that the idea of the (partial) dissolution of a union of states still informed the debate on the much broader framed separation article. To some extent, separation continued to be viewed (only) as a (potential) corollary of a previous uniting and neither should affect international treaty relations.[260] This perception is not only visible in the way the 'escape argument' is usually formulated, referring, for example, to the separation of 'two States' which should not free themselves of their treaty obligations:[261] it is also evidenced by the fact that some of the states voicing the importance of protecting treaty stability at the same time supported the

---

257 United States of America, '41st Meeting of the Committee of the Whole' (n 229) 58.
258 Denmark, '42nd Meeting of the Committee of the Whole' (n 241) 63. See also Ireland, '42nd Meeting of the Committee of the Whole' (n 241) 65.
259 The question here had been whether 'a certain degree of separate international personality by constituent territories of the State' could be considered 'as an element for determining whether treaties of a dissolved State continue to be binding on the States emerging from the dissolution'. However, in the eyes of the ILC, the 'almost infinite variety of constituted relationships [...] [rendered] it inappropriate to make this element the basic test for determining whether treaties continue in force upon a dissolution of a State.' (See 'ILC Report 1972' (n 51) 295).
260 See eg the Union of Soviet Socialist Republics when arguing against the Franco-Swiss amendment ('41st Meeting of the Committee of the Whole' (n 229) 59): 'A situation could then arise in which, if States A and B united, the continuity rule would apply in respect of existing treaties [...], but if they separated, they would enjoy complete freedom.' Similarly, Denmark ('42nd Meeting of the Committee of the Whole' (n 241) 63): 'In the case of a union of two States, their treaty régimes would be maintained, but if the new State thus formed subsequently broke up, the same treaties which had been maintained in force would no longer be applicable, which would create a legal vacuum.'
261 See eg Turkey, '41st Meeting of the Committee of the Whole' (n 229) 58; Italy, '41st Meeting of the Committee of the Whole' (n 229) 61 ('It was impossible to claim that when *two States separated* which [...] *had been joined for centuries* and had formed

clean slate exception initially provided for in draft article 33 paragraph 3 for cases that factually did not correspond to the (partial) dissolution of a union.[262]

Moreover, the idea of a former territory of a state participating – to whatever extent – in the treaty-making of that state was most likely to be found in a (federal) union. This was expressly stated by the UK representative:

> If a *federation* broke up in the future, it would not be inappropriate for any resultant successor State, which had had a voice in the formulation of the foreign policy of the federation, to continue to be bound by treaty relations.[263]

In justifying the continuity rule, the states participating in the Diplomatic Conference thus did not find relevant the visibility or degree of personality of the constituent states which the ILC had considered in its reports.[264] But in placing relevance on the participation of the people or of the part of a state which separates, the federal state with its constituent units acting as intermediaries of the will of its people comes closest to said idea. Or put differently, the characteristics that states deemed relevant to the continuity of international agreements in the case of succession could most likely be found in a federal union.

C. The Relevance of Treaty Stability in the Case of EU Withdrawal

The discussions at the diplomatic conference on draft article 33 reveal two aspects important for justifying the analogy between the EU and unions of states. Firstly, the principle of treaty stability crystallised as the rationale underlying the states' decision to opt for a strict *ipso jure* continuity rule. Secondly, on the basis of the representatives' statements, it is also possible to understand *why* they attached such great importance to this principle. What differentiated the case of a state emerging from a separation from that of a newly independent state was the fact that, in the former case, the

---

links with other States, they were beginning a completely new existence just like those emerging from decolonization.' Emphasis added).
262 See eg Turkey, '41st Meeting of the Committee of the Whole' (n 229) 58.
263 United Kingdom, ibid 60 (emphasis added).
264 As the ILC had considered and rejected (see 'ILC Report 1972' (n 51) 295).

III. On Similarities: The Relevance of the Concept of Treaty Stability

agreements in question had been concluded with the will or participation of the people or the government of the part of the territory which separated.

This characteristic can also be found in the EU and its Member States' conduct of foreign relations. In concluding international agreements with non-EU states, the EU has to follow a procedure laid out by Art. 218(2)-(8) TFEU. According to said procedure, the Council – the organ representing the Member States – plays a decisive role both in the negotiation and conclusion of international agreements. The Council decides on the opening of negotiations as well as the signing and ratification of the final agreements.[265] While the Commission or the High Representative for Foreign Affairs generally conduct the negotiations, they do so upon nomination by the Council, based on the Council's negotiating directives and under its supervision.[266] The role of the Member States in the process of treaty conclusion increases even further in the case of mixed agreements. Here, not only do Member States participate via their representative in the Council, but upon conclusion of the negotiations, they also conduct their own national procedures for the conclusion of international agreements. In doing so, the national parliaments of almost all Member States are directly involved in the conclusion of agreements through adoption of a national approval act.[267]

Thus, the EU and unions of states are similar in an aspect *relevant* to the principle of treaty stability and, in extension, the continuity rule of Art. 34

---

265 Art. 218(2) TFEU: 'The Council shall authorise the opening of negotiations, adopt negotiating directives, authorise the signing of agreements and conclude them.'
266 Art. 218(3) and (4) TFEU: '3. The Commission, or the High Representative of the Union for Foreign Affairs and Security Policy where the agreement envisaged relates exclusively or principally to the common foreign and security policy, shall submit recommendations to the Council, which shall adopt a decision authorising the opening of negotiations and, depending on the subject of the agreement envisaged, nominating the Union negotiator or the head of the Union's negotiating team. 4. The Council may address directives to the negotiator and designate a special committee in consultation with which the negotiations must be conducted.' While the Council may opt to choose another negotiator (eg a single Member State), it generally nominates the Commission and/or the High Representative, Schmalenbach (n 186) para 11.
267 In some Member States, parliamentary participation depends on the type of international agreement. Thus, the number of national (and regional) parliaments involved in the conclusion of a mixed agreement may vary, with an estimate of around 38 (including regional and bicameral parliaments), see G van der Loo, 'Less is More?: The Role of National Parliaments in the Conclusion of Mixed (Trade) Agreements' (2018) 1 *CLEER Paper Series*, 16.

VCSSRT. But how viable, overall, is it to apply the same rationale to both the separation from a union of states, on the one hand, and the withdrawal of an EU Member State, on the other hand?

The principle of treaty stability focuses especially on the interest of the treaty partners. As put by the US representative to the Diplomatic Conference,

> [f]rom the political viewpoint, it might be considered that it was not realistic that a successor State should be bound by the treaty obligations of the predecessor State [...]. But neither was it just that a great number of States should lose their treaty rights. Thus a very serious choice had to be made. Perhaps it was *better to be unjust to one State than to a very large number of States.*[268]

From the perspective of this 'very large number of States', however, the involved interests do not appear different in the case of a Member State leaving the EU instead of a (constitutional) union of states. It is the Member States' free choice to accede to the EU and to withdraw from it; in doing so, they should not be able to free themselves of obligations entered into either as individual states pre-accession or as part of the Union. Even where the Member States are not treaty parties themselves as in the case of EU-only agreements, it is arguably the intent of the treaty partner to conclude an agreement *encompassing* these Member States. Where the agreement itself no longer does so because a Member State has decided to leave the EU, the interest of the treaty partner in retaining its rights *vis-à-vis* that Member State are *prima facie* best served through a continuity of treaty relations.

There is, however, a more general problem with placing such a focus on the concept of treaty stability. At the heart of this argument lies the (constructed) consent of the separating state (or its people) and the assumed interest of the treaty partner. The argument of treaty stability thus presupposes that the treaty partner *wants* its treaty relations to be safeguarded. But what if the interest of that other party is *not* the continuation of its international agreements with a successor state? A countervailing consideration to relying on the principle of treaty stability, taking account of the *actual* interests of the successor state and the affected treaty partners may thus be another principle of treaty law: the principle of consent.

---

268 United States of America, '48th Meeting of the Committee of the Whole' (n 235) 105 (emphasis added).

IV. Countervailing Considerations: The Principle of Consent

In the context of international agreements, consent is an (if not *the*) overarching principle. When placing the law of succession within the framework of the law of treaties, making arguments with reference to the parties' consent is thus perhaps inevitable. And indeed, the principle of consent was taken into account by the ILC as well as being picked up again during the Diplomatic Conference (A.). In both instances, reference to parties' consent was thought to justify a differentiation in the treatment of bilateral and multilateral agreements. While this was successful with regard to newly independent states, an amendment seeking to introduce the principle of consent in Art. 34 VCSSRT failed at the Diplomatic Conference. Despite not being supported by Art. 34 VCSSRT's drafting history, there may be a strong case for focusing more on the principle of consent than that of treaty stability, especially in the case of bilateral agreements (B.).

A. The Irrelevance of the Principle of Consent in Drafting Art. 34 VCSSRT

At the Diplomatic Conference, most of the discussions on draft article 33 dealing with separations and the proposed Franco-Swiss clean-slate amendment to it revolved around the two dominating principles in the ILC's reports, self-determination and treaty stability.[269] The German delegation, however, proposed another amendment to the separation article based on a third principle, that of consent. In opting for an *ipso jure* continuity rule with regard to all international agreements in cases of separation, the ILC not only introduced a distinction between newly independent states and other successor states, but it also discarded a differentiation found within the part of the draft articles dealing with newly independent states. Here, the draft drew a distinction between the legal consequences of succession for bilateral and multilateral agreements that the subsequent part on uniting and separation of states lacked. The German amendment aimed to change this. In introducing the proposed text, the German representative explained '[t]hat [the] amendment was intended to establish a distinction between multilateral and bilateral treaties and to introduce into article 33

---

269 See above Part II § 6 section III.B.

the notion of consent which appeared in article 23'[270], the draft article on newly independent states and bilateral agreements of their predecessors.

For newly independent states, Art. 16 VCSSRT provides for a general clean slate approach: 'A newly independent State is not bound to maintain in force, or to become a party to, any treaty' of its predecessor. This rule is further concretised for multilateral agreements in Art. 17–23 VCSSRT and for bilateral agreements in Arts. 24–26 VCSSRT. In the case of multilateral agreements, the newly independent state 'may, by a notification of succession, establish its status as a party to any multilateral treaty'[271] of its predecessor. While it is not automatically bound to those agreements, the newly independent state thus enjoys a *unilateral* right to participation, an 'opt-in' option. In contrast, the possible continuation of a bilateral agreement between a newly independent state and its predecessor's treaty partner requires *reciprocal* consent. According to Art. 24(1) VCSSRT, a bilateral agreement 'is only considered as being in force between a newly independent State and the other State party when: (a) they expressly so agree; or (b) by reason of their conduct they are to be considered as having so agreed'. Using the same formulation, Germany intended to include a clean slate exception for bilateral agreements into the article on separation. The amendment would have inserted in draft article 33(1), stating the general continuity rule, a new subparagraph according to which

> [...] any bilateral treaty in force at the date of the succession of States in respect to the entire territory of the predecessor State is considered as being in force between the successor State and the other State party when they expressly so agree or by reason of their conduct, are to be considered as having so agreed [...].[272]

The amendment was ultimately rejected.[273] However, the fact that Art. 34 VCSSRT treats bilateral and multilateral agreements the same has been described as a 'major defect of the Convention'[274]. Dumberry, a strong

---

270 Germany, '40th Meeting of the Committee of the Whole' (n 229) 55.
271 Art. 17(1) VCSSRT.
272 For the text of the amendment, see 'UNCSSRT 1979' (n 234) 160.
273 Rejected by 57 votes to 5 with 20 abstentions ('49th Meeting of the Committee of the Whole' (n 237) 109).
274 P Dumberry, 'State Succession to Bilateral Treaties: A Few Observations on the Incoherent and Unjustifiable Solution Adopted for Secession and Dissolution of States under the 1978 Vienna Convention' (2015) 28(1) *Leiden Journal of International Law* 13, 15.

IV. Countervailing Considerations: The Principle of Consent

proponent of (re)introducing such a distinction, draws this conclusion based on the VCSSRT's drafting history. Waldock introduced the distinction between bilateral and multilateral agreements in his first reports when analysing the practice surrounding de-colonisation. As Dumberry argues, however, it was neither that practice nor (only) the principle of self-determination that informed the ILC's decision for a clean slate rule for newly independent states.[275] Instead, he claims, self-determination was the decisive factor for the ILC to opt for a clean slate *only* in the case of multilateral agreements. With respect to bilateral agreements, Dumberry argues, the clean-slate rule was justified with reference to the principle of consent.[276] But the principle of consent – unlike self-determination – undisputedly applies to newly independent states and other successor states alike. Moreover, for the treaty partners to bilateral agreements, 'it mattered little whether they had to deal with a newly independent State, or with a new State [...]. In any case, they would wish their consent to be required'[277]. Why was the same reasoning then not applied beyond the context of newly independent states? Dumberry finds this 'regrettable' and 'unexplainable'[278].

In fact, however, the fact that the ILC omitted any considerations as to a distinction between bilateral and multilateral agreements in its article on separation is not 'unexplainable'[279]. Rather, considering the ILC's reasoning with regards to newly independent states, it is only consequential. For in contrast to what Dumberry argues, Waldock had explicitly relied on practice *and* the principle of self-determination to arrive at a clean slate approach, *also* with regard to bilateral agreements.[280] However, the ILC did draw a distinction between bilateral and multilateral agreements

---

275 Ibid 23–24.
276 Ibid 24–26.
277 Germany, '40th Meeting of the Committee of the Whole' (n 229) 55.
278 Dumberry (n 274), 27.
279 Ibid.
280 'SR Waldock Fourth Report' (n 95) 150. Waldock was convinced that *practice* must be understood in that sense. In his view, 'enough evidence [had] been adduced to establish the essentially voluntary character of succession in respect of bilateral treaties' ('SR Waldock Fourth Report' (n 95) 149). But see KJ Keith, 'Succession to Bilateral Treaties By Seceding States' (1967) 61(2) *American Journal of International Law* 521, 545 who interprets the practice completely different coming to the conclusion 'that the two requirements of consistent practice and *opinio iuris* are met and that new States are to remain bound by certain categories of bilateral treaties'. For a discussion of the two positions, see MCR Craven (n 30) 145–147.

with respect to the newly independent state's ability to continue its predecessor's international agreements if it so wished. In the case of multilateral agreements, the newly independent state's right of participation through notification was justified with reference to a 'legal nexus of a certain degree between the treaty and the territory'[281], created 'by the acts of the predecessor State'[282]. In the case of bilateral agreements, however, the ILC considered the principle of consent to prevail over this 'legal nexus'. The principle of consent, thus, did not serve as a justification for the clean slate rule. Instead,

> emphasis upon mutual consent [...] was to deny the successor State the right to determine unilaterally whether bilateral agreements should continue in force, and was to suggest that their survival would ultimately be brought about by a process most closely analogous to 'novation'.[283]

Based on this understanding of the principle of consent – as a justification for requiring 'novation' – applying it to the case of separation would have made no sense. Where successor states automatically succeed to the international agreements of their predecessors, mutual consent to continue these agreements is unnecessary.[284]

B. The Relevance of the Identity of the Treaty Partner in Bilateral Agreements

The VCSSRT's drafting history does not support a clean-slate rule for bilateral agreements in cases of separation. That is not to say, however, that the lack of differentiation between bilateral and multilateral agreements may not, in fact, be 'regrettable'[285]. Much of today's criticism of Art. 34 VCSSRT reflects the reasons of the German delegation for introdu-

---

281 'SR Waldock Third Report' (n 94) 39.
282 MCR Craven (n 30) 139. For a detailed account of the discussions in the ILC revolving around the concept of such a 'legal nexus', see MCR Craven (n 30) 141–147.
283 MCR Craven (n 30) 143.
284 Similarly, the Israeli representative at the Committee of the Whole noted that the 'reasons advanced by the International Law Commission in support of the special regime established in article 23 for newly independent States were not valid in the case of separation of parts of a State.' (Israel, '42nd Meeting of the Committee of the Whole' (n 241) 64).
285 Dumberry (n 274), 27.

IV. Countervailing Considerations: The Principle of Consent

cing its clean slate-amendment for bilateral agreements. In the view of both the German delegation and scholars today, the 'particular nature'[286] of bilateral agreements makes it 'necessary to take account of the legitimate interest of the contracting parties'[287] – not in the abstract, but by making continuity of an agreement dependent on the parties' consent. This particular nature is derived from the 'personal equation'[288], the importance placed on the identity of the parties, in the context of bilateral agreements.

> Generally, a bilateral treaty was intended to regulate the rights and obligations of the parties in their mutual relations. Hence it could not be assumed that States which had agreed that a bilateral treaty should apply to a certain territory would subsequently be willing to keep it in force with respect to that territory when it had become an integral part of the territory of a new sovereign.[289]

The understanding underlying calls for a differentiation based on an agreement's laterality is, thus, that the character of a bilateral agreement places the treaty partners in a different situation in the case of succession. While a multilateral agreement is viewed as negotiated in the general interest of a variety of parties, a bilateral agreement is considered as being 'signed to preserve the *specific* interests of the two parties involved'[290]. The predecessor and the successor state, however, 'have not only different sizes and population, but also different political and economic powers'; importantly, subsequently 'they also have different interests'[291]. It is for that reason that – arguably – treaty stability may be considered to serve the general interests of states in the context of multilateral agreements, while requiring the consent of the treaty partners may better serve the specific interests of states in a bilateral context.

Some of the states participating in the Diplomatic Conference considered the exceptions to the continuity rule as already provided for in draft article 33 as catering to this concern.[292] They rejected the German

---

286 Ibid 15.
287 Germany, '40th Meeting of the Committee of the Whole' (n 229) 55.
288 Dumberry (n 274), 25 quoting the term used by the Waldock and the ILC in the part on newly independent states, see eg 'ILC Report 1974' (n 59) 237.
289 Germany, '40th Meeting of the Committee of the Whole' (n 229) 55.
290 Dumberry (n 274), 25.
291 Ibid 26.
292 See eg Hungary, '40th Meeting of the Committee of the Whole' (n 229) 56; Belarus, '41st Meeting of the Committee of the Whole' (n 229) 58; United States of America,

amendment to introduce a clean slate rule for bilateral agreements with reference to draft article 33 paragraph 2, according to which the successor state does not become bound by its predecessor's agreements if

> (a) the States concerned otherwise agree; or
> (b) it appears from the treaty or is otherwise established that the application of the treaty in respect of the successor State would be incompatible with the object and purpose of the treaty or would radically change the conditions for its operation.[293]

There is, however, an obvious difference between protecting the 'legitimate *interests* of the contracting parties'[294], as envisaged by the German amendment, and an exception limited to the narrow circumstances of incompatibility or *rebus sic stantibus*[295]. Whereas the former has a clear subjective element, the latter is restricted to a situation of an objective malfunctioning of the agreement.

What is more, the German amendment offered a clear criterion – the laterality of the agreement – and attached to it a precise legal consequence – clean slate. With a clean slate as the starting point, it was believed that 'where there was a common interest, the two States would not fail to reach agreement in order to ensure the continuity of the treaty'[296]. In contrast, all exceptions provided for in draft article 33 paragraph 2 – and transferred to Art. 34(2) VCSSRT with the same wording – depend on the successor state and the other state party eventually reaching some kind of understanding either by consenting to the disapplication of the continuity rule as such (lit. a) or agreeing on the existence of the conditions of one of the exceptions in lit. b.[297] Importantly in this regard, Art. 34(2)(b) VCSSRT is not a

---

'41st Meeting of the Committee of the Whole' (n 229) 58; Brazil, '42nd Meeting of the Committee of the Whole' (n 241) 64; Guyana, '42nd Meeting of the Committee of the Whole' (n 241) 68.

293   As in the current Art. 34 VCSSRT.
294   Germany, '40th Meeting of the Committee of the Whole' (n 229) 55.
295   The ILC explicitly drafted the second alternative of Art. 34(2)(b) along the lines of Art. 62 VCLT, see V Mikulka, 'Article 34' in G Distefano, G Gaggioli and A Hêche (eds), *La Convention de Vienne de 1978 sur la Succession d'États en Matière de Traités: Commentaire Article par Article et Études Thématiques* (Bruylant 2016) para 64.
296   Switzerland, '40th Meeting of the Committee of the Whole' (n 229) 53.
297   But see Dumberry (n 274), 28 who suggested that '[i]t may be that the ILC came to the conclusion that, in any event, the solution of continuity could never be imposed on a reluctant state'.

unilateral termination clause, but an exception to the automatic continuity rule that 'prevents the treaty from devolving to the successor State'[298]. Thus, while the exceptions in Art. 34(2)(b) may be unilaterally invoked by the successor state or the other state party[299], until both states concerned agree on the exception being fulfilled (or not), it is unclear whether a devolution of the agreement has taken place (or not). Where the rationale is to better protect the specific interests of states in the context of bilateral agreements, perhaps it is then simply more *practical* to rely on states coming together where they have an actual interest in a particular agreement.

V. Brexit Practice: Between Treaty Stability and Consent?

In many regards, the analogy between the EU and unions of states and the consequent application of Art. 34 VCSSRT to the exiting of a Member States from the EU is justified. The EU's obvious dissimilarity from constitutional unions, as considered by Waldock in his reports on state succession, are of only minor relevance to the continuity rule in cases of separation. Neither statehood nor the associated principle of sovereignty are decisive for establishing the fact of succession or for Art. 34 VCSSRT's objective of guaranteeing treaty stability. Furthermore, the EU and unions of states share characteristics which are relevant when arguing in favour of treaty stability. Where the constituent states of a union have participated in the creation of international treaty relations, they should not – by leaving the union – be able to simply sever the legal nexus thereby created.

At the same time, substantive considerations may speak against Art. 34 VCSSRT and its absolute continuity rule as such. Did the ILC perhaps wrongly – at least from the perspective of practice – favour the principle of treaty stability over the principle of consent? Furthermore, the practice that emerged from Brexit is not exactly characterised by an emphasis on stability and continuity, at least not in an automatic sense. Following the EU and the UK's approach, none of the rights and obligations stemming from EU-only and bilateral mixed agreements in any form continued to apply or devolved to the UK. With regard to many aspects of a state's international (treaty) relations, a prominent example being

---

[298] Mikulka (n 295) para 68 ('il empêche la dévolution du traité à l'État successeur', translated by the author).
[299] Ibid para 69.

trade, Brexit thus very much meant a clean slate for the UK. On the other hand, the EU and the UK did opt for a continuity approach in the case of multilateral mixed agreements in which the UK was sought to remain a party. Additionally, the UK did aim for a certain degree of stability by rolling over international agreements in which it had an interest. Could Brexit, then, perhaps be characterised as a balancing of stability and the clean slate approach, albeit with a clear bias towards the latter?

With Brexit practice not following Art. 34 VCSSRT – does that invalidate the analogy? Or does not perhaps the rule – Art. 34 VCSSRT – analogically applied rather require adapting? One indicator for the latter may be Dumberry's reference to state practice with regard to separations *after* the adoption of the VCSSRT. As he argues, differentiating between bilateral and multilateral agreements with automatic continuity only in the latter case 'is also the general position that has been adopted by states in recent years in the context of numerous examples of secession and dissolution of states'[300]. Although the VCSSRT is a treaty based on a codification project, its provisions are rarely considered customary. Its provisions may thus provide a starting point, but they are still very much capable of changing and being shaped by state practice. How does the practice in the case of Brexit then play out in comparison to more recent state practice? And could not, in the end, Brexit itself be considered as new 'state' practice?

---

300   Dumberry (n 274), 30.

§ 7 Brexit and Recent Practice. Brexit as Recent Practice?

The previous chapter (§ 6) has shown that analogical application of Art. 34 *Vienna Convention on Succession of States in Respect of Treaties*[1] (VCSSRT) to the situation of EU withdrawal is justifiable based on state practice and rationales underlying the drafting of this rule. Not only does the EU show similarities to unions of states, but also these unions and the characteristics shared by the EU were relevant to the drafting of the continuity rule for international agreements in cases of separation. Besides considering the (ir)relevance of (dis)similarities and analogy-warranting rationales, there is, however, another criterion important to justify legal reasoning by analogy. To guarantee coherence within the legal system, the analogical application of a rule must be consistent with its application in prior cases. This is especially relevant where – as in common law jurisdictions – previous case law plays an important role. In other words, to justify the analogical application of a rule, it is necessary to consider precedents. How have courts decided previous cases based on the rule, which is now to be applied analogically? And is it coherent – considering those precedents – to apply the same rule to the case at hand?

In international law, previous applications of a rule in general do not matter so much in the form of precedents. Even though the International Court of Justice (ICJ) is regularly referred to as the 'World Court', this is solely owed to its 'combination of functions', being able to 'hear cases from any region of the world, [...] to consider all substantive aspects of international law' and being 'endowed with the stature of the UN's principal judicial organ'[2]. But the Court is neither hierarchically superior to other international courts and tribunals allowing for the application of the *stare decisis* doctrine[3] nor is it itself bound to any of its previous rulings.[4]

---

1 Vienna Convention on Succession of States in Respect of Treaties (adopted 23 August 1978, entered into force 6 November 1996) 1946 UNTS 3 [VCSSRT].
2 JE Donoghue, 'The Role of the World Court Today' (2012) 47(1) *Georgia Law Review* 181, 182.
3 G Acquaviva and F Pocar, 'Stare decisis' in R Wolfrum (ed), *The Max Planck Encyclopedia of Public International Law* (Oxford University Press 2012) para 2.
4 It does, however, regularly refer to its previous case law, see eg ICJ *Case Concerning United States Diplomatic and Consular Staff in Tehran* (Judgement) [1980] ICJ Rep

§ 7 Brexit and Recent Practice. Brexit as Recent Practice?

Additionally, with regard to many aspects of international law, the ICJ has never had the chance to express an opinion or, as in the case of Art. 34 VCSSRT, avoided doing so.[5]

However, the (non-)application of a certain rule or principle by a state to a set of facts does play a role as state practice. The legal relevance of such practice varies, depending on the rule or principle under consider-

---

1980, p 3, [33]: 'in accordance with its settled jurisprudence'. See for more examples, Acquaviva and Pocar (n 3) paras 10–13. On the relevance of precedents in the ICJ's jurisprudence, see JG Devaney, 'The Role of Precedent in the Jurisprudence of the International Court of Justice: A Constructive Interpretation' (2022) 35(3) *Leiden Journal of International Law* 641.

5   The issue of state succession in respect of international agreements following a separation was raised in two different cases.
Firstly, in a case brought by Bosnia and Herzegovina against the Federal Republic of Yugoslavia the question arose as to whether and if so when Bosnia and Herzegovina had succeeded in the Genocide Convention. However, both in its decision on provisional measures and on preliminary objections the Court avoided a determination on the issue. See ICJ *Case Concerning the Application of the Convention on the Prevention and Punishment of the Crime of Genocide (Bosnia and Herzegovina v. Serbia and Montenegro)* (Preliminary Objections) [1996] ICJ Rep 1996, p 595, [23]: 'Without prejudice as to whether or not the principle of "automatic succession" applies in the case of certain types of international treaties or conventions, the Court does not consider it necessary in order to decide on its jurisdiction in this case, to make a determination on the legal issues concerning State succession in respect to treaties which have been raised by the Parties. Whether Bosnia and Herzegovina automatically became party to the Genocide Convention on the date of its accession to independence on 6 March 1992, or whether it became a party as a result – retroactive or not – of its Notice of Succession of 29 December 1992, at all events it was a party to it on the date of the filing of its Application on 20 March 1993.' For the decision in the provisional measures stage, see ICJ *Case Concerning the Application of the Convention on the Prevention and Punishment of the Crime of Genocide* (Provisional Measures) [1993] ICJ Rep 1993, p 3, [25]. On how the separate opinions addressed the issue, see A Zimmermann, *Staatennachfolge in völkerrechtliche Verträge: Zugleich ein Beitrag zu den Möglichkeiten und Grenzen völkerrechtlicher Kodifikation* (Springer 2000) 304. On the case, see also in detail MC R Craven, *The Decolonization of International Law: State Succession and the Law of Treaties* (Oxford University Press 2007) 7–16.
Secondly, in the *Gabcikovo-Nagymaros case*, Hungary challenged Slovakia's succession to a 1977 treaty between Hungary and Czechoslovakia concerning the construction and operation of a system of locks. The Court '[did] not find it necessary for the purpose of the present case to enter into a discussion of whether or not Article 34 of the 1978 Convention reflects the state of customary international law' for the 1977 treaty in question established a territorial regime as per Art. 12 VCSSRT (see ICJ *Case Concerning the Gabčíkovo-Nagymaros Project (Hungary v Slovakia)* (Judgement) [1997] ICJ Rep 1997, p 7, [123]). On the state succession aspects of the case, see J Klabbers, 'Cat on a Hot Tin Roof: The World Court, State Succession, and the Gabcikovo-Nagymaros' (1998) 11(2) *Leiden Journal of International Law* 345 and Craven, *Decolonization* (n 5) 239–244.

ation. Especially where there is no firm treaty basis – as in the case of Art. 34 VCSSRT – state practice plays an important role in shaping and subsequently, together with *opinion juris*, (dis)confirming a (emerging) customary rule of international law.[6] Thus, the practice of pre-VCSSRT unions of states – along with considerations of general principles of (treaty) law – provided the basis for the drafting of Art. 34 VCSSRT.[7] However, Art. 34 VCSSRT being a progressive development of international law at least in combining the two different situations of separation and dissolution, practice continues to play a decisive role even after the conclusion of the VCSSRT. With codification having 'ended in a relative failure'[8] – the VCSSRT currently counts just 23 treaty parties – the status of Art. 34 VCSSRT hinges upon its acceptance in state practice following the conclusion of the VCSSRT.

The law of state succession had been 'pronounced dead (or at least comatose) in the 1980s after the vogue of decolonization had passed'[9]. Starting with the early 1990s, however, new instances of state succession occurred. Several of these qualify as separations in the sense of Art. 34 VCSSRT. While pre-VCSSRT practice as regards unions of states supported the initial drafting of an automatic continuity rule, the question is whether practice following the adoption of the VCSSRT confirms it (I.). Either way, when drawing an analogy between the separation from a union of states and the exit of a Member State from the EU, these recent instances of state succession must – as a rule-creating or rule-(dis)confirming factor – be taken into account. How can Brexit practice concerning international agreements then be assessed in light of Art. 34 VCSSRT and the subsequent separation cases (II.)?

---

6 On the elements of customary international law, see ICJ *North Sea Continental Shelf Cases (Federal Republic of Germany/Denmark; Federal Republic of Germany/Netherlands)* (Judgement) [1969] ICJ Rep 1969, p 3, [77]. See also ILC, 'Draft Conclusions on Identification of Customary International Law, with Commentaries', YBILC (2018) Vol. II(2).

7 See above Part II § 5 section III.C.

8 M Koskenniemi, 'Report of the Director of Studies of the English-speaking Section of the Centre' in PM Eisemann and M Koskenniemi (eds), *State Succession: Codification Tested Against the Facts* (Martinus Nijhoff Publishers 2000) 66.

9 Ibid.

Finally, the question of 'what then?' arises. Can the practice arising from Brexit contribute to 'state'[10] practice as regards the separation from a union of states? Strictly speaking, this must be answered in the negative considering that Brexit viewed through the lens of Art. 34 VCSSRT is still not a *direct* application but an analogy. Yet, the engagement with inter-national agreements that took place in the Brexit process undeniably amounts to practice. Does Brexit then give rise to a law of succession for 'hybrid unions'[11] of states? At least for itself, the EU has certainly set a model by which it will most likely approach the issue of international agreements – and by which it will be measured – should another Member State withdraw. What does placing withdrawal from the EU in the realm of the law of succession mean beyond the specific case of Brexit (III.)?

I. Post-1978 Practice: Putting Art. 34 VCSSRT to the Test

Had practice on separation been limited when the VCSSRT was drafted, the majority of state successions happening after its adoption in 1978 concerned the disintegration of states. Compared to other articles, Art. 34 VCSSRT has thus been put to the test several times. Evaluating this state practice since the 1980s in detail would go beyond the scope of this study[12] and has been done in detail before.[13] The intent of this chapter is thus not to

---

10 As regards the post-Brexit treaty practice by the UK, the remaining Member States and non-EU treaty partners, this amounts to *state* practice. The statements and conduct of the EU do not count towards *state* practice.
11 ILC, 'Fifth Report on Succession in Respect of Treaties, by Sir Humphrey Waldock' UN Doc. A/CN.4/256 and Add.1 – 4, YBILC (1972) Vol. II 18.
12 On the difficulties to be encountered when trying to assess the practice surrounding state succession, see A Zimmermann and JG Devaney, 'Succession to Treaties and the Inherent Limits of International Law' in CJ Tams, A Tzanakopoulos and A Zimmermann (eds), *Research Handbook on the Law of Treaties* (Edward Elgar Publishing 2016) 539–540. With a special focus on 'proving' automatic continuity, *inter alia*, in the case of humanitarian agreements, see A Rasulov, 'Revisiting State Succession to Humanitarian Treaties: Is There a Case for Automaticity?' (2003) 14(1) *European Journal of International Law* 141, 154–157.
13 For detailed accounts, see T Schweisfurth, 'Das Recht der Staatensukzession: Die Staatenpraxis der Nachfolge in völkerrechtliche Verträge, Staatsvermögen, Staatsschulden und Archive in den Teilungsfällen Sowjetunion, Tschechoslowakei und Jugoslawien' in U Fastenrath, T Schweisfurth and CT Ebenroth (eds), *Das Recht der Staatensukzession* (CF Müller 1996); Koskenniemi (n 8); A Zimmermann (n 5). See also the reports by the International Law Association (ILA), ILA, 'New Delhi

I. Post-1978 Practice: Putting Art. 34 VCSSRT to the Test

meticulously analyse the practice that ensued with regard to international agreements, especially as all cases of state succession show particularities making them unique, or at least to some extent distinguishing them from previous cases. As the disintegration of states has always been an inherently political – if not violent – process,[14] their incomparableness had been one of the main points of critique against codifying the law of succession at all.[15] Instead, the following section will rely on previous accounts to provide an overview of recent practice (A.). Based thereon, some general lines can be drawn and more recent developments retraced to provide a framework for a comparison with the Brexit practice (B.).

A. The Practice: Considering Instances of Separation

Separation is defined by Art. 34(1) VCSSRT as all successions where 'a part or parts of the territory of a State separate to form one or more States, whether or not the predecessor State continues to exist'. Based on this definition, five instances of succession following the VCSSRT's adoption theoretically fall under Art. 34 VCSSRT's scope of application. These are chronologically the separation of the Union of Soviet Socialist Republics (USSR) and of the Socialist Federal Republic of Yugoslavia (SFRY) in the early 1990s, the separation of Czechoslovakia and Eritrea in 1993 and, most recently, the separation of Sudan in 2011. In practice, however, Art. 34 VCSSRT was not applicable to any of these successions. The VCSSRT was adopted in 1978 but only entered into force in 1996, thus after the majority of separations had occurred. To these cases of succession, the Convention is thus in general temporally inapplicable.[16] Moreover, even after its entry into force, it is highly questionable whether and to what extent a successor

---

Conference 2002' Committee on Aspects of the Law of State Succession – Rapport Final sur la Succession en Matiere de Traites; ILA, 'Rio de Janeiro Conference 2008' Aspects of the Law on State Succession.

14 Craven, *Decolonization* (n 5) 208.
15 See eg DP O'Connell, 'Reflections on the State Succession Convention' (1979) 39(4) *Zeitschrift für ausländisches öffentliches Recht und Völkerrecht* 725.
16 See Art. 7(1) VCSSRT: 'Without prejudice to the application of any rules set forth in the present Convention to which the effects of a succession of States would be subject under international law independently of the Convention, the Convention applies only in respect of a succession of States which has occurred after the entry into force of the Convention except as may be otherwise agreed.' Art. 7(2) and (3) VCSSRT provide for an exceptional applicability of the Convention to cases of succession that

state may actually be bound by rules on the (dis)continuity of international agreements provided for in the VCSSRT, which itself, of course, is an international agreement. What if Sudan, for example, had been a party to the VCSSRT when South Sudan separated?[17] Would South Sudan then have been subjected to a rule of treaty continuity provided for itself in an international agreement?[18]

But despite Art. 34 VCSSRT being inapplicable, the provision played an important role in the post-1978 cases of separation, and *vice versa*. Art. 34 VCSSRT provided a starting point, an orientation, for all states party to an agreement affected by a separation. Moreover, in opting for or against an automatic continuity of international agreements, states either gave support to or questioned the ILC's codification effort as regards the separation of states.

The first test case for Art. 34 VCSSRT was the breakup of the USSR, from which Russia emerged as the predecessor state continuing the USSR's identity and Azerbaijan, Armenia, Belarus, Georgia, Kazakhstan, Kyrgyzstan, Moldova, Tajikistan, Turkmenistan, Ukraine and Uzbekistan became successor states.[19] In several unilateral declarations, but also agreements among themselves, Russia *and* the successor states initially committed to fulfilling the international agreements concluded by the USSR.[20] But, despite this

---

happened prior to its entry into force, subject to reciprocal declarations of states to that effect.

17 In fact, Sudan had signed the VCSSRT on 23 August 1978, but has so far failed to ratify it (see 'United Nations Treaty Collection: Vienna Convention on Succession of States in Respect of Treaties' (12.09.2022) <https://treaties.un.org/Pages/ViewDetails.aspx?src=IND&mtdsg_no=XXIII-2&chapter=23&clang=_en>).

18 The ILC 'Commission recognized that participation by successor States would involve problems relating to the method of giving, and the retroactive effect of, consent to be bound by the convention given by the successor State.' However, it 'considered that these were questions to be answered by Governments when drafting the final clauses for inclusion in the Convention.' (ILC, 'Report of the International Law Commission on the Work of its Twenty-Sixth Session, 6 May – 26 July 1974' UN Doc. A/9610/Rev.1, YBILC (1974) Vol. II(1) 170).

19 Preceding the breakup of the USSR, the three Baltic States of Lithuania (11 March 1990), Estonia (20 August 1991) and Latvia (21 August 1991) had declared their independence from the USSR. They considered themselves the continuators of the States that had existed pre-1940 and not as successors of the USSR. This was accepted by the international community, Schweisfurth (n 13) 56.

20 For an overview, including German or English translations of the relevant statements and agreements, see A Zimmermann (n 5) 372–379. For a detailed account of the separation process, see also Schweisfurth (n 13) 56–67. On the unilateral declarations and agreements, see also below Part II § 7 section I.B.3.

unity, practice among the states varied considerably. Russia, considering itself and being accepted as the predecessor state, by and large continued the USSR's agreements, thus confirming Art. 35 VCSSRT.[21] Among the successor states, however, different approaches can be identified. While many successor states continued the USSR's multilateral agreements, a mixed practice evolved, whereby continuation was partially achieved through notifications of succession and partially through accessions.[22] With regard to bilateral agreements, '[a]lthough there seems to have been a tendency to continue to apply existing treaties in relations with the successor States, this practice is not homogenous'[23]. Moreover, continued application of bilateral agreements often involved negotiations between the parties, or, at the very least, an exchange of notes between the successor state and a treaty partner assuring each other of the intended continuity.[24] A special case was Belarus and Ukraine: having been parties to several agreements themselves, they simply continued their membership in these agreements.[25]

More or less simultaneously to the breakup of the USSR, the SFRY disintegrated, resulting in six successor states: Bosnia and Herzegovina, Croatia, North Macedonia, Slovenia and ultimately Serbia and Montenegro.[26] From

---

21 For an analysis of the USSR's practice and the practice of its treaty partners, see A Zimmermann (n 5) 380–388.
22 For an analysis of the practice of the USSR's successor states and treaty partners, see ibid 389–422.
23 V Mikulka, 'Article 34' in G Distefano, G Gaggioli and A Hêche (eds), *La Convention de Vienne de 1978 sur la Succession d'États en Matière de Traités: Commentaire Article par Article et Études Thématiques* (Bruylant 2016) para 115.
24 A Zimmermann (n 5) 421–422; Koskenniemi (n 8) 84–85; G Hafner and G Novak, 'State Succession in Respect of Treaties' in DB Hollis (ed), *The Oxford Guide to Treaties* (2nd edn, Oxford University Press 2020) 414–416.
25 Hafner and Novak (n 24) 415.
26 Initially, Serbia and Montenegro had formed the Federal Republic of Yugoslavia and had claimed to continue the personality of the SFRY. However, this claim was not accepted by the international community (see UNSC, 'On the question of membership of the Federal Republic of Yugoslavia (Serbia and Montenegro) in the United Nations' UN Doc. S/RES/777 (19 September 1992). 777). In 2003, with the enactment of a new Constitutional Charter, the Federal Republic of Yugoslavia became the State Union of Serbia and Montenegro. However, this union was dissolved following a referendum in 2006, turning Serbia and Montenegro into two independent states. The statehood of a potential seventh successor state of the SFRY, Kosovo, is still contentious, see eg A Orakhelashvili, 'Statehood, Recognition and the United Nations System: A Unilateral Declaration of Independence in Kosovo' in A von Bogdandy and R Wolfrum (eds), *Max Planck Yearbook of United Nations Law* (Brill 2008).

§ 7 Brexit and Recent Practice. Brexit as Recent Practice?

the outset, the process was accompanied by external advisory opinions[27] and unilateral declarations by several successor states[28], *inter alia*, on the question of succession to international agreements. The tenor of these statements was, sometimes with explicit reference to Art. 34 VCSSRT, that the SFRY's successor states would abide by the SFRY's international obligations, provided this proved to be an equitable solution and compatible with the new states' constitutions.[29] In the ensuing practice, the majority of successor states and of the SFRY's prior treaty partners indeed settled on a continuity of international agreements.[30] Nevertheless, the nature of the agreements – whether bilateral or multilateral – also manifested itself with the continuity of the latter appearing to have been much more automatic than with the former. Although many bilateral agreements were continued, in the majority of cases, this was accompanied by an exchange of notes between the successor state and its treaty partner.[31] These *notes verbales* could have been considered to be of a mere declaratory nature, simply confirming the already applicable automatic continuity. However, a number of such notes included linguistic caveats putting a question mark behind this theory.[32]

---

27 The EU had tasked the so-called 'Badinter Commission' with providing advisory opinions on legal questions arising from the disintegration of the SFRY. On the Commission's work, see eg MCR Craven, 'The European Community Arbitration Commission on Yugoslavia' (1996) 66(1) *British Yearbook of International Law* 333. The Commission repeatedly referred to Art. 34 VCSSRT, see eg EC Arbitration Commission, 'Opinions on Questions Arising from the Dissolution of Yugoslavia: Opinion No. 9' (1992) 31(6) *International Legal Materials* 1488, 1523: 'As the Arbitration pointed out in its first Opinion, the succession of States is governed by the principles of international law embodied in the Vienna Convention of 23 August 1978 [ie the VCSSRT] and 8 April 1983 [on state property], which all Republics have agreed should be the foundation for discussions between them on the succession of States at the Conference for Peace in Yugoslavia.'
28 For a number of statements made by the successor states in preparation of the Badinter Commission's opinion, see A Zimmermann (n 5) 306–307, fn. 325. Moreover, several successor states issued subsequent declarations or included a reference to treaty succession in their Constitutions. For an overview with German or English translations, see A Zimmermann (n 5) 308–313.
29 A Zimmermann (n 5) 308–313.
30 For an analysis of the practice of the SFRY's successor states and treaty partners, see ibid 308–334.
31 Ibid 334; Koskenniemi (n 8) 82.
32 Koskenniemi (n 8) 82–83.

I. Post-1978 Practice: Putting Art. 34 VCSSRT to the Test

The third state succession to take place in the region was the separation of Czechoslovakia into Czechia and the Slovak Republic in 1993.[33] As in the case of the SFRY, the two successor states issued statements on the topic of state succession with respect to international agreements and even included a respective provision in their constitutions.[34] In so doing, both took a position of automatic continuity for all international agreements.

> In conformity with valid principles of international law and to the extent defined by it the Czech Republic will consider itself to be bound, as of January 1, 1993, by all multilateral and bilateral treaties and agreements to which the Czech and Slovak Federal Republic was a party by that date.[35]

With regard to multilateral agreements, both states confirmed this view in sending *notes verbales* to the depositories of these agreements and informing them of their succession.[36] With regard to bilateral agreements, the practice of exchanging notes on the continued application of the agree-

---

33 For a detailed account of the separation process, see Schweisfurth (n 13) 82–85.
34 A Zimmermann (n 5) 335, 351.
35 Proclamation of the Czech National Council to all Parliaments and Nations of the World (17 December 1992) in UNGA, 'Letter Dated 31 December 1992 from the Permanent Representative of Czechoslovakia to the United Nations Addressed to the Secretary-General' UN Doc A/47/848 Annex I (1992) The Slovak proclamation is almost identical in wording: 'In conformity with valid international norms and to their applicable extent, the Slovak Republic, as one of the two successor states to the Czech and Slovak Federal Republic, shall consider itself, effective January 1, 1993, bound by the multilateral and bilateral treaties and instruments, whose signatory to the above date was the Czech and Slovak Federal Republic.' (Proclamation of the National Council of the Slovak Republic to the Parliaments and Peoples of the World (2 December 1992) in UNGA, 'Letter Dated 31 December 1992 from the Permanent Representative of Czechoslovakia to the United Nations Addressed to the Secretary-General' UN Doc A/47/848, Annex II (1992).
36 See eg the *note verbale* sent to the UN Secretary-General: 'In accordance with the relevant principles and rules of international law and to the extent defined by it, the Slovak Republic, as a successor state, born from the dissolution of the Czech and Slovak Republic assumed responsibility for its international relations, by multilateral treaties to which the Czech and Slovak Federal Republic was a party as of 31 December 1992, including reservations and declarations made earlier by Czechoslovakia as well as objections by Czechoslovakia to reservations formulated by other treaty-parties.' (United Nations Treaty Collection, 'Multilateral Treaties Deposited with the Secretary-General: Historical Information (Slovakia)' (20.12.2022) <https://treaties.un.org/pages/HistoricalInfo.aspx?clang=_en#Slovakia>). For the practice regarding further depositaries, see V Mikulka, 'The Dissolution of Czechoslovakia and Succession in Respect of Treaties' in M Mrak (ed), *Succession of States* (Kluwer Law International 1999).

ments was taken over by both successor states and the respective treaty partners, albeit with a strong tendency to assume continuity.[37]

In contrast, when Eritrea separated from Ethiopia in 1993, it seems to have operated largely on the assumption of a clean slate. Eritrea did not make any general declarations on the topic of succession nor did it notify other states of succession to any specific agreements.[38] Instead, it simply acceded to multilateral agreements, regardless of whether Ethiopia was a party, and made no effort to negotiate with the treaty partners of Ethiopia's bilateral agreements.[39] These treaty partners, in turn, also did not seem to consider Eritrea as succeeding in any bilateral agreements, even if they had generally followed a continuity approach with regard to the previous succession cases of the USSR, the SFRY and Czechoslovakia.[40]

Finally, South Sudan separated from Sudan in 2011. Prior to its independence, South Sudan had published a handbook on legal questions that would arise in connection with separation. Its section on state succession in respect of international agreements reflects the diversity of previous practice.

> An examination of international legal principles demonstrates that a successor state, such as Southern Sudan, has the option of choosing which treaties signed by the predecessor/continuing state (the Republic of Sudan) it would like to uphold. However, based on recent state practice, the international community would likely expect an independent Southern Sudan to continue the Republic of Sudan's treaty obligations. Exceptions to this presumption of continuity occur when: (1) both parties agree otherwise, (2) the treaty is not relevant to the new state's territory, or (3) continuity would frustrate the treaty's object and purpose. In advance of 2011, Southern Sudan may wish to identify all international treaties and agreements that potentially fall under such exceptions and thus would not continue to apply to Southern Sudan after independence. Furthermore, Southern Sudan may wish to consider that prior state practice indicates that it is common for successor states to provide affirmative assurances to the international community regarding their respect for the rule of law and their intentions to abide by the terms of the predecessor

---

37 For an analysis of Czech and Slovak practice and the practice of its treaty partners, see A Zimmermann (n 5) 337–351, 354–367.
38 Ibid 423–424.
39 For two exceptions, ibid.
40 See ibid with the example of Germany.

state's treaty obligations as part of the process of achieving international recognition and establishing diplomatic relations. In some instances, new states must also deposit an instrument of accession with the appropriate treaty depository to affirm a commitment to be bound by a treaty's terms.[41]

In its ambiguity, the legal advice given to South Sudan appears indicative of the state of play as regards the law of succession.[42] On the one hand, South Sudan is advised of a 'presumption of continuity' and thus the advice recommends evaluating Sudan's international agreements pre-separation whether any exceptions to such continuity apply. On the other hand, the paragraph is bracketed by statements to the contrary, suggesting an 'option of choosing' and participation in multilateral agreements through accession.

Considering these instances of separation, it appears safe to say that Art. 34 VCSSRT was not confirmed as a rule of customary international law by a uniform practice in that regard. Rather, practice since 1978 has varied, with some states only slightly deviating from the path as envisaged by Art. 34 VCSSRT and others following a completely opposite approach. Besides state practice being heterogenous, also the reception of this practice in international legal scholarship is mixed. Authors draw radically different conclusions on the state of affairs of the law of succession, in general, and the VCSSRT and Art. 34, in particular.[43] Nevertheless, in evaluating the practice and its reception, it is possible to identify some (emerging) trends.

---

41 Office of the President of the Government of Southern Sudan in collaboration with the Public International Law & Policy Group, Executive Summary ('Continuing Treaty Obligations'). See p 36–39 for a more detailed analysis of the topic of 'Continuing Treaty Obligations'.

42 On this, see Zimmermann and Devaney, Research Handbook Law of Treaties (n 12) 527.

43 See eg the complete rejection of Art. 34 VCSSRT by P Dumberry, 'State Succession to Bilateral Treaties: A Few Observations on the Incoherent and Unjustifiable Solution Adopted for Secession and Dissolution of States under the 1978 Vienna Convention' (2015) 28(1) *Leiden Journal of International Law* 13; the acknowledgment of Art. 34 VCSSRT as custom for dissolutions by Hafner and Novak (n 24) 416. On the law of succession in general, see eg the theses on (emerging) rules of custom by Schweisfurth (n 13) 230–233 and the suggestion for a complete reframing by JG Devaney, 'Making Sense of Transcendental Nonsense: A Functional Reframing of the Law of State Succession' (2022) 14 *GCILS Working Paper Series*.

B. The Evaluation: Considering the Reception of the Practice

When the International Law Commission (ILC) proceeded to codify the law of state succession in respect of international agreements, its efforts were accompanied by scholarly scepticism as regards the feasibility and usefulness of the endeavour.[44] Such criticism of the project did not die down with the completion of the ILC's work and the adoption of the VCSSRT at the Conference of States.[45] Subsequent state practice seems to prove the critics right. While Art. 34 VCSSRT might have served as 'the foundation for discussions'[46], it by no means served as an authoritative statement of the law. Instead, the practice regarding succession to international agreements in cases of separation post-1978 can be described as heterogenous and ambiguous. With regard to multilateral agreements, successor states have, for example, notified depositaries either of their succession or their accession without any indication of the reasons for their choice of means.[47] In the case of the SFRY's successor states, this has led Rasulov to describe the records of depositaries as 'devastated by incoherence'[48]. Moreover, the abundance of negotiations and exchanges of notes in the context of bilateral agreements bedevils any statement as to how they may be understood in each individual case: as merely declaratory statements needlessly confirming an automatic continuity provided for by

---

44 As summarised by Koskenniemi (n 8) 125: 'Standard criticism against attempts to codify State succession points to the extreme heterogeneity of situations, the need to avoid abstract dogmas and to apply the law in a contextually responsive fashion.'
45 See eg O'Connell (n 15).
46 EC Arbitration Commission (n 27), 1523.
47 On the practice of accession and succession notifications, see Koskenniemi (n 8) 70 who claims that '[t]he terminology used is often uncertain and there is little warrant to draw *a contrario* conclusions: the degree to which a new State's accession to a treaty can be taken as an express repudiation of succession is far from certain.' Thus, he deems it 'unclear what effect can be given to the use of technical expressions such as "accession" or "succession" in these documents [ie notifications to depositaries]. To give full formal effect to the would seem to go against the relative disregard of formality in international law [...]'. But see Rasulov (n 12), 156–157 who argues that depositary records showing that a successor state acceded to a multilateral agreement is 'best as an evidentiary source', clearly '[indicating] support for a "clean slate"' and being 'squarely irreconcilable with the concept of continuity and, hence, automatic accession'. Arguing against Koskenniemi, Rasulov claims that such '"technical expressions" *can* be relied on as being conclusive, for any other variant would indicate a denial of predictability of terminology in the international legal discourse [...]' (Rasulov (n 12), 157, emphasis added).
48 Rasulov (n 12), 146.

law or as constitutive for the continuation of these agreement which – in the absence of a customary rule of automatic continuity – would otherwise have ceased to apply to the successor state.[49]

Given these uncertainties, in vast parts of the literature on state practice following the VCSSRT's adoption, any more or less generalising statement is thus inevitably followed by caveats. An illustrative example is Zimmermann and Devaney's account of the practice surrounding the breakup of the SFRY. Referring to 'an extensive survey of relevant State practice' they conclude that '[t]hird States, as well as treaty bodies, have to a large extent, although not without exceptions, followed the approach underlying Article 34 VCSSRT with regard to all [SFRY] successor states'[50]. 'However', they continue, 'the value of this practice as a precedent is riddled with contradictions that somewhat undermine the value of the situation for the development of the law'.[51]

Nevertheless, it is possible to make out some tentative trends,[52] three of which are relevant for the evaluation of Brexit practice through the lens of the law of treaty succession. State practice evidences a differentiation between dissolutions and separations (1.) and between bilateral and multilateral agreements (2.). Moreover, it confirms a penchant of predecessor and successor states to express their respective position as regards succession publicly or at least towards their treaty partners (3.).

1. Distinguishing between Separations and Dissolutions

Firstly, in state practice, there appears to be a tendency to distinguish between instances of separation where the predecessor state continues to exist and those where it ceases to exist. In analysing state practice, most authors differentiate between dissolutions and separations, the latter – in contrast to its use in the VCSSRT – only referring to separations where

---

49 A Zimmermann and JG Devaney, 'State Succession in Treaties' in R Wolfrum (ed) (n 3) para 7. See also Koskenniemi (n 8) 82: 'Again, the exchanges of notes, protocols and treaty lists normally omit any indication as to whether they should be read in a constitutive or declaratory light.'
50 Zimmermann and Devaney, Research Handbook Law of Treaties (n 12) 529 with reference to A Zimmermann (n 5) 314–334.
51 Zimmermann and Devaney, Research Handbook Law of Treaties (n 12) 529 (footnote omitted).
52 For a list of 18 theses on the current state of customary international law in case of state succession, see Schweisfurth (n 13) 231–233.

a rump state continues to exist.⁵³ This is shared by the International Law Association (ILA) who concluded that '[r]ecent State practice shows different approaches of the successor States with regard to treaties in cases of secession and dissolution'⁵⁴. For dissolutions, different authors argue that post-1978 practice (more or less) confirms Art. 34 VCSSRT and thus an automatic continuity rule for *all* international agreements.⁵⁵ In contrast, state practice is far less consistent in cases of separation where a predecessor state continues to exist. While following the breakup of the USSR, there appeared to be a trend towards continuity in respect of the successor states, the opposite seems to have been the case with regard to Eritrea.

Thus, a differentiation which had initially been included in the ILC's draft and the deletion of which had been cause for criticism appears to re-emerge.⁵⁶ Zimmermann explains this dogmatically with reference to the interest of the other treaty partner: in his view, in cases of dissolution, the other treaty party's interest is best preserved by obliging all successor states to succeed as otherwise the other treaty party would be left with no counterpart.⁵⁷ In instances of separation, however,

> [...] the state continuing the predecessor state's identity – as in the case of the USSR the Russian Federation – will, generally, be both willing and able to continue to fulfil at least the majority of the contractual obligations of the whole state existing up to that time. Insofar as the international community has a further interest in ensuring that the successor states in particular remain bound by individual groups of agreements [...], this is taken into account by the fact that specific succession regimes

---

53 See eg A Zimmermann (n 5); Koskenniemi (n 8); Hafner and Novak (n 24).
54 ILA, 'Conclusions of the Committee on Aspects of the Law of State Succession' Resolution No. 3/2008 (2008) para 5. This is the ILA's second project on state succession. The first had predated the ILC's codification project (for a summary of its past work, see Craven, *Decolonization* (n 5) 105–113). In 1994, the ILA decided to review the issue in light of more recent state practice. Besides the final Conclusions, it published four reports on different aspects of state succession (see 'ILA New Delhi 2002' (n 13); ILA, 'Berlin Conference 2004'Aspects of the Law of State Succession – Provisional Report; ILA, 'Toronto Conference 2006'Aspects of the Law of State Succession – Economic Aspects of State Succession; 'ILA Rio de Janeiro 2008' (n 13)).
55 See eg A Zimmermann (n 5) 367; Hafner and Novak (n 24) 416.
56 See above Part II § 6 section II.B.1.
57 A Zimmermann (n 5) 431.

have been developed for this purpose, which override the otherwise applicable *clean slate* rule as a *lex specialis*.[58]

For Zimmermann, the decisive difference in the situation of separation compared to a complete dissolution is thus that the other treaty party still has its original treaty partner – the rump state – with whom to continue the agreement. Additionally, the treaty partners of the predecessor state should be left freely to decide whether or not to enter into treaty relations with additional partners.[59]

2. Distinguishing between Bilateral and Multilateral Agreements

The second differentiation is also not new to the law of state succession. The ILC's decision not to distinguish between bilateral and multilateral agreements in cases of state succession outside the context of newly independent states led to criticism of the VCSSRT[60] and is now questioned by subsequent state practice. Based on this practice, one can certainly draw a clear distinction as regards the procedure: while successor states unilaterally notify depositaries or their treaty partners of their succession or intent to accede to a multilateral agreement, bilateral agreements are overwhelmingly dealt with on a reciprocal basis.[61] The successor state and the respective treaty partner either negotiate on the continuity of these latter agreements or at least exchange notes on the issue. However, the difference in procedure seems to be more than a formality. In contrast, many authors today question the legal understanding behind such negoti-

---

58 Ibid ('[...] wird der die Identität des Vorgängerstaates fortsetzende Staat – wie im Falle der UdSSR die Russische Föderation – in aller Regel sowohl willens wie auch weiter in der Lage sein, zumindest den allergrößten Teil der vertraglichen Verpflichtungen des bis zu diesem Zeitpunkt bestehenden Gesamtstaates weiterhin zu erfüllen. Soweit die Völkerrechtsgemeinschaft ein darüber hinausgehendes Interesse hat, daß gerade auch die Nachfolgestaaten an einzelne Gruppen von Verträgen [...] gebunden bleiben, wird dem dadurch Rechnung getragen, daß hierfür spezifische Sukzessionsregime herausgebildet wurden, welche die ansonsten anwendbare *clean-slate*-Regel als *lex specialis* außer Kraft setzen.' Translated by the author). An example of such a specific succession regime, is Art. 12 VCSSRT which provides for continuity in case of localised agreements and is accepted as customary international law. A contentious example are agreements of a humanitarian character; on this, see Rasulov (n 12).
59 A Zimmermann (n 5) 431.
60 See eg Dumberry, *Succession to Bilateral Treaties* (n 43). See also above Part II § 6 section IV.
61 See above Part II § 7 section I.A.

ations and exchanges – either claiming that this practice regarding bilateral agreements is an expression of or support for a clean-slate approach.[62]

In so doing, the extent of the claims for the discontinuity of bilateral agreements with regard to the successor state vary. Zimmermann connects it to the differentiation between dissolution and separation. While in the case of separation he is hesitant to assume automatic continuity with regards to multilateral agreements, he is even more sceptical to do so with regards to bilateral agreements.[63] Although he observes that many states pushed for the successor states of the USSR to succeed in the predecessor's international agreements, they were less adamant in other cases of separation.

> In particular, it seems that affected third states still assume that in the case of separation, where a rump state continues to exist, their (expressly or implicitly declared) consent is required in order to be able to assume that at least the bilateral international agreements of the predecessor state continue to apply in relation to the successor state or states.[64]

For many authors, however, a clean slate appears to be the norm with regard to bilateral agreements in cases of both dissolution and separation.[65] As brought to the point by Tams, 'whatever the general rule, bilateral treaties are not subject to a rule of automatic succession'.[66] A similar conclusion was also reached by the ILA:

---

[62] See eg P Dumberry, 'State Succession to BITs: Analysis of Case Law in the Context of Dissolution and Secession' (2018) 34(3) *Arbitration International* 445, 450: 'the very fact that such exchanges of letters and negotiations took place [...] suggests that [the states] worked under the presumption that old [...] BITs would not have continued to apply "automatically" without their explicit consent.'. See also A Zimmermann 430–431 and analysing the wording used in exchanges of notes and declarations, see Schweisfurth (n 13) 197–201.

[63] A Zimmermann (n 5) 430–431.

[64] Ibid ('Insbesondere scheinen betroffene Drittstaaten offenbar immer noch davon auszugehen, daß es im Falle einer Separation, bei dem ein Rumpfstaat fortbesteht, ihrer (ausdrücklichen oder implizit erklärten) Zustimmung bedarf, um von einer Fortgeltung zumindest der bilateralen völkerrechtlichen Verträge des Vorgängerstaates im Verhältnis zu dem oder den Nachfolgestaaten ausgehen zu können.' Translated by the author).

[65] Dumberry, *Succession to Bilateral Treaties* (n 43); CJ Tams, 'State Succession to Investment Treaties: Mapping the Issues' (2016) 31(2) *ICSID Review* 314; Devaney, *Transcendental Nonsense* (n 43).

[66] Tams (n 65), 327 with reference to MN Shaw, 'State Succession Revisited' (1995) 34(6) *Finish Yearbook of International Law*, 67; B Stern, *La Succession d'États* (Martinus

With regard to bilateral treaties concluded by the predecessor State, practice shows that the fate of these treaties is generally decided through negotiation between the successor State and the other party, no matter the category of State succession involved.[67]

In his report for the German Society of International Law, Schweisfurth opts for a middle path. In his view, state practice does not support what may be called fully fledged automatic continuity in the sense that the successor state automatically and definitely succeeds in all its predecessor's international agreements.[68] Instead,

[r]ecent state practice suggests the emergence of a CIL norm according to which, in cases of dismemberment and secession, the bilateral treaties of the predecessor state automatically continue to apply *ad interim* to all successor states until the other contracting parties have decided with the individual successor states on the final continuation, modification, or expiration of the treaties.[69]

Thus, Schweisfurth assumes that bilateral agreements do not disappear at the instance of succession[70], but are continued for a transitional period. In his view, this transitory automatic continuity does not, however, prejudge the successor state and the other treaty party's future relation. Instead, he argues that, under emerging customary international law, successor states

---

Nijhoff Publishers 1996) 315–316; J Klabbers and others (eds), *State Practice Regarding State Succession and Issues of Recognition* (Kluwer Law International 1999) 116; P Dumberry, 'An Uncharted Question of State Succession: Are New States Automatically Bound by the BITs Concluded by Predecessor States Before Independence?' (2015) 6(1) *Journal of International Dispute Settlement* 74, 78–82.

67 'ILA State Succession Resolution' (n 54) para 8.
68 Schweisfurth (n 13) 220.
69 Ibid ('Die jüngste Staatenpraxis spricht für die Herausbildung einer VGR-Norm, derzufolge in Dismembrations- und Sezessionsfällen die bilateralen Verträge des Vorgängerstaates für alle Nachfolgestaaten automatisch *ad interim* fortgelten, bis die anderen Vertragsparteien mit den einzelnen Nachfolgestaaten über die endgültige Fortgeltung, die Modifizierung oder das Außerkrafttreten der Verträge entschieden haben.' Translated by the author, emphasis added).
70 Art. 2(1)(e) VCSSRT defines a 'date of succession' ('the date upon which the successor State replaced the predecessor State [...]'). But see Devaney, *Transcendental Nonsense* (n 43) 5–6.

and the other treaty parties are 'entitled and obliged'[71] to negotiate the fate of bilateral agreements, with no obligation to continue them.[72]

Whatever the precise scope or form of a discontinuity practice with respect to bilateral agreements may be, its legal justification is the principle of consent. The need for a consensual continuation of bilateral agreements is not only emphasised in the literature.[73] A lack of consent was also invoked by Hungary in the *Gabcikovo-Nagymaros* case to argue that Slovakia had not succeeded in a Hungarian-Czechoslovakian agreement.[74] The ICJ evaded the issue.[75] However, (at least implicit) consent seems to have been the decisive factor for international investment arbitral tribunals when faced with questions of state succession in respect of international agreements. As *Devaney* argues,

> [t]ribunals have exerted significant time and effort evaluating the behaviour of certain states and the general context in an attempt to discern whether there was any evidence for whether the states desired to keep the relevant rights and obligations in force.[76]

The discussion in the ILC and during the Diplomatic Conference of States was focused on treaty stability.[77] However, with seemingly neither state practice nor *opinio juris* supporting Art. 34 VCSSRT's rule of *automatic* continuity as regards bilateral agreements, the facilitation of an agreement between the states concerned seems to have become the path to achieving this goal. The starting point is often the positioning of the predecessor and successor states.

3. Devolution Agreements, Unilateral Declarations and Good Faith Negotiations

Finally, state practice following the adoption of the VCSSRT did, in fact, confirm a practice that was already widespread before the ILC's codifica-

---

71 Schweisfurth (n 13) 224 ('berechtigt und verpflichtet', translated by the author).
72 Ibid 223–224.
73 See above Part II § 6 section IV.B.
74 ICJ *Case Concerning the Gabčíkovo-Nagymaros Project (Hungary v Slovakia)* (Memorial of Hungary) [1994] ICJ Rep 1997, p 7, 325–327. On Hungary's argument, see Klabbers (n 5), 351–352.
75 See above Part II § 7 fn. 5.
76 Devaney, *Transcendental Nonsense* (n 43) 21.
77 See above Part II § 6 section III.

tion and is mirrored by Arts. 8 and 9 VCSSRT: the conclusion of so-called devolution agreements between predecessors and their successor states and the issuance of unilateral declarations by successor states on the question of treaty succession. These agreements and declarations can take a variety of forms. In general, the predecessor state, where one exists, and the successor state(s) therein express their position as regards the effect of the succession on international agreements. Compared to *notes verbales* notifying succession in the context of multilateral agreements, these agreements and declarations are usually of a more general nature, not addressing a certain agreement or treaty partner.[78] Moreover, in contrast to notifications of succession, neither devolution agreements nor unilateral declarations are in anyway binding on the other parties to an agreement. While this follows from the principle of *res inter alios acta*, it is also confirmed in the VCSSRT. With respect to devolution agreements, Art. 8(1) provides that

> [t]he obligations or rights of a predecessor State under treaties in force in respect of a territory at the date of succession of States do not become the obligations or rights of the successor State towards other States Parties to those treaties by reason only of the fact that the predecessor State and the successor State have concluded an agreement providing that such obligations or rights shall devolve upon the successor.

Likewise, Art. 9(1) VCSSRT clarifies that no agreements devolve upon a successor state 'by reason only of the fact that the successor state has made a unilateral declaration'. Notwithstanding any such agreements or unilateral declarations, 'the effects of the succession of States on treaties which [...] were in force in respect of the territory in question are governed by the present Convention'[79].

An extensive practice of devolution agreements as well as joint and unilateral declarations can be found in the context of the USSR's breakup. Art. 12 of the *Charter of the Commonwealth of Independent States*[80] (CIS Charter), founded by Russia, Belarus and Ukraine, and later joined by all further successors except Georgia[81], provided that '[t]he High Contracting

---

78 See eg the practice of the USSR and its successor states described below in this section.
79 Cp Art. 8(2) and Art. 9(2).
80 Agreements Establishing the Commonwealth of Independent States (9 December 1991) 1992 (31) ILM 138, 142 [CIS Agreement ILM 1992].
81 For the accession agreement, see CIS Agreement ILM 1992 147.

Parties undertake to discharge the international obligations incumbent on them under treaties and agreements entered into by the former Union of Soviet Socialist Republics'. At the same time, Art. 13 CIS Charter clarified that '[t]his Agreement shall not affect the obligations of the High Contracting parties towards third States'. Reference in the CIS Charter to international agreements was followed by a joint declaration addressed to the USSR's treaty partners whereby '[t]he States participating in the Commonwealth [guaranteed] in accordance with their constitutional procedure the discharge of the international obligations deriving from treaties and agreements concluded by the former Union of Soviet Socialist Republics'[82]. However, in a final joint statement, the CIS states departed from their previous approach. In a Memorandum of Understanding, they expressed their view that each successor state would *decide* on its participation in multilateral agreements and *negotiate* a solution for bilateral agreements of the USSR.[83] Subsequently, several successor states individually expressed their position on treaty succession in statements or even in (constitutional) laws.[84]

When dealing with devolution agreements and unilateral declarations, the ILC noted that they were

> of interest from two separate aspects. The first is the extent to which, if any, they are effective in bringing about a succession to or continuance of the predecessor State's treaties; and the second is the evidence which they may contain of the views of States concerning customary law governing succession of States in respect of treaties.[85]

The first question has been conclusively clarified with Arts. 8, 9 VCSSRT being accepted as customary international law.[86] Evidence of the successor state's position is, however, interesting beyond the second aspect mentioned by the ILC. Besides being *legally* relevant in terms of identifying state practice and *opinio juris*, the issuance of a statement by a successor state or the inclusion of a paragraph on state succession in the successor state's (constitutional) law may also serve a *non-legal* purpose.

---

82 For the Declaration of Alma Ata, see CIS Agreement ILM 1992 148–149.
83 Memorandum of Understanding on the Question of State Succession in Respect Treaties; for a French version, see Klabbers and others (eds) (n 66) 377.
84 On these unilateral declarations, see A Zimmermann (n 5) 388–390.
85 'ILC Report 1974' (n 18) 183.
86 Schweisfurth (n 13) 193; A Zimmermann (n 5) 822; Hafner and Novak (n 24) 408–409.

What most authors rejecting a continuity rule for (bilateral) international agreements in the case of separation – whether for lack of practice or out of considerations of principle – do agree on is the desirability, if not necessity, for the states concerned to negotiate on the fate of these agreements in good faith.[87] Schweisfurth even argues that the practice following the adoption of the VCSSRT has developed – if not even confirmed – a customary obligation in that regard. In his view, not only is a 'uniform practice of negotiations by all the states concerned discernible'[88], but also *opinio juris* suggesting that states had felt obliged to conduct them.[89] If, however, negotiations are necessary – and even obligatory – because the international law on substantive questions of succession is far from settled, it is in the very interest of the successor state to clarify its approach on the matter.

Thus, in many instances of state succession, 'it was the successor state(s) which initially defined the conditions under which it (they) were prepared to succeed to treaty relations'[90]. Of course, where negotiations are common, taking an early stance by no means guarantees the intended outcome. Taking the example of the EU, '[a]n overview of the Community position on the succession in respect of treaties confirms that it is indeed important to have the initiative in matters of succession to treaties, but that it is not decisive'[91]. However, where the other treaty party has not yet made its own (final) assessment of the situation arising from the state succession, there is a chance for the successor state to influence said position (even avoiding negotiations) or, at least, to start negotiations on its own terms.

---

87 Schweisfurth (n 13) 224; Hafner and Novak (n 24) 427. Showing a widespread practice of (re)negotiations in the context of investment treaties, Tams (n 65), 328–331.
88 Schweisfurth (n 13) 224 ('Es ist daher eine einheitliche Übung der Verhandlungen aller betroffener Staaten erkennbar.' Translated by the author).
89 Ibid with reference to a guideline by the EU foreign ministers on state recognition in Eastern Europe (available at German Federal Government, 'Beschlüsse der EG-Außenminister zur Anerkennung neuer Staaten: Außerordentliche EPZ-Ministertagung in Brüssel (Bulletin 144–91)' (*Press Release*, 19.12.1991) <https://www.bundesregierung.de/breg-de/service/bulletin/beschluesse-der-eg-aussenminister-zur-anerkennung-neuer-staaten-ausserordentliche-epz-ministertagung-in-bruessel-787304>).
90 PJ Kuijper, 'The Community and State Succession in Respect of Treaties' in D Curtin and T Heukels (eds), *Institutional Dynamics of European Integration* (Martinus Nijhoff Publishers 1994) 640.
91 Ibid 639.

II. Brexit and Succession Practice: Applying a New Template

Considering the practice of state successions in respect of international agreements since the VCSSRT's adoption in 1978, it is clear that Art. 34 VCSSRT providing for automatic continuity in cases of separation – regardless of whether the predecessor state continues to exist – has not emerged into customary international law. While there is a general tendency to ensure stability in international relations, in practice this has not been achieved by relying on an automatic devolution of international agreements. Instead, states have taken active measures in this regard – from notifications of succession to accessions and negotiations. Thus, the VCSSRT has been described as 'a useful point of reference for the practitioner's selective use'[92], its underlying rationales guiding states. A concrete outcome has, however, regularly been reached through case-by-case approaches.

What does this mean with regard to Brexit? How does the way in which the EU and the UK dealt with international agreements correspond with the VCSSRT's rationales and the practice that followed the Convention's adoption? It would be pure speculation to suggest that the EU, its Member States or the UK intended their practice to correspond with or deliberately copy state practice arising from state successions. However, when re-considering Brexit practice through the lens of state succession, it is found to feature a whole range of commonalities. For one, these pertain to the process of dealing with international agreements in the context of Brexit which appears reminiscent of state successions (A.). But beyond procedural inferences, (emerging) rules and principles applied in the realm of state succession could also offer an explanation for the substantive decisions taken in the context of Brexit (B.).

A. Procedural Similarities? From Unilateral Declarations to Rollovers

Reconsidering the Brexit process through the lens of state succession, it is first noteworthy that both the EU and the UK addressed the topic of international agreements very early on in the withdrawal process. In the UK, the effects of Brexit on, for example, trade agreements were pointed to even

---

92 Ibid 640.

before the referendum on its EU membership took place.[93] The EU devoted a whole paragraph to the topic in its very first Brexit guidelines following the UK's notification under Art. 50 TEU.[94] Noticeable is, however, not only the early engagement with the topic but also the manner. The EU and UK both continuously emphasised the need – especially for the UK but also for them together – to approach non-EU treaty partners and address the effect of Brexit on the respective agreement(s) with them. However, the envisaged thrust of such talks with non-EU treaty partners soon changed.

While the UK initially referred to the need to conduct negotiations with treaty partners,[95] the EU pushed for a '*common* approach towards third country partners, international organisations and conventions concerned'[96]. It was, thus, between the EU and the UK that an exchange of statements and position papers took place addressing the effect of their separation on international agreements with non-EU treaty partners and possible transitional measures.[97] Thus, when the EU and the UK latter in the Brexit process finally approached non-EU treaty partners – in talks but also through a common *note verbale*[98] – they did so *after* having already communicated their common stance on the effect of Brexit on their international agreements.

A second important aspect is the inclusion of the topic in the *UK-EU Withdrawal Agreement*[99] (UK-EU WA), addressing the consequences of the

---

[93] UK Government, 'Why the Government believes that Voting to Remain in the EU is the Best Decision for the UK' Booklet Providing Important Information about the EU Referendum on 23 June 2016 (6 April 2016) 8.

[94] European Council, 'Guidelines following the United Kingdom's Notification under Article 50 TEU' (29 April 2017) EUCO XT 20004/17 para 13.

[95] On the UK's different strategies towards treaty partners, see UK Government, 'International Agreements if the UK leaves the EU without a Deal', Guidance Note (5 November 2019).

[96] 'EU Brexit Guidelines' (n 94) para 13 (emphasis added).

[97] See on the EU side the ibid and EU Commission, 'Internal EU27 Preparatory Discussions on the Framework for the Future Relationship' International Agreements and Trade Policy (6 February 2018) TF50(2018) 29. See the UK's technical guidance notes, UK Government, 'Technical Note' International Agreements during the Implementation Period (8 February 2018); 'UK Guidance Note' (n 95).

[98] EU Commission, 'Cover Letter and Note Verbale on the Agreement on the Withdrawal of the United Kingdom of Great Britain and Northern' (5 December 2018) COM(2018) 841 final.

[99] Agreement on the Withdrawal of the United Kingdom of Great Britain and Northern Ireland from the European Union and the European Atomic Energy Community (12 November 2019) OJ C384 I/1 [UK-EU WA].

UK's withdrawal from the EU. Art. 129 UK-EU WA dealing with '[s]pecific arrangements relating to the Union's external action' provides that 'the United Kingdom shall be bound by the obligations stemming from the international agreements concluded by the Union, by Member States acting on its behalf, or by the Union and its Member States acting jointly'. This is noteworthy, firstly, because such a provision – as the EU and the UK very well know – does not have any effect whatsoever on the non-EU treaty partners to these international agreements. The fact that they nevertheless chose to include it suggests a similar motive as Waldock ascribed to devolution agreements which are also a *res inter alios acta* for the treaty partners: 'to allocate responsibility for existing treaty relations between the parties, not to create any new rights and obligations *vis-à-vis* third States'[100].

The second noteworthy aspect of Art. 129 UK-EU WA is that the allocation of responsibility made therein pertains to a time-limited transition period, during which the EU and its Member States committed to treating the UK internally as if it were still a part of the Union.[101] As an external corollary, the EU and its Member States sought to affect a sort of *ad interim* continuation of international agreements which are – in their view – affected by Brexit. In so doing, the transition period served a similar purpose but also created similar problems as found in the context of state succession.

On the one hand, Art. 129 UK_EU WA 'essentially [provided] a space until the end of the transition period for the necessary arrangements to be made'[102]. During Brexit negotiations, the EU took the position that until the UK had withdrawn from the EU, it would not be able to conclude international agreements in an area of EU competence.[103] Thus, the Withdrawal Agreement stipulated that the UK could use the transition period to 'negotiate, sign and ratify international agreements entered into in its own capacity in the areas of exclusive competence of the Union'[104]. Successor states in cases of state succession face a similar dilemma. Whether intending to provide for stability in treaty relations or to negotiate new

---

100 Craven, *Decolonization* (n 5) 125.
101 Cp Art. 126 UK-EU WA.
102 M Cremona, 'The Withdrawal Agreement and the EU's International Agreements' (2020) 45(2) *European Law Review* 237, 248.
103 On this in detail, RA Wessel, 'Consequences of Brexit for International Agreements Concluded by the EU and its Member States' (2018) 55 (Special Issue) *Common Market Law Review* 101, 106–113.
104 Art. 129(4) UK-EU WA.

agreements, pre-succession, the successor state is legally not in a position to make arrangements for its future external relations. The predecessor state is still responsible for the international relations of the soon-to-be successor state. Thus, in cases of state succession – as also happened in the case of Brexit – it regularly takes time for the successor states to consolidate its treaty relations.

On the other hand, the (legal) character of the transition phase following Brexit with regard to international agreements is just as obscure as that following a state succession. Following the EU and the UK's position of applying a (sort of) clean-slate approach with regard to certain agreements, there is no legal basis on which non-EU treaty partners were obliged to continue to apply these international agreements in respect of the UK.[105] While the EU and the UK could ask non-EU treaty partners to treat the UK *as if* it were a Member State, the only legal commitment was between the EU and the UK with the UK being obliged *vis-à-vis* the EU – not non-EU treaty partners – to fulfil its obligations arising from these agreements.[106] The application of the international agreements between the UK and non-EU treaty partners would then amount more to a practical than legal solution. This view was, for example, expressed by the United States (US) in regard to the *EU-US Air Transport Agreement*[107]. In a statement on Brexit, the US took note of the EU's position that the Air Transport Agreement continued to apply to the UK during the transition period.[108] The statement continued that

> [a]lthough the United States *does not share this view as a legal matter*, during the transition period the United States has endeavored, and will continue to endeavor, wherever possible, to afford the UK the same treatment it would receive, in this case, if the U.S.-EU ATAs applied to it, subject to relevant legal and policy considerations. [...]
>
> We expect that, *for all practical purposes* and to maintain the current transatlantic market, the status quo for the UK will remain until the

---

105 See also Cremona (n 102), 247–248.
106 See also ibid 248.
107 Air Transport Agreement between the United States of America, of the one part, and the European Community and its Member States, of the other part (25 May 2007) OJ L134/5 [EU-US Open Skies].
108 US Government, 'U.S. Statement on Brexit and U.S.-EU ATAs: U.S.-EU Joint Committee – 23rd Meeting' (3 December 2020) <https://www.state.gov/u-s-statement-on-brexit-and-u-s-eu-atas/>.

§ 7 Brexit and Recent Practice. Brexit as Recent Practice?

transition period ends. Preparations are under way to ensure that, after that date, the air transport agreement that the United States and the UK have negotiated bilaterally and signed will govern U.S.-UK civil aviation relations.[109]

In many instances of state succession, arguably a similarly practical road was pursued. Given that it regularly takes time for successor states to come to terms with which of its predecessor's international agreements may be of interest to it, a final settlement of the issue is often preceded by a continued application of the agreements.[110] However, if states do not consider international agreements to automatically devolve to the successor state, such a continued application – even if limited in time – appears just as questionable. Alternatively, one could follow Schweisfurth that an *ad interim* continuation of international agreements following a separation has emerged as a rule of customary international law.[111] In that case, the UK may have benefited from the practical experience that its treaty partners had with such solutions.

Finally, the outcome of the Brexit process with regard to international agreements and how this was achieved is interesting from the perspective of the law of succession. While the UK did not opt for a continuity approach in the sense of an *automatic* continuation of all international agreements, it has preserved a large number of international treaty relations. This result has been achieved by recourse to a potpourri of legal instruments: simple notification and continued participation,[112] accession

---

109 Ibid (emphasis added).
110 See Schweisfurth (n 13) 220–224. This approach is also not uncommon for the EU itself. Following Algeria's independence from France, EU law – as previously applicable to Algeria – continued to be applied on a de facto basis. Several EU documents show that the EU institutions and the Member States were aware that this extension of EU law lacked a legal basis. Nevertheless, the EC Council of Ministers had agreed to treat Algeria 'as a de facto member state of the Community' (document not publicly available, quoted from KK Patel, *Project Europe: A History* (Cambridge University Press 2020) 212). Finally, in 1976 the EU and Algeria concluded a Cooperation Agreement (Agreement between the Member States of the European Coal and Steel Community and the People's Democratic Republic of Algeria (27 September 1978) OJ L263/119 [Algeria-EC Agreement]), normalising their relationship. On this, see KK Patel (n 110) 212–220.
111 Schweisfurth (n 13) 220.
112 See 'EU Note Verbale' (n 98) on the continuation of multilateral mixed agreements.

to (multilateral) agreements[113] and by conducting a practice of rolling over (bilateral) agreements[114]. In so doing, the UK's approach not only mirrors the diversity of approaches found in the state practice with regard to successions in general and separations in particular since the VCSSRT's adoption: regularly successor states chose different methods of preserving treaty relations, often without an apparent reason for the differentiation. The UK's experience also confirms a hypothesis regularly brought forward by critics of a strict automatic continuity rule in cases of state succession: a continuity rule is not needed to ensure the continuation of treaty relations because where such continuation is desired, it is regularly achieved.[115]

What remains then is the question of why the continuation of many international treaty relations had to be achieved through such diverse measures as notifications, accessions and rollovers at all. Why was continuation of these agreements not simply assumed in the first place? How is the EU and UK's 'out means out' approach to be evaluated against the rules of the VCSSRT and – even more importantly – the practice that followed its adoption?

---

113 See eg the UK's accession to the Agreement on Government Procurement (signed on 12 April 1979, entered into force 1 January 1981) 1235 UNTS 258 [GPA]) as a 'party in its own right' (WTO, 'Accession of the United Kingdom to the Agreement on Government Procurement in its own Right' Decision of the Committee on Government Procurement of 27 February 2019 (28 February 2019) GPA/CD/2).

114 See eg Agreement establishing an Association between the United Kingdom of Great Britain and Northern Ireland and the Republic of Chile (30 January 2019) CS Chile No. 2/2019 [UK-Chile AA]; Partnership and Cooperation Agreement Establishing a Partnership between the United Kingdom of Great Britain and Northern Ireland, of the one part, and the Republic of Uzbekistan, of the other part (31 October 2019) CS Uzbekistan No. 1/2019 [PCA UK-UZB]; Agreement on Trade Continuity between the United Kingdom of Great Britain and Northern Ireland and Canada (9 December 2020) CS Canada No.1/2020 [UK-Canada Trade Continuity Agreement]; Trade Continuity Agreement between the United Kingdom of Great Britain and Northern Ireland and the United Mexican States (15 December 2020) CS Mexico No.1/2021 [UK-Mexico Trade Continuity Agreement].

115 See eg the argument made by Switzerland in opposing the ILC's draft for Art. 34 VCSSRT: 'It might be asked, however, whether there would not be practical disadvantages in adopting that course [of a clean-slate rule] and whether the proposed amendment [on a clean-slate rule] would not have the effect of creating a vacuum in international relations by causing the extinction of treaties whose maintenance would be in the interests of the new State and of third States. [The Swiss Representative] believed that in reality there was no such danger and that where there was a common interest, the two States would not fail to reach agreement in order to ensure the continuity of the treaty.' (UNCSSRT, 'Official Records' 40th Meeting of the Committee of the Whole (2 August 1978) UN Doc. A/CONF.80/C.1/SR.40 53).

B. Brexit and International Agreements: Between Continuity and a Clean Slate?

With the EU losing a Member State and the UK subsequently forming a state outside the Union, the situation of Brexit can be compared to a state succession through separation. For separations, the VCSSRT provides for the automatic continuity of all international agreements, both as regards the predecessor state (Art. 35) and the successor state (Art. 34). State practice following the adoption of the VCSSRT shows, however, that as regards the successor states, this rule has not gained the status of customary international law. Instead, while successor states generally show a certain tendency to continue the international agreements of their successor states it is unclear whether they do so more out of political or economic motivations, and not out of a belief that they are legally obliged to do so. This is especially so in the case of separations in the narrower sense, that is, in instances of separation where the predecessor state continues to exist. While some authors argue that Art. 34 VCSSRT may be customary for complete dissolutions, for successor states separating from a rump state no general presumption of continuity exists, especially not as regards bilateral international agreements.[116]

In how far, then, is the practice visible in the case of Brexit explainable when applying the template of Arts. 34, 35 VCSSRT and subsequent state practice? To start with the EU itself, translated into state succession terms, the Union would represent the predecessor state. As such, it confirmed its continued participation in all international agreements to which it is a party at the beginning of the Brexit process.[117] While this was initially done in the form of internal documents, the EU later implicitly reaffirmed this position through a *note verbale* to its treaty partners, specifying the assumed adverse effect of Brexit *only* on the UK's participation in international agreements.[118] The position taken by the EU with regard to its status as a party to international agreements corresponds with Art. 35 VCSSRT which states that 'any treaty which at the date of the succession of States was in force in respect of the predecessor State continues in force in respect of its remaining territory'. It is also in line with the post-1978

---

116 See above Part II § 7 section I.
117 'EU Brexit Guidelines' (n 94) para 13.
118 'EU Note Verbale' (n 98) 3.

II. Brexit and Succession Practice: Applying a New Template

practice of Russia and Ethiopia, which, as rump states, continued their international agreements, thus confirming Art. 35 VCSSRT.

In respect of the UK – the successor state – and its participation in international agreements concluded by the EU, or by the EU together with the UK, the evaluation of practice is more complex. Here, both the EU and the UK took a more differentiated approach, distinguishing between EU-only, bilateral mixed and multilateral mixed agreements. With regard to the first two, they applied what could be called a clean-slate approach: following Brexit, the UK would automatically no longer participate in these agreements regardless of whether or not it had previously been a party itself.[119] In contrast, the EU and the UK assumed a position of automatic continuity in respect of all multilateral mixed agreements.[120] To cushion the effect of Brexit for the EU's treaty partners, both the EU and the UK emphasised the necessity to seek negotiations with all treaty partners.[121] Where the UK had an interest in continuing agreements that fell under the clean-slate approach, it 'novated'[122] the treaty relationship by acceding to or rolling over these agreements.

The approach taken by the EU and the UK does not conform with Art. 34 VCSSRT. Even though the UK, contrary to its initial position, developed a strong interest in at least temporarily pursuing many of the EU's treaty relations, it is far from continuing *all* international agreements that applied to it during its EU membership. Moreover, even where it does continue an international agreement, oftentimes this did not happen *automatically* but by a new – or in the case of bilateral mixed agreements renewed – expression of consent. To a large extent, the Brexit practice is thus coined by a (initial) discontinuity of international agreements. The exception is multilateral mixed agreements, which the UK simply continued following Brexit.

Can the UK then be said to have differentiated between bilateral and multilateral agreements as was done by many successor states following the VCSSRT's adoption? The UK's practice of acceding to some multilateral agreements – namely multilateral agreements which the EU had concluded

---

119 'EU Internal Preparatory Discussions' (n 97) 4–5; 'UK Guidance Note' (n 95).
120 'EU Internal Preparatory Discussions' (n 97) 4–5; 'UK Guidance Note' (n 95).
121 'EU Brexit Guidelines' (n 94) para 13; 'UK Guidance Note' (n 95).
122 Waldock used this expression regarding the possibility for newly independent states to agree with treaty partners on the continued application of the predecessor's agreements (cp eg 'SR Waldock Fifth Report' (n 11) 7).

§ 7 Brexit and Recent Practice. Brexit as Recent Practice?

as EU-only agreements – speaks against such an assumption.¹²³ At the same time, the fact that the UK did continue the multilateral mixed agreements rebuts any attempt to view Brexit as completely following clean-slate presumptions. What then can be made of the UK's practice? Does the comparison with state succession perhaps provide a reasonable solution but ignorant of practice?

Neither Art. 34 VCSSRT nor state practice subsequent to its adoption can fully explain Brexit practice with regard to international agreements. Furthermore, neither the VCSSRT nor subsequent separations have produced a settled, widely accepted and followed rule on succession in cases of separation. Instead, what guided the ILC in drafting Art. 34 VCSSRT and what continues to guide discussions on state practice in the context of state succession since then are much more generally accepted principles rather than precise rules. Outside the context of decolonisation, these are namely the two principles of treaty stability and of consent. While the ILC has laid great importance on the stability of treaty relations, the principle of consent, whereby no state should be bound by international obligations which it did not itself enter into, has guided the practice of separations after 1978.¹²⁴ Accordingly, the ILC has favoured a rule of continuity, while more recent practice leans towards a clean slate.

At the same time, the ILC did not altogether ignore the question of consent. It was in the context of consent that the ILC discussed the relevance of the participation of a state's separating part in the predecessor's treaty-making prior to its succession, the prime example coming from the practice of union of states.¹²⁵ In the view of the Commission, where the successor state – prior to separation – had participated in the treaty-making of the predecessor state, consent of the successor state could be presumed.¹²⁶ (Presumed) Participation thus served the ILC to justify continuity, even though the successor state had not expressed its consent to be bound in these sense of Art. 11 *Vienna Convention on the Law of Treaties*¹²⁷ (VCLT).¹²⁸

---

123 See the case of the UK's accession to the GPA above § 1 section II.D.
124 See above Part II § 7 section I.
125 See above Part II § 6 section III.B.
126 See above Part II § 6 section III.B.
127 Vienna Convention on the Law of Treaties (adopted 23 May 1969, entered into force 27 January 1980) 1155 UNTS 331 [VCLT].
128 Art. 11 VCLT: 'The consent of a State to be bound by a treaty may be expressed by signature, exchange of instruments constituting a treaty, ratification, acceptance, approval, or by any other means if so agreed.'

II. Brexit and Succession Practice: Applying a New Template

Based on these considerations and more recent state practice, a default assumption may be formulated: a successor state to a separation starts its life with a clean slate *if* an automatic continuation of the international agreements of its predecessor is not justified. Automatic continuity could be justified where the successor state's lack of consent is overridden by its strong previous participation in the agreement's making. Here, the principle of consent thus serves to protect the successor state from unwanted obligations except where such protection is not called for. Balanced in this way, the two principles of treaty stability and consent can, in fact, be transferred to the situation of EU withdrawal and serve well to explain Brexit practice. Importantly, the starting point for considering the effect of Brexit on international agreements would shift. So far, the question has mostly been regarding why the UK has *not* continued to participate in all international agreements – especially in those where it was itself a party. Viewed from the perspective of state succession, however, the initial assumption would be that of a clean slate and the initial question should be why the UK *should* as a successor state continue any of the EU's international agreements. Where is there a participation link creating a legal nexus between the UK as a former EU Member State and the EU's international agreements that would justify such continuation?

Regardless of whether they are concluded with one or more non-EU treaty partners or not, participation of the EU's Member States in the making of EU-only agreements is limited. The Council, consisting of representatives of the Member States, is tasked with authorising the negotiations and with signing and concluding international agreements.[129] Thus, the Member States have the first and final say on the conclusion of an international agreement. However, Art. 218(8) TFEU provides that, in general, '[t]he Council shall act by a qualified majority throughout the procedure'.[130] While the representatives may make their Member State's interests heard, this is not necessarily reflected in the Council's final decision. The Council's decision to conclude an international agreement is explicitly not the decision of the Member States, but the decision of an EU organ, predicated

---

129 Cp Art. 218 TFEU.
130 Exceptions, where unanimity is required, are 'when the agreement covers a field for which unanimity is required for the adoption of a Union act as well as for association agreements and the agreements referred to in Article 212 with the States which are candidates for accession' (Art. 218(8) sentence 2 TFEU). Sentence 3 also provides for unanimity for the EU's accession to the European Convention on Human Rights.

§ 7 Brexit and Recent Practice. Brexit as Recent Practice?

on the participation of further EU institutions, such as the Commission and the Parliament.[131] Moreover, externally the EU is usually represented by the Commission or the EU's High Representative. The EU's internal process of treaty-making and its external posture, taken together, emphasise its individual legal personality, distinct from its Member States. Thus, while Member States are represented in the Council, there is no strong participation link between the UK, in its former capacity as an EU Member State, and international agreements concluded solely by the EU.

This is different in the case of mixed agreements. While the process of concluding these agreements likewise follows Art. 218 TFEU, the Member States play a very decisive – if unwritten – role. Besides being represented internally in the Council, a representative of the Member States may also join the Commission in representing the EU externally in the negotiations.[132] Crucially, however, the Member States conclude mixed agreements alongside the EU, in many cases even including national parliamentary participation.[133] Based on this exceptionally strong participation link, one must not presume consent. Rather, the UK has actually consented to be bound by these agreements. Considering this, the principle of consent does not speak against obliging the UK to continue mixed international agreements in the interest of treaty stability.

In practice, however, the UK only did so with regard to multilateral mixed agreements. That, however, may again be explained with reference to the principle of consent. If and when the principle of consent is taken into the equation, as it seems to be increasingly the case in more recent state practice, it is not only the consent of the successor state that must be put into the balance. One also has to consider the treaty partners. While earlier participation in the (internal) treaty-making process of its predecessor may override the successor state's lack of consent, it certainly cannot do so with regard to the predecessor's treaty partners. Thus, even where continuation of an agreement may be justifiable from the perspective of the successor

---

131 Cp Art. 218 TFEU.
132 K Schmalenbach, 'Article 218' in C Calliess and M Ruffert (eds), *EUV/AEUV: Das Verfassungsrecht der Europäischen Union mit Europäischer Grundrechtecharta* (6th edn, CH Beck 2022) para 5. For a detailed account of the joint negotiation in the context of environmental agreements, see V Rodenhoff, *Die EG und ihre Mitgliedstaaten als völkerrechtliche Einheit bei umweltvölkerrechtlichen Übereinkommen* (Nomos 2008) 258–270.
133 G van der Loo, 'Less is More?: The Role of National Parliaments in the Conclusion of Mixed (Trade) Agreements' [2018] CLEER Paper Series 1.

state, an exception is often made if the treaty partner's consent pertained to being bound in relation to one or several specific states (or other treaty parties).

Of course, bilateral mixed agreements, as all mixed agreements, feature a high degree of participation of the Member States. At the same time, however, bilateral mixed agreements are characterised by another feature often referred to as speaking against an automatic continuity in case of succession: the 'personal equation'[134] of the parties. Although the bilateral mixed agreements are formally multipartite agreements, they essentially create a relationship between one or more non-EU states and the 'EU Party'[135]. Where one thus lays importance on the identity of the treaty partner in bilateral agreements, the same argument may be made as regards bilateral mixed agreements. Although the EU and its Member States are formally several parties, their identity in the agreement is that of the EU Party. It is with that EU Party that the non-EU state arguably intended to enter into a treaty relation, not individually with the organisation or the individual states behind that party. The reason often given for treating truly bilateral agreements – agreements between two parties – differently from multilateral agreements may thus likewise be used to justify the discontinuity of bilaterally structured agreements such as bilateral mixed agreements.

III. Brexit and the Law of Succession: Match or Misfit?

The previous two chapters (§§ 5, 6) set out to answer a general question: can the law of treaty succession be applied by analogy to the situation of a Member State leaving the EU? This chapter (§ 7) took a more concrete approach: can recent practice on state succession and the practice surrounding Brexit be compared? And can the former perhaps even explain some of the latter? As has been shown, it is certainly possible to use the principles of consent and treaty stability and to balance them in a manner that not only largely accords with recent state practice but also accommodates EU specificities. At the same time, both the initial analogy and the ensuing

---

134 'ILC Report 1974' (n 18) 237.
135 See on the use of this term in bilateral mixed agreements above Part I § 4 section I.B.1 and section II.B.1.c. See in detail, S Schaefer and J Odermatt, 'Nomen est Omen?: The Relevance of "EU Party" In International Law' in N Levrat and others (eds), *The EU and its Member States' Joint Participation in International Agreements* (Hart Publishing 2021).

§ 7 Brexit and Recent Practice. Brexit as Recent Practice?

comparison between treaty practice in recent cases of state successions and Brexit is certainly not free from points of criticism. To conclude this chapter, thus, two possible main points of criticism shall be addressed.

The first pertains to the initial comparison between the EU and unions of states. Considering the evolution of the ILC's draft away from a provision specifically on *unions* of states to an article on separations from *states* in general, the starting point for the analogy can be questioned. This is all the more the case since the practice of these unions neither accords with more recent practice nor appears completely comparable with the situation of Brexit. After all, the whole practice of unions of states, on which the ILC based its Art. 34 VCSSRT, is related to the *complete* dissolution of unions.[136] Of what worth is the comparison to unions then when Brexit obviously does not lead to the dissolution of the EU, but only a separation of the UK?

The answer is given by more recent state practice. For one, most post-1978 instances of disintegration compared to Brexit practice above pertain to unions of states. The USSR, the SFRY and Czechoslovakia were all what Waldock would have defined as federal unions.[137] Thus, also the more recent practice on the effects of a state's disintegration on international agreements relates to composite actors. Moreover, the difference in pre- and post-1978 practice may precisely be explained by the fact that the ILC could only consider cases of *complete* dissolutions of unions of states. Many writers today argue, however, that there is a difference between dissolutions and separations of only part of a union's territory which does not only show in practice but can also be dogmatically explained.[138] Thus, Hafner and Novak argue that post-1978 practice in fact confirms Art. 34 VCSSRT as a customary rule, but only as regards dissolutions.[139] In contrast, instances

---

136 Arguably, the United Arab Republic may have formed an exception. Founded by Egypt and Syria, Syria later announced its withdrawal from the union. While Syria resumed its pre-union identity, Egypt continued the identity of the United Arab Republic. Thus, one could consider the withdrawal of Syria as case of separation in the narrower sense, with Egypt remaining as the rump state. On the other hand, it is logically difficult not to speak of a dissolution of the union, when one of two parts forming the union leaves. The exact categorisation of this succession was also contemplated by Waldock, see 'SR Waldock Fifth Report' (n 11) 38–39. On this see also R Young, 'The State of Syria: Old or New?' (1962) 56(2) *American Journal of International Law* 482.
137 For Waldock's definition of unions of states, see 'SR Waldock Fifth Report' (n 11) 18. See also above Part II § 5 section III.A.
138 A Zimmermann (n 5) 431.
139 Hafner and Novak (n 24) 416.

III. Brexit and the Law of Succession: Match or Misfit?

of mere separations from a union – such as the disintegration of the USSR – are not only more comparable to the situation of Brexit, but, as shown above, also showed similar practice with regard to international agreements.

The second obvious point of criticism concerns, as is so often the case, the EU's practice of concluding mixed agreements. The co-conclusion of international agreements is not only unique in the realm of international organisations but also unheard of in the context of unions of states. Certainly, the constituent states of some unions conclude international agreements, some of which are also concluded by the union itself. The practice of Belarus and Ukraine to conclude international agreements alongside the USSR while still being constituent states of the union is a prime example.[140] However, such instances may perhaps be described as a *parallel*, but certainly not as joint conclusions of international agreements. The closest one could perhaps get to the Belarussian and Ukrainian practice may be the EU's multilateral mixed agreements, where the conclusion is not necessarily synchronised and the EU and its Member States do not form an 'EU Party'[141]. However, even here, a variety of treaty designs and instruments, such as declarations of competence, 'regional economic integration organisation' and disconnection clauses,[142] often ensure the jointness of the EU and its Member States.

What then to make of these kinds of international agreements, which never previously needed to be considered in the context of succession? One possibility is to deny their peculiarity and simply treat them for what they formally still are: multilateral agreements between 29+ treaty parties – the EU, its now 27 Member States and at least one none-EU state. The other option is to accept their distinctive features and attempt to deal with them within the means and categories available. Thus, the previous section addressed the fact that the UK had consented to be bound by mixed agreements alongside the EU under the aspect of pre-separation participation. But does this participation link regarding mixed agreements – the UK's status as a party under international law – rather harm the analogy instead of explaining its application? If the UK is already a party, why apply rules and principles for succession?

---

140 Ibid 415.
141 In the sense described above Part I § 4 section I.B.1 and section II.B.1.c.
142 On these treaty instruments, see J Odermatt, *International Law and the European Union* (Cambridge University Press 2021) 69–88.

Firstly, based on the VCSSRT's definition,[143] a factual succession takes place also with regards to mixed agreements. It is this fact that differentiates the EU's mixed agreements from the agreements concluded by Belarus and Ukraine while still constituent states of the USSR. Belarus and Ukraine concluded agreements in those areas of international relations that they were responsible for even prior to separation.[144] Thus, when separating from the USSR, the two states did not replace the USSR regarding its responsibility, at least in respect of these agreements. The reason that the EU's mixed agreements are co-concluded is, however, precisely because the responsibility for the international relations in the agreement's subject area is divided between the EU and its Member States. When withdrawing from the EU, the UK replaces the EU in competences that the EU exercised in respect of these agreements. Especially in many bilateral mixed agreements, trade agreements being the prominent example, the share of exclusive Member State competences is meanwhile hardly discernible.[145]

As with agreements solely concluded by a predecessor state, the question thus arises how this change in responsibilities affects the successor state's rights and obligations. One possibility would be that the leaving Member State – upon gaining full responsibility for the subject areas covered by the agreements – takes over all rights and obligations, becoming a 'full'[146] party to these agreements. The other possibility would be that upon replacement, the former Member State starts its life outside the EU with a clean slate – at least where continued participation fails due to the lack of a strong participation link or the existence of a strong personal equation.

But can the answer – as given in respect of bilateral mixed agreements – really be that the UK loses its status *as a party* under international law? Notably, the wording of the clean-slate rule as formulated in the VCSSRT does not exclude this. Where a clean slate is applied,[147] the successor state

---

143 Cp Art. 2(1)(b) VCSSRT. On the definition, see above at Part II § 6 section II.A.
144 A Zimmermann (n 5) 392, 397; Hafner and Novak (n 24) 416.
145 On Member States' limited competences in trade agreements, see ECJ, Case 2/15 *FTA Singapore* [2015] EU:C:2017:376.
146 As opposed to a party that has concluded the whole agreement but is only competent – or responsible – for parts of it. On the extent to which the EU and its Member States become parties – ie bound – to mixed agreements, see above at Part I § 3 section III.C.2 and in more detail Schaefer and Odermatt (n 135) 134–138.
147 In the VCSSRT, the clean slate rule is applied only to newly independent states. However, differences only arise as to the applicability – whether it should also apply to cases of dissolution and separation – not as regards the content of the rule.

III. Brexit and the Law of Succession: Match or Misfit?

is not bound to maintain in force, or to become a party to, any treaty by reason only of the fact that at the date of the succession of States the treaty was in force in respect of the territory to which the succession of States relates.[148]

This formulation does not define *why* the agreement was in force for the territory prior to succession nor does it explicitly limit the rule to agreements of the predecessor (alone). Nevertheless, the purpose of the cleanslate rule is indisputably that 'any new state would come into existence unburdened by commitments *of its predecessor*'[149]. Of course, it is possible to argue that the mixed agreements are *not* commitments of (only) the predecessor – the EU – for the UK participated in the making of the agreement as a party. But does it really make sense to maintain this formalistic view given Brexit practice?

Certainly, the EU views bilateral mixed agreements as *EU* agreements, even though the Member States are parties alongside it. The European Court of Justice (ECJ) since its *Haegeman* judgement and the UK-EU Withdrawal Agreement frame international agreements as respectively an 'integral part of *EU* law'[150] and 'Union law'[151]. In bilateral mixed agreements, the EU and its Member States, in the words of Advocate General Tesauro form a 'single contracting party'[152], the Member States often being said to have entered these agreements only in their capacity as Member States of the EU.[153]

This has not gone unnoticed by non-EU treaty partners. In describing the US experience with mixity, Olson, then Legal Adviser in the US State Department, points to several EU treaty practices which 'raise anew questions of whether the party status of Member States is simply a façade based

---

148 Cp Art. 16 VCSSRT.
149 P Janig, 'The 1978 Vienna Convention, the Clean Slate Doctrine and the Decolonization of Sources' (2018; published 2021) 23 *Austrian Review of International and European Law* 143 (emphasis added). See also Craven, *Decolonization* (n 5) 30–33.
150 ECJ, C-181/73 *R. & V. Haegeman v Belgian State* [1974] ECLI:EU:C:1974:41, [5] (emphasis added). On the judgement and its implications, see RA Wessel, 'International Agreements as an Integral Part of EU Law: Haegeman' in G Butler and RA Wessel (eds), *EU External Relations Law: The Cases in Context* (Hart Publishing 2022).
151 Art. 2(a) UK-EU WA.
152 ECJ, C-53/96 *Hermès International v FHT Marketing Choice BV* (Opinion of the Advocate General Tesauro) [1998] ECLI:EU:C:1997:539, [15].
153 On their status in mixed agreements, see above at Part I § 3 section III.C.2 and § 4 section I.B.1.

on a technicality of internal European law, but in fact barely concealing the fact that the Union is the only real EU party'[154]. Against this background, it is even more remarkable that, to the author's knowledge, no non-EU state has rejected the EU and UK's position on the effect of Brexit on international agreements. Furthermore, the UK's practice of rollover agreements shows that most EU treaty partners accepted the proposition that they needed to re-conclude their international agreements with the UK, *even* in cases where under international law the UK had already formally consented to be bound. In so doing, whether intended or not, the practice of these states cannot but be read as leaning towards the EU's view that in bilateral mixed agreements, the EU and its Member States form *one* party.

It would be wrong to claim that the practice of dealing with international agreements in the case of Brexit is identical with state practice in instances of separation. And it would be more than speculative to suggest that the EU, the UK or any of their treaty partners, in fact, had the law of state succession in mind when considering the effects of Brexit on international agreements and the practical steps to be taken. Neither the EU nor the UK ever elaborated on the legal reasons for taking certain procedural steps or assuming a certain position with respect to the different categories of international agreements. Nevertheless, the steps taken and the positions assumed fit surprisingly well within the framework of the rules, principles and practices of state succession. Based on this finding, one is tempted to conclude that applying the law of state succession to the EU and EU withdrawal is not only a justifiable analogy, but it is one that may even be confirmed by actual practice. This is more than any attempt at explaining Brexit practice based on treaty law can claim.

---

154 P Olson, 'Mixity from the Outside: the Perspective of a Treaty Partner' in C Hillion and P Koutrakos (eds), *Mixed Agreements Revisited: The EU and its Member States in the World* (Hart Publishing 2010) 346.

Concluding Remarks: Towards a Law of EU Succession

Part I demonstrated that the law of treaties as codified in the *Vienna Convention on the Law of Treaties* (VCLT) cannot explain many aspects of the EU and the UK's treaty practice following the UK's withdrawal from the EU. Some of the international agreements affected by Brexit were concluded by the EU Member States *inter se* and very much mirror the practice of convention-making in the context of other international organisations. However, the vast majority of the international agreements in question were concluded by the EU – often together with its Member States – with non-EU states. In contrast to *inter se* agreements, these external agreements are 'much more "state-like"'[1]. In examining these agreements, *Part II* explored an alternative approach: applying the law of state succession by analogy.

The basis for this analogy is the comparison of the EU and unions of states. Not only do they share many similarities, but the characteristics of unions of states shared by the EU are precisely those that decisively shaped the law of state succession as codified in the *Vienna Convention on Succession of States in Respect of Treaties* (VCSSRT). According to Art. 34 VCSSRT, in cases of separation – the situation comparable to EU withdrawal – the international agreements of the predecessor automatically remain in force for the successor state(s). While this rule has not been confirmed by state practice following the adoption of the VCSSRT, the principles guiding states in instances of separation are still very much transferrable to the EU and an exit therefrom. Additionally, weighing of the principle of consent, on one hand, against treaty stability, on the other, could even help explain why – at least in the eyes of the EU and the UK – EU-only and bilateral mixed agreements ceased to apply to the UK post-Brexit while it remained a party to multilateral mixed agreements.

The crucial argument for placing EU withdrawal in the context of succession, however, is one of legal policy. That the exit of the UK from the EU had effects on international agreements concluded with external partners is a fact that is visible today in treaty databases and depositary registries. Brexit has set a precedent, and, given the remarkable consistency in EU

---

1 J Odermatt, *International Law and the European Union* (Cambridge University Press 2021) 62.

treaty practice, the EU and its Member States will likely adhere to the same approach in the event of another Member State withdrawal. Thus, inevitably, international law has to engage with the (state) practice Brexit created, and the possibility of further EU exits. For both aspects, drawing an analogy to state succession is the most promising.

There are certainly parts of Brexit practice that can be explained without reference to the rules and principles of succession. Indisputably, under international treaty law, the application of EU-only agreements to the UK ended with Brexit. To these agreements the UK itself was never a party, their application being a matter purely of EU, not international, law. Consequentially, following Brexit, the UK acceded to those EU-only agreements that it had a continued interest in. At the same time, practice following the adoption of the VCSSRT shows that accession is a method that is also regularly chosen by successor states to ensure their continued participation in a multilateral agreement, regardless of the automatic continuity rule that Art. 34 VCSSRT provides for. Thus, while under the law of succession, one could argue that the UK would automatically succeed into the rights and obligations flowing from multilateral agreements previously concluded by the EU, the fact that the UK chose to deposit instruments of *accession* instead of notifications of *succession* is not an anomaly.

Similarly, the continued participation of the UK as a party to multilateral mixed agreements can be explained both under international treaty law and the law of succession. From the perspective of treaty law, withdrawal from the founding treaty of an international organisation does not ensue automatic consequences for *other* international agreements, especially when concluded with non-member states. From the viewpoint of the law of succession, the fact that the UK had expressly consented to these agreements prior to its EU exit speaks for their automatic continuity following its exit.

In contrast, the termination of the UK's participation in bilateral mixed agreements cannot be justified under general treaty law nor based on the text or structure of the respective agreements. *Pacta sunt servanda* as long as an agreement has not been validly terminated. Such termination, however, did not take effect automatically with the UK's withdrawal from the EU nor has it been validly effected by the UK in accordance with the provisions on denunciation in bilateral mixed agreements or the VCLT. While international treaty law thus offers no explanation of Brexit practice with regard to bilateral mixed agreements, the law of state succession arguably does. Although generally emphasising the importance of treaty stability, in the context of bilateral relations, the law appears to develop in the direction of a clean slate, especially in cases of separation.

This presents international (and European) lawyers with three options. Firstly, one could continue to evaluate the Brexit practice from the viewpoint of international treaty law, as many authors did prior to the UK's withdrawal. As regards bilateral mixed agreements, this would mean accepting that the practice is not justifiable according to the law as it stands. The second option is to view the effect of Brexit on international agreements as unregulated by international law, a novel practice of a *sui generis* subject. These two options are harmful – for the EU and international law – further burdening the often strained relationship between the legal orders and potentially playing into recurring claims of EU exceptionalism.[2] To this, the third option – placing Brexit in the context of succession – offers a real alternative.

Drawing an analogy to unions of states recognises that the questions arising in the context of the UK's withdrawal from the EU are new. So far, no state has ever separated from an international legal subject such as the EU – whether considered a regional (economic) integration organisation, hybrid union or *sui generis* – that featured a treaty-making practice comparable to that of the EU. At the same, drawing an analogy allows the application of existing rules and principles, instead of accepting a legal lacuna. Such an analogical extension of the rules applicable to states to other international legal subjects is nothing new. As Bordin has shown, the comparison between states and international organisations significantly shaped two ILC codification projects.[3] In the case of the VCLT-IO this may have been 'eased by the fact that practice at the time showed that international organisations concluded agreements relying on rules and procedures that did not differ from those codified in VCLT 1969'[4]. This cannot not, however, be said of the *Draft Articles on the Responsibility of*

---

[2] On these claims, see M Lickova, 'European Exceptionalism in International Law' (2008) 19(3) *European Journal of International Law* 463; G Nolte and HP Aust, 'European Exceptionalism?' (2013) 2(3) *Global Constitutionalism* 407; T Isiksel, 'European Exceptionalism and the EU's Accession to the ECHR' (2016) 27(3) *European Journal of International Law* 565. On the strained relationship in the context of the EU-UK Withdrawal Agreement, see S Peers, 'The End – or a New Beginning?: The EU/UK Withdrawal Agreement' (2021) 39(1) *Yearbook of European Law* 122.

[3] FL Bordin, *The Analogy between States and International Organizations* (Cambridge University Press 2019) 39–43.

[4] Ibid 40.

Part II: Brexit and the Law of Succession

International Organizations[5] (DARIO). Nevertheless, 'the commentary to the [DARIO] largely justifies extending rules from the [Articles on State Responsibility] on the ground that there would be "little" or "no" reason to distinguish between States and international organizations with respect to the rule or issue concerned'[6].

Finally, drawing an analogy to apply the law of state succession to the EU is the most reasonable solution. This would mirror the reverse situation of Member State accession, where it has been argued that '[t]he rationale [for the functional succession doctrine] was borrowed from the idea of "state succession". Since the Union is not a "state", the concept had to be applied analogously.'[7] Moreover, the law of state succession is also best suited to address the challenges which are common to state succession and withdrawal from the EU. This is illustrated by looking at two central characteristics of the law of succession.

The first pertains to the circumstances under which the law of succession becomes relevant: 'the law of state succession always occurs in highly politicized contexts'[8]. Thus, a certain politisation of the legal questions arising from state succession is not only accepted but inherent to the system. The law of state succession may not (yet) be dealing with this in a perfect way. Given the often major (political) disruptions preceding the replacement of one state by another with respect to a certain territory, the VCSSRT is frequently criticised as lacking flexibility. The Convention's commitment to one approach – automatic continuity – for all cases of state succession outside the context of decolonisation seems too rigid and detached from reality. But the acknowledgement of the 'political transformations'[9] triggering the questions of succession at least allows us to look for suitable solutions and flexible approaches. The law of treaties as codified in the VCLT, in

---

5 ILC, 'Draft Articles on the Responsibility of International Organizations' UN Doc A/66/10, YBILC (2011) Vol. II(2).
6 FL Bordin (n 3) 41 providing a whole list of examples of articles in the DARIO to which this statement applies.
7 R Schütze, 'The "Succession Doctrine" and the European Union' in R Schütze (ed), *Foreign Affairs and the EU Constitution: Selected Essays* (Cambridge University Press 2014) 110.
8 A Rasulov, 'Revisiting State Succession to Humanitarian Treaties: Is There a Case for Automaticity?' (2003) 14(1) *European Journal of International Law* 141, 148–149.
9 Cp M Koskenniemi, 'Report of the Director of Studies of the English-speaking Section of the Centre' in PM Eisemann and M Koskenniemi (eds), *State Succession: Codification Tested Against the Facts* (Martinus Nijhoff Publishers 2000) 66.

contrast, is largely immune from political events,[10] and needs to provide for rigid rules. While it allows the treaty parties the autonomy to adapt its rules, they must do so *prior* to the conclusion of an agreement. In contrast, the law of state succession requires flexibility in situations which the parties have precisely *not* provided for in advance. In those instances, it

> seems that both successor and third States tend to prefer ad hoc political solutions rather than fixed and somewhat rigid rules. And indeed, in most situations such political solutions can be seen as constituting a relatively unproblematic way of resolving State succession-related issues that arise.[11]

For Koskenniemi, the significance of the law of state succession thus does not lie in 'ready-made solutions to particular problems', but 'in two other directions'[12]. Firstly, 'State succession enables the articulation, in legal terms, of the character, direction and limits of political transformation'[13], 'creating a sense of the importance of the change and the need for stability'[14]. Secondly, 'it may be that the very flexibility of State succession makes it possible to manage sometimes dangerous political conflicts in an innovative way' and 'to combine continuation at the level of abstract status with important changes at the level of specific rights and duties'[15].

Undoubtedly, the situation following the UK's Brexit referendum and the subsequent Art. 50 notification can be described as highly politicised. The UK's withdrawal from the EU is a process of disintegration unprecedented in the EU's history. In this transformative process, even if not a *state* succession, both of Koskenniemi's points hold true. Given the consequences on international agreements as assumed by the EU and the UK, the absence of legal language and justifications is striking. No publicly available EU or UK statements or documents attempt to explain their approach in legal terms. Instead, the language used by the EU in its Brexit guidelines and negotiating directives, and ultimately the respective provisions of the UK-EU

---

10 An exception is a fundamental change of circumstances as provided for in Art. 62 VCLT.
11 A Zimmermann and JG Devaney, 'Succession to Treaties and the Inherent Limits of International Law' in CJ Tams, A Tzanakopoulos and A Zimmermann (eds), *Research Handbook on the Law of Treaties* (Edward Elgar Publishing 2016) 539.
12 Koskenniemi (n 9) 66.
13 Ibid.
14 Ibid 68.
15 Ibid.

Withdrawal Agreement, created 'ambiguity' rather than living up to 'the EU's commitment to clarity and legal certainty for (among others) the EU's international partners'[16].

Formulations such as 'no longer covered by' did not clarify the exact legal consequences expected regarding whether the agreement would no longer apply to the UK or if the UK would cease to be a party, nor do they provide any information on possible underlying legal considerations. While a difference continually appears to be made between describing the UK as being a party 'in its capacity as a Member State'[17] and referring to 'agreements the UK signed in its own right'[18], no explanation is given as to why and how this (perceived) difference in status plays out when the UK leaves the EU. In the end, the EU and the UK did find a (political) solution. Indeed, the status of international agreements following Brexit appears to be one of the few issues on which they did not disagree. Together, they found innovative solutions, many of which – knowingly or unknowingly – mirrored succession practices. But by not actively taking recourse (by analogy) to state succession, dealing with international agreements in the context of Brexit lacked the 'conceptual matrix'[19] which the law of state succession could have provided.

The second central characteristic of the law of succession that enables it to address the challenges faced by states *and* the EU in situations of disintegration is its objective. The aim of the law of state succession is a balancing of interests that exist both in the case of *state* succession *and* the withdrawal from the EU. When initially drafting the VCSSRT, the focus of both the ILC and the majority of states participating in the Diplomatic Conference lay on the stability of treaty relations. Outside the context of decolonisation, continuity in international relations, the stability of the international community and the protection of the other treaty parties' interests led the Commission and the participating states to provide for the automatic continuity of all international agreements for successors states. States should not be able to escape their pre-succession international commitments either through uniting or a separation. That these considerations

---

16 M Cremona, 'The Withdrawal Agreement and the EU's International Agreements' (2020) 45(2) *European Law Review* 237, 244.
17 UK Government, 'Technical Note' International Agreements during the Implementation Period (8 February 2018) para 2.
18 UK Government, 'International Agreements if the UK leaves the EU without a Deal', Guidance Note (5 November 2019).
19 Koskenniemi (n 9) 66.

equally applied to modern forms of (economic) unions which members of the Commission believed to be on the horizon was explicitly recognised. The EU (to some extent) takes this into account in its handling of the pre-accession agreements of its Member States. Equally, the interests of non-EU treaty partners could and should have played a greater role during the Brexit process.

The focus of UK treaty practice in the context of Brexit lay less on stability and more on the principle of consent. Instead of relying on any form of automatic continuity, the UK often resorted to reciprocal solutions, such as rollover agreements. The principle of consent has also played an increasing role in state succession practice since 1978. It, too, may serve to protect other treaty parties' interests. It may be against a *treaty partner's* interest to have a treaty relation with a new successor state forced upon it, especially in the context of bilateral agreements. Conversely, one can also cite the lack of consent of the successor state in arguing in favour of a clean slate rather than the presumption of automatic continuity. Thus, the crux of automatic continuity is seen in the question of whether and, if so, how it can be overcome that neither the successor state nor the treaty partner have consented to an agreement.

In attempting to answer this question, the number of treaty parties and the agreement's structure – both potentially indicative of a 'personal equation'[20] – still play a role. If an agreement is to be continued by a successor state, 'the treaty or treaties must be removed as far as possible from the personality of the states parties'[21]. For multilateral agreements of a more personal character, and especially for bilateral agreements, the link between consent and the identity of the treaty parties thus remains an obstacle to automatic continuity that for many authors has yet to be overcome.

> The more intimate the legal relationship with the 'self' of the State – the case of political treaties – the less reason there is to maintain them: the more generalizable or 'objective' a legal relationship – territorial and boundary régimes, 'law-making treaties' – the easier it is to argue that the successor should be bound.[22]

---

20 ILC, 'Report of the International Law Commission on the Work of its Twenty-Sixth Session, 6 May – 26 July 1974' UN Doc. A/9610/Rev.1, YBILC (1974) Vol. II(1) 237.
21 Rasulov (n 8), 151.
22 Koskenniemi (n 9) 122.

Part II: Brexit and the Law of Succession

In the light of the importance that the EU and the UK placed on their joint identity as the 'EU Party' in bilateral mixed agreements, the participation of the Member States in these agreements being intimately linked with their capacity as Member States, it is obvious to see how a focus on the principle of consent in cases of succession may appeal to the EU.

Yet, it is another development in the law of state succession – paired with the continuous development of the EU itself – that makes it essential to include the EU in any further considerations on this field of international law: the shift of attention in recent scholarship on state succession toward the content of agreements rather than solely their laterality or structure. Thus, to assume the continuity of multilateral agreements by pointing to the number of treaty partners no longer suffices. True, the identity of the treaty partner may potentially be less relevant in multilateral agreements. Nevertheless, the simple absence of a 'personal equation' is no longer considered enough to overcome the absence of consent. Rather,

> in order to qualify for automatic succession, the treaty or treaties at issue must be, by virtue of their purpose and functions, directly related to international values of the greatest importance, sufficient to override the principles of sovereignty and consent.[23]

The agreements generally discussed as falling within this description are 'multilateral conventions of humanitarian character' which, according to Jennings, count to 'the necessary working capital of international jural relationships that a new State needs at the outset'[24]. To what extent this has already been confirmed by state practice is again obscured by the difficult to ascertain practice of post-1978 successions.[25] While some argue that there is 'a clear movement toward the formation of a rule of customary international law, according to which successor states are obliged to confirm the continuity of international human rights treaties and of conventions on humanitarian law in armed conflicts'[26], others have come to the conclusion

---

23 Rasulov (n 8), 151.
24 RY Jennings, *General Course on Principles of International Law* (Martinus Nijhoff Publishers 1967) 442–443.
25 See also the caveat made by Jennings: 'Whether the distinction between these and other kinds of treaty can yet be expressed in terms of legal criteria is more than doubtful.' (ibid 444–445).
26 T Schweisfurth, 'Das Recht der Staatensukzession: Die Staatenpraxis der Nachfolge in völkerrechtliche Verträge, Staatsvermögen, Staatsschulden und Archive in den Teilungsfällen Sowjetunion, Tschechoslowakei und Jugoslawien' in U Fastenrath, T

that *opinio juris* 'is not anywhere close'[27] to an automatic succession in multilateral agreements of a humanitarian character.[28]

This has not, however, prevented scholars from further engaging with the idea of protecting individuals from the potentially negative effects of a state succession on international agreements. With regard to Bilateral Investment Treaties (BITs), Tams has thus proposed to reconsider their nature. Instead of viewing them as bilateral agreements, which in his view do not automatically devolve to a successor state, he proposes to consider BITs as agreements vesting third parties – the investors – with rights.[29] Thus, as a 'human rights analogy'[30], 'one could perhaps argue that foreign investors making an investment when a BIT applies should acquire the right to have that investment protected by the BIT after the State succession has taken place'[31].

At the same time, the EU's treaty practice has greatly evolved, said evolution not only pertaining to the subject matter which has 'widened'[32].

> The (then) Community began by concluding bilateral agreements largely regulating trade liberalization [...]. The EU's treaty practice expanded rapidly when it concluded agreements in the field of CFSP. It is no longer confined to the economic arena, and now concludes agreements in the field of energy, development, human rights, security and the environment.[33]

Additionally, the types of international agreements have changed, with the EU being the only international organisation to conclude law-making agreements. There are, as Reuter put it, 'ordinary international organiza-

---

Schweisfurth and CT Ebenroth (eds), *Das Recht der Staatensukzession* (CF Müller 1996) 233.

27 Rasulov (n 8), 168.
28 On the question, see also MT Kamminga, 'State Succession in Respect of Human Rights Treaties' (1996) 7(4) *European Journal of International Law* 469; N el-Khoury, 'Human Rights Treaties and the Law of State Succession in the Event of Secession' in E de Wet and KM Scherr (eds), *Max Planck Yearbook of United Nations Law Online* 23 (Brill Nijhoff 2020); J Tropper, 'Succession into Human Rights Treaties' in C Binder and others (eds), *Elgar Encyclopedia of Human Rights* (Edward Elgar Publishing 2022).
29 CJ Tams, 'State Succession to Investment Treaties: Mapping the Issues' (2016) 31(2) *ICSID Review* 314, 335.
30 Ibid 336.
31 Ibid 335.
32 J Odermatt (n 1) 68.
33 Ibid.

tions' and 'international organizations exercising State functions'. The EU represents the latter. The more the EU engages in areas traditionally associated with statehood and the more it emancipates itself from its origins as an economic union, the greater the relevance of present-day questions on state succession to further EU (dis)integration.

As posited by some states at the Diplomatic Conference, it is comparably easy to accept that states wishing to continue a treaty relation will find a way to do so, regardless of a rule requiring automatic continuity when the agreements in question concern, for example, trade or transport. But beyond that, '[m]odern States are embedded in an intensive set of commonly shared values and interests governing their social life, all of which are the product of very dense treaty relations'[34]. And this 'social life' is no longer restricted to states. The 'international society can no longer be – if it ever could have been – conceived as a society merely of States'[35]. The EU increasingly promotes values and rights, intending to protect individuals not only via its own legal order, but also through its participation in international agreements: 'once focused mainly on issues such as trade, the EU is now an active treaty partner in fields such as international security, human rights, health and environmental protection.'[36]

A withdrawing Member State should not be able to escape this social life to the creation of which it contributed in the context of its EU membership. Treaty practice following Brexit shows that formal consent by a Member State cannot necessarily serve as a guarantee for this. As a Member State the UK ratified over 150 bilateral mixed agreements; following its EU withdrawal, it no longer felt bound by them. Non-EU states may accept the proposition that Brexit terminated international commitments entered into by the UK and agree to renegotiations. Individuals, in contrast, require protection from the adverse consequences of disintegration – be it a separation from a state or withdrawal from the EU.

34　G Hafner and G Novak, 'State Succession in Respect of Treaties' in DB Hollis (ed), *The Oxford Guide to Treaties* (2nd edn, Oxford University Press 2020) 407.
35　Ibid.
36　J Odermatt (n 1) 60.

Summary and Outlook

In the past, lyrical approximations of a Member State's withdrawal from the European Union have referred readers to a famous song by the American band *The Eagles*.[1] Brexit has demonstrated that the EU is, in fact, not a 'Hotel California': you can check out anytime you like and you can really leave.[2] Since January 31, 2020, the UK is no longer a Member State of the EU. While the process of leaving was certainly not completed at that date, the EU and the UK have undergone a thorough and often painful disintegration. From a legal perspective, withdrawal from the EU has rightly been described as a disentangling of legal orders.[3] Brexit profoundly affected the legal order of the EU, the UK, and the remaining Member States, all of which for decades had primarily known but one direction: further integration.

In addition, Brexit demonstrated that withdrawal from the EU also concerns the *international* legal order. With a Member State leaving the EU's legal order, international law not only (re)gains relevance in the future relations between that state and the EU and its remaining Member States. International law also plays a role in the immediate withdrawal situation. Brexit raised the question of the effect of a withdrawal from the EU on

---

1 RA Wessel, 'You Can Check out Any Time You like, but Can You Really Leave?' (2016) 13(2) *International Organizations Law Review* 197 with reference to the song 'Hotel California' (*The Eagles*, 1976). Friel employs the same notion when referring to the EU as the 'archetypal cockroach motel: a motel where you can check in, but not check out.' (see RJ Friel, 'Secession from the European Union: Checking Out of the Proverbial "Cockroach Motel"' (2003) 27(2) *Fordham International Law Journal* 590, 590).

2 In the first footnote of his editorial, Wessel also quotes the final verse of the song. With debates in the UK on the future relationship with the EU having increased in the last months, the verse may have gained some prophetic weight: 'Last thing I remember, I was running for the door / I had to find the passage back to the place I was before / Relax, said the night man / We are programmed to receive / You can check out any time you like / But you can never leave.'

3 See eg J Odermatt, 'Brexit and International Law: Disentangling Legal Orders' (2017) 31 *Emory International Law Review Recent Developments* 1051; T Fajardo, 'Disentangling the UK from EU Environmental Agreements after Brexit: The Challenges Posed by Mixed Agreements and Soft Law' in J Santos Vara, RA Wessel and PR Polak (eds), *The Routledge Handbook on the International Dimension of Brexit* (Routledge 2020).

Summary and Outlook

international agreements concluded by the EU and its Member States in the context of their EU membership. Unlike many other withdrawal issues, this dimension of the UK's exit not only concerned the EU, the UK, and its Member States. It also affected over 150 non-EU states with which the EU and its Member States are connected through a network of international agreements covering an abundance of subject matters, ranging from development to trade, from environmental protection to transport.

Despite its relevance to actors within and outside the EU, the issue of withdrawal from the EU and its impact on international agreements had not received any (scholarly) attention before the UK's EU referendum. This gradually changed with the start of the Brexit negotiations. However, upon their completion, scholars did not engage in a thorough critical assessment of the vast amount of withdrawal-related treaty practice, despite the differences between this practice and the outcome they had predicted. This study closed this gap in two respects: first, by describing how the EU, the UK, and non-EU states addressed the effect of Brexit on their international agreements and, secondly, by evaluating this practice against the background of international law.

The Practice

From an EU perspective, international agreements concluded by the Union or its Member States in the context of their EU membership can be divided into three categories: EU-only, mixed, and *inter se* agreements. Their fate – respectively, the future of the UK's participation in these agreements – post-Brexit formed part of the EU-UK withdrawal negotiations. Both advocated an approach whereby EU-only agreements would cease to apply to the UK and the UK would cease to be a party to bilaterally structured mixed and *inter se* agreements. The UK's status as a party would remain unaffected only in multilateral mixed agreements. For all the international agreements thought to be negatively affected by Brexit, the EU and the UK aimed for transitional arrangements, *inter alia*, in the UK-EU Withdrawal Agreement. In general, these transitional arrangements consisted of a commitment by the UK to the EU to continue to fulfil its obligations under these agreements for a limited period of time.

This meant that the UK – where it had a continued interest in an EU-only, bilateral mixed, or *inter se* agreement – needed to (re)conclude the agreement through accession or an agreement with the respective treaty partner(s). The latter approach led to a practice of rollover agreements, where the UK and its treaty partners essentially copy-pasted international agreements of the EU (and its Member States) instead of (re)negotiating (new) agreements. The UK's accession to multilateral agreements and its (re)conclusion of bilateral agreements both show that many states worldwide at least accepted the UK's position that legal steps were necessary to preserve their treaty relations – regardless of whether the UK had been a party to an agreement itself pre-Brexit or the agreements had applied to it merely through EU law.

Irrespective of any legal assessment, this practice is relevant for European external relations and international law. For the EU, Brexit has set a precedent. The EU's treaty practice is characterised by a high degree of consistency. Ever since the first enlargement round in 1972, the EU has tackled the opposite question – the effect of *accession* to the EU on international agreements – in the same manner. Judging from this, it will presumably show the same uniformity in addressing the impact of *withdrawal* from the EU on international agreements should future exits occur. From an international law perspective, the way the treaty parties handled their international agreements in the wake of Brexit represents (state) practice, an element essential in shaping the international legal order. How it does so – in a rule-creating or rule-confirming, or even a rule-modifying or -contesting manner – depends on the legal evaluation of the practice.

The Legal Evaluation

The EU-only, mixed and *inter se* agreements being *international* agreements, the rules applicable to them and by which, accordingly, the effect of an EU withdrawal must be judged are those of *international* law. For an international lawyer, while acknowledging EU specificities, the most natural view of the Union is that of an international organisation. Accordingly, the exit of a Member State constitutes the withdrawal from a multilateral agreement, the organisation's founding treaty. Most scholarly contributions engaging with the effect of withdrawal from the EU on international agreements reflect this. While this approach may be legally correct, international institutional and treaty law applicable to the withdrawal from an international organisation cannot explain the *actual* treaty practice surrounding Brexit.

First, terminating a state's membership in an international organisation generally has no automatic consequences for international agreements concluded by the organisation or the withdrawing member state in the context of its membership. Art. 70 *Vienna Convention on the Law of Treaties* (VCLT), stipulating the consequences of treaty denunciation, does not provide for any effects of the withdrawal from *one* international agreement – here, the EU Treaties – on *other* international agreements. In contrast, Art. 70(1)(b) VCLT and customary principles such as *res inter alios acta* protect any legal situation created outside the denounced treaty – such as another international agreement.

Secondly, the EU, its Member States, and their treaty partners did not *explicitly* provide for the effect of EU withdrawal on their international agreements. As Art. 70 VCLT acknowledges, it lies in the autonomy of the treaty parties to deviate from the default consequences of treaty termination. Thus, all parties to an international agreement can agree that membership in one agreement should necessarily be linked to membership in another agreement. In practice, withdrawal from an international organisation quite regularly entails the termination of membership in other international agreements, either because the organisation's founding treaty or the other international agreements so provides. A prominent recent example is Russia's exclusion, respectively withdrawal, from the Council of Europe, which effected the termination of its membership in the European Convention on Human Rights.[4] However, the EU Treaties, as well as the EU-only, mixed, and *inter se* agreements are silent on the issue of withdrawal. Although the UK-EU Withdrawal Agreement addresses the effect of Brexit on international agreements, it is not an agreement between *all* parties.

Thirdly, neither the mixed nor *inter se* agreements contain an *implicit* resolutory condition terminating a Member State's party status upon EU withdrawal. Especially bilateral mixed, but also some *inter se* agreements contain provisions – such as the definition of the parties or the territorial scope of application – establishing a close connection between the Member States' participation in these agreements and their EU membership. Loss of EU membership thus changes the circumstances of these agreements and may affect their continued performance by the withdrawing state. However, as Art. 62 VCLT shows, this does not entail automatic consequences but, under narrow conditions, an invokable denunciation right.

---

4 Art. 58 ECHR provides: 'Any High Contracting Party which shall cease to be a member of the Council of Europe shall cease to be a Party to this Convention under the same conditions.' On Russia, see CoE, 'The Russian Federation is excluded from the Council of Europe' (*Press Release*, 16.03.2022) <https://www.coe.int/en/web/portal/-/the-russian-federation-is-excluded-from-the-council-of-europe> and, subsequently, CoE, 'Russia ceases to be party to the European Convention on Human Rights' (*Press Release*, 16.09.2022) <https://www.coe.int/en/web/portal/-/russia-ceases-to-be-party-to-the-european-convention-on-human-rights>.

Finally, reference to a fundamental change of circumstances as per Art. 62 VCLT cannot justify the automatic termination of all bilateral mixed and *inter se* agreements for the UK. Art. 62 VCLT only provides a subsidiary right of denunciation if an international agreement does not itself include a termination provision. However, many bilateral mixed and *inter se* agreements provide a right of and procedure for denunciation. Moreover, the exceptional nature of Art. 62 VCLT, manifested in its narrow conditions, requires a case-by-case analysis. Pointing to the structure of an agreement – as bilateral mixed or *inter se* – does not suffice. Moreover, neither the UK nor any other treaty party indeed invoked Art. 62 VCLT.

Correct from the perspective of international treaty law is thus the EU and the UK's statement that the EU-only agreements cease to apply to the UK. During its EU membership, these agreements bound the UK only via Art. 216 TFEU and, thus, as a matter of EU law. However, treaty law as applied in the context of withdrawal from an international organisation offers no legal explanation why a Member State – as suggested in the case of Brexit – should lose its status as a party under international law in bilateral mixed and *inter se* agreements. A withdrawing Member State remains a party to these agreements unless it actively denounces them.

Against this background, Brexit practice could be seen as contesting – if not violating – the rules of international law applicable to the withdrawal from an international organisation and to international agreements concluded within their framework. However, besides not being able to explain the Brexit practice, the comparison between exiting the EU and prior withdrawals from international organisations can, in many respects, also be questioned for its adequacy. Both the EU itself and its treaty-making practice have earned the attribute 'state-like'. Where states undergo a disintegration process, the VCLT's rules are expressly *not* applicable. Instead, the effect of a territorial change on a state's international agreements is regulated by the rules contained in the *Vienna Convention on Succession in Respect of Treaties* (VCSSRT) or their customary equivalents.

Few authors have hinted at the possibility of applying the law of succession as an alternative legal framework to EU accession or withdrawal. It has never been examined in depth. This may be because of the apparent hurdle to applying the law of *state* succession: the EU not being a state. However, it is possible to compare the EU to unions of states, themselves formed through a uniting of previously independent states, and to whom the rules of succession apply. Where two subjects share similarities, drawing an analogy is a method commonly employed in legal reasoning and previously

Summary and Outlook

utilised in international jurisprudence and practice. Transferring the rules applicable to a separation of states to an exit from the EU is not only legally possible; it also offers a convincing alternative explanation for the Brexit practice.

Firstly, the law of state succession in respect of treaties inherently offers a better starting point than the law of treaties to capture the effects of a Member State withdrawing from the EU. International treaty law has been described as a 'flat earth', often inadequate for dealing with layered subjects.[5] In contrast, the law of state succession in respect of treaties is capable of dealing with composite international actors. The practice on the formation and separation of unions of states as composite – or layered – actors heavily shaped and continues to influence the rules and principles of succession to international agreements.

Secondly, the most significant dissimilarity between unions of states and the EU – the latter's lack of statehood – does not hurt the analogical application of the rules on succession to unions to withdrawal from the EU. For the law of *state* succession, the exact locus of sovereignty and, accordingly, the statehood of a composite actor is not as relevant as its title may suggest. This concerns the determination that succession has taken place and the law applicable to it. Regarding the first, neither the VCSSRT nor customary international law still defines the *fact* of succession as narrowly as a change of sovereignty. Instead, the definition is now broader, specifically to avoid controversies on the precise locus of sovereignty. As regards the applicable law, a closer look at those unions whose separations provided the underlying state practice shows that their statehood was often far from settled. Thus, the rules and principles on succession in respect of international agreements applicable in cases of separation stem from composite actors, which, in fact, may not have been states themselves.

Thirdly, the principles that guide state practice in cases of separation from a union of states are just as relevant in the case of EU withdrawal. The VCSSRT and its article on separation, in particular, do not enjoy broad acceptance. Moreover, so far, no customary international law on the effect of separation on international agreements has emerged. However, from the VCSSRT's drafting history and state practice, two guiding, yet contradictory principles can be identified: the principle of treaty stability and of consent. On the one hand, no state should be able to escape treaty

---

[5] See CM Brölmann, 'A Flat Earth?: International Organizations in the System of International Law' (2001) 70 *Nordic Journal of International Law* 319.

obligations, whether by joining or leaving a union. This is especially the case where the separating state has participated in the treaty-making of the union. There is no justification for why the same rationale should not apply to the EU. The Member States' participation in the EU's treaty-making is not only formalised in Art. 218 TFEU, but regularly even takes the shape of co-conclusions. On the other hand, no state should be bound by international obligations it has not consented to, especially where the agreement puts great weight on the identity of the treaty parties. Especially in bilateral agreements, the presumption is that treaty parties tailored their agreement to the union's specific size, population, political and economic powers. The same applies to the EU's bilateral external relations. Whether EU-only or mixed agreement, the interest and consent of the EU's treaty partners pertain to the size, population, and economy of the EU as a whole, not to an individual former Member State.

Finally, applying the principles of treaty stability and consent to the situation of EU withdrawal explains the actual Brexit practice. In state practice, the principles of treaty stability and consent are balanced. Separation of parts of a union neither leads to an automatic continuity of all international agreements for the successor state nor to a completely clean slate. Evidence for this is the successor states' mixed practice of succession notifications, accessions, exchanges of notes, and (re)negotiations. Similarly, the UK post-Brexit practice cannot be assigned to one approach – continuity or clean slate – but must be understood as a mixture of the two underlying principles. The UK continued multilateral mixed agreements, which are characterised by a high degree of participation and a lower relevance of treaty partner identity; it did not continue those international agreements characterised either by a low degree of prior participation – as in EU-only agreements – or a high relevance of the treaty partner identity – as in bilateral mixed agreements.

Viewed from the perspective of the law of succession, the Brexit practice of the UK and its treaty partners can fulfil two functions. It can be regarded as state practice that lays the foundation for the emergence of a law of treaty succession upon withdrawal from an 'international organisation […] exercising State functions'[6]. Alternatively, Brexit practice could be considered as confirming an already emerging rule on succession: namely, for separations from unions of states.

---

6 P Reuter, *Introduction to The Law of Treaties* (2nd edn, Kegan Paul International 1995) 114.

Summary and Outlook

Outlook

At the time of writing this study, no concrete next exit from the EU is in sight. Still, every once in a while, a new disintegration scenario flickers on the horizon. Some of them are only partly comparable to Brexit. Like the UK's exit, the separation of a part of a Member State's territory – such as, for example, Catalonia from Spain – would result in a decrease in the EU's territory. This, too, would raise questions about the effect on international agreements concluded by the EU and its Member States. Catalonia – in contrast to the UK – not having been a state before separation, its EU exit would, however, most likely entail different legal consequences and a different practice. However, time and again, discussions concerning the possible exit of another Member State from the EU surface – be it talks of a 'Polexit', triggered by a rule of law crisis in Poland, or of a 'Dexit', as prompted by the *Alternative for Germany*'s party manifesto for the 2024 EU parliamentary elections. None of these possibilities seems very likely, let alone imminent. Nevertheless, the EU and its treaty partners would be well advised to prepare for them.

It is highly possible that the EU and its Member States – should another withdrawal take place – would simply repeat the Brexit practice. This time, they would even have the advantage of being able to refer their treaty partners to their previous acceptance of this practice. At the same time, given the legal evaluation of this practice, a simple repetition would risk again placing EU withdrawal in a grey area: caught somewhere between disrespecting the law of treaties and advancing a law of – possibly EU-specific – succession. To avoid this, there are two possible ways of moving forward.

One possibility is for the EU, its Member States, and its treaty partners to provide for the consequences of an EU withdrawal in their international agreements. Just as a growing number of bilateral mixed agreements include provisions on an automatic accession of a new EU Member State, the treaty parties could also agree on an automatic withdrawal in the case of an EU exit. The same holds true for Member States' *inter se* agreements. Conversely, this would mean accepting that a withdrawing Member State remains a party to those international agreements that are silent on the issue. By opting for this approach, the EU would return to the fold of international institutional and treaty law, where either the treaty parties by means of their contractual autonomy accommodate the unique features of an international organisation, or the relationship between the organisation and its member states constitutes a *res inter alios acta* for their treaty partners.

However, so far, there is no indication of a change in the EU's treaty practice. International agreements concluded or even negotiated after Brexit still do not address the issue of EU withdrawal.[7] Should this continue to be the case, the second alternative – for which this study laid the groundwork – gains (even more) importance: assessing EU withdrawal from the viewpoint of the law of succession in respect of international agreements.

In the past, the law of state succession played a role 'in the reproduction of the political transformation in Europe and in the management of the diplomatic problems that [...] ensued'[8]. It 'provided a conceptual matrix by which one could reproduce in legal terms and in regard to legal relationships the ideas of transformation, collapse and renewal'[9]. While this assessment refers to the creation of new states following the breakup of Czechoslovakia, the Soviet Union and Yugoslavia, another 'transformation of Europe'[10] did not result in statehood[11]: the EU is not a state and, consequently, Brexit is not a case of *state* succession. Nonetheless, recourse to the law of state succession can help 'reproduce in legal terms'[12] the consequences of this disintegration for 'legal relationships'[13], particularly international agreements. Crucially, placing EU withdrawal in the context of succession does not imply reopening Pandora's box of discussing the nature of the EU and its legal order. The EU does not need to be a state to apply rules of succession in respect of international agreements to a Member State's withdrawal. Drawing an analogy between the EU and unions of states makes their application possible. Moreover, the recent developments

---

7 See eg Framework Agreement between the European Union and its Member States, of the one part, and Australia, of the other part (3 October 2022) OJ L255/3; Framework Agreement on Comprehensive Partnership and Cooperation between the European Union and its Member States, of the one part, and the Kingdom of Thailand, of the other part (23 December 2022) OJ L330/72.
8 M Koskenniemi, 'Report of the Director of Studies of the English-speaking Section of the Centre' in PM Eisemann and M Koskenniemi (eds), *State Succession: Codification Tested Against the Facts* (Martinus Nijhoff Publishers 2000) 66.
9 Ibid.
10 JH Weiler, 'The Transformation of Europe' (1991) 100(8) *The Yale Law Journal* 2403.
11 See also JH Weiler, 'Europe: The Case Against the Case for Statehood' (1998) 4(1) *European Law Journal* 43.
12 Koskenniemi (n 8) 66.
13 Ibid.

Summary and Outlook

in the EU's treaty practice *and* the law of succession also make such an application necessary.

The EU has developed into a global actor. This goes hand in hand with a continuous expansion of its treaty-making – geographically, quantitatively, and qualitatively. The EU concludes international agreements that, because of their nature or their subject matter, have traditionally been conceived of as falling within the domain of states. The dynamic increase in the EU's competences has not only made this possible; it has also made it necessary. The more competences Member States transfer to the EU, the more important it becomes to integrate the Union into multilateral treaty fora. This strengthens a rules-based international community: the EU cannot act state-like but not be subject to the same 'working capital of international jural relationships'[14]. Additionally, the EU's expanding treaty practice promotes and enhances the rights of individuals, be it in the form of investment or human rights protection.

At the same time, this development raises a question that is also increasingly posed in the context of the law of state succession: how to minimise the effects of 'transformation, collapse and renewal'[15] on international agreements particularly worthy of protection? With state practice on successions in respect of international agreements in the last decades favouring a clean slate, scholarly contributions seek to achieve *de jure* continuity to those agreements indispensable for 'State social life'[16] and the protection of the individual. The more the law of state succession evolves in this direction and the more the EU concludes such international agreements, the less possible and reasonable it becomes to consider one without the other.

When drafting the VCSSRT, the International Law Commission predicted the proliferation of new economic unions. As Ustor stated, the 'Commission was legislating for the future' with 'the growing need to allow for unions of states' already visible in a 'general trend towards integration throughout the world'[17]. The Commission was right in its general assessment: today, the EU has become synonymous with this trend and a model for deeper regional integration. However, the Commission did not act on

---

14 RY Jennings, *General Course on Principles of International Law* (Martinus Nijhoff Publishers 1967) 442–443.
15 Koskenniemi (n 8) 66.
16 G Hafner and G Novak, 'State Succession in Respect of Treaties' in DB Hollis (ed), *The Oxford Guide to Treaties* (2nd edn, Oxford University Press 2020) 407.
17 ILC, 'Summary records of the Twenty-Fourth Session 2 May-7 July 1972' UN Doc. A/CN.4/Ser.A/1972, YBILC (1972) Vol. I 166.

its prediction: it limited its draft to states and excluded hybrid unions, such as the EU, from the scope of the law of succession. The UK's withdrawal from the EU illustrates why this was wrong – and provides the opportunity to righten that wrong.

References

Literature

Ackrén Maria and Jakobsen Uffe, 'Greenland as a Self-Governing Sub-National Territory in International Relations: Past, Current and Future Perspectives' (2015) 51(4) Polar Record 404–412.

Acquaviva Guido and Pocar Fausto, 'Stare decisis' in Rüdiger Wolfrum (ed), *The Max Planck Encyclopedia of Public International Law* (Oxford University Press 2012).

Allen Nicholas, 'Brexit Means Brexit: Theresa May and post-referendum British Politics' (2018) 13 British Politics 105–120.

Allot Philip, 'Adherence to and Withdrawal from Mixed Agreements' in David O'Keeffe and Henry G Schermers (eds), *Mixed Agreements* (Kluwer 1983) 97–121.

Armstrong Kenneth A, *Brexit Time: Leaving the EU – Why, How and When?* (Cambridge University Press 2017).

Ascensio Hervé, 'Article 70: Consequences of the Termination of a Treaty' in Olivier Corten and Pierre Klein (eds), *The Vienna Conventions on the Law of Treaties* (vol II, Oxford University Press 2011).

Aust Anthony, *Modern Treaty Law and Practice* (2nd edn, Cambridge University Press 2007).

Azaria Danae, 'The Working Methods of the International Law Commission: Adherence to Methodology, Commentaries and Decision-Making' in United Nations, *Seventy Years of the International Law Commission: Drawing a Balance for the Future* (Brill Nijhoff 2021) 172–197.

Bartels Lorand, 'The UK's Status in the WTO Post-Brexit' in Robert Schütze and Stephen Tierney (eds), *The United Kingdom and the Federal Idea* (Hart Publishing 2018) 227–249.

Beaud Olivier, 'La notion de pacte fédératif: Contribution à une théorie constitutionnelle de la Fédération' in Jean-François Kervégan and Heinz Mohnhaupt (eds), *Gesellschaftliche Freiheit und vertragliche Bindung in Rechtsgeschichte und Philosophie* (Klostermann 1999).

Bernhardt Rudolf, 'International Organizations: Internal Law and Rules' in Rudolf Bernhardt (ed), *International Organizations in General: Universal International Organizations and Cooperation* (Elsevier Science Publishers 1983) 142–145.

Bernier Ivan, *International Legal Aspects of Federalism* (Longman 1973).

Binder Christina and Hofbauer Jane A, 'The Perception of the EU Legal Order in International Law: An In- and Outside View' in Marc Bungenberg and others (eds), *European Yearbook of International Economic Law 2017* (Springer 2017) 139–202.

Bleckmann Albert, 'Analogie im Völkerrecht' (1977) 17(2) Archiv des Völkerrechts 161–180.

References

–, 'The Mixed Agreements of the EEC in Public International Law' in David O'Keeffe and Henry G Schermers (eds), *Mixed Agreements* (Kluwer 1983) 155–165.

Bordin Fernando Lusa, *The Analogy between States and International Organizations* (Cambridge University Press 2019).

Brewer Scott, 'Exemplary Reasoning: Semantics, Pragmatics, and the Rational Force of Legal Argument by Analogy' (1996) 109(5) Harvard Law Review 923–1028.

–, 'Indefeasible Analogical Argument' in Hendrik Kaptein and Bastiaan David van der Velden (eds), *Analogy and Exemplary Reasoning in Legal Discourse* (Amsterdam University Press 2018) 33–48.

Brölmann Catherine M and others, 'Exiting International Organizations: A Brief Introduction' (2018) 15(2) International Organizations Law Review 243–263.

Brölmann Catherine M, *The Institutional Veil in Public International Law: International Organisations and the Law of Treaties* (Hart Publishing 2007).

–, 'A Flat Earth?: International Organizations in the System of International Law' (2001) 70 Nordic Journal of International Law 319–340.

–, 'Brexit en bestaande verdragsverplichtingen' (2017) 95(25) Nederlands Juristenblad 1748–1750.

–, 'The 1986 Vienna Convention on the Law of Treaties: The History of Draft Article 36*bis*' in Jan Klabbers and René Lefeber (eds), *Essays on the Law of Treaties: A Collection of Essays in Honour of Bert Vierdag* (Brill Nijhoff 1998) 121–140.

Brownlie Ian, 'The Calling of the International Lawyer: Sir Humphrey Waldock and His Work' (1984) 54(7) British Yearbook of International Law 7–74.

Bühler Konrad, 'State Succession, Identity/ Continuity and Membership in the United Nations' in Pierre Michel Eisemann and Martti Koskenniemi (eds), *State Succession: Codification Tested Against the Facts* (Martinus Nijhoff Publishers 2000).

Burgess Michael, *Federalism and European Union: The Building of Europe, 1950–2000* (Routledge 2000).

Busse Christian, *Die völkerrechtliche Einordnung der Europäischen Union* (C Heymanns 1999).

Calliess Christian, 'Article 1 TEU' in Christian Calliess and Matthias Ruffert (eds), *EUV/AEUV: Das Verfassungsrecht der Europäischen Union mit Europäischer Grundrechtecharta* (6th edn, CH Beck 2022).

Casteleiro Andrés Delgado, 'EU Declarations of Competence to Multilateral Agreements: A Useful Reference Base?' (2012) 17(4) European Foreign Affairs Review 491–509.

Chestermann Simon, 'Rule of Law' in Rüdiger Wolfrum (ed), *The Max Planck Encyclopedia of Public International Law* (Oxford University Press 2012).

Christiansen Thomas and Reh Christine, *Constitutionalizing the European Union* (Bloomsbury Publishing 2017).

Comella Victor F, 'Does Brexit Normalize Secession' (2018) 53(2) Texas International Law Journal 139–152.

Cotran Eugene, 'Some Legal Aspects of the Formation of the United Arab Republic and the United Arab States' (1959) 8(2) International & Comparative Law Quarterly 346–390.

Craven Matthew C R, *The Decolonization of International Law: State Succession and the Law of Treaties* (Oxford University Press 2007).

–, 'The European Community Arbitration Commission on Yugoslavia' (1996) 66(1) British Yearbook of International Law 333–413.

Crawford James, 'State' in Rüdiger Wolfrum (ed), *The Max Planck Encyclopedia of Public International Law* (Oxford University Press 2012).

–, 'The Contribution of Professor DP O'Connell to the Discipline of International Law' (1980) 51(1) British Yearbook of International Law 1–87.

–, 'The Current Political Discourse Concerning International Law' (2018) 81(1) The Modern Law Review 1–22.

–, *Creation of States in International Law* (2nd edn, Oxford University Press 2007).

Cremona Marise, 'External Relations of the European Union: The Constitutional Framework for International Action' in Paul Craig and Grainne de Búrca (eds), *The Evolution of EU Law* (3rd edn, Oxford University Press 2021) 431–479.

–, 'The Withdrawal Agreement and the EU's International Agreements' (2020) 45(2) European Law Review 237–250.

De Witte Bruno, 'EU Law: Is it International Law?' in Catherine Barnard and Steve Peers (eds), *European Union Law* (3rd edn, Oxford University Press 2020) 177–197.

–, 'The European Union as an International Legal Experiment' in Grainne de Búrca and Joseph H Weiler (eds), *The Worlds of European Constitutionalism* (Cambridge University Press 2012) 19–56.

Denza Eileen, *The Intergovernmental Pillars of the European Union* (Oxford University Press 2005).

Devaney James Gerard, 'Making Sense of Transcendental Nonsense: A Functional Reframing of the Law of State Succession' (2022) 14 GCILS Working Paper Series.

–, 'The Role of Precedent in the Jurisprudence of the International Court of Justice: A Constructive Interpretation' (2022) 35(3) Leiden Journal of International Law 641–659.

Donoghue Joan E, 'The Role of the World Court Today' (2012) 47(1) Georgia Law Review 181–202.

Dorau Christoph, *Die Verfassungsfrage der Europäischen Union: Möglichkeiten und Grenzen der europäischen Verfassungsentwicklung nach Nizza* (Nomos 2001).

Dörr Oliver, 'Article 47 TEU' in Eberhard Grabitz, Meinhard Hilf and Martin Nettesheim (eds), *Das Recht der Europäischen Union* (82nd supplement, CH Beck 2024).

–, 'Article 50 TEU' in Eberhard Grabitz, Meinhard Hilf and Martin Nettesheim (eds), *Das Recht der Europäischen Union* (82nd supplement, CH Beck 2024).

Dougan Michael, *The UK's Withdrawal from the EU: A Legal Analysis* (Oxford University Press 2021).

References

Douma Wybe, 'Come Fly With Me?: Brexit and Air Transport' in Juan Santos Vara, Ramses A Wessel and Polly Ruth Polak (eds), *The Routledge Handbook on the International Dimension of Brexit* (Routledge 2020) 90–103.

Dumberry Patrick, 'An Uncharted Question of State Succession: Are New States Automatically Bound by the BITs Concluded by Predecessor States Before Independence?' (2015) 6(1) Journal of International Dispute Settlement 74–96.

–, 'State Succession to Bilateral Treaties: A Few Observations on the Incoherent and Unjustifiable Solution Adopted for Secession and Dissolution of States under the 1978 Vienna Convention' (2015) 28(1) Leiden Journal of International Law 13–30.

–, 'State Succession to BITs: Analysis of Case Law in the Context of Dissolution and Secession' (2018) 34(3) Arbitration International 445–462.

Eckes Christina and Wessel Ramses A, 'An International Perspective' in Robert Schütze and Takis Tridimas (eds), *The Oxford Principles of European Union Law: The European Union Legal Order* (Oxford University Press 2018) 74–102.

Eeckhout Piet, *External Relations of the European Union: Legal and Constitutional Foundations* (Oxford University Press 2004).

Ehlermann Claus-Dieter, 'Mixed Agreements: A List of Problems' in David O'Keeffe and Henry G Schermers (eds), *Mixed Agreements* (Kluwer 1983) 3–21.

el-Khoury Naiade, 'Human Rights Treaties and the Law of State Succession in the Event of Secession' in Erika de Wet and Kathrin Maria Scherr (eds), *Max Planck Yearbook of United Nations Law Online* (Brill Nijhoff 2020).

Epping Volker, 'Die Europäische Union: Noch international Organisation oder schon Staat?: Zur Vision der Vereinigten Staaten von Europa' in Christoph Brüning and Joachim Suerbaum (eds), *Die Vermessung der Staatlichkeit: Europäische Union – Bund – Länder – Gemeinden. Symposium zu Ehren von Rolf Grawert anlässlich seines 75. Geburtstages* (Duncker & Humblot 2013) 13–28.

Ermacora Felix, 'Confederations and Other Unions of States' in Rudolf Bernhardt (ed), *Encyclopedia of Disputes Installment* (Elsevier Science Publishers 1987) 60–65.

Everling Ulrich, 'Sind die Mitgliedstaaten der Europäischen Gemeinschaft noch Herren der Verträge?: Zum Verhältnis von Europäischem Gemeinschaftsrecht und Völkerrecht' in Rudolf Bernhardt and others (eds), *Völkerrecht als Rechtsordnung, Internationale Gerichtsbarkeit, Menschenrechte: Festschrift für Hermann Mosler* (Springer 1983) 173–191.

Fahey Elaine and Mancini Isabella, 'Introduction: Understanding the EU as a Good Global Actor: Whose Metrics?' in Elaine Fahey and Isabella Mancini (eds), *Understanding the EU as a Good Global Actor: Ambitions, Values and Metrics* (Edward Elgar Publishing 2022) 1–17.

Fajardo Teresa, 'Disentangling the UK from EU Environmental Agreements after Brexit: The Challenges Posed by Mixed Agreements and Soft Law' in Juan Santos Vara, Ramses A Wessel and Polly Ruth Polak (eds), *The Routledge Handbook on the International Dimension of Brexit* (Routledge 2020) 270–283.

Fastenrath Ulrich, *Lücken im Völkerrecht: Zu Rechtscharakter, Quellen, Systemzusammenhang, Methodenlehre und Funktionen des Völkerrechts* (Duncker & Humblot 1991).

Feist Christian, *Kündigung, Rücktritt und Suspendierung von multilateralen Verträgen* (Duncker & Humblot 2001).

Forsyth Murray, *Unions of States: The Theory and Practice of Confederation* (Leicester University Press 1981).

Fressynet Isabel, 'The Legal Impact of Brexit on the Comprehensive Economic Trade Agreement (CETA) Between the European Union and Canada' in Jennifer A Hillman and Gary N Horlick (eds), *Legal Aspects of Brexit: Implications of the United Kingdom's decision to withdraw from the European Union* (Georgetown Law 2017) 69-78.

Friel Raymond J, 'Providing a Constitutional Framework for Withdrawal from the EU: Article 59 of the Draft European Constitution' (2004) 53(2) International & Comparative Law Quarterly 407-428.

–, 'Secession from the European Union: Checking Out of the Proverbial "Cockroach Motel"' (2003) 27(2) Fordham International Law Journal 590-641.

Gareis Sven Bernhard, Hauser Gunther and Kernic Franz, *The European Union – A Global Actor?* (Verlag Barbara Budrich 2012).

Gatti Mauro, 'Art. 50 TEU: A Well-Designed Secession Clause' (2017) 2(1) European Papers – A Journal on Law and Integration 159-181.

Geiger Rudolf and Kirchmair Lando, 'Article 1 TEU' in Rudolf Geiger, Daniel-Erasmus Khan, Markus Kotzur and Lando Kirchmair (eds), *EUV/AEUV: Vertrag über die Europäische Union und Vertrag über die Arbeitsweise der Europäischen Union* (7th edn, CH Beck 2023).

Giegerich Thomas, 'Article 61' in Oliver Dörr and Kirsten Schmalenbach (eds), *Vienna Convention on the Law of Treaties: A Commentary* (2nd edn, Springer 2018).

–, 'Article 62' in Oliver Dörr and Kirsten Schmalenbach (eds), *Vienna Convention on the Law of Treaties: A Commentary* (2nd edn, Springer 2018).

Golding Martin, 'Argument by Analogy in the Law' in Hendrik Kaptein and Bastiaan David van der Velden (eds), *Analogy and Exemplary Reasoning in Legal Discourse* (Amsterdam University Press 2018) 123-136.

Götting-Biwer Friedemann, *Die Beendigung der Mitgliedschaft in der Europäischen Union* (Nomos 2000).

Gradoni Lorenzo, 'Article 2' in Giovanni Distefano, Gloria Gaggioli and Aymeric Hêche (eds), *La Convention de Vienne de 1978 sur la Succession d'États en Matière de Traités: Commentaire Article par Article et Études Thématiques* (Bruylant 2016).

Grawert Rolf, 'Staatsvolk und Staatsangehörigkeit' in Josef Isensee and Paul Kirchhof (eds), *Handbuch des Staatsrechts der Bundesrepublik Deutschland* (3rd edn, CF Müller 2004).

Gruber Joachim, 'Europäische Schulen: Ein in die EG integriertes Völkerrechtssubjekt' (2005) 65 Zeitschrift für ausländisches öffentliches Recht und Völkerrecht 1015-1032.

Hafner Gerhard and Novak Gregor, 'State Succession in Respect of Treaties' in Duncan B Hollis (ed), *The Oxford Guide to Treaties* (2nd edn, Oxford University Press 2020) 396-427.

Hall William Edward, *A Treatise on International Law* (8th edn, Clarendon Press 1924).

References

Hallstein Walter, *Der unvollendete Bundesstaat: Europäische Erfahrungen und Erkenntnisse* (Econ-Verlag 1969).

Harbo Florentina, 'Secession Right – An Anti-Federal Principle?: Comparative Study of Federal States and the EU' (2008) 1(3) Journal of Politics and Law 132–148.

Harhoff Frederik, 'Greenland's Withdrawal from the European Communities' (1983) 20(1) Common Market Law Review 13–33.

Hay Peter, *Federalism and Supranational Organizations: Patterns for New Legal Structures* (Illinois University Press 1966).

Heesen Julia, *Interne Abkommen: Völkerrechtliche Verträge zwischen den Mitgliedstaaten der Europäischen Union* (Springer 2015).

Heintschel von Heinegg Wolff, 'Treaties, Fundamental Change of Circumstances' in Rüdiger Wolfrum (ed), *The Max Planck Encyclopedia of Public International Law* (Oxford University Press 2012).

Helfer Laurence R, 'Exiting Treaties' (2005) 91(7) Virginia Law Review 1579–1648.

–, 'Part VI Avoiding or Exiting Treaty Commitments: Terminating Treaties' in Duncan B Hollis (ed), *The Oxford Guide to Treaties* (2nd edn, Oxford University Press 2020) 624–640.

Heliskoski Joni and Kübek Gesa, 'A Typology of EU Mixed Agreements Revisited' in Nicolas Levrat and others (eds), *The EU and its Member States' Joint Participation in International Agreements* (Hart Publishing 2021) 23–42.

Heliskoski Joni, 'EU Declarations of Competence and International Responsibility' in Malcolm D Evans and Panos Koutrakos (eds), *The International Responsibility of the European Union: European and International Perspectives* (Hart Publishing 2013) 189–212.

–, *Mixed Agreements as a Technique for Organizing the International Relations of the European Community and its Member States* (Kluwer Law International 2001).

Herbst Jochen, 'Observations on the Right to Withdraw from the European Union: Who are the "Masters of the Treaties"?' (2005) 6(11) German Law Journal 1755–1759.

Herrmann Christoph, 'Brexit, WTO und EU-Handelspolitik' (2017) 24 Europäische Zeitschrift für Wirtschaftsrecht 961–967.

Hillion Christophe, 'Accession and Withdrawal in the Law of the European Union' in Anthony Arnull and Damian Chalmers (eds), *The Oxford Handbook of European Union Law* (Oxford University Press 2017) 126–152.

–, 'Withdrawal under Article 50 TEU: An Integration-Friendly Process' (2018) 55(Special Issue) Common Market Law Review 29–56.

Isiksel Turkuler, 'European Exceptionalism and the EU's Accession to the ECHR' (2016) 27(3) European Journal of International Law 565–589.

Jacqué Jean-Paul, *Droit institutionnel de l'Union Européenne* (4th edn, Editions Dalloz 2006).

Jaeger Thomas, 'Reset and Go: The Unitary Patent System post-Brexit' (2017) 3 International Review of Intellectual Property and Competition Law 254–285.

Janig Philipp, 'The 1978 Vienna Convention, the Clean Slate Doctrine and the Decolonization of Sources' (2018; published 2021) 23 Austrian Review of International and European Law 143–161.

Jellinek Georg, *Die Lehre von den Staatenverbindungen* (Alfred Hölder 1882).

Jennings Robert Yewdall, *General Course on Principles of International Law* (Martinus Nijhoff Publishers 1967).

Kaddous Christine and Touré Habib Badjinri, 'The Status of the United Kingdom Regarding EU Mixed Agreements after Brexit' in Nicolas Levrat and others (eds), *The EU and its Member States' Joint Participation in International Agreements* (Hart Publishing 2021) 271–285.

Kammerhofer Jörg, 'Uncertainty in the Formal Sources of International Law: Customary International Law and Some of Its Problems' (2004) 15(3) European Journal of International Law 523–553.

Kamminga Menno T, 'State Succession in Respect of Human Rights Treaties' (1996) 7(4) European Journal of International Law 469–484.

Kamto Maurice, 'The Working Methods of the International Law Commission' in United Nations, *Seventy Years of the International Law Commission: Drawing a Balance for the Future* (Brill Nijhoff 2021) 198–214.

Kant Immanuel, 'Perpetual Peace: A Philosophical Sketch' in Hans Siegbert Reiss (ed), *Kant: Political Writings* (2nd edn, Cambridge University Press 1991) 93–130.

Kaspiarovich Yuliya and Levrat Nicolas, 'European Union Mixed Agreements in International Law under the Stress of Brexit' (2021) 13(2) European Journal of Legal Studies 121–150.

Kaspiarovich Yuliya and Wessel Ramses A, 'Unmixing Mixed Agreements: Challenges and Solutions for Separating the EU and its Member States in Existing International Agreements' in Nicalos Levrat and others (eds), *The EU and its Member States' Joint Participation in International Agreements* (Hart Publishing 2021) 287–304.

Kaufmann Stefan, *Das Europäische Hochschulinstitut: Die Florentiner »Europa-Universität« im Gefüge des europäischen und internationalen Rechts* (Duncker & Humblot 2003).

Keith Kenneth J, 'Succession to Bilateral Treaties By Seceding States' (1967) 61(2) American Journal of International Law 521–548.

Kellerbauer Manuel and Klamert Marcus, 'Article 351 TFEU' in Manuel Kellerbauer, Marcus Klamert and Jonathan Tomkin (eds), *The EU Treaties and the Charter of Fundamental Rights: A Commentary* (Oxford University Press 2019).

Kent April, 'Brexit and the East African Community (EAC)-European Union Economic Partnership Agreement (EPA)' in Jennifer A Hillman and Gary N Horlick (eds), *Legal Aspects of Brexit: Implications of the United Kingdom's decision to withdraw from the European Union* (Georgetown Law 2017) 59–68.

Kim Jin Woo Jay, 'Is the United Kingdom Still a Party to the EU-Korea FTA after Brexit?' in Jennifer A Hillman and Gary N Horlick (eds), *Legal Aspects of Brexit: Implications of the United Kingdom's decision to withdraw from the European Union* (Georgetown Law 2017) 41–58.

References

Kiss Alexandre Charles, 'L'extinction des traités dans la pratique française' (1959) 5 Annuaire Français de Droit International 784–798.

Klabbers Jan and others (eds), *State Practice Regarding State Succession and Issues of Recognition* (Kluwer Law International 1999).

Klabbers Jan, 'Cat on a Hot Tin Roof: The World Court, State Succession, and the Gabcikovo-Nagymaros' (1998) 11(2) Leiden Journal of International Law 345–355.

–, 'The European Union in the Law of International Organizations: Misfit or Model?' in Ramses A Wessel and Jed Odermatt (eds), *Research Handbook on the European Union and International Organizations* (Edward Elgar Publishing 2019) 25–41.

–, *An Introduction to International Institutional Law* (2nd edn, Cambridge University Press 2009).

–, *International Law* (3rd edn, Cambridge University Press 2021).

–, *Treaty Conflict and the European Union* (Cambridge University Press 2010).

Kochenov Dimitry (ed), *EU Law of the Overseas: Outermost Regions, Associated Overseas Countries and Territories, Territories sui generis* (Kluwer Law International 2011).

Koskenniemi Martti, 'Report of the Director of Studies of the English-speaking Section of the Centre' in Pierre Michel Eisemann and Martti Koskenniemi (eds), *State Succession: Codification Tested Against the Facts* (Martinus Nijhoff Publishers 2000) 65–132.

Koutrakos Panos, 'International Agreements Concluded by Member States Prior to their EU Accession: Burgoa' in Graham Butler and Ramses A Wessel (eds), *EU External Relations Law: The Cases in Context* (Hart Publishing 2022) 133–143.

–, 'Managing Brexit: Trade Agreements Binding on the UK pursuant to its EU Membership' in Juan Santos Vara, Ramses A Wessel and Polly Ruth Polak (eds), *The Routledge Handbook on the International Dimension of Brexit* (Routledge 2020) 75–89.

–, 'Negotiating International Trade Treaties After Brexit' (2016) 41(4) European Law Review 475–478.

–, 'Three Narratives on the United Kingdom's Trade Agreements post-Brexit' in Adam Łazowski and Adam Jan Cygan (eds), *Research Handbook on Legal Aspects of Brexit* (Edward Elgar Publishing 2022) 403–421.

–, *EU International Relations Law* (Hart Publishing 2006).

Krämer Hans R, 'Greenland's European Community (EC)-Referendum: Background and Consequences' (1982) 25 German Yearbook of International Law 273–289.

Krieger Heike, 'Article 65' in Oliver Dörr and Kirsten Schmalenbach (eds), *Vienna Convention on the Law of Treaties: A Commentary* (2nd edn, Springer 2018).

Kuijper Pieter Jan and Paasivirta Esa, 'EU International Responsibility and its Attribution: From the Inside Looking Out' in Malcolm D Evans and Panos Koutrakos (eds), *The International Responsibility of the European Union: European and International Perspectives* (Hart Publishing 2013) 35–72.

Kuijper Pieter Jan, 'International Responsibility for EU Mixed Agreements' in Christophe Hillion and Panos Koutrakos (eds), *Mixed Agreements Revisited: The EU and its Member States in the World* (Hart Publishing 2010) 208–227.

–, 'The Community and State Succession in Respect of Treaties' in Deirdre Curtin and Ton Heukels (eds), *Institutional Dynamics of European Integration* (Martinus Nijhoff Publishers 1994) 619–640.

–, 'The European Courts and the Law of Treaties: The Continuing Story' in Enzo Cannizzaro (ed), *The Law of Treaties Beyond the Vienna Convention* (Oxford University Press 2011) 256–278.

Larik Joris, 'Instruments of EU External Action' in Ramses A Wessel and Joris Larik (eds), *EU External Relations Law: Text, Cases and Materials* (Bloomsbury Publishing 2020) 101–137.

Lauterpacht Hersch (ed), *Oppenheim's International Law: A Treatise* (vol 1, 8th edn, Longmans, Green and Co. Ltd. 1955).

Łazowski Adam and Wessel Ramses A, 'The External Dimension of Withdrawal from the European Union' (2016) 4 Revue des Affaires européennes 623–638.

Łazowski Adam, 'Copy-Pasting or Negotiating?: Post-Brexit Trade Agreements between the UK and non-EU Countries' in Juan Santos Vara, Ramses A Wessel and Polly Ruth Polak (eds), *The Routledge Handbook on the International Dimension of Brexit* (Routledge 2020) 117–132.

Lenk Hannes, 'The Member States' Duty to Denounce Anterior Treaties: Commission v Portugal (Maritime Policies)' in Graham Butler and Ramses A Wessel (eds), *EU External Relations Law: The Cases in Context* (Hart Publishing 2022).

Lickova Magdalena, 'European Exceptionalism in International Law' (2008) 19(3) European Journal of International Law 463–490.

Lütz Susanne and others (eds), *The European Union As a Global Actor: Trade, Finance and Climate Policy* (Springer 2021).

Mancini Federice G., 'Europe: The Case for Statehood' (1998) 4(1) European Law Journal 29–42.

Maresceau Marc, 'A Typology of Mixed Bilateral Agreements' in Christophe Hillion and Panos Koutrakos (eds), *Mixed Agreements Revisited: The EU and its Member States in the World* (Hart Publishing 2010) 11–29.

McNair Arnold D, *The Law of Treaties* (Clarendon Press 1961).

Meessen Karl Matthias, 'The Application of Rules of Public International Law within Community Law' (1976) 13(4) Common Market Law Review 485–501.

Messenger Gregory, 'EU-UK Relations at the WTO: Towards Constructive Creative Competition' in Juan Santos Vara, Ramses A Wessel and Polly Ruth Polak (eds), *The Routledge Handbook on the International Dimension of Brexit* (Routledge 2020) 136–147.

Mikulka Václav, 'Article 34' in Giovanni Distefano, Gloria Gaggioli and Aymeric Hêche (eds), *La Convention de Vienne de 1978 sur la Succession d'États en Matière de Traités: Commentaire Article par Article et Études Thématiques* (Bruylant 2016).

–, 'The Dissolution of Czechoslovakia and Succession in Respect of Treaties' in Mojmir Mrak (ed), *Succession of States* (Kluwer Law International 1999) 109–125.

Mögele Rudolf, 'Article 218' in Rudolf Streinz (ed), *EUV/AEUV: Vertrag über die Europäische Union, Vertrag über die Arbeitsweise der Europäischen Union, Charta der Grundrechte der Europäischen Union* (3rd edn, CH Beck 2018).

References

Mosely Philip E, 'Iceland and Greenland: An American Problem' (1940) 18(4) Foreign Affairs 742–746.

Nettesheim Martin, 'Article 1 TEU' in Eberhard Grabitz, Meinhard Hilf and Martin Nettesheim (eds), *Das Recht der Europäischen Union* (82nd supplement, CH Beck 2024).

Nolte Georg and Aust Helmut P., 'European Exceptionalism?' (2013) 2(3) Global Constitutionalism 407–436.

O'Connell David Patrick, 'Reflections on the State Succession Convention' (1979) 39(4) Zeitschrift für ausländisches öffentliches Recht und Völkerrecht 725–739.

–., *State Succession in Municipal Law and International Law: International Relations* (vol II, Cambridge University Press 1967).

Odendahl Kerstin, 'Article 29' in Oliver Dörr and Kirsten Schmalenbach (eds), *Vienna Convention on the Law of Treaties: A Commentary* (2nd edn, Springer 2018).

Odermatt Jed, 'Brexit and International Law: Disentangling Legal Orders' (2017) 31 Emory International Law Review Recent Developments 1051–1075.

–, 'Brexit and International Legal Sovereignty' in Juan Santos Vara, Ramses A Wessel and Polly Ruth Polak (eds), *The Routledge Handbook on the International Dimension of Brexit* (Routledge 2020) 316–328.

–, 'Unidentified Legal Object: Conceptualizing the European Union in International Law' (2018) 33(2) Connecticut Journal of International Law 215–247.

–, *International Law and the European Union* (Cambridge University Press 2021).

Oeter Stefan, 'Föderalismus und Demokratie' in Armin von Bogdandy and Jürgen Bast (eds), *Europäisches Verfassungsrecht: Theoretische und dogmatische Grundzüge* (2nd edn, Springer 2009) 73–120.

Olson Peter, 'Mixity from the Outside: the Perspective of a Treaty Partner' in Christophe Hillion and Panos Koutrakos (eds), *Mixed Agreements Revisited: The EU and its Member States in the World* (Hart Publishing 2010) 331–348.

Orakhelashvili Alexander, 'Statehood, Recognition and the United Nations System: A Unilateral Declaration of Independence in Kosovo' in Armin von Bogdandy and Rüdiger Wolfrum (eds), *Max Planck Yearbook of United Nations Law* (Brill 2008) 1–44.

–, 'The Idea of European International Law' (2006) 17(2) European Journal of International Law 315–347.

Paasivirta Esa and Kuijper Pieter Jan, 'Does one Size fit All?: The European Community and the Responsibility of International Organizations' (2005) 36 Netherlands Yearbook of International Law 169–226.

Patel Kiran Klaus, *Project Europe: A History* (Cambridge University Press 2020).

Pauwelyn Joost, Wessel Ramses A and Wouters Jan, 'When Structures Become Shackles: Stagnation and Dynamics in International Lawmaking' (2014) 25(3) European Journal of International Law 733–763.

Pechstein Matthias, 'Article 1 TEU' in Rudolf Streinz (ed), *EUV/AEUV: Vertrag über die Europäische Union, Vertrag über die Arbeitsweise der Europäischen Union, Charta der Grundrechte der Europäischen Union* (3rd edn, CH Beck 2018).

Peers Steve, 'The End – or a New Beginning?: The EU/UK Withdrawal Agreement' (2021) 39(1) Yearbook of European Law 122–198.

Pellet Alain, 'Article 38' in Andreas Zimmermann and others (eds), *The Statute of the International Court of Justice: A Commentary* (2nd edn, Oxford University Press 2012).

Petti Alessandro and Scott Joanne, 'International Agreements in the EU Legal Order: International Fruit' in Graham Butler and Ramses A Wessel (eds), *EU External Relations Law: The Cases in Context* (Hart Publishing 2022) 21–34.

Polak Polly Ruth, 'EU Withdrawal Law After Brexit: The Emergence of a Unique Legal Procedure' in Juan Santos Vara, Ramses A Wessel and Polly Ruth Polak (eds), *The Routledge Handbook on the International Dimension of Brexit* (Routledge 2020) 58–71.

Rasulov Akbar, 'Revisiting State Succession to Humanitarian Treaties: Is There a Case for Automaticity?' (2003) 14(1) European Journal of International Law 141–170.

Reuter Paul, *Introduction to The Law of Treaties* (2nd edn, Kegan Paul International 1995).

Robinson James Harvey, 'Review: Staatenbund und Bundesstaat by J. B. Westerkamp' (1894) 4 The Annals of the American Academy of Political and Social Science 145–149.

Rodenhoff Vera, *Die EG und ihre Mitgliedstaaten als völkerrechtliche Einheit bei umweltvölkerrechtlichen Übereinkommen* (Nomos 2008).

Rudolf Walter, 'Federal States' in Rüdiger Wolfrum (ed), *The Max Planck Encyclopedia of Public International Law* (Oxford University Press 2012).

Ruffert Matthias and Walter Christian, *Institutionalisiertes Völkerrecht: Das Recht der Internationalen Organisationen und seine wichtigsten Anwendungsfelder* (2nd edn, CH Beck 2015).

Ruffert Matthias, 'Article 288 TFEU' in Christian Calliess and Matthias Ruffert (eds), *EUV/AEUV: Das Verfassungsrecht der Europäischen Union mit Europäischer Grundrechtecharta* (6th edn, CH Beck 2022).

Schaefer Sabrina and Odermatt Jed, 'Nomen est Omen?: The Relevance of "EU Party" In International Law' in Nicolas Levrat and others (eds), *The EU and its Member States' Joint Participation in International Agreements* (Hart Publishing 2021) 131–150.

Schermers Henry G and Blokker Niels, *International Institutional Law: Unity within Diversity* (5th edn, Martinus Nijhoff Publishers 2011).

Schermers Henry G, 'A Typology of Mixed Agreements' in David O'Keeffe and Henry G Schermers (eds), *Mixed Agreements* (Kluwer 1983) 23–33.

Schmalenbach Kirsten, 'Article 2' in Oliver Dörr and Kirsten Schmalenbach (eds), *Vienna Convention on the Law of Treaties: A Commentary* (2nd edn, Springer 2018).

–, 'Article 218' in Christian Calliess and Matthias Ruffert (eds), *EUV/AEUV: Das Verfassungsrecht der Europäischen Union mit Europäischer Grundrechtecharta* (6th edn, CH Beck 2022).

–, 'Article 351' in Christian Calliess and Matthias Ruffert (eds), *EUV/AEUV: Das Verfassungsrecht der Europäischen Union mit Europäischer Grundrechtecharta* (6th edn, CH Beck 2022).

References

Schmitt Carl, *Verfassungslehre* (11th edn, Duncker & Humblot 2017).

Schmitz Thomas, *Integration in der Supranationalen Union: Das europäische Organisationsmodell einer prozeßhaften geo-regionalen Integration und seine rechtlichen und staatstheoretischen Implikationen* (Nomos 2001).

Schönberger Christoph, 'Die Europäische Union als Bund: Zugleich ein Beitrag zur Verabschiedung des Staatenbund-Bundesstaat-Schemas' (2004) 129(1) Archiv des öffentlichen Rechts 81–120.

Schütze Robert, 'On "Federal Ground": The European Union as an (Inter)national Phenomenon' in Robert Schütze (ed), *Foreign Affairs and the EU Constitution: Selected Essays* (Cambridge University Press 2014).

–, 'The "Succession Doctrine" and the European Union' in Robert Schütze (ed), *Foreign Affairs and the EU Constitution: Selected Essays* (Cambridge University Press 2014) 91–119.

–, *European Constitutional Law* (2nd edn, Cambridge University Press 2015).

–, *From Dual to Cooperative Federalism: The Changing Structure of European Law* (Oxford University Press 2009).

Schweisfurth Theodor, 'Das Recht der Staatensukzession: Die Staatenpraxis der Nachfolge in völkerrechtliche Verträge, Staatsvermögen, Staatsschulden und Archive in den Teilungsfällen Sowjetunion, Tschechoslowakei und Jugoslawien' in Ulrich Fastenrath, Theodor Schweisfurth and Carsten Thomas Ebenroth (eds), *Das Recht der Staatensukzession* (CF Müller 1996).

Schwerdtfeger Angela, 'Austritt und Ausschluss aus Internationalen Organisationen: Zwischen staatlicher Souveränität und zwischenstaatlicher Kooperation' (2018) 56(1) Archiv des Völkerrechts 96–126.

Shaw Malcolm N and Fournet Caroline, 'Article 62' in Olivier Corten and Pierre Klein (eds), *The Vienna Conventions on the Law of Treaties* (vol II, Oxford University Press 2011).

Shaw Malcolm N, 'State Succession Revisited' (1995) 34(6) Finish Yearbook of International Law 34–98.

Silvereke Siri, 'Withdrawal from the EU and Bilateral Free Trade Agreements: Being Divorced is Worse?' (2018) 15(2) International Organizations Law Review 321–340.

Simma Bruno and Pulkowski Dirk, 'Of Planets and the Universe: Self-contained Regimes in International Law' (2006) 17(3) European Journal of International Law 483–529.

Singh Nagendra, *Termination of Membership of International Organisations* (Praeger 1958).

Steiger Dominik and Günther Wiebke, 'Brexit: What's Public International Law Got to Do with it' in Karl August Prinz von Sachsen Gessaphe, Juan J Garcia-Blesa and Nils Szuka (eds), *Legal Implications of Brexit* (MV Wissenschaft 2018) 93–120.

Steiger Heinhard, *Staatlichkeit und Überstaatlichkeit: Eine Untersuchung zur rechtlichen und politischen Stellung der Europäischen Gemeinschaften* (Duncker & Humblot 1966).

Stein Klaus D, *Der gemischte Vertrag im Recht der Außenbeziehungen der Europäischen Wirtschaftsgemeinschaft* (Duncker & Humblot 1986).

Steinberger Eva, 'The WTO Treaty as a Mixed Agreement: Problems with the EC's and the EC Member States' Membership of the WTO' (2006) 17(4) European Journal of International Law 837–862.

Stern Brigitte, *La Succession d'États* (Martinus Nijhoff Publishers 1996).

Sunstein Cass R, 'On Analogical Reasoning' (1993) 106(3) Harvard Law Review 741–791.

Tams Christian J, 'State Succession to Investment Treaties: Mapping the Issues' (2016) 31(2) ICSID Review 314–343.

Thiele Alexander, 'Der Austritt aus der EU: Hintergründe und rechtliche Rahmenbedingungen eines „Brexit"' (2016) 51(3) Europarecht 281–304.

Thürer Daniel and Burri Thomas, 'Secession' in Rüdiger Wolfrum (ed), *The Max Planck Encyclopedia of Public International Law* (Oxford University Press 2012).

Tomuschat Christian, 'Liability for Mixed Agreements' in David O'Keeffe and Henry G Schermers (eds), *Mixed Agreements* (Kluwer 1983) 125–132.

Tropper Johannes, 'Succession into Human Rights Treaties' in Christina Binder and others (eds), *Elgar Encyclopedia of Human Rights* (Edward Elgar Publishing 2022) 332–338.

Vahl Marius and Grolimund Nina, 'Integration without Membership: Switzerland's Bilateral Agreements with the European Union' (Brussels 2006), CEPS.

Van der Loo Guillaume, 'Less is More?: The Role of National Parliaments in the Conclusion of Mixed (Trade) Agreements' (2018) 1 CLEER Paper Series 1–34.

Villiger Mark Eugen, 'Article 62' in Mark Eugen Villiger (ed), *Commentary on the 1969 Vienna Convention on the Law of Treaties* (Martinus Nijhoff Publishers 2008).

–, 'Article 70' in Mark Eugen Villiger (ed), *Commentary on the 1969 Vienna Convention on the Law of Treaties* (Martinus Nijhoff Publishers 2008).

Voland Thomas, 'Auswirkungen des Brexit auf die völkervertraglichen Beziehungen des Vereinigten Königreichs und der EU' (2019) 79(1) Zeitschrift für ausländisches öffentliches Recht und Völkerrecht 1–42.

Von Juraschek Franz, *Personal- und Realunion: Das rechtliche Verhältniss zwischen Oesterreich und Ungarn* (C Heymanns 1878).

Vöneky Silja, 'Analogy in International Law' in Rüdiger Wolfrum (ed), *The Max Planck Encyclopedia of Public International Law* (Oxford University Press 2012).

Waltemathe Arved, *Austritt aus der EU: Sind die Mitgliedstaaten noch souverän?* (Lang 2000).

Walter Christian, 'Subjects of International Law' in Rüdiger Wolfrum (ed), *The Max Planck Encyclopedia of Public International Law* (Oxford University Press 2012).

Webb Dominic, 'UK Progress in Rolling over EU Trade Agreements' (13 December 2019), Briefing Paper Number 7792 <https://researchbriefings.files.parliament.uk/documents/CBP-7792/CBP-7792.pdf>.

Weiler Joseph H, 'Europe: The Case Against the Case for Statehood' (1998) 4(1) European Law Journal 43–62.

References

–, 'The External Legal Relations of Non-Unitary Actors: Mixity and the Federal Principle' in David O'Keeffe and Henry G Schermers (eds), *Mixed Agreements* (Kluwer 1983) 35–83.

–, 'The Transformation of Europe' (1991) 100(8) The Yale Law Journal 2403–2483.

Weiss F, 'Greenland's Withdrawal from the European Communities' (1985) 10 European Law Review 173–185.

Wessel Ramses A, 'Can the EU Replace its Member States in International Affairs?: An International Law Perspective' in Inge Govaere and others (eds), *The European Union in the World: Essays in Honour of Professor Marc Maresceau* (Martinus Nijhoff Publishers 2014) 129–147.

–, 'Close Encounters of the Third Kind: The Interface between the EU and International Law after the Treaty of Lisbon' (2013) 8 SIEPS Reports.

–, 'Consequences of Brexit for International Agreements Concluded by the EU and its Member States' (2018) 55 (Special Issue) Common Market Law Review 101–132.

–, 'International Agreements as an Integral Part of EU Law: Haegeman' in Graham Butler and Ramses A Wessel (eds), *EU External Relations Law: The Cases in Context* (Hart Publishing 2022) 34–44.

–, 'Studying International and European Law: Confronting Perspectives and Combining Interests' in Inge Govaere and Sacha Garben (eds), *The Interface Between EU and International Law: Contemporary Reflections* (Hart Publishing 2019) 73–98.

–, 'You Can Check out Any Time You like, but Can You Really Leave?' (2016) 13(2) International Organizations Law Review 197–209.

Westerkamp Justus Bernhard, *Staatenbund und Bundesstaat: Untersuchungen über die Praxis und das Recht der modernen Bünde* (Brockhaus 1892).

Wittich Stephan, 'Article 70' in Oliver Dörr and Kirsten Schmalenbach (eds), *Vienna Convention on the Law of Treaties: A Commentary* (2nd edn, Springer 2018).

Wolfrum Rüdiger, 'International Law' in Rüdiger Wolfrum (ed), *The Max Planck Encyclopedia of Public International Law* (Oxford University Press 2012).

Young Richard, 'The State of Syria: Old or New?' (1962) 56(2) American Journal of International Law 482–488.

Zedalis Rex J, 'An Independent Quebec: State Succession to NAFTA' (1996) 2(4) Law and Business Review of the Americas 3–27.

Ziegler Katja S, 'The Relationship between EU Law and International Law' in Anna Södersten and Dennis M Patterson (eds), *A Companion to European Union Law and International Law* (Wiley Blackwell 2016) 42–61.

Zimmermann Andreas and Devaney James Gerard, 'State Succession in Treaties' in Rüdiger Wolfrum (ed), *The Max Planck Encyclopedia of Public International Law* (Oxford University Press 2012).

–, 'Succession to Treaties and the Inherent Limits of International Law' in Christian J Tams, Antonios Tzanakopoulos and Andreas Zimmermann (eds), *Research Handbook on the Law of Treaties* (Edward Elgar Publishing 2016) 505–540.

Zimmermann Andreas, 'Secession and the Law of State Succession' in Marcelo G Kohen (ed), *Secession: International Law Perspectives* (Cambridge University Press 2006).

–, *Staatennachfolge in völkerrechtliche Verträge: Zugleich ein Beitrag zu den Möglichkeiten und Grenzen völkerrechtlicher Kodifikation* (Springer 2000).

Cases

ECJ NV Algemene Transport en Expeditie Onderneming van Gend & Loos v Netherlands Inland Revenue Administration (1963) C-26/62 ECLI:EU:C:1963:1.

–, International Fruit Company NV and others v Produktschap voor Groenten en Fruit (1972) C-21 to 24/72 ECLI:EU:C:1972:115.

–, R. & V. Haegeman v Belgian State (1974) C-181/73 ECLI:EU:C:1974:41.

–, Yvonne van Duyn v Home Office (1974) C-41/74 ECLI:EU:C:1974:133.

–, Parti écologiste "Les Verts" v European Parliament (1986) C-294/83 ECLI:EU:C:1986:166.

–, Draft agreement between the Community, on the one hand, and the countries of the European Free Trade Association, on the other, relating to the creation of the European Economic Area (1991) Opinion 1/91 ECLI:EU:C:1991:490.

–, Hermès International v FHT Marketing Choice BV (1998) Case C-53/96 EU:C:1998:292.

–, Hermès International v FHT Marketing Choice BV (Opinion of the Advocate General Tesauro) (1998) C-53/96 ECLI:EU:C:1997:539.

–, A. Racke GmbH & Co. v. Hauptzollamt Mainz (1998) C-162/96 ECLI:EU:C:1998:293.

–, Commission of the European Communities v Portuguese Republic (Joined opinion of Advocate General Mischo) (1999) C-62/98 and C-84/98 ECLI:EU:C:1999:509.

–, Commission of the European Communities v Portuguese Republic (2000) C-84/98 ECLI:EU:C:2000:359.

–, Creation of a Unified Patent Litigation System (2011) Opinion 1/09 ECLI:EU:C:2011:123.

–, Accession to the ECHR (2014) Opinion 2/13 ECLI:EU:C:2014:2454.

–, FTA Singapore (2015) Case 2/15 EU:C:2017:376.

–, FTA Singapore (Opinion of the Advocate General Sharpston) (2017) Opinion 2/15 EU:C:2016:992.

–, Wightman (2018) C-621/18 ECLI:EU:C:2018:999.

–, Governor of Cloverhill Prison and Others (Opinion of the Advocate General Kokott) (2021) C-479/21 PPU ECLI:EU:C:2021:899.

German Federal Constitutional Court Maastricht (1993) 2 BvR 2134/92, 2 BvR 2159/92 BVerfGE 89, 155.

ICJ Reparation for Injuries Suffered in the Service of the United Nations (Advisory Opinion) (1949) ICJ Rep 1949, p 174.

References

–, International Status of South-West Africa (Advisory Opinion) (1950) ICJ Rep 1950, p 128.
–, Case Concerning the Aerial Incident of July 27th, 1955 (Israel/Bulgaria) (Preliminary Objections) (1959) ICJ Rep 1959, p 127.
–, North Sea Continental Shelf Cases (Federal Republic of Germany/Denmark; Federal Republic of Germany/Netherlands) (Judgement) (1969) ICJ Rep 1969, p 3.
–, Fisheries Jurisdiction (United Kingdom v Iceland) (Jurisdiction) (1973) ICJ Rep 1973, p 3.
–, Fisheries Jurisdiction Case (Federal Republic of Germany v Iceland) (Jurisdiction) (1973) ICJ Rep 1973, p 3.
–, Case Concerning United States Diplomatic and Consular Staff in Tehran (Judgement) (1980) ICJ Rep 1980, p 3.
–, Interpretation of the Agreement of 25 March 1951 between the WHO and Egypt (Advisory Opinion) (1980) ICJ Rep 1980, p 96.
–, Case Concerning Military and Paramilitary Activities in and against Nicaragua (Nicaragua v United States of America) (Jurisdiction and Admissibility) (1984) ICJ Rep 1984, p 392.
–, Case Concerning Military and Paramilitary Activities in and against Nicaragua (Nicaragua v United States of America) (Merits) (1986) ICJ Rep 1986, p 4.
–, Case Concerning the Application of the Convention on the Prevention and Punishment of the Crime of Genocide (Provisional Measures) (1993) ICJ Rep 1993, p 3.
–, Case Concerning the Gabčíkovo-Nagymaros Project (Hungary v Slovakia) (Memorial of Hungary) (1994) ICJ Rep 1997, p 7.
–, Case Concerning the Application of the Convention on the Prevention and Punishment of the Crime of Genocide (Bosnia and Herzegovina v. Serbia and Montenegro) (Preliminary Objections) (1996) ICJ Rep 1996, p 595.
–, Case Concerning the Gabčíkovo-Nagymaros Project (Hungary v Slovakia) (Judgement) (1997) ICJ Rep 1997, p 7.
–, Case Concerning the Land and Maritime Boundary between Cameroon and Nigeria (Cameroon v Nigeria) (Preliminary Objections) (1998) ICJ Rep 1998, p 275.
–, Case Concerning the Arrest Warrant of 11 April 2000 (Judgement) (2002) ICJ Rep 2002, p 3.
–, Case Concerning the Arrest Warrant of 11 April 2000 (Dissenting Opinion of Judge van den Wyngaert) (2002) ICJ Rep, p 137.
–, Case Concerning Application of the Convention on the Prevention and Punishment of the Crime Genocide (Bosnia and Herzegovina v Serbia and Montenegro) (Judgement) (2007) ICJ Rep 2007, p 43.
ITLOS Responsibilities and Obligations of States Sponsoring Persons and Entities with respect to Activities in the Area (Advisory Opinion) (2011) ITLOS Rep 10.
PCA Muscat Dhows Case (France v Great Britain) (Award) [1905] [1961] XI RIAA 83 (1961).

–, Russian Claim for Interest on Indemnities (Damages Claimed by Russia for Delay in Payment of Compensation Owed to Russians Injured During the War of 1877–1878) (Russia v Turkey) (Award) (1912) XI RIAA 421 (1961).

–, Difference between New Zealand and France Concerning the Interpretation or Application of Two Agreements Concluded on 9 July 1986 between the Two States and Which Related to the Problems Arising from the "Rainbow Warrior" Affair (New Zealand v France) (1990) 20 RIAA 217.

PCIJ Case of the S.S. Wimbledon (United Kingdom, France & Italy v. Germany) (Judgement) (1923) Series A No 1.

–, Delimitation of the Polish-Czechoslovakian Frontier (Question of Jaworzina) (Advisory Opinion) (1923) Series B No 8.

–, Certain German Interests in Polish Upper Silesia (Judgement) (1926) Series A No. 7 Series A No 7.

–, The Case of the S.S. Lotus (Judgement) (1927) Series A No. 10 Series A No 10.

–, Customs Regime between Germany and Austria (Individual Opinion) (1931) Series A/B No. 41 Series A/B No 41.

–, Free Zones Case of Upper Savoy and the District of Gex (Judgement) (1932) Series A/B No. 146 Series A/B No 146.

UK Supreme Court R (on the Application of Miller and Another) v Secretary of State for Exiting the European Union (2017) UKSC 5.

International Agreements and Legislation

Agreement between the Member States of the European Coal and Steel Community and the People's Democratic Republic of Algeria (27 September 1978) OJ L263/119.

Agreement establishing an association between the European Community and its Member States, of the one part, and the Republic of Chile, of the other part (30 December 2002) OJ L352/3.

Agreement establishing an Association between the European Economic Community and Greece (18 February 1963) OJ L26/294.

Agreement establishing an Association between the European Union and its Member States, on the one hand, and Central America on the other (15 December 2012) OJ L346/3.

Agreement establishing an Association between the United Kingdom of Great Britain and Northern Ireland and the Republic of Chile (30 January 2019) CS Chile No. 2/2019.

Agreement Establishing the Common Fund for Commodities (adopted on 27 June 1980, entered into force 19 June 1989) 1538 UNTS 3.

Agreement Establishing the World Trade Organization (adopted on 15 April 1994, entered into force 1 January 1995) 1867 UNTS 4.

Agreement on a Unified Patent Court (20 June 2013) OJ C175/1.

References

Agreement on Government Procurement (signed on 12 April 1979, entered into force 1 January 1981) 1235 UNTS 258.

Agreement on Maritime Transport between the European Community and its Member States, of the one part, and the government of the People's Republic of China, of the other part (21 February 2008) OJ L46/25.

Agreement on Relations between the International Labour Organization and the European Economic Community (27 April 1959) OJ 27/521.

Agreement on the Withdrawal of the United Kingdom of Great Britain and Northern Ireland from the European Union and the European Atomic Energy Community (12 November 2019) OJ C384 I/1.

Agreement on Trade Continuity between the United Kingdom of Great Britain and Northern Ireland and Canada (9 December 2020) CS Canada No.1/2020.

Agreements Establishing the Commonwealth of Independent States (9 December 1991) 1992 (31) ILM 138.

Air Transport Agreement between the United States of America, of the one part, and the European Community and its Member States, of the other part (25 May 2007) OJ L134/5.

Articles of Agreement of the International Bank for Reconstruction and Development (adopted 27 December 1945, entered into force 27 December 1945) 2 UNTS 134.

Articles of Agreement of the International Development Association (adopted 29 January 1960, entered into force 24 September 1960) 439 UNTS 249.

Articles of Agreement of the International Finance Corporation (adopted 25 May 1955, entered into force 20 July 1956) 264 UNTS 117.

Articles of Agreement of the International Monetary Fund (adopted 27 December 1945, entered into force 27 December 1945) 2 UNTS 39.

Association Agreement between the European Union and the European Atomic Energy Community and their Member States, of the one part, and Ukraine, of the other part (29 May 2014) OJ L161/3.

Comprehensive Economic and Trade Agreement between Canada, of the one part, and the European Union and its Member States, of the other part (14 January 2017) OJ L11/23.

Consolidated Version of the Treaty on European Union (26 October 2012) OJ C326/13.

Consolidated Version of the Treaty on the Functioning of the European Union (26 October 2012) OJ C326/47.

Constitution of the International Labour Organisation (adopted on 1 April 1919, entered into force 28 June 1919) 15 UNTS 40.

Convention Defining the Statute of the European Schools (17 August 1994) OJ L212/3.

Convention establishing the Multilateral Investment Guarantee Agency (adopted on 11 October 1985, entered into force 12 April 1988) 1508 UNTS 99.

Convention for European Economic Cooperation (adopted on 16 April 1948, entered into force 28 July 1948) 888 UNTS 141.

Convention for the Protection of Human Rights and Fundamental Freedoms (adopted 4 November 1950, entered into force 3 September 1953) 213 UNTS 221.

International Agreements and Legislation

Convention on the Grant of European Patents (adopted 5 October 1973, entered into force 7 October 1977) 1065 UNTS 199.

Convention on the Rights and Duties of States (adopted 26 December 1933, entered into force 26 December 1934) 165 LNTS 19.

Convention Setting up a European University Institute (9 February 1976) OJ C29/1.

Cooperation Agreement on a Civil Global Navigation Satellite System (GNSS) between the European Community and its Member States, of the one part, and the Republic of Korea, of the other part (19 October 2006) OJ L288/31.

Council Decision (86/283/EEC) of 30 June 1986 on the association of the overseas countries and territories with the European Economic Community (1 July 1986) OJ L175/1.

Decision of the European Council (2010/718/EU) of 29 October 2010 amending the status with regard to the European Union of the island of Saint-Barthélemy (29 October 2010) OJ L325/4.

Draft Convention on the Law of Treaties (adopted 20 February 1928)1935 (29) AJIL 657.

Draft Treaty establishing a Constitution for Europe (18 July 2003) OJ C169/1.

European Convention on the Suppression of Terrorism (adopted on 10 November 1976, entered into force 27 January 1977) CoE No. 090.

Exchange of Letters between Mr Walter Hallstein, President of the Commission of the European Community, and Mr Jacques Fouques-Duparc, Chairman of the Central Commission for the Navigation of the Rhine, on cooperation between the EEC and the Central Commission for the Navigation of the Rhine (4 August 1961) OJ 53/1027.

Framework Agreement between the European Union and its Member States, of the one part, and Australia, of the other part (3 October 2022) OJ L255/3.

Framework Agreement on Comprehensive Partnership and Cooperation between the European Union and its Member States, of the one part, and the Kingdom of Thailand, of the other part (23 December 2022) OJ L330/72.

Internal Agreement between the Representatives of the Governments of the Member States of the European Union meeting within the Council, on the Financing of European Union Aid under the Multiannual Financial Framework for the Period 2014 to 2020, in Accordance with the ACP-EU Partnership Agreement, and on the Allocation of Financial Assistance for the Overseas Countries and Territories to which Part Four of the Treaty on the Functioning of the European Union applies (6 August 2013) OJ L210/1.

International Cocoa Agreement (adopted on 25 June 2010, provisionally applied since 1 October 2012) 2871 UNTS 3.

International Tropical Timber Agreement (adopted on 27 January 2006, entered into force 7 December 2011) 2797 UNTS 75.

Partnership Agreement between the Members of the African, Caribbean and Pacific Group of States, of the one part, and the European Community and its Member States, of the other part (23 June 2000) OJ L317/3.

Partnership Agreement between the Members of the African, Caribbean and Pacific Group of States of the one part, and the European Community and its Member States, of the other part (15 December 2000) OJ L317/3.

References

Partnership and Cooperation Agreement Establishing a Partnership between the United Kingdom of Great Britain and Northern Ireland, of the one part, and the Republic of Uzbekistan, of the other part (31 October 2019) CS Uzbekistan No. 1/2019.

Political Dialogue and Cooperation Agreement between the European Union and its Member States, of the one part, and the Republic of Cuba, of the other part (13 December 2016) OJ L337I/3.

Protocol on Integrated Coastal Zone Management in the Mediterranean (4 February 2009) OJ L34/19.

Statute of the Council of Europe (signed on 5 May 1949, entered into force 3 August 1949) 87 UNTS 103.

Statute of the International Court of Justice (adopted 24 October 1945, entered into force 18 April 1946) 33 UNTS 993.

Statute of the Permanent Court of International Justice (adopted 13 December 1920, entered into force 8 October 1921) Serie D – No. 1.

Stepping Stone Economic Partnership Agreement between Ghana, of the one part, and the European Community and its Member States, of the other part (21 October 2016) OJ L278/3.

Strategic Partnership Agreement between the European Union and its Member States, of the one part, and Japan, of the other part (24 August 2018) OJ L216/4.

The European University Institute (EU Exit) Regulations 2022 (25 November 2022) 2022 No. 1231.

Trade Agreement between the European Union and its Member States, of the one part, and Colombia and Peru, of the other part (21 December 2012) OJ L354/3.

Trade and Cooperation Agreement between the European Union and the European Atomic Energy Community, of the one part, and the United Kingdom of Great Britain and Northern Ireland, of the other part (30 April 2021) OJ L149/10.

Trade Continuity Agreement between the United Kingdom of Great Britain and Northern Ireland and the United Mexican States (15 December 2020) CS Mexico No.1/2021.

Treaty concerning the Accession of the Kingdom of Denmark, Ireland, the Kingdom of Norway and the United Kingdom of Great Britain and Northern Ireland to the European Economic Community and to the European Atomic Energy Community and Act concerning the Conditions of Accession and the Adjustments to the Treaties 27 March 1972.

Treaty establishing the European Coal and Steel Community (adopted 18 April 1951, entered into force 23 July 1952) 261 UNTS 140.

Treaty establishing the European Economic Community (adopted on 25 March 1957, entered into force 1 January 1958) 294 UNTS 3.

Treaty Establishing the European Economic Community (adopted on 25 March 1957, entered into force 1 January 1958) 294 UNT 3.

United Nations Convention on the Law of the Sea (adopted 10 December 1982, entered into force 16 November 1994) 1836 UNTS 3.

United Nations Framework Convention on Climate Change (adopted on 9 May 1992, entered into force 21 March 1994) 1771 UNTS 107.

Vienna Convention on Succession of States in respect of State Property, Archives and Debts (adopted 8 April 1983, not yet in force) A/CONF.117/14.

Vienna Convention on Succession of States in Respect of Treaties (adopted 23 August 1978, entered into force 6 November 1996) 1946 UNTS 3.

Vienna Convention on the Law of Treaties (adopted 23 May 1969, entered into force 27 January 1980) 1155 UNTS 331.

Vienna Convention on the Law of Treaties between States and International Organizations or between International Organizations (adopted and opened for signature 21 March 1986) UN Doc A/CONF.129/15.

Documents and Miscellaneous Sources

Council of the European Union, 'Directives for the Negotiation of an Agreement with the United Kingdom of Great Britain and Northern Ireland setting out the Arrangements for its Withdrawal from the European Union' (Brussels 22 May 2017) XT 21016/17 ADD 1 REV 2.

EC Arbitration Commission, 'Opinions on Questions Arising from the Dissolution of Yugoslavia: Opinion No. 9' (1992) 31(6) International Legal Materials 1488.

EU Commission, 'Internal EU27 Preparatory Discussions on the Framework for the Future Relationship: International Agreements and Trade Policy' (6 February 2018) TF50(2018) 29.

–, 'Cover Letter and Note Verbale on the Agreement on the Withdrawal of the United Kingdom of Great Britain and Northern' (5 December 2018) COM(2018) 841 final.

European Council, 'Guidelines following the United Kingdom's Notification under Article 50 TEU' (Brussels 29 April 2017) EUCO XT 20004/17.

ILA, 'Berlin Conference 2004: Aspects of the Law of State Succession – Provisional Report'.

–, 'New Delhi Conference 2002: Committee on Aspects of the Law of State Succession – Rapport Final sur la Succession en Matiere de Traites'.

–, 'Rio de Janeiro Conference 2008: Aspects of the Law on State Succession'.

–, 'Toronto Conference 2006: Aspects of the Law of State Succession – Economic Aspects of State Succession'.

–, 'Conclusions of the Committee on Aspects of the Law of State Succession: Resolution No. 3/2008' (2008).

ILC, 'Survey of International Law in Relation to the Work of Codification of the International Law Commission: UN Doc. A/CN.4/1/Rev.1' (1949), YBILC.

–, 'Second Report on the Law of Treaties, by Gerald Fitzmaurice, Special Rapporteur: UN Doc A/CN.4/107' (1957), YBILC Vol. II.

–, 'First Report on the Law of Treaties, by Sir Humphrey Waldock, Special Rapporteur: UN Doc A/CN.4/144 and Add. 1' (1962), YBILC Vol. II.

References

–, 'Summary Records of its 14th Session (24 April-29 June 1962): UN Doc A/CN.4/SR.647' (1962), YBILC Vol. I.
–, 'Report by Manfred Lachs, Chairman of the Sub-Committee on Succession of States and Governments: UN Doc. A/CN.4/160 and Corr.1' (1963), YBILC Vol. II.
–, 'Second Report on the Law of Treaties, by Sir Humphrey Waldock, Special Rapporteur: UN Doc. A/CN.4/156 and Add.1 – 3' (1963), YBILC Vol. II.
–, 'Reports of the International Law Commission on the Work of its 18th Session (4 May-19 July 1966): UN Doc A/CN.4/191' (1966), YBILC Vol. II.
–, 'Summary Records of the 18th Session (4 May – 19 July 1966): UN Doc. A/CN.4/Ser.A/1966' (1966), YBILC Vol. I(2).
–, 'First Report on Succession of States and Governments in Respect of Treaties, by Sir Humphrey Waldock: UN Doc A/CN.4/202' (1968), YBILC Vol. II.
–, 'Report of the International Law Commission on the work of its twentieth session, 27 May-2 August 1968: UN Doc. A/7209/Rev.1' (1968), YBILC Vol. II.
–, 'Second Report on Succession in Respect of Treaties, by Sir Humphrey Waldock: UN Doc. A/CN.4/214 and Add. 1 & 2' (1969), YBILC Vol. II.
–, 'Third Report on Succession in Respect of Treaties, by Sir Humphrey Waldock: UN Doc. A/CN.4/244 and Add. 1' (1970), YBILC Vol. II.
–, 'Fourth Report on Succession in Respect of Treaties, by Sir Humphrey Waldock: UN Doc A/CN.4/249' (1971), YBILC Vol. II(1).
–, 'Fifth Report on Succession in Respect of Treaties, by Sir Humphrey Waldock: UN Doc. A/CN.4/256 and Add.1 – 4' (1972), YBILC Vol. II.
–, 'Report of the International Law Commission on the Work of its Twenty-Fourth Session, 2 May – 7 July 1972, Official Records of the General Assembly, Twenty-seventh session, Supplement No.10: UN Doc. A/8710/Rev.1' (1972), YBILC Vol. II.
–, 'Summary records of the Twenty-Fourth Session 2 May-7 July 1972: UN Doc. A/CN.4/Ser.A/1972' (1972), YBILC Vol. I.
–, 'First Report on Succession of States in Respect of Treaties, by Sir Francis Vallat, Special Rapporteur: UN Doc. A/CN.4/278 and Add.1 – 6' (1974), YBILC Vol. II(1).
–, 'Report of the International Law Commission on the Work of its Twenty-Sixth Session, 6 May – 26 July 1974: UN Doc. A/9610/Rev.1' (1974), YBILC Vol. II(1).
–, 'Tenth Report on the Question of Treaties concluded between States and International Organizations or between two or more International Organizations, by Paul Reuter, Special Rapporteur: UN Doc A/CN.4/341 and Add.1 & Corr.1' (1981), YBILC Vol. II(1).
–, 'Report of the International Law Commission on the Work of its 34th Session (3 May-23 July 1982): UN Doc A/37/10' (1982), YBILC Vol. II(2).
–, 'Third Report on State responsibility, by Roberto Ago, Special Rapporteur: UN Doc. A/CN.4/246 and Add.1 – 3' (2000), YBILC Vol. II(1).
–, 'Articles on the Responsibility of States for Internationally Wrongful Acts' (2001), YBILC Vol. II(2).

Documents and Miscellaneous Sources

–, 'Conclusions of the Study Group on the Fragmentation of International Law: Difficulties arising from the Diversification and Expansion of International Law' (2006), YBILC Vol. II.

–, 'Draft Articles on the Responsibility of International Organizations: UN Doc A/66/10' (2011), YBILC Vol. II(2).

–, 'Draft Conclusions on Identification of Customary International Law, with Commentaries' (UN Doc. A/73/10) (2018), YBILC Vol. II(2).

Miller V, 'Legislating for Brexit: EU External Agreements' (5 January 2017), Briefing Paper Number 7850.

Office of the President of the Government of Southern Sudan in collaboration with the Public International Law & Policy Group, 'South Sudan: A Guide to Critical Post-2011 Issues, Legal Handbook' (December 2009).

Praesidium de la Convention européenne, 'Titre X: L'appartenance à l'Union: CONV 648/03' (2 April 2003).

Swiss Federal Department of Foreign Affairs/Federal Department of Economic Affairs, 'Bilateral Agreements Switzerland-EU' (Bern August 2009).

UK Government, 'The Process for Withdrawing from the European Union' (London February 2016) Cm 9216.

–, 'Why the Government believes that Voting to Remain in the EU is the Best Decision for the UK: Booklet Providing Important Information about the EU Referendum on 23 June 2016' (6 April 2016).

–, 'The United Kingdom's Exit from and New Partnership with the European Union: White Paper' (2 February 2017) Cm 9417.

–, 'Technical Note: International Agreements during the Implementation Period' (8 February 2018).

–, 'EU Exit: Taking back control of our borders, money and laws while protecting our economy, security and Union' (November 2018) Cm 9741.

–, 'International Agreements if the UK leaves the EU without a Deal' (5 November 2019), Guidance Note.

–, 'Written Questions, Answers and Statements: European University Institute' (tabled on 22 September 2022; answered on 11 October 2022) UIN 54450.

UK House of Commons, 'Oral Evidence: Costs and Benefits of EU Membership for the UK's Role in the World' (8 December 2015) HC 545.

–, 'Global Britain: Sixth Report of Session 2017–19' (6 March 2018) HC 780.

UK House of Lords, 'Brexit and the EU budget: European Union Committee – 15th Report of Session 2016–17' (4 March 2017) HL Paper 125.

UN Conference on the Law of Treaties, 'Official Records of the UN Conference on the Law of Treaties (Summary Records of the Plenary Meetings and of the Meetings of the Committee of the Whole): First Session, 26 March – 24 May 1968' (A/CONF.39/11).

UN Secretariat, 'Succession of States in Respect of Bilateral Treaties – Study prepared by the Secretariat: UN Doc. A/CN.4/229' (1970), YBILC Vol. II.

References

–, 'Succession of States in Respect of Bilateral Treaties – Second and Third Studies prepared by the Secretariat: A/CN.4/243 and Add.1' (1971), YBILC Vol. II(2).

UN Conference on Succession of States in Respect of Treaties, 'Official Records: 3rd meeting of the Committee of the Whole' UN Doc. A/CONF.80/C.1/SR.3.

–, 'Official Records: 37th Meeting of the Committee of the Whole' (31 July 1978) UN Doc. A/CONF.80/C.1/SR.37.

–, 'Official Records: 38th Meeting of the Committee of the Whole' (1 August 1978) UN Doc. A/CONF.80/C.1/SR.38.

–, 'Official Records: 39th Meeting of the Committee of the Whole' (1 August 1978) UN Doc. A/CONF.80/C.1/SR.39.

–, 'Official Records: 40th Meeting of the Committee of the Whole' (2 August 1978) UN Doc. A/CONF.80/C.1/SR.40.

–, 'Official Records: 41st Meeting of the Committee of the Whole' (2 August 1978) UN Doc. A/CONF.80/C.1/SR.41.

–, 'Official Records: 42nd Meeting of the Committee of the Whole' (3 August 1978) UN Doc. A/CONF.80/C.1/SR.42.

–, 'Official Records: 47th Meeting of the Committee of the Whole' (7 August 1978) UN Doc. A/CONF.80/C.1/SR.47.

–, 'Official Records: 48th Meeting of the Committee of the Whole' (8 August 1978) UN Doc. A/CONF.80/C.1/SR.48.

–, 'Official Records: 49th Meeting of the Committee of the Whole' (8 August 1978) UN Doc. A/CONF.80/C.1/SR.49.

–, 'Official Records: 13th Plenary Meeting' (21 August 1978) UN Doc. A/CONF.80/SR.13.

–, 'Official Records (Volume III): Documents of the Conference' (1979) UN Doc. A/CONF.80/16/Add.2.

UN General Assembly, 'Future Work in the Field of the Codification and Progressive Development of International Law: UN Doc. A/Res/16/1686' (18 December 1961).

–, 'Letter Dated 31 December 1992 from the Permanent Representative of Czechoslovakia to the United Nations Addressed to the Secretary-General: UN Doc A/47/848, Annex II' (1992).

–, 'Letter Dated 31 December 1992 from the Permanent Representative of Czechoslovakia to the United Nations Addressed to the Secretary-General: UN Doc A/47/848 Annex I' (1992).

United Nations, 'Final Clauses of Multilateral Treaties: Handbook' (2nd edn, United Nations Publications 2005).

United Nations, 'Summary of Practice of the Secretary-General as Depositary of Multilateral Treaties' (UN Doc. ST/LEG/7/Rev.1).

UN Security Council, 'On the question of membership of the Federal Republic of Yugoslavia (Serbia and Montenegro) in the United Nations: UN Doc. S/RES/777' (19 September 1992).

WTO, 'Accession of the United Kingdom to the Agreement on Government Procurement in its own Right: Decision of the Committee on Government Procurement of 27 February 2019' (28 February 2019) GPA/CD/2.